INTRODUCING
WORLD
MISSIONS

Encountering Mission
A. Scott Moreau, Series Editor

INTRODUCING
WORLD
MISSIONS

A Biblical, Historical,
and Practical Survey

A. SCOTT MOREAU
GARY R. CORWIN
GARY B. McGEE

Baker Academic

A Division of Baker Book House Co
Grand Rapids, Michigan 49516

Published by Baker Academic
a division of Baker Book House Company
P.O. Box 6287, Grand Rapids, MI 49516-6287
www.bakeracademic.com

Printed in the United States of America

Library of Congress Cataloging-in-Publication Data

Moreau, A. Scott, 1955–
    Introducing world missions : a biblical, historical, and practical survey / A. Scott Moreau, Gary R. Corwin, Gary B. McGee.
       p.   cm. — (Encountering mission)
    Includes bibliographical references and indexes.
    ISBN 0-8010-2648-2 (cloth)
    1. Missions. I. Corwin, Gary, 1948– II. McGee, Gary B., 1945– III. Title. IV. Series.
BV2061.3.M67 2003
266—dc21
                                       2003052201

Contents

Preface

Introducing World Missions was written for prospective missionaries as well as for those who are interested in missions but may serve in other capacities in God's work. The idea of becoming a missionary can be exciting and frightening at the same time. Living in a remote location, learning a new language, and possibly being cut off from those at home are all daunting for many people. Forging new friendships across cultures, the thrill of seeing a new church planted and leadership developing, and helping God's people grow and develop in their walk with Christ are all exciting prospects for the missionary. Doing all of this in an increasingly uncertain world filled with indifference or even danger is a sobering prospect.

Introducing World Missions is the first in a projected series of eight books focusing on mission from an evangelical perspective. For many years, J. Herbert Kane's textbooks, including The Making of a Missionary, Understanding Christian Missions, Christian Missions in Biblical Perspective, A Concise History of the Christian World Mission, Life and Work on the Mission Field, and The Christian World Mission: Today and Tomorrow, have been widely used in seminaries and Bible colleges as introductory texts. With the passing of time, however, his classic works have become dated, and it was recognized by Baker Book House that the time had come to develop a series of books to replace Kane's gifts to the mission community.

This first book of the series is intended to be a general introduction to contemporary missions. Written as a textbook, its focus is on providing students in introductory missions courses with a broad overview as well as occasional deeper explorations. Typical introductory missions classes include not only prospective missionaries, but also students who might not become missionaries themselves but who need to understand contemporary missions as part of their anticipated pastoral roles. Although our focus here has been on the former, we also wrote with the latter in mind.

The book is divided into five major sections through which mission is encountered. First comes the biblical and theological encounter, which lays the foundation for the rest of the book. In part 1 we argue that the evangelistic mandate of winning people to

Christ must be at the core of any theology of mission that hopes to remain true to the biblical orientation. Contemporary practices and thinking about missions are best understood in light of their historical context, and part 2 is a freshly written overview of the history of God's work through the church in missions.

Introducing the contemporary student to mission requires pragmatic information in addition to the foundations laid, and the last three parts of the book tackle practical issues and current challenges from different perspectives. Part 3 explores missions from the perspective of the prospective missions candidate and others who share in the task. What does it mean to be called as a missionary, and what is involved in getting from here (the missionary's home) to there (the country or location of service)? Part 4 carries the story further by looking at the challenges that will face any "sent one." These span a spectrum of personal and family issues, strategic and ministry issues, and the requirements of adjusting to a new culture and all kinds of new relationships. Part 5 concludes the book with an exploration of contemporary challenges to missions, a survey of the missionary encounter with the non-Christian religions of the world, and a brief projection of what lies in the future for missions.

To supplement the text, we have added four additional sets of materials. They were designed to help the teacher get the most out of the book. Two relate to the text of the book itself, and two are available electronically.

First, most of the chapters include a case study. Case studies help the readers dig more deeply into a selected issue that fits the discussion in the chapter. Our case studies leave the reader with a dilemma

for which a solution should be sought. For every case study in the book there are numerous good solutions and numerous bad ones. Having students wrestle with the dilemmas presented in the case study engages them in the learning process. Case dilemmas help students learn how to draw from theory in light of practical problems faced on the field.

If you are a teacher, we encourage you to use the case studies in ways that fit your objectives for the class. Students might write an essay on possible solutions to a case as a homework assignment. Alternately, class discussion of the case studies can be used to determine student awareness of the issues raised. Students can be formed into small groups to work together in developing possible solutions to get them to think more deeply about the issues involved. For further help, including a worksheet that can be used with the case studies and to focus discussion, teachers are invited to see the supporting instructor's manual for the text (see below). Hiebert and Hiebert (1987), from whose work many of the case studies in this book were drawn, also provide helpful ways to use case studies as teaching devices.

Our second set of additional materials is the numerous sidebars scattered throughout the book. Most offer deeper thinking on a particular issue being discussed in the text and come with accompanying questions for discussion and reflection. The rest are focused examples of churches from across the United States that exemplify excellence in an area being presented. These latter sidebars we call "Church Models That Work." They are drawn from Tom Telford's *Today's All-Star Missions Churches,* a book that we highly recommend.

Third, a CD-ROM containing the entire *Evangelical Dictionary of World Missions* is attached to the back of the book. Teachers may require students to read particular articles relevant to each chapter or have them read other articles for additional research or reflection.

Finally, an instructor's manual has been created to support the teacher who adopts the book as a required text. If you do so, and notify Baker Academic of the adoption, you will receive a copy of the manual on CD-ROM. The materials include further case study helps and additional cases, important historical documents, downloadable PowerPoint presentations for each chapter of the book, more discussion-generating questions, and suggested readings from the *Evangelical Dictionary of World Missions* for each chapter. If you are a teacher, we invite you to take advantage of these supporting resources.

Because of a lack of consensus among those writing about mission, it is necessary to give a quick explanation of the way *mission* and *missions* are used in this book. Essentially, the term *missions* refers to the specific work of churches and agencies in the task of reaching people for Christ by crossing cultural boundaries. The term *mission,* however, is broader, referring to everything the church is doing that points toward the kingdom of God (Moreau 2000b). We will return to this discussion in greater depth in chapters 1 and 5. Our aim throughout the book has been to be consistent in using *mission* in the broader sense of the term, and *missions* for the more narrow. Where we quote authors who use these terms differently than we do in this text, we have chosen not to change their original wording.

Finally, as authors, we offer our deepest gratitude to Baker Book House for the opportunity not only to write this book, but also for their ongoing commitment to mission as evidenced in their support for the entire series. We also gratefully acknowledge the role that our spouses play in our lives—alternately encouraging, chastising, cajoling, challenging, and, ultimately, bearing with us as we work through the calling we as authors have to encourage God's people through writing.

Missions in the Modern World

INTRODUCTION

If you are reading this book, chances are you are interested in missions. Maybe you already sense a call from God to go somewhere. Maybe you are interested in other cultures. Maybe you want to go into ministry but not mission and still hope to support mission in some way. Mission has changed dramatically in the past few decades, and we hope to introduce you to the changes and provide you with information that will help you understand what is involved in either being a missionary or being involved in supporting God's missionary work. To start, a brief survey of the modern world will help set the context. After that, we provide you with some exploratory thoughts on mission and missionaries that will set the stage for the rest of the book.

WHAT IN THE WORLD?

The world today is both frightening and fascinating. Wars—including wars of independence (Chechnya), civil wars (Liberia), ethnic wars (Rwanda, Bosnia), religious wars (Iran and Iraq), and, most recently, terrorist wars—seem to flare up on a regular basis everywhere. Millions follow the stories with morbid interest on television, in newspapers and magazines, and via the Internet. Perhaps the most frightening element of wars in the twenty-first century is that the technology to manufacture and deploy weapons of mass destruction is no longer limited to governments; wealthy individuals with a vendetta and the technical know-how can control the ability to kill by means undreamed of a few decades ago.

The very technology that cures diseases previously thought incurable also can be used to revive old diseases, make new ones, or even manufacture machine-based diseases (through nanobots) against which flesh and blood may very well be completely defenseless. As if that were not enough, apparently new diseases such as AIDS and Ebola have arisen in the past fifty years that have devastated whole populations. AIDS is projected to reduce life expectancy in several African nations from over fifty-five years to less than thirty-five years by 2010, and many Asian countries appear to be facing parallel consequences. Patrick Johnstone points out,

SIDEBAR 1.1
NEW AND IMPORTANT TERMS USED IN MISSION

New terms for missionary working and thinking seem to be coined daily. The following ones, with basic definitions, are used throughout the book. Additionally, many of them are discussed more fully in relevant sections of the book.

10/40 Window: An imaginary rectangular window between the 10th and 40th latitudes, bordered around Africa, the Middle East, and Asia. This window contains the bulk of the unreached peoples in the world and the bulk of the non-Christian religions.

4/14 Window: Developed as a spin-off from the 10/40 Window, this refers to the age at which children are most likely to commit their lives to Christ as well as the ages at which they are most vulnerable.

Conciliar Movement: Among contemporary churches this refers to the churches and denominations that have joined together under various ecumenical organizations, especially the World Council of Churches and the National Council of Churches. These organizations provide a platform for cooperative work through ecumenical councils or assemblies without actually binding the constituent denominations into a single organization.

Contextualization: The core idea is that of taking the gospel to a new context and finding appropriate ways to communicate it so that it is understandable to the people in that context. Contextualization refers to more than just theology; it also includes developing church life and ministry that are biblically faithful and culturally appropriate.

Creative Access Country: Formerly referred to as a *closed country*, a creative access country is a nation-state in which traditional missionary work is illegal or banned. Missionaries who want to work in such countries must be creative in the means they utilize for entry and residence.

Ecumenical Movement: Parallel to the conciliar movement, this generally refers to the twentieth-century phenomenon of Protestant churches and denominations working together in the context of the World Council of Churches with a goal of achieving some type of external unity (see Ritschl 1991).

Holistic Mission: Mission that takes into account the whole of human needs: spiritual, social, and personal. Holistic mission includes evangelism and church planting as well as development and social transformation.

Incarnational Mission: Just as Christ was incarnated as a person, so missionaries, it can be said, need to incarnate themselves into a new context. They cannot come as newborns, but they can learn the language and culture of their new context in such a way that they can behave like one who was born in that context.

Indigenous Church: A church that fits well into the local culture. Traditionally, this is defined in terms of "three selfs": self-governing (not dependent on outside agencies to make decisions), self-supporting (not needing outside funding to carry on its work), and self-propagating (able to evangelize within its own culture effectively). More recently, self-theologizing—the ability to develop its own theological understandings from Scripture—has been added to the criteria.

Indigenous Missionary: A missionary from what once was considered to be a receiving nation. This term tends to be used broadly of both indigenous evangelists (who do not cross cultural boundaries) and indigenous missionaries (who may cross significant boundaries even though they stay within their country of residence).

In Malawi 6 people an hour die of AIDS, which is over 50,000 a year. The economic devastation is horrific with deaths most prevalent among the most economically active part of the population and with an expected 10 million AIDS orphans in Africa by the year 2000. (Johnstone 1998, 258)

Mainline Denominations: The prominent denominations of the nineteenth and twentieth centuries in North America and Europe, including various branches within the Episcopal (Anglican), Presbyterian (and other Reformed groups), Methodist, Lutheran, and United Church of Christ traditions.

Majority World: Several terms have been used to describe the non-Westernized world, including *developing world, Africasia* (McGavran 1970, 9), *third world, two-thirds world, underdeveloped world,* and *world A.* The terminology is still in flux, with political agendas tied to most of the terms. In this book the term *majority world* is used to refer to this area.

Mobilizer: A person who energizes a church or group of people and its resources for mission. This may be an outsider (a mission agency representative, a missionary, a consultant) or an insider (a missions pastor, an elder, a member of the church missions committee, a Bible study leader).

Nonresidential Missionary: A missionary who, for whatever reason, is unable to live permanently in the country or among the people group that is the main focus of his or her ministry. This tends to be the case more often in creative access countries.

People Groups: A people group usually is defined by ethnic or linguistic terms. It is estimated that there are some twelve thousand distinct languages and dialects and as many as twenty-four thousand people groups in the world today.

Restricted Access Country: An older term referring to the same thing as a creative access country.

Shalom: The Hebrew word for *peace* in the Old Testament, where it refers to wholeness, completeness, and soundness. It is a holistic term, extending to include spiritual peace (salvation), physical peace (healing), psychological peace (wholeness), and social peace (justice and freedom from war).

Short-Term Missions: This usually refers to trips with a mission focus that range from one week to one or two years. They may be organized by churches, agencies, or even individuals for a variety of reasons (English-language camps, church building projects, evangelistic campaigns).

Spiritual Warfare: Reflects the reality that Satan does not want unbelievers to come to Christ or believers to live fruitful, holy lives. The warfare that Christians face involves Satan and his hosts constantly trying to maneuver them toward spiritual lethargy or depression while they seek to live the abundant life that Jesus promised.

Syncretism: The replacement of core or important truths of the gospel with non-Christian elements (Moreau 2001c).

Tentmaking: A term coined from Paul's stay at Corinth when he made tents so as to not be a burden to the Corinthian church. Tentmaking is the practice of using paid employment to gain and maintain entry in a cross-cultural setting. Tentmakers work as professionals and engage in ministry activities in addition to their wage-earning work.

Transformation: Working to change society by transforming its unjust structures into more just ones. In the twentieth century evangelicals typically did not think of transformation as appropriate missionary work. However, advocates of transformation rightly note that the historical fights against the slave trade, infanticide, widow burning, and foot binding are all examples of transformational mission.

Unreached Peoples: People groups (see above) that currently have no access to the gospel. They are "hidden" not in the sense that they are invisible, but in the sense that there is no way, given current conditions, that they can hear the gospel in their own language in a way that makes sense to them.

As bad as these circumstances are, there are equally frightening religious realities. When the Taliban ruled, Afghanistan's legal code was notorious among human rights advocates. Converting to Christianity, preaching the gospel, and proselytizing were illegal, and all carried a penalty of death. In Indonesia by the end of 2000 the death toll from Muslim-Christian clashes was over four thousand, the vast bulk of whom were Christian villagers slaughtered by Muslim jihadists. An additional four thousand were forcibly converted to Islam, and forty-one thousand were made homeless refugees in Mindanao. Christians and missionaries in India have been growing increasingly concerned at extremist statements and actions by the Hindu nationalist Bharatiya Janata Party. The burning of a train carrying Hindu pilgrims in February 2002 sparked Muslim-Hindu clashes in which more than six hundred died. In 1997 two Filipino prisoners in Saudi Arabia were beheaded apparently for evangelizing other Filipino cellmates. Harassment and persecution of Filipinos there, including deportation and jail sentences for attending Bible studies in private homes, have been steady ever since.

In Pakistan the death penalty is imposed on anyone who demeans Muhammad, and reportedly, Muslims who have disagreements with Christians take advantage of this law to get rid of their antagonists. In Colombia rebel forces closed three hundred churches, killing twenty-five evangelical pastors in a six-month span in 1999. In Nigeria Brother Andrew's ministry, Open Doors, reported that six hundred Christians were killed and two hundred churches were burned from 1982 to 1996. In Peru Christian pastors were targeted throughout the 1980s and 1990s by Shining Path guerillas. More than six hundred of them were killed primarily because they preached against the insurgents and gave their flocks strength to say no when coerced to join. The evangelical church, though less than 7 percent of the population, suffered over half of the casualties.

However, Christians not only are being persecuted, but also are persecuting. At times, unfortunately, people who claim the name of Christ are the ones who persecute others, even others who also claim Christ's name. Pentecostals in Chiapas, Mexico, have been harassed for years and denied justice by Catholic officials. By 1999 some thirty-five thousand had been forced to flee as refugees. Orthodox leaders and politicians in Romania, Bulgaria, Georgia, and Russia have been working to enact and enforce laws banning or restricting newer religious movements, including evangelical and Pentecostal groups. What in the world is happening?

QUESTIONS OF TRUTH

In the realm of ideas the encroachment of postmodern thinking is eroding traditional ideas of truth. Since the gospel is a message of truth, this will have a potentially huge impact on the missionary effort. Truth is no longer thought to be absolute. In 2001 pollster George Barna found that only 33 percent of Americans accept the idea of absolute moral truth (Barna and Hatch 2001, 80). His poll indicated that born-again Christians do better, but still only 49 percent of them accept that moral truth is absolute. For centuries motivation for missionary work has been founded on the truth of the gospel and the need to communicate that truth to people who do not follow Jesus. If Barna's polls accurately reflect American thinking, then motivation for future missionary work by Americans may be in serious trouble. What will the perceived need for the missionary enterprise be twenty years from now?

In addition to an erosion of the idea of absolute truth, other religious systems offer competing and well-articulated views of the world. While missionaries have long gone out from American locations to the rest of the world, the rest of the world now is coming to North America, where universities and colleges are teeming with people in search of higher education unavailable in their own countries. Many, having completed their education, choose to stay and settle in North America. Mosques and temples are slowly becoming a normal part of the American suburban landscape. Many of these are being built not for outreach purposes but to service the needs of immigrant communities that are not ready to give up the faith of their home countries. This is a time of unprecedented opportunity; rather than being a world away, people of non-Christian faiths are the next-door neighbors of American Christians.

This influx, however, has had a by-product. As Americans have come increasingly into contact with people of other faiths, questions have arisen about issues of salvation. Is Jesus the only way to heaven? Aren't there many paths to God? Can't other religions produce good and virtuous people? A Barna survey in 2000 of adult Americans showed that 44 percent agreed with the statement, "It does not matter what religious faith you follow because they all teach the same thing" (Barna Research Online 2000a). Even among those who have had a born-again Christian experience, 31 percent agreed with the statement, "A good person can earn his/her way into heaven" (Barna Research Online 2000a).

GLOBALISM AND TRIBALISM

In the 1996 book *Jihad vs. McWorld*, Benjamin R. Barber proposes two axial principals of our age: globalism and tribalism. He explains in a 1992 *Atlantic Monthly* article,

The tendencies of what I am here calling the forces of Jihad and the forces of McWorld operate with equal strength in opposite directions, the one driven by parochial hatreds, the other by universalizing markets, the one re-creating ancient subnational and ethnic borders from within, the other making national borders porous from without. They have one thing in common: neither offers much hope to citizens looking for practical ways to govern themselves democratically. (Barber 1992)

These forces are not unseen in missions. At times the Western dominance in finances and technology can reduce mission efforts to a McDonald's approach ("McMissions"?). North American Christians may "extra-value meal" their methodologies as packaged approaches that look the same everywhere in the world. They also may demand immediate service and solutions for spiritual problems. Within this same outlook many mission agencies focus their efforts on developing churches composed of a single demographic group. Such an approach can result in churches isolated from diversity and insulated by their ethnicity.

SPELUNKING IN THE CAVE OF MISSIONS

Spelunking is the exploration of caves. For many, mission is like an unexplored cave. Full of dark tunnels and twists and turns, and largely unmapped, mission bewilders them with talk of unreached people groups, contextualization, creative access nations, spiritual warfare, nonresidential missionaries, indigenous missionaries, tentmaking, and so on.

This may also be the experience of many of the readers of this book. To help you understand the core vocabulary related to

SIDEBAR 1.2
SO YOU WANT TO BE A MISSIONARY?

Jim Reapsome
(Reapsome 1999, 53–55 [used with permission])

Be sure you are sent by the owner of the harvest—the Lord Jesus Christ—to work in his fields. You will go because his harvest is bountiful and his workers are scarce. You will go because others have prayed for you to be sent by him.

Be sure you have Jesus' authority to do his work. You must be in step with the Lord's program, policies, and practices. This is much more important than having some organization's authority to do its work.

Be sure Jesus knows you by name, and that he knows all about you, warts and all. You are his companion and friend. He wants to live in you and bear fruit in, within, and through you. You are his plan and program to bring in his harvest.

Be sure you know Jesus' commission and the message he wants you to proclaim. You will find this only in closest communion with him in his words and in prayer. Your calling is to listen before you work, to meditate before you lift a hand.

Be sure you know the full scope of working in the harvest, because the fields are full of helpless, harassed, hurting people for whom few others—especially those in power—have any compassion at all. Their needs are total—spiritual and physical. They must be touched as well as taught, brought to spiritual life in God's kingdom as well as to physical wholeness and health here and now.

Be sure you know that working for Jesus is not work for hire. You did not earn your way onto his work force, and therefore you must not expect wages from him.

Be sure you trust Jesus to give you all you need to survive in the fields. Don't load yourself up with a lot of stuff you think you will need.

Be sure you learn from Jesus how to size up the harvest. Pray to enter the lives of those who will welcome you. Don't be surprised, however, because some parts of the field are not ripe. In fact, some people will reject the workers who bring peace.

Be sure you know you will be working like a sheep among wolves. You will work in weakness, not power. Ask Jesus to teach you how to survive and be a proficient harvester, despite the risks of being caught off guard, or trusting your own cleverness.

Be sure you are prepared for persecution at the hands of religious and political leaders. This will be for the sake of Jesus, so you can testify to him. This is a tough way to harvest, but it is the Lord's way. The Holy Spirit will speak through you, so don't worry about this in advance.

Be sure you are prepared for frightful consequences of your harvesting. Not everyone will be happy. Families will be split by betrayals and even death. You will be hated for your allegiance to Jesus, but don't quit because he will save you. If persecution in one place gets really bad, go to another place.

Be sure you don't put yourself above Jesus. Expect to share his lot in every way. He didn't come for appreciation, respect, and power. He came to seek and to save the lost, and for that he was called the devil. He said his workers should expect much worse.

These are not my instructions. They come from Jesus himself (Matt. 9:35–10:25).

REFLECTION
AND DISCUSSION

1. What is your first reaction to these observations?
2. Which observations are the most challenging to you? Why?
3. What would you say to a new Christian who tells you that she or he wants to be a missionary?

mission, it is important at least to explain the basic ideas behind the most important terms. In our discussion below we introduce those terms. In sidebar 1.1 we provide a list of concise definitions for terms used in modern mission circles, many of which are discussed in greater detail later in the book. This will provide the foundation you need not only for reading the rest of this book, but also for reading mission books in general.

Mission and Missions

The first distinction made in contemporary mission studies is between *mission* and *missions*. Until the mid-1900s no distinction was made between the two. Generally, the preferred term was *missions*. Out of the work of the International Missionary Council, however, came the recognition that biblical discussion of the idea of mission was not limited to what the church was doing, since God has always been active everywhere in the world (Potter 1991) (we will expand on this idea later). Essentially, *missions* has been relegated to the specific work of the church and agencies in the task of reaching people for Christ by crossing cultural boundaries. By contrast, *mission* is broader, referring to everything the church is doing that points toward the kingdom of God (see Cardoza-Orlandi 2002, 31–48; Moreau 2000b).

Missio Dei

Missio Dei is another term used of mission. Taken from the Latin for "mission of God," its central idea is that God is the one who initiates and sustains mission. At most, the church is God's partner in what is his agenda. This term was coined in part to refute the traditional idea that mission is centered on the church and to express that mission actually is centered on God. In essence, it "refers to everything God does for the communication of salvation" (Stransky 1991) without neglecting the important role that God has assigned to the church in that process.

Missiology

Missiology is the academic study of missions, mission, and *missio Dei*. Missiology has three central concerns: (1) the identity or nature of mission, (2) the goal of mission, and (3) the means or method of mission. To get at those concerns, missiology includes the study of the nature of God, the created world, and the church and the ways they interact. Thus, theology and the social sciences play important roles in missiological thinking. As an academic discipline it is relatively new and not completely settled (see Moreau 2001a).

Missionary

Since the understanding of the role of missionaries has changed dramatically over the past century, we need to discuss what a missionary is. The types of work that are called missionary service are almost unlimited today. From Filipino domestic servants working in the Middle East to Brazilian church planters in Portuguese-speaking Africa, from European health workers in Latin America to American microenterprise specialists working in Asia, there are a multitude of Christians working cross-culturally on every continent and from every continent. In one sense they all have the opportunity to work out the general call of God that all Christians share—the call to urge people to respond to Christ and to live lives reflecting his kingdom. The question remains, however, Are they rightly called "missionaries"? Traditionally, a missionary was a person who crossed cultural boundaries to establish new outreach on behalf of Jesus and plant new bodies of local believers. How are we to understand the new generation of cross-cultural workers who are engaged in effective ministries but do not correspond to the traditional idea of what a missionary is? Additionally, what is the difference between those

> *A missionary is a prepared disciple whom God sends into the world with his resources to make disciples for the kingdom.*
> Ada Lum (1984, 21)

who cross cultures for a short time (from a week to a year or so) and those who go for longer stays (several years to life)? Are both missionaries?

When you think of the word *missionary,* what do you imagine? Spiritual giants who look death in the face on a regular basis? People who give up vacation time to build homes in another city? Or, from a more negative view, people who sign their lives away with no chance to ever change their career? Hardy explorers who can't sit still? Religious zealots who travel far and wide searching for potential converts? Some of these misunderstandings are part of American culture, while others typically are found in churches. It will be helpful first to look at these misunderstandings as a backdrop so that what a missionary actually is can be seen more clearly. In addition, sidebar 1.2 provides helpful instructions and insights from Jim Reapsome, the former editor of *Evangelical Missions Quarterly* and *World Pulse.*

Misunderstanding 1: Missionaries are superspiritual. This may be the most common misunderstanding of all. Some assume that the commitment required to become a missionary puts people who follow that call into a category of supersaints. Others assume that the strangeness and the hardships of life in other parts of the world constantly put missionaries on their knees, and this results in a higher spirituality. The simple reality is that missionaries are human and that some go into missionary work with mixed motives resulting in mixed spirituality. Sometimes missionaries themselves make the problem worse by what they communicate to those at home (either through newsletters, Web sites, or preaching or teaching while on furlough). Missionaries are not superhuman in their faith, and the other members of the church could benefit from knowing this; it might help them see that they too perhaps could serve as missionaries.

A corollary to this misunderstanding is that missionaries never have spiritual or psychological problems. However, the recent rapid growth of member-care emphasis in mission agencies, together with some of the data developed on missionary attrition and burnout (Taylor 1997b; Whittle 1999), indicates that this simply is not true. Mission agencies have responded to the fact that missionaries hurt just like other people by making available services for those who are seeking to deal with personal pain or anguish. We will return to this topic in chapter 15.

Part of the problem here is that the missionaries themselves may feel that they are not supposed to suffer from anxiety, depression, or paranoia—after all, they are missionaries! However, God does not separate out missionaries as a class to be shielded supernaturally from pain or distress. As missionary counselor Scott Hicks points out, missionaries have tended to normalize the idea that their marriages have no problems. Thus, it is unnatural for them to go for help when they have difficulties, and they may delay until it is too late (Hicks 2001). Missionaries do hurt, and they do need help to cope with what life brings. Being aware of that from the beginning may help you, or missionaries you know, recognize more quickly when it's time to seek help in processing overwhelming events or feelings.

Misunderstanding 2: Missionaries are misfits in their own cultures. More typical of skeptics is the characterization of missionaries as those who simply are unable to fit into their home culture; moving to another culture is little more than a way to alleviate the discomfort of home.

It is true that at times the way missionaries dress and act can reinforce that stereotype. Missionaries typically are not up on the latest in fashion trends (though they may be quite stylish in their country of service, where tastes may differ radically from those of their home country). However, with the globalization of fashion (and the economy), that is slowly becoming a thing of the past.

It is also true that at times even normal communication at home seems hard for missionaries, especially if they have been well adjusted in their place of service and are going through reentry shock in readjusting to their home culture. The simple reality is that some missionaries truly are misfits in their home cultures; but certainly that stereotype does not apply to the majority of those engaged in cross-cultural service.

Misunderstanding 3: Missionaries are little more than adventure seekers. Missionaries also have been characterized as glory-bound adventure seekers who feel that the grass is greener on the other side—as long as that other side is anywhere but home. But although the life of a missionary indeed can be adventuresome, and many of the missionary heroes of the past were explorers and adventurers, the glory of adventure seeking often fades quickly in the face of learning a difficult language, adjusting to a new culture, and working with teammates who can be as cantankerous as they are loving.

Misunderstanding 4: Missionaries are always good with languages. Although being adept with languages certainly can make the

> *Had I cared for the comments of people, I should never have been a missionary.*
> C. T. Studd (Grubb 1933, 196)

missionary experience much more fruitful and valuable, missionaries (like the general population) vary in language skills. Some work diligently for years to achieve a basic level of fluency, while others seem to pick up the ability to communicate clearly by osmosis. Language learning, like culture learning, is a task that the cross-cultural worker will be engaged in throughout life. We will return to this subject in chapter 10.

The good news is that contemporary techniques for learning a second language help students to focus on methods that match their individual areas of strength rather than force them all into a single methodological mold. This makes it possible for those who are less gifted in language aptitude to learn fruitfully how to communicate in a new language, even though they still need time and hard work to be successful.

One of the realities of the urbanization and globalization of the world is that

English has been moving toward being a "world" language (though with countless variations). Urban settings are themselves polyglot, and missionaries who work among people with no common language have found at times that English is appropriate for ministry. This reality should be handled with care; we are not advocating that a missionary plan on avoiding the acquisition of a second language. Nevertheless, it is true that in certain locations language learning does not always occupy the core strategic role that it played prior to contemporary times.

Misunderstanding 5: Missionaries always have a very strong call from God. This misunderstanding builds on the idea that God's call is always identifiable through a tangible event (a dream or vision, an audible voice, an irresistible urge of some type). We will treat this topic in greater depth in chapter 9, but for now, suffice it to say that God's calls on the lives of his people are as varied as the people themselves, and it is wise not to box him into a particular method.

Misunderstanding 6: Missionaries are (bigoted) cultural imperialists. As with the third misunderstanding, this one tends to be perpetrated by those most threatened by the whole idea of mission. There has been an element of truth in this claim, especially in view of the stories of the early missionaries and their attitudes toward the people whom they sought to reach. Although today's Christians must be careful not to judge eighteenth- and nineteenth-century missionaries in light of twenty-first-century sensitivities, they should not shrink from the plain fact that missionaries, like all people, have biases and prejudices.

Particularly tempting to the missionary is the notion that he or she has been sent as an "expert" who is expected to have answers to religious questions. After all, the missionary typically comes to teach and reach rather than to listen and learn. Yet almost all contemporary missions training is geared toward helping the missionary to be successful in listening and learning, for that is the key to a heart of service.

Misunderstanding 7: Missionaries are no longer needed. Some say that the day of the missionary is dead. Perhaps this is a lingering side effect of the call for a cessation of missions that came in ecumenical circles in the early 1970s. It may be due to the recognition of the increasingly pluralistic attitude and growing global nature of the church. The reader may be surprised to know that the authors essentially agree that missionaries are no longer needed—if the missionaries we have in mind are the intrepid explorer, or the commercially minded person who serves in a neocolonial role, or

> *If every Christian is already considered a missionary, then all can stay put where they are, and nobody needs to get up and go anywhere to preach the gospel. But if our only concern is to witness where we are, how will people in unevangelized areas ever hear the gospel? The present uneven distribution of Christians and opportunities to hear the gospel of Christ will continue on unchanged.*
>
> C. Gordon Olson (1998, 12)

the "big man" who demands that things be done his (or her) way at the expense of indigenous sensitivities.

God's work of bringing all people to worship him is far from finished, and thus the need for missionaries will be present until the consummation of history. One of the exciting realities of our day, however, is that the Western missionary is no longer the only one toiling in God's harvest fields. Indeed, the evidence is clear that Western missionaries have become a minority in God's labor force. Even so, the need is for all peoples who have viable churches to be directly engaged in the task of sending their own laborers, and Western churches are not exempt from this responsibility.

A corollary to this misunderstanding is that missionaries, especially Western missionaries, cost too much. We will discuss this subject more fully later, but for now, three important arguments will help clear some of the fog surrounding this misunderstanding. First, Western churches are not exempt from the responsibility to send workers into the harvest field simply because laborers from the West cost more. Second, if Western churches were to turn away from sending out missionaries and only send money to support less expensive missionaries from non-Western settings, the zeal of the church soon would decline and even the flow of money would be in danger of drying up. Third, although God commands Christians to be good stewards, he never asks them to determine their role purely in light of monetary considerations. God's focus is on reaching people, not on attaining the greatest efficiency in the process. The "most bang for the buck" is not God's ultimate standard of judgment on how to carry out our missionary obligation.

Misunderstanding 8: Missionaries always go overseas. This misunderstanding focuses on the idea that unreached people are always "over there," and the missionary has the task of going to where they are. Immigration and urbanization patterns have resulted in many arrivals in North America who rep-

resent cultures that currently have little or no viable witness for Christ. While away from home, whether as students or professionals or refugees, people tend to be more receptive to the good news of the gospel than when they are in their home cultures with all of their support structures intact. At one time, *home missions* referred to pockets of indigenous people needing to be reached within the home country. Today, the meaning is much broader, and it includes work among resettled urban populations (e.g., Indians in Chicago, Cubans in Miami, Chinese in Los Angeles, Bosnians in New York) as well as work among international students present in every major university in North America.

Misunderstanding 9: Missionaries live in "the bush." This misconception comes from a stereotype of pioneer missionary work carried out in remote jungles in Africa, highland villages in Papua New Guinea, or the Amazon basin in South America. Although many missionaries live and minister in remote rural settings, urbanization is changing that situation quite dramatically.

Soon more than half of the world's population will live in cities (Barrett, Kurian, and Johnson 2001, 2:541), and some mission agencies are beginning the difficult process of changing deployment based on this reality. Urban mission can range from helping the desperately poor in Manila, to dealing with bureaucracies in São Paulo, to meeting the needs of executives in Nairobi—a bewildering set of challenges that requires the very best of our efforts if the world's megalopolises are to have an effective gospel witness. Although it is true that much of the Bible translation work left to be finished is focused on rural pockets of people, our attention is commanded by the simple fact that half of the world's popula-

CASE STUDY: KIDNAPPED!

Paul G. Hiebert
(Hiebert and Hiebert 1987, 230–32 [used with permission])

"We have to decide now," said Gerald, chairman of the mission's executive committee. "It is Wednesday, and it takes two days to get the money to the kidnappers. The deadline they gave us was Sunday."

"I vote against paying the ransom," said James. "If we give in now, it will encourage terrorists everywhere to kidnap missionaries for ransom. Besides, we can't agree to their condition that we take our missionaries out of Mindanao and abandon our new converts. That would sentence them to persecution, possibly even death."

"I know," said Sarah, "but what about Mark? I believe they will kill him, just as they did Pastor Manuel last week. They mean business! And what about Rachel and the children? What about all the relatives and the members of the Hansons' church? They will never forgive us if Mark is killed. I can't blame them. I know how I would feel if someone let a person I loved die. I am convinced we must negotiate with the kidnappers on the ransom. If necessary, we can move the missionaries to Devao. They would be safe in the city, and the young Christians in the villages could still meet with them when necessary."

Gerald realized he held the deciding vote. The committee had discussed the various possibilities many times over the past three weeks since the kidnapping took place. Now they had to make a decision.

The crisis began when the executive committee of the Mindanao Muslim Mission received word that the Reverend Mark Hanson, one of their missionaries, and Pastor Manuel had been kidnapped by the Islamic Jihad, a radical Muslim movement in the Philippines. Mrs. Hanson was in Manila with her two young children when the kidnapping occurred. The kidnappers demanded $50,000 and a promise that the missionaries would leave the area. They gave the mission two weeks to respond. The year before, the general board of the mission had adopted a policy not to negotiate with terrorists, so the executive committee rejected the ultimatum. At the end of the two weeks, it received word that the kidnappers had killed Pastor Manuel and had set a new deadline for Mark Hanson's death two weeks hence.

Immediately after the kidnapping, the mission had informed the relatives and Hanson's church of the mission policy regarding kidnapping. Although they agreed that paying the ransom

---

tion is packed together in sprawling urban landscapes, desperately seeking work, educational opportunities, and a better life than the countryside offers.

Misunderstanding 10: Missionaries sign their lives away forever. Some people think that once you become a missionary, you are stuck for life, and for them, the idea of making a lifetime commitment is too overwhelming to contemplate. Although a permanent missionary commitment perhaps was truer of the missionaries of previous centuries, it certainly does not hold in the same way today. As we will see in chapter 9, God's call to ministry can be fulfilled in numerous ways, of which traditional missionary work is only one.

CONCLUSION

Those who seek to follow God's leading into cross-cultural missionary service face a more rapidly changing and dangerous world than ever before. This is a time in North America when the willingness to sacrifice in the service of Christ is harder to

would only encourage terrorism in the future, they encouraged the mission to continue negotiating with the kidnappers for Mark's release. Special prayer sessions were organized in the churches for both Mark and Pastor Manuel.

After Pastor Manuel was executed, however, the family members urged the mission to pay the ransom secretly. When the executive committee reaffirmed the board policy, the family members, with the help of the pastor of Mark's home church, began to raise the money and contact the terrorists on their own. They also called upon the United States government to urge the Philippine government to seek Mark's release. Some of the church members, unhappy with the committee's action, said they would withdraw their support if the mission did not negotiate to save Mark's life. They also contacted members in other churches, who then phoned the mission office to express their concern for Mark Hanson's life.

The U.S. State Department contacted the mission and urged it not to pay the ransom. It offered to assist the mission board by putting pressure on the Philippine government, but the mission, wishing to avoid a close identification with the United States government, asked it to wait.

When the press heard of the kidnapping, newspaper reports began to appear—branding all Muslims as fanatics and terrorists, and calling on the government of the United States to offer commandos to the Philippine regime to recapture Reverend Hanson. Despite the mission's pleas that the press keep silent on the matter, so as not to antagonize the kidnappers and other Muslims, inflammatory articles continued to appear in the local papers.

The executive committee kept in contact with the kidnappers through its field director in the Philippines and tried to negotiate

a peaceful settlement. But the kidnappers remained adamant—the mission would have to pay the money and leave the area. If they refused, there would be other reprisals. None of the missionaries would be safe.

Gerald contacted the chairman of the mission board, who pointed out that there was no time to call a board meeting. Besides, the board members knew little about the situation. He said that the executive committee was authorized to act in times of emergency.

Now, as Gerald looked at James and Sarah, he thought of Mrs. Hanson and her children, and of the mission and its commitment to evangelize the Muslims in Mindanao. If a nation expected its people to die for the nation, should the church not expect Christians to give their lives for the cause of Christ? But did this situation call for such a sacrifice? Gerald breathed a prayer before he spoke....

find than in centuries past. The case study for this chapter—"Kidnapped!"—draws on this reality to show that missionaries and mission agencies have to be ready to respond to crisis situations.

There also are greater opportunities than ever before. Missionaries know of and can have access to literally millions of people who have yet to hear the claims of Christ through a variety of means—radio, satellite, Internet, video—that the apostle Paul never could have imagined.

As we introduce you to both the challenges and the opportunities, our prayer is that you will have the foundation necessary to make wise decisions about mission service, or if you are not so called, to help you counsel and guide others whom God brings across your path who are seeking his will in reaching the nations.

PART 1

Encountering Mission in the Scriptures

The Bible tells the story of God's work for and among all the peoples of the world. The fact that the word *mission* does not appear anywhere in the Bible, then, does not mean that the Bible is not a missionary text through and through.

In the Bible a divine drama is played out through the lives of numerous people, spanning thousands of years, who respond to God's call and choose to walk his path. This drama can be divided into a series of acts following the lives of the people it portrays as they struggle with the reality of a broken world and their own yearnings to connect to the One in whose image they are made.

Each scene in the drama is full of twists and turns, including various plots and sub-plots. Some characters, such as God, Christ, the Spirit—as well as Satan, the enemy of humankind—are found throughout the narrative. Others make quick entrances and exits, leading lives that reflect God's image to a bleeding world.

In the four chapters comprising this first part of the book we explore this divine drama. Chapter 2 focuses on the Old Testament, and chapters 3 and 4 present the story in the New Testament. Chapter 5 begins the work of putting it all together, showing what is necessary for a theology of mission that honors biblical teaching and briefly surveying selected areas of that theology.

Encountering Mission in the Old Testament

INTRODUCTION

Can a clear case for Christian mission be made from the Old Testament? Evangelical missiologists resoundingly answer yes—but then, they would be expected to give this answer since their livelihood depends on it! Are they being fair to the Old Testament? A commonly held view in popular culture in North America is that the God of the Old Testament is the God of anger and wrath, and only in the New Testament is the God of love found. Some Old Testament scholars argue that Israel had no responsibility toward the nations, and the New Testament should not be read into the Old (see, e.g., Dobbie 1962). If this is true, then one would not expect to find much on mission in the Old Testament.

Fortunately, it is not true. As we will show in this chapter, from the very opening words of the Bible important themes in mission appear that are expanded throughout the Old Testament. They lay the foundation for what is found more explicitly about mission in the New Testament. Old Testament scholar Christopher Wright explains the Old Testament orientation toward mission:

> First, it presents the mission and purpose of God with great power and clarity and with universal implications for all humanity. Second, the Old Testament shaped the very nature of the mission of the New Testament church, which, indeed, felt compelled to justify its mission practice from the Scriptures we now call the Old Testament. (Wright 2000)

Mission in the Old Testament is best encountered by exploring it as a divine drama in four acts: (1) the creation and the fall, (2) God's calling and setting apart a people for himself, (3) God's work in rescuing his people, and (4) God's work in sending his people into exile. The encounter with the New Testament presented in chapters 3 and 4 will introduce you to three more acts in this drama. We do not intend to support any theological structure by dividing the biblical story into seven acts, and, as an illustration, sidebar 2.1 gives different ways to structure the drama.

ACT 1: THE CREATION AND THE FALL

In the first statement in Genesis God is seen as the sovereign creator of the universe. What God creates is "very good" (Gen. 1:31); it is good because goodness finds its reference in the character of God himself, and whatever he creates will, by definition, be good.

God Creates

That God is the creator of the universe establishes his concern for the people he creates. That concern is not limited by racial, political, gender, economic, or religious boundaries. Wherever one goes in the world, God is already there. He is intimately interested in every person in the world right from the start, and that interest does not change over time. Because of this intense interest in every person, God is in the process of making himself known long before missionaries arrive on the scene. Mission is *God's* project, and he graciously allows Christians to take part in it. As we saw in chapter 1, this idea is captured by the term *missio Dei* (see McIntosh 2000). It indicates that although the church plays a central role in mission, it does not play the only role.

The fact that God created Adam and Eve put them (and us) in his debt—a debt that never can be fully repaid. All people owe their very existence to God. He does not ask for repayment, but he does ask for acknowledgment. God is the inventor of creation. To put it in today's terms, God owns the patent. Like all patent owners, he deserves the royalties for his inventive work. In this case, the royalties given to God are simply our glorification of him through delighting in him (Piper 1993) and in all that he made.

This is the foundation for mission and is implicit in the creation story.

From the beginning, Adam and Eve were set apart from the rest of creation. God made nothing else in his image (Gen. 1:26–27). Although the exact meaning of being made "in God's image" is debated in theological circles, at least three implications are clear. First, the image of God is linked to the command to have dominion over the rest of creation. God is the King of kings, but human beings are his vice-regents.

Second, every human being is significant in God's eyes simply because God made him or her. You are significant. It is natural that you want to experience that significance, and the history of our race shows the great creativity, as well as perversity, in our attempts to connect to the One whose image we all bear. The tragedy of the story is that, like flies returning to garbage, over and over again people connect to the idols made in their hearts rather than to the One who made them (Keyes 1992).

Third, being made in God's image and given subsequent responsibilities as a race, we have a purpose in living: we are to glorify God by delighting him as we exercise dominion over creation and are fruitful and multiply. This responsibility to exercise worshipful and respectful dominion over creation has been called the *cultural mandate* (Adrian 1967, 21). It comes before the fall and continues on in the midst of a broken world. Dyrness summarizes:

> This then is the commission given to man and woman: to serve creation and one another in their daily work, to build a social world centering on the family. All these tasks, however humble, have their intrinsic value. All of this done with integrity glorifies God, or at least God cannot be

SIDEBAR 2.1
THE DIVINE DRAMA—HOW MANY ACTS?

In *Let the Earth Rejoice! A Biblical Theology of Holistic Mission,* William Dyrness (1983) developed the idea of exploring mission in the Bible as a divine drama. He splits that drama into five acts, while we divide the story into seven acts. The following table shows the breakdown of the two approaches.

DRAMA IN FIVE ACTS	DRAMA IN SEVEN ACTS
ACT 1: Creation (Genesis 1–50)	**ACT 1:** The Creation and the Fall (Genesis 1–11)
ACT 2: The Exodus (Exodus through preexilic history, writing, and prophets)	**ACT 2:** Calling a People through Abraham (Genesis 12–50)
ACT 3: The Exile (exilic and postexilic history, writing, and prophets)	**ACT 3:** Rescuing and Separating a People: The Exodus and the Monarchy (Exodus through preexilic history, writing, and prophets)
ACT 4: Jesus Christ: The Coming of the Kingdom (Matthew through Jude)	**ACT 4:** Maintaining God's Holiness: The Exile (exilic and postexilic history, writing, and prophets)
ACT 5: The Consummation (Revelation)	**ACT 5:** Saving a People: Jesus the Messiah (Matthew through John)
	ACT 6: Gathering a People: The Church (Acts through Jude)
	ACT 7: Renewing All Creation: The Consummation (Revelation)

REFLECTION AND DISCUSSION

1. What are other ways in which the story of God's work in the Bible might be divided?
2. What factors help you decide how to separate one act from another in the scriptural story?
3. Might people of different cultures divide the story in ways that make sense to them?

glorified if all this is left undone. (Dyrness 1983, 36)

Our purpose as people made in God's image remains even after the fall and the flood, as God repeats the command to multiply and subdue the earth in Gen. 9:1–7. The covenant that God established with Noah and his sons encompasses all humankind (Gen. 9:8–19).

Adam and Eve Fall; God Pursues

Being creatures with choice, Adam and Eve try to bypass God's plan for them by listening to the enticing ideas of the serpent. They fall. As a result of their blatant denial of respect for their creator, God judges them and the serpent.

In essence, the story of mission from that time on has been the story of God reaching out to humans, who are asked to choose sides. The conflict between God and the serpent, or Satan, is not a dualistic battle. Satan's defeat was provided for even in God's judgment against Adam and Eve. Eve will produce offspring who will fatally wound

> There was no "mission" in the Garden of Eden and there will be no "mission" in the new heavens and the new earth (though the results of "mission" will be evident). From the first glimmer of the gospel in Genesis 3:15 to the end of this age, however, mission is necessitated by humanity's fall into sin and need for a Saviour, and is made possible only by the saving initiative of God in Christ.
>
> Andreas Köstenberger
> and Peter O'Brien (2001, 251)

the serpent (Gen. 3:15). This initial promise of salvation, known as the *protoevangelium* (Peters 1972, 83–86), is the promise that Jesus will come for all people. However, this does not come without a battle, as Dyrness notes:

> Mission, if it is to succeed, must involve conquest; there will be battles and casualties. For the struggle of God in history is with the powers of evil, and his people

will become involved in this battle when they join themselves to him. (Dyrness 1983, 117)

Throughout the rest of this first act in the divine drama the consequences of the fall are evident. Brother murders brother (Gen. 4:1–16), and all of humankind rebels in wickedness so that God destroys all but a remnant (Gen. 6–9). At the same time, however, a veiled reminder of the initial promise given in Gen. 3:15 reappears after the flood in Gen. 9:27, when God promises to dwell in the tents of Shem (Kaiser 2000, 17). This is a hint that God's blessing to all people would come through a particular people (Dyrness 1983, 45), which will unfold in the following acts of the drama.

Ultimately, the nations themselves fall (Gen. 11:1–9). This last piece of the story clearly shows that the effect of the choice of our progenitors is not limited to individuals. Entire societies are infected. For example, people are divided by language and consequently culture. This splitting serves as a protection against the prospect of unchecked sin made possible by a common language ("better division than collective apostasy" [Kidner 1967, 110]). Linguistic and cultural barriers remain today and are great obstacles to the missionary task.

After the fall, in their search to connect to the significance of being image bearers of their creator, people build idolatrous systems designed to create a name for themselves. The story of the tower of Babel exemplifies this orientation to life. As a people, we are so broken that we do not recognize that God longs to give us names he has chosen and to fill us with the sense that we belong to him so that we may properly delight in him.

In this act of the divine drama all of the main characters are introduced. God starts it all. He pursues Adam and Eve after the fall and promises the solution to their (and our) brokenness. Adam and Eve choose a path opposite to God's clear instruction, and they suffer the consequences. They are broken in how they relate to God, each other, and even themselves. Satan tempts Adam and Eve to deny God, and as a result his doom is pronounced. Jesus also appears, although in shadow form, through the promise of a battle between Eve's offspring and those of the serpent. A hint appears that although God's intention is for all humankind, his method will focus on a particular people.

With the fall comes banishment from the garden and from intimate contact with the creator. Individuals have fallen, but so have whole societies. The curtain closes on this act with a world of people scattered and unable to communicate with each other. With people broken, separated from the creator, and successfully lured by a clever enemy, the stage is set for the story of redemption played out through the rest of the drama.

ACT 2: CALLING A PEOPLE THROUGH ABRAHAM

In the opening of the second act God calls Abraham in the first phase of the story of his reaching out to us. The call is found in Gen. 12:1–3:

> The LORD had said to Abram, "Leave your country, your people and your father's household and go to the land I will show you. I will make you into a great nation and I will bless you; I will make your name great, and you will be a blessing. I will bless those who bless you, and whoever curses you I will curse; and all peoples on earth will be blessed through you."

God thus calls Abraham to leave his land and people to go to a land to be shown by God. There, God will make Abraham into a great nation and bless him. Three blessing promises are given by God, all with the same purpose in mind. First, God will make Abraham into a great nation, a promise tied to the land to which God calls him. Second, God will give Abraham a great name. The purpose of both blessings is that Abraham be a blessing to others. The third blessing and purpose clarify that although Abraham is the means, he is not the goal. It is through him that others will be blessed by blessing, but the purpose goes beyond Abraham: *"all peoples on earth* will be blessed" (emphasis ours). God's universal intent now is to be manifest through an individual and the people who come from that individual.

Paul echoes this in the New Testament. In Rom. 4:13 he identifies Abraham as "heir of the world." In Gal. 3:8 he argues that the promise in Gen. 12 foreshadows the gospel going to all nations.

In the first act of the drama the universal nature of God's love and concern is clearly seen. They establish that God's goal is not limited to any person or people. In this second act, however, the particular method that God will use to express universal concerns is in focus. Although God's method is to work through a particular person and the people who come from him, his intention remains universal, as Old Testament scholar Walter Kaiser notes:

> The fact remains that the goal of the Old Testament was to see both Jews and Gentiles come to a saving knowledge of the Messiah who was to come. Anything less than this goal was a misunderstanding and an attenuation of the plan of God. God's eternal plan was to provide salvation for

all peoples; it was never intended to be reserved for one special group, such as the Jews, even as an initial offer! (Kaiser 2000, 10)

In Abraham, then, God manifests his reign. Through him the kingdom revealed in creation and rejected by Adam and Eve is restored and begins its advance. Abraham is blessed not only for his sake, but also for ours. God's missionary heart is evident as he begins the process of rolling back the kingdom of darkness and seeking his lost creation. No wonder Paul asserts that the Abrahamic covenant stands throughout the ups and downs of Israel's history as the proper foundation for God's ultimate salvation blessing in his Son (Gal. 3:14; Williams 1989, 70–76).

Kaiser maintains that this is the Old Testament version of the Great Commission (Kaiser 1996; 2000, 13). Abraham was chosen, and through him Israel was called to become the people of God. The initial choice of Abraham, however, was for the benefit of all peoples (Gen. 12:3; 22:18), as Kaiser argues,

> The sweep of all the evidence makes it abundantly clear that God's gift of a blessing through the instrumentality of Abraham was to be experienced by nations, clans, tribes, people groups, and individuals. It would be for every size group, from the smallest people group to the greatest nation. (Kaiser 2000, 19)

The nations will not be blessed in some automatic fashion, however. John Stott explains, "Now we are Abraham's seed by faith, and the earth's families will be blessed only if we go to them with the Gospel. That is God's plain purpose" (Stott 1999, 9). God's call is not solely for our blessing, but is also a call to service on behalf of humanity (Adrian 1967, 25).

The rest of Genesis works out God's call of Abraham, through the lives of Isaac, Jacob, and Joseph, until the chosen people are in Egypt enjoying the blessings of God's protection as a result of Joseph's faith and wisdom.

At the end of the Genesis story, a further clarification of the promise made in the garden is given. The identity of the one foreshadowed to come through Eve in Gen. 3:15 and hinted at in the line of Shem in Gen. 9:27 is now further narrowed to the line of Judah, fourth son of Jacob, Abraham's grandson (Gen. 49:9–12; see Kaiser 2000, 47).

ACT 3: RESCUING AND SEPARATING A PEOPLE: THE EXODUS AND THE MONARCHY

As the third act opens, God's people find themselves in Egypt rather than in the land promised to Abraham. God knows that they probably would remain content to live in Egypt forever, but the time has come for them to claim the heritage that Abraham had received by faith. It is time again for God to intervene. Now God will take his people out of Egypt and place them in the land from which they would serve as a blessing to the peoples of the world.

Through God's mighty hand, Israel is rescued from Egypt. It is in this process that a national identity is forged and the descendants of Abraham are forced to take sides. Even so, Exod. 12:38 refers to the whole group as a "mixed multitude" (NASB), indicating a group made up not just of Abraham's descendants but also others who wished to join them (Dyrness 1983, 60). Thus, even in the forging of Israel's

SIDEBAR 2.2
MISSION IN PSALM 67

Psalm 67 has long been known for its "whole world" perspective on God's blessing. The psalmist extols God to the ends of the created order, offering three reasons that God's community is called to prove his purposes in blessing them. First, everyone in that community has experienced God's grace and knows that God offers it to all people—if only the rest would come to know that same grace (vv. 1–3). Second, God rules in righteousness and guides all the earth—it is time for the whole earth to acknowledge his just leading (vv. 4–5). Third, God has been good to his community— the nations need to see this and come to know his goodness as well (vv. 6–7).

Psalm 67

> ¹May God be gracious to us and bless us
>   and make his face shine upon us,
> ²that your ways may be known on earth,
>   your salvation among all nations.
> ³May the peoples praise you, O God;
>   may all the peoples praise you.
> ⁴May the nations be glad and sing for joy,
>   for you rule the peoples justly
>   and guide the nations of the earth.
> ⁵May the peoples praise you, O God;
>   may all the peoples praise you.
> ⁶Then the land will yield its harvest,
>   and God, our God, will bless us.
> ⁷God will bless us,
>   and all the ends of the earth will fear him.

REFLECTION AND DISCUSSION

1. As you meditate on the psalm, write out the implications for the nations in your own words as a meditative prayer to God.
2. In addition to the land yielding its harvest, in what other ways will God bless his people if they praise him before the nations?

national identity the universal nature of God's concern is found.

Several decades later, with the rescue complete and the lessons of unbelief and a resulting forty-year wilderness detour behind them, Israel moves into the promised land. The people are sternly warned by Moses of the consequences of intermingling with the nations they find inhabiting Canaan. The greatest danger lies in turning from God to worship false gods, and unfortunately, that possibility recurs as a reality throughout the monarchy that is established.

Again and again throughout the monarchial period, the time of the divided kingdom, and the subsequent exiles, the people turn their backs on God. He alternately disciplines and extends mercy to them. The discipline is a stark reminder of God's unwillingness to share the glory due him with any rival. God's acts of mercy demonstrate his love not only for those he has called, but also for every people he has created.

Several mission themes are interwoven in this act of the divine story. We will briefly explore three of them: (1) the universality of God's intent, (2) the purpose of God's people as light for the Gentiles, and (3) the narrowing of the means of deliverance from a people to a person.

God's Universal Intent

Although the story of rescue and separation involves one people in particular, the fact of God's universal intent through that one people remains clear. Just as God called one person (Abraham) to be a blessing for the whole world, so now he begins with one land (Israel) to renew the whole earth (Dyrness 1983, 79). Israel is only the starting point of a universal program of God.

This is seen in several ways. For example, strangers were allowed to enter in among the people of Israel, and they were to be loved as the Israelites loved themselves (Lev. 19:33–34). Foreigners were expected (and allowed) to come to the temple to worship (1 Kings 8:41–43). God's house was not confined to Israel alone; it was to be a house of prayer for all nations (Isa. 56:6–7). God was to uphold Israel so that all the people of the world would know that he is God (1 Kings 8:59–60).

The psalms, not often thought of as missionary in focus, clearly relate God's universal intent. As missiologist George Peters points out, a universal note can be found in more than 175 references in the psalms. He goes so far as to assert, "the Psalter is one of the greatest missionary books in the world" (Peters 1972, 116). Peters advises the reader to study Pss. 2, 33, 66, 72, 98, 117, and 145. To this list Kaiser adds Pss. 67, 96, and 100 (Kaiser 2000, 30). Missionary and Old Testament professor W. Creighton Marlowe discusses terminology of active outreach found in Pss. 46, 49, 57, 67, 96, 105, 108, 119, and 145 (Marlowe 1998, 447), and Kaiser notes,

> Over and over again the psalmists called on all the peoples of all the lands and nations to praise the Lord (Pss. 47:1; 67:3, 5; 100:1; 117:1). Even more directly, these ancient singers of Israel urged their people to tell, proclaim, and make known the mighty deeds of Yahweh (Pss. 9:11; 105:1) and to join in singing praises to God from all the nations (Pss. 18:49; 96:2–3). The psalmists themselves offer to sing God's praises among the nations (Pss. 57:9; 108:3). The expected result would be that all the ends of the earth would turn to the Lord and all the families on earth would bow down in worship to him (Pss. 22:27; 66:4; 86:9). (Kaiser 2000, 37)

Psalm 67:1–7, for example, is a request that God bless Israel so that when the peoples of the world look at Israel, they will see God's hand and come to know God (see Kaiser 1999, 15–16).

The preexilic prophets add their voices in proclaiming a universal thrust for mission. Joel prophesies the outpouring of God's Spirit on all people (2:28) and God's coming judgment of all nations (3:11–12). Amos predicts that God's restoration will involve all the nations that bear his name

---

SIDEBAR 2.3
"SENT" IN THE OLD TESTAMENT

Since mission essentially means to send someone, an examination of what people are sent to do in the Bible will help clarify what the mission of the Christian is. The following are side-by-side summaries of two such studies (May 1959, 23; McDaniel 1998, 16–19).

MAY	McDANIEL
1. It is God who sends; the initiative in sending or mission lies with God.	1. The Old Testament presents a picture of God as the divine, sovereign Lord, who sends in order to convey and accomplish his will on earth.
2. The purpose in sending is twofold: first, to deliver his people from their enemies, both spiritual and material; second, to bring back his people to himself.	2. God exiles sinners and sends a variety of agents to punish wrongdoers.
3. Those whom God sends are always related to this twofold purpose: kings, judges, and leaders to deliver his people; prophets and afflictions to bring them back to himself.	3. God also sends benefit and salvation.
4. There is little or no suggestion that God's sending extends beyond his own people: it is to Israel that God sends judges, prophets, and afflictions, either to deliver or to bring back to himself. Nor is there any suggestion that Israel itself is sent by God to deliver the other nations and bring them to God, except perhaps in the famous Servant Songs of Isaiah.	4. God does send people, and most often the person sent is a prophet who promises those held captive that God will send a savior and champion to free them.

REFLECTION AND DISCUSSION

1. What implications are there for mission in the way God sends in the Old Testament?
2. How might these insights be helpful in developing a theology of mission?

(9:11–12). Habakkuk declares that the whole earth will be filled with the knowledge of God, as waters cover the sea (2:14). Micah looks to the day when the nations will come to worship God (4:1–4). Jonah preaches, against his will, to the Assyrians; to God's delight and Jonah's chagrin, they repent. Zephaniah prophesies universal judgment (3:8) and restoration of God's people before the eyes of all nations (3:20).

The most significant missionary message in the Old Testament prophets comes from Isaiah. He declares that God's servant will be a light for the Gentiles and that all the earth will see his salvation (42:6; 49:6) and be full of the knowledge of him (11:6–9). He also foretells the coming of the Servant of the Lord.

The Purpose of God's People: A Light for the Gentiles

Isaiah calls Israel a "light for the Gentiles" (Isa. 42:6; 49:6). God did not bring Israel out of Egypt without reason; God's people are to serve in a mediatorial role. They are God's priests out of the whole world (Exod. 19:5–6), which makes them the servants of God (see also Deut. 14:1–2).

In Exod. 19:4–6 God tells Moses to announce to Israel that because he himself brought Israel out of Egypt, they will be his special possession, his kingdom of priests, his holy nation. By designating them as his "special possession," God shows that he places a high value on people. As his "kingly priests," "the whole nation was to function on behalf of the kingdom of God in a mediatorial role in relation to the nations" (Kaiser 1999, 13). As a "holy nation," they were wholly God's, set apart for his service, not for their own ends.

Israel (specifically Jerusalem) was to serve as the center to which other nations would come, a light to the nations. This truth led missiologists to speak of the centripetal (inward focused) nature of mission in the Old Testament (see Adrian 1967; Peters 1972, 21–25). This centripetal impetus, however, was not the only mission direction seen in the Old Testament. In fact, Kaiser argues that the Old Testament thrust was for Israel to go out and bring religious teaching to the nations (Kaiser 2000, esp. 36–38; see also Marlowe 1998). God sends (see sidebar 2.3) Abraham to a new land, Moses to lead the people back to the land while exhibiting God's wonders to Egypt, and Jonah to preach repentance to the hated Assyrians in Nineveh. The fact that the Israelites fail to live up to God's expectations should not deter present-day readers from seeing that they had a responsibility to go and be a blessing in order to present God to any people who did not know him.

The Means of Deliverance: From a People to a Seed

The final theme in this act is that the promise first given in Gen. 3:15 is narrowed down from a particular people to a particular person who will redeem Israel and provide hope for the nations. Isaiah in particular, through the Servant Songs in chapters 40–55, describes God's Suffering Servant. An intermingled picture of corporate and individual identity, the Servant Songs portray a suffering one who will come to bring healing to the nations. Wright's summary is worth noting:

> The mission of the Servant would be one of justice, gentleness, enlightenment, and liberation (Isa. 42:1–9). But it would also involve rejection and apparent failure (Isa. 49:4; 50:6–8) in the task of restoring Israel to God. In response to that, his mission would be extended to include the nations to the ends of the earth (Isa. 49:6). In that way, the mission of the Servant would be the fulfillment of the mission of Israel itself. (Wright 2000)

In the third act of the divine drama of mission the universal intent of God is developed through a particular people. Individuals from among the people of Israel, especially the prophets, are sent by God to call the people to repentance and deliverance. Israel as a nation is to serve in the same capacity among the rest of the nations of the world. Unfortunately, Israel fails to live up to God's call, and as a result the next act in the divine drama is one of brokenness and scattering.

ACT 4: MAINTAINING GOD'S HOLINESS: THE EXILE

As Adam and Eve were expelled from the garden, so also Israel is expelled from the land. More than just a judgment, however, this is God's way of "clearing the deadwood" out so that his purposes will be accomplished. The prophets of the exile and later do not stop proclaiming God's provision through the coming messiah. They strongly declare the universal nature of God's continuing work. Jeremiah announces that all the nations will be gathered to Jerusalem and that they will not walk in the stubbornness of their hearts anymore (3:17). He also announces God's new covenant, when all God's people will know him (31:27–37). Ezekiel prophesies that the heathen will know that he is God (36:22–23). Zechariah looks ahead to a day when many nations would join God's people (2:11).

In the midst of the exile God continues to provide signs of hope. He is still interested in the peace of the nations. He wants them to repent and be spared from the judgment they deserve. Jerusalem, when it is rebuilt, will be a source of praise among the nations.

At the same time, a more solidified and hopeful picture now emerges of one coming who will fulfill God's promise and rescue Israel, a hope not lost during the centuries of the exile. His coming is the next act in the divine drama unfolded through Scripture.

CONCLUSION

The drama of mission in the Old Testament brings all of the main characters into the play. God, humanity, and a shadowy accuser engage in a conflict of cosmic proportions. The savior, who will crush the head of the accuser, has been promised.

Mission in the Old Testament involves the individual and the community of God's people cooperating with God in his work of reversing what took place as a result of the fall. They do this by participating in God's covenant of peace (*shalom*—wholeness, completeness, soundness [Isa. 54:10]), which is entered by faith in God (Gen. 15:6), including trusting in his power to totally deliver, and by living a life of obedience in the light of his word (Mic. 6:8), no matter what the cost (Gen. 22:1–18). The picture of the drama painted in the Old Testament becomes a backdrop for the continuation as God further unfolds his story for the nations in the New Testament.

The case study that concludes this chapter focuses not on the divine drama, but on the fact that the ability to communicate the biblical message clearly in a new culture depends on how well key terms that express the divine drama are interpreted. Perhaps the most important words to be chosen are those that translate into the new language the various Hebrew and Greek terms for *God* found in the Bible, and the case study illustrates some of the issues involved in the decision-making process.

CASE STUDY: A WORD FOR GOD

Paul G. Hiebert
(Hiebert and Hiebert 1987, 155–57 [used with permission])

Ivan threw up his hands. "What is more important—" he asked his colleague, "that people think of God as 'ultimate reality,' or that they think of him as a 'person' with whom they can communicate? Each of these, by itself, is a half-truth. Yet somehow it seems to me that we must choose between two words that carry these two meanings when we translate the word God into Telugu. What shall we do?"

After joining the Union Bible Society, Ivan had been asked to assist in a new translation of the Bible into Telugu. After settling down in the city of Hyderabad, he began to work with Yesudas, a high-caste convert who was also assigned to the project. Together the two had worked out many of the difficult problems they faced in translating the Bible into this South Indian language. But the most stubborn one remained unsolved. What word would they use for "God"? The choice they made was critical, for the nature of God lies at the very heart of the biblical message. To use the wrong term for "God" would seriously distort the Christian message. But although there are many Telugu terms for "god," none conveyed the biblical meaning.

At first Ivan suggested, "Let's use the term *deva*. That is the word the people use when they speak of 'god' in general terms."

But Yesudas pointed out, "The *devas* are the highest form of personal beings, but they are not the ultimate reality. Like all things in the universe, they are *maya,* or passing phenomena. In the end, they, too, will be absorbed into the ultimate reality or Brahman. Moreover, they do both good and evil. They fight wars with each other and with the demons, commit adultery, and tell lies. Finally, in Hinduism 'all life is one.' In other words, gods, humans, animals, and plants all have the same kind of life. Consequently, *devas* are not fundamentally different from humans. They are more powerful and live in the heavens. But they sin, and when they do, they are reborn as humans, or animals, or even ants." Yesudas added, "Hindus claim that *devas* often come to earth as *avatars* to help humans in need, but because there is no difference between them it is like kings helping their commoners or saints helping their disciples. We, therefore, can use neither *deva* nor *avatar,* for both destroy the biblical meaning of the 'incarnation.'"

"If that is the case, why not use the term *parameshwara*?" Ivan suggested. "That means 'highest of the deities.'"

Yesudas replied, "Yes, but this carries the same connotations as *deva*. In fact, all Telugu words for 'god' implicitly carry these Hindu beliefs! We have no word that means a supreme being who is the ultimate reality and the creator of the universe. Moreover, there is no concept of 'creation' as found in the Bible. The world itself is an illusion that does not really exist."

Ivan took another approach to the problem. "Why not use the concept of *brahman* itself? After all, *brahman* is ultimate reality—that which existed before all else and will exist when all else has ceased to be."

Yesudas objected. *"Brahman,"* he said, "may be ultimate reality, but it is a force, not a person. True, some philosophers speak of *sarguna brahman,* of *brahman* in a personal form. But even he is only a manifestation of *nirguna brahman,* which is an insular, impersonal force. It makes no sense to say that *nirguna brahman* reveals itself to gods and humans, just as it makes no sense to say that a dreamer speaks as a real person in his dream. Similarly, humans have no way of knowing about or communicating with *nirguna brahman.* Moreover, nothing really exists outside of *brahman.* The heavens and earth are not creations that exist apart from it. They are projections of *brahman* in much the same way that a dream is a projection of the dreamer. So, in fact, we are all simply manifestations of the same ultimate reality. This destroys the biblical idea of a creator and a real but contingent creation."

"What shall we do then?" asked Ivan. "Perhaps we could use the English word 'God' or the Greek word *Theos* and introduce it into the translation. In time the word would become familiar, and it would not carry within it the implicit Hindu theology found in Telugu words."

"How can we do that?" asked Yesudas. "When we preach in the villages, no one will understand those foreign words. We must use words the people understand. Isn't that what the early church did when it took the Greek words for 'god' and gave them new Christian meanings?"

Ivan countered, "Even if we do use *deva* or *brahman* and try to give them a Christian meaning, they will still be given Hindu meanings by the Hindus. And since the Hindus make up ninety percent of the population, how can a small Christian community maintain its own definitions of these words when the linguistic pressures for accepting the Hindu connotations are so great?"

"Well," said Yesudas, "we're back to square one. Should we use *deva,* or *brahman,* or 'God'? We have to use one of these."

The two discussed the matter for a long time, for they knew that their choice would influence both the evangelistic outreach of the church and also the extent to which the church would understand and be faithful to the biblical concept of God in the next fifty or hundred years. Finally they decided to …

3

Encountering Mission in the Gospels

INTRODUCTION

Proverbs 13:12 reads, "Hope deferred makes the heart sick, but a longing fulfilled is a tree of life." Hope in a messiah was generated by the promise that God gave immediately after the fall of Adam and Eve. After thousands of years of waiting, God's people are finally to realize that hope. Their sick hearts are about to become trees of life.

In the New Testament the One promised long ago by God comes in the person of Jesus. "Sending" was an important element in the Old Testament picture of mission. It is even more clearly central in the New Testament. God sent Jesus (John 20:21). In turn, Jesus returns to God and sends the Spirit to his followers (John 15:26; 16:7). In the power of the Spirit they are sent by Jesus into the world to proclaim God's kingdom and call people to glorify the King of kings through a worshipful lifestyle (John 20:21–22; Acts 1:8). This truly is good news for all people.

As a collection of documents telling the story of Jesus, the Gospels do not contain a systematic theology of mission. However, "The New Testament is a missionary book

in address, content, spirit and design. . . . The New Testament is theology in motion more than theology in reason and concept. It *is* 'missionary theology'" (Peters 1972, 131 [emphasis ours]).

In this chapter and the next we explore the rest of the divine drama in three acts. In act 5, Jesus saves a people. In act 6, the church is established. Finally, in act 7, all is consummated and the curtain is drawn on mission.

ACT 5: SAVING A PEOPLE: JESUS THE MESSIAH

In this act, seen through the Gospels, God at last answers the hopes that the prophets had planted, nurtured, and stirred in his people. However, the fulfillment of their hopes comes in an unexpected way. Jesus did not come as a conquering king ready to take over Rome. Rather, he came as a humble teacher prepared to die on behalf of his people.

Each of the four Gospels was written with a specific purpose in mind. These various perspectives reflect each author's view of Christ's purpose and are in turn reflected in the different versions of the missionary commission of Christ found in the Gospel accounts.

Matthew

Matthew splits the story of God's history of salvation into four missional epochs or time periods (Harvey 1998b, 122): (1) the prophets proclaiming the promise of Jesus, (2) Jesus' own redemptive mission fulfilling the promise of the prophets, (3) the commissioning of the disciples to make disciples of all nations, and (4) the angelic mission at the return of Christ to separate the righteous from the unrighteous.

Today, the church stands in Matthew's third epoch, and three passages in his Gospel stand out as exemplars of that epoch: 9:35–38; 24:14; 28:16–20.

MATTHEW 9:35–38

Jesus went through all the towns and villages, teaching in their synagogues, preaching the good news of the kingdom and healing every disease and sickness. When he saw the crowds, he had compassion on them, because they were harassed and helpless, like sheep without a shepherd. Then he said to his disciples, "The harvest is plentiful but the workers are few. Ask the Lord of the harvest, therefore, to send out workers into his harvest field." (Matt. 9:35–38)

In this first exemplar text, Jesus' compassion on those separated from God and his urge to see them rescued are clearly seen. Also obvious is an intimate connection between "preaching the good news of the kingdom" and "healing every disease and sickness" (cf. 4:23). Jesus' sense of compassion for the people comes as a result of his ministry among them of preaching,

teaching, and healing. Through his ministry among the broken and hurting, Jesus sees the people as God sees them.

Jesus' work as portrayed by Matthew includes teaching in the synagogues, preaching the good news of the kingdom, and healing people. It is by these that the "harassed and helpless" are harvested. Jesus' healings include expulsion of demons, as seen in the story of the healing of the mute demoniac (9:32–34) told immediately before the report of Jesus' ministry and his charge

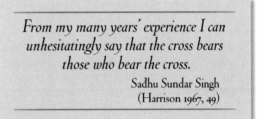

From my many years' experience I can unhesitatingly say that the cross bears those who bear the cross.

Sadhu Sundar Singh
(Harrison 1967, 49)

to his disciples. People feel swallowed up by sin and by the hurts of life. Jesus calls his followers to release and heal them.

The Christian's part in the drama is not simply to watch Jesus from the audience. He commands the disciples to petition God to send out laborers into the harvest. Then, as now, the laborers are few, while the crop to be harvested is huge. The source of the problem is not that the crop is huge, but that harvesters are lacking. Jesus not only commands the disciples to pray that God would raise up more harvesters, but also sends them out to show how serious he is (10:1–23). They themselves are an answer to the prayer that they are commanded to pray.

Christ's command has an urgency not usually captured in today's translations. First, the harvest often was a metaphor for the end times, and every farmer knew the importance of getting a harvest in once it was ready. Second, the Greek word translated as "send out" means to thrust violently (it is also used for expelling demons from people). A farmer who hired laborers to harvest the crop, knowing the importance of gathering in the harvest before it rots, might not be gentle in getting lackadaisical workers out into the field.

The fact that two thousand years have intervened since this event took place does not lessen the urgency. Today's Christians are still to pray that God would "expel" laborers—and be ready to be sent themselves.

MATTHEW 24:14

And this gospel of the kingdom will be preached in the whole world as a testimony to all nations, and then the end will come. (Matt. 24:14)

This second exemplar text expresses the scope of the gospel. Today, the influence of religious pluralism has resulted in calls from many to curtail Christian evangelistic activities. "Since all religions ultimately are expressing the same truth," many people reason, "why go and antagonize people by telling them that their religion is false?" In sharp contrast, the statement of Jesus stands as a beacon to those who follow him: Christians must preach the good news of Jesus to the whole world. No other option is available for those who claim to follow Christ.

Jesus' statement intimately links Christians reaching all nations with his return. Theologian George Ladd explains the core issues in preaching about Jesus among all people as a central theme in God's view of contemporary history:

The ultimate meaning of history between the Ascension of our Lord and His return in glory is found in the extension and working of the Gospel in the world. . . . The divine purpose in the nineteen hundred years since our Lord lived on earth is found in the history of the Gospel of the Kingdom. The thread of meaning is woven into the missionary program of the Church. (Ladd 1974, 133)

How does the church know when it has accomplished what Jesus expects? What does he mean by saying that the gospel will be preached as a testimony to "all nations"?

The Greek words translated as "all nations" have a variety of possible interpretations. The one typically used in mission over the past thirty years among evangelical missionaries is "people groups." This orientation has given rise to the current "Adopt-A-People" campaign and has guided most evangelical missionary strategy during that time. We explore this further in sidebar 3.1.

MATTHEW 28:16–20

Then the eleven disciples went to Galilee, to the mountain where Jesus had told them to go. When they saw him, they worshiped him; but some doubted. Then Jesus came to them and said, "All authority in heaven and on earth has been given to me. Therefore go and make disciples of all nations, baptizing them in the name of the Father and of the Son and of the Holy Spirit, and teaching them to obey everything I have commanded you. And surely I am with you always, to the very end of the age." (Matt. 28:16–20)

The third exemplar text is Matthew's report of the Great Commission. In mission circles this certainly is the most widely used version of Jesus' commission to his follow-

---

SIDEBAR 3.1
THE MEANING OF "ALL NATIONS"

In recent years proponents of church growth have advocated that the evangelical church generally has misunderstood "all nations" in a modern sense rather than grasping the original one (see, e.g., McGavran 1970, 62). This assumption is in the background of mission strategizing today, and uncovering it is critical to understanding current mission strategies and interests. For the most thorough explanation and defense of this idea, see John Piper's *Let the Nations Be Glad!* (1993, 167–218).

Essentially, the term used by Jesus has a range of possible meanings. The main options include:

1. *All the non-Jews*, which would be momentous for the early disciples. That salvation was for all was a new concept for them, extending into Acts and brought to a head at the Jerusalem council (Acts 15).

2. *Nation-states* as they were understood at the time of the writing of the New Testament. Essentially, they were somewhat fluid geographic spheres of influence rather than the sharply bounded political states of today.

3. *Ethnic groups* (the Greek word translated "nations" is *ethnē*). The primary idea is that of ethnic (or ethnolinguistic) groups, and all the "nations" refers to all the ethnolinguistic groups in the world.

4. *The whole of humanity in a general sense.* Advocates of this view say that to force the text to undergird a sociological "people group" strategy to fulfill the Great Commission is to take it beyond its intended meaning (see Verkuyl 1978, 106; Carson 1984, 596; Bosch 1983, 235–40).

REFLECTION AND DISCUSSION

1. Discuss how understanding the Great Commission through each of these options would impact the mission of the church.
2. How does one choose from among the options?
3. Which option do you think is the appropriate interpretation? Why?

---

ers (cf. Mark 16:14–18; Luke 24:36–49; John 20:19–23), and it merits close attention.

Before discussing the passage itself, we should point out that the church by and large did not use it as a motivation for mission prior to 1792, when William Carey published *An Enquiry into the Obligations of Christians to Use Means for the Conversion of the Heathens.* In this booklet Carey laid the foundation for contemporary mission societies. His ideas were so influential that many call him the "father of modern Protestant missions," even though Protestant missions (and mission societies) had been founded long before his work was published (as we will see in chapter 7).

The great Reformers in Europe had largely understood this passage to be lim-

ited to the twelve apostles (Bosch 1983, 218; Culver 1984, ix–xvi). It was Carey's thinking on the Great Commission, made concrete by his visionary work, that launched what eventually became today's missionary societies and agencies.

The first distinction of Matthew's version of the Great Commission is the fact that all authority has been given to Jesus. *All* is a key word in this passage, being used four times: Jesus has been given *all* authority; the disciples must go to *all* the nations; the disciples must teach them to obey *all* things; Jesus is with the disciples *all* the days (for discussion, see Bosch 1983, 229).

First, Jesus has all authority in heaven over angels, demons, Satan, and any rulers and authorities in heavenly places. He also

---

SIDEBAR 3.2
DOES DISCIPLESHIP INCLUDE JUSTICE?

Through much of the twentieth century evangelicals tended to think of discipleship in terms of personal piety and evangelistic zeal. South African missiologist David Bosch, in agreement with this, writes that the core of what Jesus taught is summarized in the command to love God and people (Matt. 19:16–26). However, he interprets this in a way that challenges our thinking. "But Jesus radicalizes these commandments in a specific direction: To love one's neighbors means to have compassion on them . . . and to see that justice is done" (Bosch 1983, 234). Bosch proposes, "To become a disciple is to be incorporated into God's new community through baptism *and to side with the poor and the oppressed.* To put it differently, it is to love God and our neighbor" (Bosch 1983, 235 [emphasis ours]).

REFLECTION AND DISCUSSION

1. Do you agree with Bosch? Why or why not? Support your position by drawing on Scripture and theological reflection.
2. If Bosch is right, what are the implications for Christian mission?

---

has all authority on earth over kings, rulers, leaders, and all people. This gives him the divine right, as ruler over all, to give all Christians their marching orders.

His use of *therefore* shows the connection between the authority and the order. In this is seen the "dawning of the new age of messianic authority" (Carson 1984, 595). The risen Jesus is completely qualified to give orders. He can impel (or expel, as we saw in Matt. 9:35–38) his disciples into the harvest fields.

Despite the impression often given in the English translations of the New Testament, the foundational command of Matthew's Great Commission is not "go" but "make disciples." A legitimate question to ask is, What is a disciple? In the Bible the central idea of discipling is that of learning in the context of a relationship. Throughout the New Testament discipleship always involves attachment to a person, and most often that person was Jesus. In its most technical sense it is applied to the twelve apostles (Matt. 10:1). More broadly it is used of those who follow him during his earthly ministry (John 6:60–66) and of Christians in general (Acts 14:28; 15:10, 19).

In terms that make the best sense of Jesus' Commission, disciples are people who have a deep, abiding commitment to a person (Christ), not simply a philosophy. They hold to Jesus' teaching (John 8:31–32); they love one another (John 13:35) and help each other (Matt. 10:42); they bear fruit for Christ (John 15:8) and are partners with him in service (Luke 5:1–11). All of these, when done in godly fashion, are acts of worship that glorify God the creator.

Disciples are the family of Jesus (Matt. 12:46–50), putting him ahead of all other earthly commitments (Matt. 8:21–22; Luke 14:26–27) to the extent that they are willing to suffer for the sake of the gospel (Matt. 10:17–23). Michael Wilkins clearly expresses what discipleship involves:

> Jesus declared that to be a disciple is to become like the master (Matt. 10:24–25; Luke 6:40). Becoming like Jesus includes going out with the same message, ministry, and compassion (Matt. 10:5ff.), practicing the same religious and social traditions

(Matt. 12:1–8; Mark 2:18–22), belonging to the same family of obedience (Matt. 12:46–49), exercising the same servant-hood (Matt. 20:26–28; Mark 10:42–45; John 13:12–17), experiencing the same suffering (Matt. 10:16–25; Mark 10:38–39), and being sent in the same way to the same world (John 20:21). (Wilkins 2000)

From a missionary perspective, an intriguing element of making disciples of all nations is the implied demand of crossing cultures and discipling those who are different from us. We will return to the implications of this in later chapters.

Three auxiliary or attendant activities are attached to the command to make disciples: going, baptizing, and teaching to obey. "Going" sometimes is seen as a com-

> *Sent by the one who has all authority, who enables them to overcome any obstacle, and who is always present with them, Jesus' followers are to make disciples of all the nations, disciples who are obedient in carrying out the task entrusted to them.*
>
> John Harvey (1998b, 136)

mand, with some justification (see Carson 1984, 595; Bosch 1983, 229–30; O'Brien 1976, 72–73; Culver 1984, 150–52). Even if "going" is not technically a command, Christians certainly are not simply to sit and wait for people to come to them. A natural part of making disciples is going to new places where there are no disciples. This is an overt shift from what the disciples thought about letting the nations come to Israel and learn of God. Today, there can be no doubt that Christians are to take the

initiative and cross boundaries of all types (geographic, political, ethnic, linguistic) to make disciples.

Having gone (in the specific use of Matthew's Great Commission), those who are sent use, as the means of making disciples, baptizing and teaching to obey. But do not think that these two are the only elements of discipleship, for the grammar will not sustain this (see sidebar 3.2). Though these are not the sole means, they do characterize the discipleship process (Carson 1984, 597).

The basic thrust in baptizing is to initiate people into the Christian faith. Although Matthew's formula is Trinitarian, all of the baptisms in Acts are performed only in Jesus' name. Matthew's intention through Jesus' words is not to set a rigid rule for the means of baptism (such rules too easily move toward legalism), but to ground the need for baptism as the appropriate Christian ritual that embodies repentance from sin and entrance into allegiance to Christ.

Finally, making disciples includes teaching them to obey all the things that Jesus commanded. Don Williams comments,

> And what is it that Jesus commands? In sum, in the context of Matthew, it is to preach the gospel of the kingdom, cast out demons, and heal the sick. To be a disciple of Jesus is to bear his message and continue his ministry. Nothing less will do. (Williams 1989, 131)

These commands are universal, applying to all cultures and times. They were relevant to the first disciples, they remain relevant today, and they will be relevant until Christ returns.

Christians are not simply to teach, but to teach to obey. Memorizing Scripture and being able to argue the finer points of theology are not enough. Christ's followers must obey what they know and teach others to do the same. The form of this command sets in motion a generational effect. Every generation of disciples has the holy obligation to teach the next generation to obey the teachings of Jesus.

Finally, Jesus attaches the promise of being with his disciples to the end of the age. The original, translated literally, says, "I will be with you the whole of every day" (Moule 1959, 34). He is with his followers to protect them, encourage them, and watch them as they engage in the process of discipling others.

Mark

Mark's Gospel is perhaps the least Gentile-focused of the four (see discussion in Köstenberger and O'Brien 2001). However, the contributions he brings to the divine drama of mission are the realities of discipleship failure together with persecution and suffering.

Suffering is interwoven throughout Mark's Gospel (e.g., 8:31, 34; 9:49; 13:9–13; 14:36). He vividly portrays the fact that mission takes place in a hostile world (Williams 1998, 137). It is in this light that the passion and death of Jesus give meaning to all the other traditions about him—his death is an "enacted rite of salvation" (Dyrness 1983, 139). That it was a Gentile who acknowledges Jesus as the Son of God (15:39) shows that the ransom Jesus paid for many (10:45) was acknowledged by them and that his death and the preaching of the good news in the whole world belong together (Hahn 1965, 118).

Although the version of the Great Commission commonly noted in Mark (16:14–18) is not found in the oldest manuscripts, it is congruent with the character of the rest of Mark's Gospel. In it the focus is on Jesus' power over those that are hostile toward God as a vehicle for preaching the good news to all creation (or all the nations [13:10]).

That power, however, does not mean that mission will go forth without suffering, as Joel Williams notes:

> In our own time the mission of the church is presented on occasion in triumphant terms, in which Christian soldiers march ever onward and God's kingdom swiftly spreads from shore to shore. . . . The teaching of Mark's gospel on mission can serve as a corrective to an unrealistic optimism. The witness of believers may occur in a world that is indifferent or even openly hostile, and the proclamation of the gospel may take place in the context of difficulty and persecution. Instead of offering more effective or successful methods, Mark points to the way of the cross, the path of self-sacrifice and humble service. (Williams 1998, 150)

Another crucial facet of Mark's Gospel account is that he vividly illuminates the persistent failures of the disciples: "Jesus' disciples, far from being a potent missionary force during Jesus' earthly ministry, are consistently shown to fail in their efforts to understand the true nature of Jesus' identity, the meaning of the cross and the thrust of his mission" (Köstenberger and O'Brien 2001, 86).

There is good news, however: even though the disciples struggle and fail to consistently recognize Jesus for who he is, he still drafts them into full partnership with him (Köstenberger and O'Brien 2001, 83). Perhaps this theme reflects Mark's feelings about his own failure as a missionary (see Acts 15:37–38).

Whether or not this is true, it expresses the truth that God does continue to use failures to accomplish his purposes. This message of discipleship failure, then, is one of encouragement. If God could use people who time and again failed to understand and believe Jesus to turn the world upside down, then there is hope that God can use you and me. Our role in the divine drama of mission does not end with a single failure or even a series of failures, for God is bigger than our failures and can use them for his purposes. This is truly good news for missionaries.

Luke

In Luke's carefully researched account Jesus fulfills the Old Testament promises and offers salvation to the lowly (Dyrness 1983, 150). Together with Acts, the Gospel of Luke provides the most clearly delineated picture of mission in the Bible (Köstenberger and O'Brien 2001, 111). The fact that Luke's Gospel was written to Theophilus (a Greek name) is an indication of Luke's personal commitment to going beyond the house of Israel and bringing Christ to the nations.

In Luke, Jesus is not only the sent one, but also the sender of others. This is clearly portrayed in two key passages: Luke 4:18–19 and 24:46–48.

JESUS THE SENT ONE

The Spirit of the Lord is on me, because he has anointed me to preach good news to the poor. He has sent me to proclaim freedom for the prisoners and recovery of sight for the blind, to release the oppressed, to proclaim the year of the Lord's favor. (Luke 4:18–19)

Possibly the most discussed passage in Luke in contemporary mission is Jesus' disclosure of his task as the sent one in 4:18–19. Central to Jesus' understanding is that it is the Spirit on him and anointing him to carry out his mission. Thus, mission comes out of the anointing and sending of the Spirit, not our own initiative.

Jesus' use of words from the Book of Isaiah in this declaration incorporates four infinitives to mark the nature of what he was sent to do: *to preach* good news to the poor, *to proclaim* freedom to the prisoners and recovery of sight for the blind, *to release* the oppressed, and *to proclaim* the year of God's favor. That three of the four are related to preaching is an indication of the thrust of the means of Jesus accomplishing his mission, and yet, "For Luke the spiritual is primary, yet the liberation it brings is holistic" (Larkin 1998, 160).

First, Jesus was sent to preach good news to the poor, "the people who are most in need of divine help and who wait upon God to hear his word" (Marshall 1978, 183). Most contemporary scholars limit discussion to those who are in a state of economic destitution (see Green 1994, 60–65), but in the context of Isaiah the reference is to "the eschatological community, the suffering exiles or faithful in Israel who have been spiritually oppressed" (Köstenberger and O'Brien 2001, 117).

Second, Jesus was sent to proclaim freedom to the prisoners and recovery of sight to the blind. Is this freedom physical, sociopolitical (political, economic, and social liberation), spiritual (release from sin, demons), or in some sense all three? "Prisoners" are literally captives of war (see Luke 21:24). In favor of not limiting the interpretation to the literal is that the audience to whom Jesus declared Isaiah's prophecy to be fulfilled were not themselves in captivity. The term is also used in the New Testament as a metaphor for being dominated (e.g., by the power of sin in Rom. 7:23, and by Christ in Eph. 4:8). Luke nowhere presents a literal war captive being freed by Jesus. Thus, Jesus' intention most likely was metaphorical, and the liberation envisioned is freeing "people who were captives to guilt (see 7:41–50), to the crushing and bruising power of Satan (see 8:26–39), to the love of money (e.g., 19:1–10) and so forth" (Gooding 1987, 82).

Jesus' proclaiming work also included recovery of sight to the blind, a miracle he literally accomplished (Luke 7:21–22; 18:35–43). This also figuratively means to forgive, and Luke later recorded that Jesus commissioned Paul to open the eyes of Gentiles so that they would receive forgiveness (Acts 26:15–18; see Gooding 1987, 82–83), so it is not limited to the physical recovery of sight (Marshall 1978, 184).

Third, Jesus was sent to release the oppressed. Since the poor, the captives, and the blind are all in the category of the oppressed, this does not add new meaning to the message, but encapsulates the emphasis of the whole. Luke 7:22–23 cites several ways that Jesus actually fulfilled this mission (Liefeld 1984, 867).

Fourth, Jesus was sent to proclaim the year of God's favor. Release has come today in the person of Jesus. It is not limited to the end times, though the final outworking of the "Year of Jubilee" (see Lev. 25:13) will come then.

Isaiah's original statement also declared that the sent one would proclaim "the day of vengeance of our God," which Jesus omits in his recitation. The omission was startling to his audience, for the Jews familiar with this passage expected not only their own release, but also the destruction of their enemies. Contemporaries of Jesus promised a Jubilee

(an economic event in which all debts were forgiven) as a rallying cry to call people to the day of God's vengeance, which was to be exacted by overthrowing the occupying powers (Larkin 1998, 161).

By omitting the reference to God's vengeance, however, Jesus indicates that his Jubilee Year focuses on reconciliation rather than revenge, and this reconciliation is extended even to God's enemies (Bosch 1991, 110–11).

JESUS THE SENDING ONE

Luke portrays Jesus not only as the sent one, but also as the sending one. During his earthly ministry he sent the disciples out twice to the house of Israel (9:1–6; 10:1–16). The symbolic nature of sending out seventy disciples should not be overlooked. In Jewish tradition humankind was thought to encompass seventy nations and seventy languages in the world, and "the sending of the seventy emissaries is an implicit claim that Jesus' message must be heard not only by Israel but by all men" (Ladd 1974, 114; see also Liefeld 1984, 940). After his death and resurrection, Jesus, in Luke's version of the Great Commission, tells the disciples that they will be his witnesses to the whole world (see Larkin 1998, 165):

> He told them, "This is what is written: The Christ will suffer and rise from the dead on the third day, and repentance and forgiveness of sins will be preached in his name to all nations, beginning at Jerusalem. You are witnesses of these things. (Luke 24:46–48)

In contrast to Matthew, Luke presents Jesus' commission as a statement of fact and promise rather than a command. It sets forth "in a nutshell, Luke's entire understanding of Christian mission" (Bosch 1991, 91). At least six elements are included: (1) Jesus' life, death, and resurrection come to fulfill Scripture so that (2) the message of forgiveness and repentance will be preached (3) to all nations, (4) beginning in Jerusalem; (5) and the disciples themselves will become Jesus' witnesses (6) after they receive the promised power from God. This whole framework resurfaces in Acts 1:8, which outlines the book that serves as the sequel to Luke (Bosch 1991, 91).

Luke shows why Jesus was sent. He also shows the connection between Jesus' sending and ours. Christians are now the sent ones, with the explicit obligation to be witnesses to the life, death, and resurrection of Christ and to the need for repentance and the possibility of forgiveness of sin. This message is to go to all nations in God's power. That, for Luke, is Christian mission.

John

In John's Gospel God is the center of mission; it is he who so loved the world that he sent his unique son (3:16). Some argue that the book itself is primarily an evangelistic treatise (Erdmann 1998, 206–8). If so, it certainly follows that there would be a strong mission theme in the Fourth Gospel.

While God is the center of mission, Jesus is the focus of mission (Köstenberger and O'Brien 2001, 203). He is the sent one—the unique one who shares deity with God (1:1), came from the Father (1:18), does what he was sent to do (5:36) and thus glorifies God (1:14; 13:31–32), returns to the father (13:1), and now sends those who follow him to continue his work (20:21).

In John's Gospel the mission of Jesus' followers is seen only through the lens of his mission. John's version of the commission thus is founded on a striking parallel: as Jesus was sent, so he sends us (20:21; cf. 17:18).

John Stott notes, "If then, we are to understand the nature of the church's mission, we have to understand the nature of the Son's!" (Stott 1975a, 68). What, then, was Jesus sent to do?

John's Gospel is rich in the vocabulary of *send*—the term and its derivatives appear almost sixty times in twenty chapters. A quick look at the passages shows that John's perspective on why Jesus was sent is clear: to save the world (3:17); to do God's will (4:34); to finish God's work (5:36; 9:4), which includes believing in the one whom God sent (6:29); to work for the honor of the one who sent him (7:18); to tell what he heard from God to the whole world (8:26; 12:47–50) and in that way make God known to the world (17:25–26).

In his prayer for the disciples Jesus notes that because they believed the words he brought, they knew that God indeed had sent him (17:8). In that sense, Jesus sends the disciples out as he was sent. Their task is also clear: to make God known to the world in the same way Jesus did, glorifying God and telling the world what they learned through the one who sent them. That remains our task today.

CONCLUSION

In all four Gospels, then, the themes of the sending of Jesus and his subsequent sending of Christians are clear. Today's world is filled with pain. That pain finds its ultimate source in our sin and separation from God, as a species and as individuals. Jesus was sent to effect reconciliation between God and humanity, offering hope

CASE STUDY:
LILY LIU'S BAPTISM

James Chuang
(Hiebert and Hiebert 1987, 152–54 [used with permission])

"What do they know about baptism? How can I bend God's command in order to please them?" Reverend Smith asked himself. As a young missionary to Taiwan, he had been looking forward to his first baptism in the small Baptist church outside Taipei when Lily's parents had come to his home, furious and demanding that he not baptize their daughter, Lily, the next day.

Reverend Smith thought back to what he knew of the bright young woman. Lily had grown up in a Buddhist home, seeing idols and smelling incense all her life. She first heard of Christianity from the Smiths when they moved in next door. They soon became friends. Not only Lily but also her entire family welcomed the new neighbors. After four years of fighting doubts and opposition, Lily made a solid decision for Christ. Her testimony was so dynamic that the youth group elected her to be their first woman president.

Mr. Liu was a faithful Buddhist who checked each evening upon his return from work to see whether the incense before the images was lit. As a bus driver, he did not want to offend his ancestors lest they cause him to have an accident. Like other bus drivers he also scattered paper money along the road when he drove over dangerous mountain roads in order to protect himself from the spirits of those who had died there in past accidents. Mrs. Liu, too, took their religion seriously. She was a loving mother who cooked, washed, cleaned, and said prayers for her children. Once she refused to allow a worker sent by the telephone company to put up a pole in front of her house because, she said, it might block the passage of her gods.

Although neither Mr. nor Mrs. Liu were Christians, they attended the church services on occasion. They also allowed Lily to participate freely in church activities. But they drew the line at baptism. Mr. Liu told Pastor Smith, "I like what you teach, but what do you think my ancestors will say if I accept your religion? They would be very upset, and how can I do anything to displease my ancestors?" He likewise refused to allow Lily to violate family tradition. Moreover, he needed her to worship his spirit after his death so that he would be cared for in his afterlife. Mrs. Liu's opposition to the baptism centered around Lily's marriage. Only two percent of Taiwan's population were Christians, and it would be much harder to find Lily a husband if she were a Christian.

Reverend Smith pondered the situation, for he knew that Lily would arrive shortly to seek his direction. Should he advise her to ignore her parents' orders? This would surely destroy the relationships he and his wife had so carefully cultivated with Mr. and Mrs. Liu and the other neighbors. Or should he suggest that she wait, thus denying her the opportunity to give a public testimony of her faith in Christ?

---

of eternal life through the forgiveness of sins. People receive that hope by repenting, committing themselves to Christ, and being baptized in his name. Having been forgiven, they are in turn sent to proclaim that good news to others, preaching to all the peoples of the world the opportunity to be reconciled with God through Christ. Those who respond are to glorify the King of kings through living worshipful lives—lives that are in tune with God and his will for the world. That, at the core, is the mission of the church. In the next act of the divine drama mission is enacted as the church brings the good news to a hurting world.

"Lily Liu's Baptism," the case study for this chapter, illustrates a central issue in the New Testament story of a person coming to Christ. In many parts of the world baptism is rightly seen as a watershed event. Christians recognize it as a crucial part of incorporation into the body of Christ. In areas where other religions dominate, especially Islam and Hinduism, however, it is seen as an affront to the religion from which the convert has come. In those cases it can lead to rejection, ostracism, persecution, and even martyrdom of the one being baptized. The case study illustrates the difficulty of putting the call of Christ to baptism ahead of the obligations of family and culture, in this instance in a Buddhist setting. This is part of the divine drama of mission, enacted through the lives of those following Christ.

4

Encountering Mission
in the New Testament Church

INTRODUCTION

The divine drama does not end with the death and resurrection of Jesus. Jesus' followers having been commissioned, Luke picks up the story in the second volume of his historical account, the Book of Acts. In it he traces the earliest establishment and expansion of the Christian church—much of it through seemingly serendipitous trials and tribulations rather than directed, purposeful evangelism. In this act of the divine drama the church is both the center and the agent for the kingdom of God in the world, and the story of the church as portrayed in Acts *is* the story of God's mission. That story continues to focus on sending and going into the world, calling peoples of all nations, tongues, and tribes to glorify God through living worshipful lives.

ACT 6: GATHERING A PEOPLE: THE CHURCH

Luke outlines early in Acts the direction in which this part of the story will take us: beginning in Jerusalem, then to all of Judea and Samaria, and finally to the ends of the earth (1:8).

The consistent failures of the disciples in Mark are seen in Acts as well, though not quite as conspicuously. Again, this is good news for us: God chooses to use ordinary people, not supersaints, to accomplish his work of calling the world to glorify him.

Jerusalem Reached

After the Spirit comes, the early church is privileged to see many Jews who come to Jerusalem from around the world respond to Peter's inspired preaching by placing their trust in Christ at Pentecost (2:1–41). However, even such a vivid illustration of God's concern for the whole world does not seem to shake the apostles enough to move them beyond the boundaries of Jerusalem. Over the next several chapters (3–7) Luke recounts how they evangelize among Jerusalem's Jewish population. This population includes both those born into Jewish heritage and those who came to the Jewish faith from Gentile backgrounds.

One of the first problems that the members of the young church have to address is an unequal distribution of food among widows, apparently along ethnic and linguistic lines. They solve it by assigning deacons of Gentile descent to ensure that the Gentile-descended widows' needs are met (6:1–6). Though they consolidate their gains in the fledgling church, and rejoice in what God is doing, they still do not seem to truly grasp the idea that Christ is for those beyond the borders of Judaism and that they themselves have a responsibility to live out this truth.

Judea and Samaria Reached

Stephen, one of those chosen to ensure that food is properly distributed, preaches forcefully in the power of the Holy Spirit and is martyred (6:8–7:60). A fiery persecutor named Saul looks on with approval (8:1). This event opens the doors of a broader persecution, with Saul as the chief antagonist, and the church scatters (8:1–3; 11:19).

Luke then tells a story of Philip, one of the scattered, to illustrate the results of the scattering. At last the church is now moving out of Jerusalem to all of Judea and Samaria. Philip, whose name indicates his Greek heritage, successfully brings the good news across a cultural boundary by preaching in Samaria (8:5). The Samaritans, historically related to the Jews, are a mixed lot who are seen by the Jews as "half-breeds," not fully Jewish but not completely Gentile.

They respond to Philip's preaching, and accompanying signs and wonders affirm their conversion. The church in Jerusalem, apparently still not understanding, sends Peter and John to check things out and ensure that the conversions are real (8:14–17). The stories brought back by Peter and John are enough to convince the Jerusalem church leaders that even Samaritans can come to faith. Christians in our time

have a hard time recognizing how great a shift this was for the first Christians. Even so, God had not yet finished expanding their horizons.

In preparation for what is to come, Luke relates the story of Saul, the witness of Stephen's martyrdom and now the main enemy of the early church (9:1–31). Because of the vigor and success of Saul's persecution, the church must scatter for safety. An unintended result of that scattering is that Jesus is preached more broadly. Thus, even before Saul's miraculous conversion, one result of his work is the spread of the church.

That conversion, told three times in Acts (9:1–19; 22:3–21; 26:1–23), becomes a central event for the expansion of the church. In it Luke sets the stage for the person who will be the center of the story of Acts from chapter 13 on.

Before that, however, Luke returns the thread of the narrative to the apostle Peter. By now, having seen the conversion of Samaritans himself, Peter is at least open to the wonder of what God is about to do. Leaving no room for doubt, however, God gives Peter a vision that forces him to open the door for Gentiles to convert (10:9–16). Cornelius comes to Christ, and the stage is finally set for the ends of the earth to be reached. Unlike Peter, Cornelius does not need three repetitions of the same vision to be convinced of what God is saying to him (10:1–8).

To the Ends of the Earth

After Peter is imprisoned and then escapes, Luke's focus dramatically switches. Now in Antioch, rather than Jerusalem, a multiethnic church is described. Luke set the stage by earlier relating the story of the development of the church in Antioch from those scattered by persecution (11:19–29). In this story the Jerusalem church sent Barnabas to Antioch to see what was happening. Encouraged by what he saw, he went to Tarsus to get Paul, and the two of them lived and ministered in Antioch for a year, after which they were sent to Jerusalem to bring an offering from Antioch to help out with famine relief (11:27–29; 12:24–25). Though often overlooked, the journeys from Tarsus to Antioch and from Antioch to Jerusalem and back form Paul's first missionary experiences.

It is while they are in Antioch, away from Jerusalem, that God sets Paul and Barnabas aside for the special task of going throughout the world proclaiming the gospel (13:1–3). God wants to *send* them out from the Antioch church to the ends of the earth. The door that was opened through Peter is the one they travel through in their ministry—the Gentiles now are in focus, though not without obstacles to be overcome. Paul and Barnabas begin their ministry as itinerant evangelists who call people everywhere in the then known world to repent and give themselves to Christ.

Every student of mission sooner or later encounters the accounts of Paul's missionary journeys. It is tempting to read too much into the journeys, treating them as though they are carefully planned itineraries managed with military precision. Luke's account is more realistic. In a blend of Spirit-led decisions and divine revelations, Paul moves from one city to another, preaching Christ everywhere he goes. As Roland Allen noted some time ago, in the relatively short span of roughly a decade, Paul could confidently say that all of Asia (as he knew it) was reached for Christ, and he was planning to go further west, apparently in the expectation that the newly planted churches would carry on just fine without him (Allen 1927, 3).

Here, a quick detour to introduce Paul before discussing his missionary journeys will help set the stage. Reading through Acts, one is quickly struck by the fact that an obscure person who participates in the persecution of the church (7:54–8:3; 9:1–2) is turned around by Jesus and eventually moves to center stage in the drama portrayed in Acts. It is obvious that this man is special in God's early work of spreading the gospel.

What was it like for Paul (then Saul) when he was blinded on the road to Damascus? Put yourself in his position. You set out on a journey full of importance—you have a special role in stamping out this new sect on behalf of Judaism. Along the way you are confronted by a vision of the very person whose followers you are pursuing. You are struck blind and have to be humbly led into the city in which you had planned on carrying out your campaign (9:1–8). Keep in mind that Paul did not know that his blindness would last only for three days. What do you suppose he thought about during that time? What would you have thought about?

Whatever the answer, Paul's entire life is now turned upside down. The people he was hounding now must accept his conversion, and for the rest of his life he is dedicated to the one who appeared to him on the road to Damascus.

If a contemporary missionary followed Paul's schedule and itinerary, burnout would be a real danger. Four major trips occupy the rest of his life, including hardships everywhere he goes, care and concern for the fledgling congregations planted at almost every stop along the way, and a burning desire to preach Christ where he was not known.

Many extensive treatments of Paul's journeys exist (see, e.g., Allen [1912] 1962, 1927; Longenecker 1971; Bruce 1977; Pollock 1972; Boyd 1995; Bolt and Thompson 2000). We will focus on highlights rather than details and draw out lessons of importance for today from Paul's work two thousand years ago.

PAUL'S FIRST JOURNEY (ACTS 13:4–14:28)

Paul's first journey was a round trip from Antioch north and east into Asia Minor (see map 4.1).

A pattern set in Paul's first journey can be seen throughout the rest of his missionary career. Paul begins his ministry in each new city by first preaching in the synagogue—not

surprising, since he wanted to reach his own people for Christ wherever possible. Having heard the message, some of those in the Jewish communities accept the new teaching and others reject it. Those who reject Paul's message in turn influence the larger Jewish community to reject, and often to persecute, Paul.

At this stage Paul turns to the Gentiles and meets them where they are (Longenecker 1971, 47–48). They typically are more responsive to the message he brings, and those who come in faith are integrated into the new church that is planted.

Prior to Paul's first journey, Gentiles generally came to Christ only through significant contact with Jews as proselytes. Now

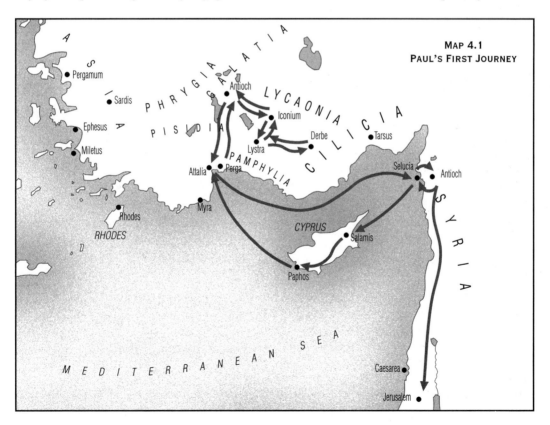

MAP 4.1
PAUL'S FIRST JOURNEY

they have their own channels through which the gospel can be offered. The breakthrough is found in the story of Sergius Paulus (13:6–12), the Gentile Roman proconsul who listened to Paul preach away from the context of a synagogue. From this time on Luke refers to Saul as Paul, the Roman version of his name (13:9). Perhaps by this Luke hints at the shift in Paul's thinking. Paul's call was to the Gentiles rather than to the Jews, and this is demonstrated by Luke calling him Paul (Longenecker 1971, 43).

The city of Derbe is as far as Paul and Barnabas go on this journey. Winning "a large number of disciples" (14:21) there, they turn around and retrace the journey back through Lystra, Iconium, and (Pisidian) Antioch to Perga. Modern Christians may wonder what Paul's feelings were as he returned to Lystra, where recently he had been stoned and left for dead, but Luke offers no related comments. Perhaps it was a "nonissue" for Paul, though that seems humanly impossible to us.

As they returned through each city, they visited the recently planted churches, building them up, appointing elders, and entrusting those churches to the Lord with prayer and fasting. The "encouraging" that Paul and Barnabas do is something that many today might not find so encouraging: "We must go through many hardships to enter the kingdom of God" (14:22).

In revisiting the very cities from which he so recently escaped, Paul demonstrates his courage and stick-to-itiveness. He had indeed gone through many hardships for the sake of the kingdom. His life was a living object lesson to the believers. They too need to endure hardships, not letting persecution dominate the way they live or how they preach Christ. Paul, after all, is their model.

Rather than return to Cyprus, Paul and company travel to Attalia and sail from there directly to Antioch, where they stay for a while. Luke notes that they report how God had opened a door to the Gentiles—a reminder of the change that was taking place as the gospel stretched beyond the borders of Judaism.

It took Paul and Barnabas roughly three years to cover almost fifteen hundred miles on this journey (Boyd 1995, 112). Churches were planted in at least nine cities along the way; the gospel was taking root in new territories.

PAUL'S SECOND JOURNEY (ACTS 15:36–18:22)

While Paul and Barnabas are still in Antioch, some Jewish converts arrive from Judea. They begin teaching that Gentiles

> *Paul sees mission in holistic, even cosmic terms. The glory of God, the reign of Christ, the declaration of the mystery of the gospel, the conversion of men and women, the growth and edification of the church, the defeat of the cosmic powers, the pursuit of holiness, the passion for godly fellowship and unity in the church, the unification of Jews and Gentiles, doing good to all but especially to fellow-believers—these are woven into a seamless garment. All the elements are held together by a vision in which God is at the centre and Jesus Christ effects the changes for his glory and his people's good.*
>
> Donald A. Carson (2000, 182)

must be circumcised if they are to be genuine followers of Christ. Paul and Barnabas immediately dispute their claims. Eventually the fight grows to the extent that members of both sides of the debate are commissioned by the Antioch church to carry the question to Jerusalem, where the apostles and elders can resolve the issue.

At the council in Jerusalem, James's and Paul's arguments win the day. Circumcision is not a necessary precondition for Christian faith, and Gentiles do not have to enter the house of Christianity through the doors of Judaism. The apostles, however, affirm some basic prohibitions that Gentiles should observe once they have committed themselves to Christ: they must avoid things polluted by idols, sexual impurity, meat from animals that were strangled to death, and blood (15:19–20, 29).

However these prohibitions might be interpreted today, the main emphasis was that faith in Christ was open to Gentiles apart from them having to enter through Judaism (especially the rite of circumcision). New Testament scholar I. Howard Marshall states, "The story of the mission is at the same time the story of how these two groups [Jews and Gentiles] were able to form one people of God without the Gentiles having to submit to circumcision and in effect become Jews in order to become Christians" (Marshall 2000, 99). If this is true, then the Jerusalem council is a pivotal point for missionary thinking and provides a model for missionaries today in wrestling with issues of contextualization.

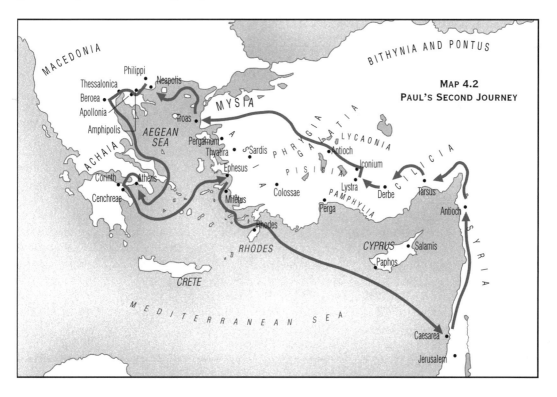

MAP 4.2
PAUL'S SECOND JOURNEY

After the meeting Paul and Barnabas return to Antioch, with a letter from the council in hand, to report to the Antioch church the good news of the decision. After reporting, they remain in Antioch, teaching and evangelizing.

"Some time later" (15:36) Paul feels a need to follow up on the believers from their previous journey. He mentions the need to Barnabas, but the two are unable to agree whether to include John Mark, who had deserted them before they had finished their first journey.

Their disagreement becomes so acute that Paul splits from Barnabas and John Mark. After noting that the latter two sail off to Cyprus (15:39), Luke does not mention them again. Paul chooses Silas as his new partner. Silas, a prophet from Jerusalem, was a Roman citizen (16:37), which provides an added benefit for Paul. The two of them embark on Paul's second missionary journey, and the rest of Luke's narrative follows Paul's travels and ministry.

Paul's first concern on the second journey is to follow up on the churches planted during his first journey. This is the third time the churches see their founder, and he and Silas satisfy themselves that the fledgling churches are growing. They present to those churches the decision made at the Jerusalem council.

In Derbe Paul picks up Timothy as a traveling companion. Interestingly, in light of the decision made at the Jerusalem council, Paul has Timothy circumcised. Luke is careful to note, however, that salvation was not the issue at stake, but rather the ability to preach successfully to local Jewish audiences who knew Timothy had a Greek father and had not previously been circumcised. Clearly seen in this action is Paul's concern to avoid placing unnecessary communica-tion barriers that could prevent people from giving the gospel a fair hearing.

Once the initial follow-up in the Galatian region is completed, Paul turns to travel north and east, deeper into Asia. However, the Holy Spirit does not allow him to go there, but instead leads him west toward

> *God's part is to put forth power; our part is to put forth faith.*
> Andrew Bonar (Loane 1970, 119)

Europe. The implications of this turn of events are staggering. Paul is used by God to open Europe to the gospel, changing the course of history. Luke does not explain why God did not allow Paul to head further into Asia. Europe was to be impacted forever by the momentous course of events recorded in five short verses (16:6–10).

Having crossed the Aegean Sea, Paul moves south through present-day Greece, finally settling in Corinth. Along the way churches are planted in Philippi (16:11–40), Thessalonica (17:1–9), Beroea (17:10–14), and Athens (17:15–34).

Much has been made of Paul's sermon on Mars Hill in Athens. In it he points out that he has seen the pantheon of Greek gods in Athens. He is especially interested that the city has an altar to an unknown god. It is this God he wants to reveal. As he preaches, he draws on poets known to the Athenians, using their ideas as contact points for the gospel.

Luke's comments seem to indicate that the response to Paul's proclamation was mixed, with the number of those who re-sponded positively being small (17:32–34). Strengthening that perception is that Paul later wrote to the Corinthians that he came to them (from Athens) not with wisdom, but with weakness and trembling (1 Cor. 2:1–5). Perhaps, having tried cultural wisdom as a bridge in Athens, Paul decided that such an approach was not always the best one to take. Because this is an inference we make, caution must be exercised in drawing implications for mission today. Whatever else may be said, it is clear that Paul was willing to experiment with new methods and possibly cast them aside when they did not produce fruit to his satisfaction (see 1 Cor. 9:19–23).

Paul remains in Corinth for some time, and then he sets sail back across the Aegean Sea to Ephesus after taking a Nazirite vow in Cenchreae (18:18). He is well received in Ephesus and, after promising to return, departs for Jerusalem. There, he takes the time needed to greet the church and then departs for his home base in Antioch.

Altogether it took Paul three and one-half years to cover the almost three thousand miles of his second journey (Boyd 1995, 148). Over the course of this journey Luke mentions five more cities in which churches were planted—all west of Paul's previous work, and now across the Aegean Sea as well. It seems likely that Paul wrote 1 and 2 Thessalonians over the course of this journey.

PAUL'S THIRD JOURNEY (ACTS 18:23–21:19)

After staying in Antioch for an unspecified period of time, Paul once again decides that it is time to visit the churches he planted. Luke glosses over the follow-up work in Galatia and Phrygia, simply noting that Paul strengthened "all the disciples" in those regions.

Paul fulfills the promise made during his second journey to the Jews in Ephesus,

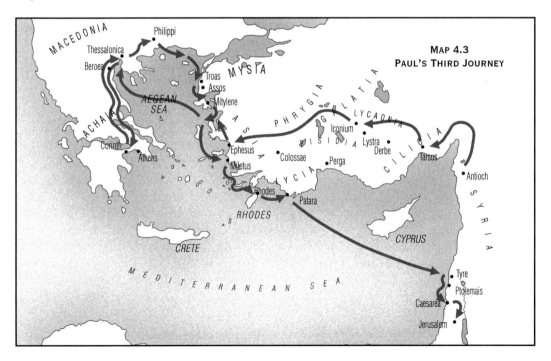

MAP 4.3
PAUL'S THIRD JOURNEY

arriving there over land after visiting the churches in Galatia. He stays in Ephesus more than two years—the longest residential stretch of his missionary journeys. While Paul is there, God performs "extraordinary miracles" through him, possibly because of the pervasiveness of magical practices and beliefs found in Ephesus at the time (see Arnold 1992).

After the events at Ephesus Paul resolves "in the Spirit" (19:21 NRSV) to travel through Macedonia and Achaia, apparently to revisit the churches planted on his second missionary journey. He makes his way south to Greece, encouraging the believers along the way.

After several months in Greece he decides to sail across the Aegean Sea (as on his second journey), but a plot against him makes him decide to return by land through Macedonia instead. Reaching Philippi, Paul sails to Troas, where he remains one week. Hoping to reach Jerusalem by the day of Pentecost, he decides to forgo a stop at Ephesus, figuring that it will delay him too long.

Instead, after landing in Miletus, some thirty miles south of Ephesus (Bruce 1988, 387), he sends a message to the Ephesian elders to meet him there. Once they arrive, he delivers his farewell to them before setting sail for Jerusalem. He travels to Jerusalem knowing by the Holy Spirit that imprisonment and persecutions await him, and that he would not see his friends from Ephesus again. Setting sail, he arrives in Tyre, and the disciples there tell him "through the Spirit" (21:4) not to go to Jerusalem. Apparently, they mistake the knowledge that he faces trials there for the conviction that he should not go (Grudem 1988). Paul, however, exercising his apostolic authority, overrides them and continues his journey. Warnings

of what is to come are given once again after they arrive in Caesarea, this time through Agabus the prophet. Again, Paul overrides the local believers' urgent insistence that he avoid Jerusalem (Grudem 1988).

Once Paul reaches Jerusalem, he reports in detail to the Jerusalem elders what God had accomplished among the Gentiles. This report formally concludes Paul's third missionary journey.

Altogether it took Paul roughly four years to cover the almost four thousand miles of his third missionary journey (Boyd 1995, 148). The third journey was a close parallel to the second one. The primary differences between the two trips are these: (1) Paul travels by land through Achaia and Macedonia (contemporary Greece) to Troas rather than sailing across the Aegean Sea from the southern tip of Achaia; and (2) the journey closes at Jerusalem rather than Antioch. Although the chronology of the actual writing of his epistles is difficult to establish with any certainty, it is possible that he wrote 1 and 2 Corinthians, Galatians, and Romans during this journey.

PAUL GOES TO ROME—IN CHAINS

After Paul's initial report, the elders in Jerusalem explain that they have a problem (21:20–25). They tell Paul that Asian Jews have come into Jerusalem portraying him as one who forsakes the law of Moses and thereby the very fabric of Judaism. The elders propose that Paul participate in a Jewish ritual (paying for the completion of a Nazirite vow taken by several believers in Jerusalem) to dispel the rumors.

Paul agrees and does as requested (21:26). Unfortunately, the plan backfires, and Paul has to be rescued from an angry mob by the local Roman guard (21:27–36). Thus begins the story of the trial that eventually takes him on his final trip, this time to Rome.

On the way to Rome, at almost every stop, Paul is given opportunities to share Christ. His preaching touches religious leaders (23:1–11), governors (24:1–21), kings (25:23–26:23), sailors (27:13–26), and superstitious islanders (28:1–10). The physical chains are no impediment to Paul's spiritual vitality and ability to communicate Christ. In fact, they enable him to travel even farther than on his missionary journeys. Luke closes this act in the divine drama in mission with Paul under house arrest but able to preach freely: "Boldly and without hindrance he preached the kingdom of God and taught about the Lord Jesus Christ" (28:31). As a final note, it is most likely that while in Rome Paul wrote Philemon, Colossians, Ephesians, Philippians, 1 and 2 Timothy, and Titus.

Lessons from Paul's Life and Ministry

In all, Paul's missionary journeys encompass over a decade of his life during which the gospel spread throughout four important provinces in Asia Minor and on contemporary European soil. What missionary lessons can be learned from Paul (see sidebar 4.1 for additional discussion)?

First, the maximum duration Paul remained at a single location was less than three years. In that sense, Paul was an itinerant missionary rather than a residential one. He moved from place to place planting new churches but did not stay long enough to become the permanent pastor (see Gilliland 1983, 33; but see also the warning of taking this too far in Marshall 2000, 102). Thus, although Paul's missionary career certainly must be seen as an example of what a mis-

sionary life can be, it should not be seen as the "norm" for all missionaries.

Second, Paul's strategy was far more focused on a willingness to obey the Holy Spirit than on the detailed and programmatic strategic planning practices seen in Western mission agencies of today. Herbert Kane asks whether Paul had an actual strategy that he followed. His own answer is that Paul indeed did have a strategy, but only "if we take the word to mean a flexible *modus operandi* developed under the guidance of the Holy Spirit and subject to His direction and control" (Kane 1976, 73). Examples of divine guidance in Paul's life include his

> *Paul was a theologically driven missionary and a missiologically driven theologian. His theology was missiological and his missionary endeavours were theological. May Paul's gospel of the crucified and risen Christ and his willingness to embody it through his own endurance of suffering on behalf of others be our "consuming passion" as well.*
>
> Scott Hafemann (2000, 141)

"conversion vision; the activity of Ananias; the summons by Barnabas; the guidance at the Antioch prayer meeting; another vision in the temple; the dream of the man of Macedonia; the prophecies by Agabus and others; the vision in Corinth; and the vision on the ship" (Marshall 2000, 101). The human side is seen in the initiation of the second missionary tour coming from Paul's desire to return to visit churches established during the first journey.

Third, Paul certainly was an evangelist, but he was an evangelist with a goal in mind.

SIDEBAR 4.1
CHARACTERISTICS OF PAUL'S MISSIONARY METHODS

REFLECTION
AND DISCUSSION

In studying Paul's missionary journeys, we find it helpful to extract patterns or activities that stretch across his missionary activity. Here, we offer lists from three scholars who reflect on Paul's methods, each drawn from years of study and careful attention to the issues at hand. As you examine each of these lists, consider the questions below as starting points for discussion on Paul's methods and what application they have for missionary work today.

Pauline New Testament scholar Paul Bowers lists the seven patterns found in Paul's missionary career that characterize Paul's missionary method. Missiologist and missionary to China J. Herbert Kane lists nine characteristics of Paul's missionary work. Professor of missiology and former missionary to Sri Lanka Roger Greenway identifies seven key methods Paul used. Look at the chart to compare the findings of each of these scholars with the others.

Read through each of Paul's missionary journeys (Acts 13:4–14:28; 15:36–18:22; 18:23–21:19) and compare what you find with the lists below.

1. What might you add to these characteristics?
2. What might you omit from any of the lists?
3. Discuss how each of the characteristics impacts the way you think about your own future missionary work.

BOWERS (1993, 610)	KANE (1976, 74–85)	GREENWAY (1999, 62–68)
1. Paul is committed to introducing the gospel where it has not yet been heard, to a pioneering function at the frontiers of the Christian expansion.	1. Paul maintained close contact with the home base.	1. Paul confronted people with the saviorhood and lordship of Christ and urged them to submit their hearts and lives to him.
	2. Paul confined his efforts to four provinces.	2. Paul focused on families and households in both evangelism and outreach into society.

New Testament scholar and missionary Paul Bowers points out that Paul's primary concern went beyond winning people to Christ; his ministry focus was on forming communities of Christians throughout the regions he traveled as a means of spreading the gospel to the whole world (see Bowers 1993, 609; Köstenberger and O'Brien 2001, 180–81). Even more broadly, Paul had a goal of developing mature believers so that they might both experience what was already theirs in Christ and become fully fit in preparation for Christ's return (Peterson 2000, 200).

Fourth, Paul was willing to change the message based on the audience. His circumcision of Timothy demonstrated that the messenger has a responsibility to avoid building unnecessary obstacles to the hearing of the gospel. His appeal to poets and shrines in Athens as contact points for the gospel demonstrated his willingness to meet people where they were as a starting point to bridge to the gospel.

Fifth, there were definite limits to Paul's contextualization. He and Barnabas being mistaken for Roman deities in Lystra was

BOWERS (1993, 610)	KANE (1976, 74–85)	GREENWAY (1999, 62–68)
2. He understands this commitment to imply geographical movement in the proclamation of the gospel.	3. Paul concentrated on large cities.	3. Paul stressed the importance of planting and nurturing churches and communities of faith, worship, fellowship, and service.
3. He conceptualizes such movement in terms of specific geographical areas.	4. Paul made the synagogue the scene of his chief labors.	4. Paul concentrated on developing local leaders in the churches and placing them in charge as soon as possible.
4. Paul attempts to canvass these areas in a roughly contiguous sequence, from east to west.	5. Paul preferred to preach to responsive peoples.	5. Paul used the natural "bridges" of family relatives, friends, and other contacts in spreading the gospel.
5. Within that compass Paul seeks to establish Christian communities in the main population centers of each region.	6. Paul baptized converts on confession of their faith.	6. Paul started "house churches" everywhere he went. These house churches became living cells of the body of Christ. Paul used a large number of "fellow workers" (called "lay people" today) to spread the gospel and minister in the house churches.
6. Paul's missionary commitment includes nurturing such communities toward mature stability.	7. Paul remained long enough in one place to establish a church.	
	8. Paul made ample use of fellow workers.	
7. Once he takes this to be accomplished, Paul feels that he has "no more room" for his particular missionary calling in these areas, and is prepared to move on.	9. Paul became all things to all men.	7. Paul taught believers to promote justice, truth, and mercy in society and to care for the Lord's earth.

not acceptable to him; nor was the demand that Gentiles be circumcised as part of the conversion process.

Sixth, Paul focused his attention on planting churches and moving on to new areas. Though the churches Paul planted had an ongoing relationship with him, they were expected to stand independently of his presence. He avoided developing a dependence relationship with the churches he planted, instead giving them enough to stand on their own feet with Christ's power. Modern Christians do well to pay close attention to Roland Allen's penetrating summary of Paul's methods (see sidebar 4.2).

Seventh, the content of Paul's preaching essentially was the story of Jesus. It parallels the story accounts seen in the four Gospels (see Wenham 2000; Seccombe 2000). With the exception of his approach in Athens, Paul chose to focus on the history rather than philosophy, on the simple story rather than intellectual discourse.

Eighth, Paul tended to work as the leading member of a team of people rather than trying to go it alone on his journeys. Practi-

SIDEBAR 4.2
PAUL'S MISSIONARY PRINCIPLES

Roland Allen penned the classic text *Missionary Methods: St. Paul's or Ours?* in 1912, and his book is still used in mission classes today. In it he explores Paul's methodology in planting churches, comparing and contrasting Paul's methods with the (Anglican) methods prevalent in Allen's day. That the book remains in print is a testimony to the fact that Allen's analysis remains relevant in spite of the almost one hundred years of change that have transpired.

What follows is a section from the book in which he summarizes the most important lessons learned from his study about Paul's methods in church planting and development (pp. 151–52):

We have seen that the secret of the Apostle's success in founding churches lay in the observance of principles which we can reduce to rules of practice in some such form as this.

1. All teaching to be permanent must be intelligible and so capable of being grasped and understood that those who have once received it can retain it, use it, and hand it on. The test of all teaching is practice. Nothing should

be taught which cannot be so grasped and used.
2. All organization in like manner must be of such a character that it can be understood and maintained. It must be an organization of which the people see the necessity; it must be an organization which they can and will support. It must not be so elaborate or so costly that small and infant communities cannot supply the funds necessary for its maintenance. The test of all organizations is naturalness and permanence. Nothing should be established as part of the ordinary church life of the people which they cannot understand and carry on.
3. All financial arrangements made for the ordinary life and existence of the church should be such that the people themselves can and will control and manage their own business independently of any foreign subsidies. The management of all local funds should be entirely in the hands of the local church which should raise and use their own funds for their

own purposes that they may be neither pauperized nor dependent on the dictation of any foreign society.
4. A sense of mutual responsibility of all the Christians one for another should be carefully inculcated and practiced. The whole community is responsible for the proper administration of baptism, ordination and discipline.
5. Authority to exercise spiritual gifts should be given freely and at once. Nothing should be withheld which may strengthen the life of the church, still less anything be withheld which is necessary for its spiritual sustenance. The liberty to enjoy such gifts is not a privilege which may be withheld but a right which must be acknowledged. The test of preparedness to receive the authority is the capacity to receive the grace.

REFLECTION
AND DISCUSSION

For each of Allen's five lessons, discuss the impact on the views you have of mission and how it should be carried out.

cal considerations may have applied. Travel in Paul's day was far more dangerous than in many parts of the world today (Winter 2000), and traveling in groups was one of the best ways to ensure safety. Although initially Paul and his named companions (Barnabas and later Silas) were colleagues, later he was the one in charge, and the companions were helpers rather than colleagues (Marshall 2000, 106).

Ninth, persecution was a crucial part of Paul's circumstances (see Hafemann 2000), but it did not deter him from proclaiming the gospel. He lived through the very thing about which he warned the churches on the follow-up leg of his first journey: the path of the kingdom is a path of hardships (14:22). Hardships did not deter Paul, and they are not to deter missionaries today. The reality that more Christians were martyred in the twentieth century than in all previous centuries combined (Barrett, Kurian, and Johnson 2001, 2:229) stands as a stark reminder that what Paul said twenty centuries ago still applies in many parts of the world today.

Tenth, Paul was flexible in his financing. Occasionally he depended on the hospitality of God's saints (Acts 16:14–15) or the contributions of various churches (Phil. 4:16), but most typically he generated his own income through making tents (Acts 18:1–4; 20:33–34; 1 Cor. 9:3–18). Though Paul's practices were flexible, Roland Allen notes that there were some boundaries for him:

> There seem to have been three rules which guided his practice: (1) that he did not seek financial help for himself; (2) that he took no financial help to those to whom he preached; (3) that he did not administer local church funds. (Allen [1912] 1962, 49)

Encountering Mission in the Epistles

The various epistles that comprise the rest of our New Testament were written as occasional letters. Prompted by a certain occasion, event, or concern about a church, a community, or an individual, each epistle tends to focus on the specific issues facing the intended audience. They were written to address concrete situations rather than as general treatises, and so they tend not to offer systematic treatments of topics except when those topics are of immediate concern to the readers.

One looks in vain for a focus on a theology of mission in any epistle. However, interwoven among them are the great themes of mission already seen in the rest of the Scrip-

> *There is perhaps little theology of missions as such in the New Testament because it is in its totality a missionary theology, the theology of a group of missionaries and a theology in missionary movement. Thus it does not present a theology of missions, it is a missionary theology.*
>
> George Peters (1972, 131)

tures. For the purposes of our discussion we will focus our attention on five selected themes seen in these epistles that continue the divine drama of mission. For each theme we cite only a sampling of the possible supporting ideas and verses available.

THEME 1: GOD'S MERCY EXTENDS TO ALL PEOPLE

Although Paul's specific calling was to reach the Gentiles (Rom. 1:5; 15:17–19), the very fact that Gentiles were included indicated that the offer of the gospel was a universal offer. Jesus died for all (Rom. 5:18–19; 2 Cor. 5:15), and God wants all to be saved (1 Tim. 2:4; 2 Pet. 3:9). Therefore the offer of salvation extends to all—to Gentiles and Jews, slave and free, men and women (Gal. 3:28). All are given the opportunity to worship the King of kings. The amazing vision given to John of the gathered throng before God's throne, which includes people "from every nation, tribe, people and language" (Rev. 7:9), indicates that God's offer will be accepted among all peoples (though not by every person) of the world before the end.

THEME 2: MISSION INVOLVES A MESSAGE

The message is from God (Rom. 1:1), and the content of that message is central (Gal. 1:6–8). It incorporates the centrality of Jesus (Rom. 1:3–4; 2 Cor. 5:19, 21), the reality of every person's estrangement from God (Rom. 3:23), the fact of his coming judgment (1 Thess. 1:9–10), and the need to respond (2 Cor. 5:11–21) as empowered by God's grace (Eph. 2:8–9). The idea that salvation comes through works undermines God's plan of redemption (Rom. 10:3; Gal. 2:21; Eph. 2:8–9; Phil. 3:9), though works are intimately related to the Christian life (Eph. 2:10; James 2:14–26).

Jesus is the reality of God's plan for people (Col. 2:8–12). Because Jesus came as a humble, obedient servant, God chose to exalt him above all others (Phil. 2:6–11; Heb. 2:9). He is the Lamb of God, slain before the foundation of the world (Rev. 13:8) and now seated at the right hand of God (Eph. 1:20). Though the message is constant, the means to communicate that message must adapt to fit the situation and the people being reached (1 Cor. 9:22–23).

THEME 3: MISSION FACES A SUPERNATURAL OPPONENT

Mission and spiritual warfare are inextricably intertwined. The unbelieving world or domination system (Wink 1992) is under Satan's sway, being held captive to his schemes. He blinds those in the domination system (2 Cor. 4:4). They are dead in their trespasses and sins (Eph. 2:1–3) and are slaves to his tactics and nature (Gal. 4:3, 9). For a season Satan and his hosts are allowed to continue to exert authority here on earth in his domain of darkness (Col. 1:13; Eph. 2:1–3).

The reality underlying the limitations on Satan's activity is framed by the fact that Jesus is successful in his mission to destroy the works of Satan (1 John 3:8) and set people free from fear of the power of death (Heb. 2:14–15). Though it is true that Jesus completely defeated Satan and his forces at the cross (Col. 2:15–22), that total defeat has not yet been fully manifested (Heb. 2:8), although it will be in God's timing (1 Cor. 15:24–26).

Christians, having been declared a new creation (2 Cor. 5:17), are God's children (Rom. 8:15–17; Eph. 1:4–5), are given Christ's authority (Col. 2:10), and are called to engage in the kingdom conflict (Eph. 6:12) in the power of the Holy Spirit (2 Cor. 10:3–5). They do this by submitting to God and resisting Satan (James 4:4–9; 1 Pet. 5:5–9).

THEME 4: GOD IS SOVEREIGNLY IN CHARGE OF MISSION

The sovereignty of God is clearly in evidence. He is a loving (Rom. 5:8) "Daddy" (Rom. 8:15–16; Gal. 4:4–6), yet still the immortal, invisible, eternal King of kings (1 Tim. 1:17; 6:14b–16), who is over all, in all, and through all (Eph. 4:6), and in whom all things hold together (Col. 1:17). He created and governs the world (Acts 17:24–28), and gives generously to all he created (James 1:5–8, 17) while working all things toward good for those who love him (Rom. 8:28–30).

As the Sovereign One, God's plans for peace (1 Cor. 14:33a) cannot be thwarted. His foolishness is greater than human wisdom; his weakness is greater than human strength (1 Cor. 1:25). He is the one from whom all things come and for whom all people live

(1 Cor. 8:6), and ultimately the one whom all nations will worship (Rev. 15:3–4).

THEME 5: WE ARE CHRIST'S AMBASSADORS

In Christ, Christians have been given a new position as (1) a chosen race (1 Pet. 2:9–12) (or elect generation [from Isa. 43:20]); (2) a royal priesthood (Exod. 19:6), sharing in the kingly ruling with Christ (Stibbs 1959, 104); (3) a holy nation (Exod. 19:6); and (4) a people for God's own possession (based on Hos. 1:6–10; 2:23). There is a purpose for the Christian's position: to proclaim the excellencies (virtues or eminent qualities) of God. Michael Lawson notes,

> While God's people await the coming of their King, they are not passive. They are a people with a purpose. Corporately, they are to "declare the wonderful deeds of him who called you out of darkness into his marvelous light." In short, God's people are to be a sign of the kingdom. (Lawson 1987, 135)

God works in Christians (Phil. 2:12–13), enabling them to grow (1 Cor. 3:7) and to do the works already prepared for them (Eph. 2:8–10). Based on their submission to Christ, they do not wage just a defensive battle, but actively and offensively engage the enemy of their souls using God's rules of engagement. These include overcoming evil with good (Rom. 12:21) and returning curses with blessings (1 Pet. 3:8–12) as God's ambassadors (2 Cor. 5:18–21). New Testament scholar Philip Hughes points out, "This ministry with its message of reconciliation is, in the ultimate issue, the one thing needful for our world in all circumstances and in every generation" (Hughes 1962, 206).

Buttressing this idea is the logical chain that Paul presents in Rom. 10:6–17: (1) people can call on Christ only if they have already believed in him; (2) they can believe in him only if they have heard him; (3) they can hear him only if someone proclaims the message; and (4) the message can be proclaimed only if God commissions someone to proclaim it (adapted from Cranfield 1985, 262). Culver emphasizes the gist: "There is no plainer statement of the mandate in all of literature, biblical or otherwise. Some must go with the gospel to the people who have not yet heard it and others must send them!" (Culver 1984, 121).

ACT 7: RENEWING ALL CREATION: THE CONSUMMATION

The first act of creation foreshadows the final act in that God has promised to replace the current sinful order with a new, glorified one. The consummation will restore the universe to the order that the world had at the time God declared, "It is good."

Not surprisingly, the final act of the divine

> *Jesus told us plainly that the world will become a most unpleasant place and evil will multiply and even apparently triumph, but at the same time [Christ's] people will multiply and spread across the face of the earth. Everything is heading towards a climax—both evil and good. It will be high tide at midnight.*
>
> Patrick Johnstone (1998, 87)

drama of mission in the Bible is the most difficult to describe. Ultimately, John Piper

CASE STUDY:
A GROUP CONVERSION

Paul G. Hiebert
(Hiebert and Hiebert 1987, 158–60 [used with permission])

Mark looked at the chief and elders before him and at the more than two hundred men, women, and children crowding behind them. "Have they all really become Christians? I can't baptize them if they don't each decide for themselves!" he said to Judy, his wife.

Mark and Judy Zabel had come to Borneo under the Malay Baptist Mission to start a new work in the highlands. They spent the first year building a thatched house, learning the language, and making friends with the people. The second year they began to make short treks into the interior to villages that had never heard the gospel. The people were respectful, but with a few exceptions none had shown any real interest in the gospel. Woofak was always around and had been from the beginning. In time he had become a believer, but few of the others took him seriously. He was something of a village maverick. And there had been Tarobo and his wife and four others. By the end of the third year, the worship services were made up of these seven baptized believers, Mark and Judy, a few passersby, and a dozen children.

That year an epidemic had spread through the highlands. For weeks Judy and Mark went through the villages, praying with the sick and dispensing medicines, until they thought they could go on no more. They wept with families faced with death and told them of the God who loved them and had conquered death itself. One village in particular had suffered greatly from the disease. Though the people seemed to appreciate the love shown by the two missionaries, they had shown no particular interest in the gospel.

Three months later, two elders from this village had come to the mission home, wanting to see the missionaries. "Can you come to our village and tell us more about your God?" they asked. "We want to know more about him."

Mark and Judy were excited. Their many hours on the trail in the rain and the weary days of ministering to the people were bearing fruit. Taking some food, water, changes of clothes, cots and nets, they set out for the distant village.

It was almost dark when they arrived. The village chief invited Mark into the men's long house where all the adult males of the village were gathered. Judy joined the women, who sat in front of their huts discussing the decision the village elders were about to make. She sensed that there had been much

---

is right: mission is a temporary activity of the church that will cease when the roster of worshipers is complete.

> When this age is over, and the countless millions of the redeemed fall on their faces before the throne of God, missions will be no more. It is a temporary necessity. But worship abides forever. (Piper 1993, 11)

One very clear element of the consummation is the portrayal of the extent of the kingdom of God. An uncountable multitude of people from "every nation, tribe, people and language" (Rev. 7:9) will stand before God; no one will escape the consequences of the end of history. This is a vivid reminder that our current missionary task extends to every person on the planet.

When the divine drama closes, mission will come to an end. The passion of the Christian until that time is to be intimately involved in the process of urging others to recognize their state of separation from

discussion in the village before she and Mark had been invited to come. Now there was a feeling of excitement and uncertainty in the air. Some of the women wanted to know more about this new God. Others said that it was best to stay with their ancestors who cared for them in the spirit world, and with the tribal gods who had helped them to be victorious over their enemies in the past.

In the long house the chief asked Mark to tell them more about his God. For three hours Mark told the men about the Jesus Way and answered their questions. Then the chief asked Mark to sit down on a log. Mark noticed that the men broke up into smaller groups, each made up of men from the same lineage. For half an hour there was a loud debate as men argued for and against following the new God. The arguments died down, and then the leaders from the various lineages gathered with the chief. Again there was a heated discussion. Finally the chief came to Mark and said, "We have all decided to follow the Jesus Way. We want to be baptized like Woofak and Tarobo."

Although it was late, neither Mark nor Judy could sleep after the meeting. The decision of the village, especially the way it was made, had caught them totally by surprise. They knew that tribal people often made important decisions, such as moving their villages or raiding neighboring tribes, by discussion and group consensus. But they never dreamed that people might use this method to choose a new god. All their theological training in their church and Bible College had taught the young missionaries that people had to make personal decisions to become followers of Christ. Here the group leaders had decided for all. What did that mean? Was it a valid decision, especially when it was clear from the debates that some had opposed the choice? How could they baptize the whole village when not all were agreed? Then again, what did it mean in Acts when the jailer believed and Paul immediately baptized him and his whole household? Moreover, if they did not accept the villagers as Christians, the villagers might return to their old gods. Judy and Mark knew that they had to do something before they left the next day.

As Mark and Judy searched for an answer, suddenly the great spirit gong in the men's long house rang out. Hurrying over to find out what was going on, Mark found the chief and asked him why they were summoning the tribal spirits, now that they had become Christians. "Don't worry," the chief said. "We are calling them to tell them to go away because now we have a new God."

Judy and Mark were still uncertain as they finally fell asleep, bone-tired and knowing that they would have to give the chief and the village an answer in the morning.

God, to repent, and to commit themselves to Christ and thereby join the great throng around the throne worshiping God forever. This urging is done by the way Christians live, as reflections of God's glory in a dark world. It also is done by the way Christians speak, imploring people to be reconciled to God through Christ. Finally, this urging is done by the way Christians live out the firstfruits of God's coming kingdom through acts that show his love and compassion, his desire for justice to rule the nations, and his infinite mercy graciously extended to all.

Every person's life path is to point toward the consummation of the divine drama of mission. May God give us all the strength to live faithfully his vision of learning to delight in him as our loving, merciful, creating redeemer!

CONCLUSION

As we have seen, the story of mission is presented through the panorama of Scripture. From beginning to end, the themes of God's deep love for all people, our subsequent rebellion against him, Christ's sacrificial giving of himself, our responsibility to worship God by reflecting his glory, and calling the nations to repentance have been clear and compelling. In light of the events and emphases of the divine drama, what should be a corresponding theology of mission? That question we will take up in the next chapter.

In the case study for this chapter we explore the process of conversion, one of the great themes in the New Testament drama. One question that missionaries face in many cultures is whether or not it is possible for groups of people to convert at the same time. North Americans are accustomed to the idea of individual conversion, and the case study challenges them to consider what should be done when an entire group wants to convert.

5

Encountering Mission Theology

INTRODUCTION

To many people, the word *theology* conjures up images of dusty tomes lining towering bookshelves. The connection between theology and real life is lost somewhere in the library entryway. Even so, theology does have an essential role to play. Good theology is not about endless debates over the nature of God or predestination, but about establishing grounds for what people do and providing reasons for the way Christians minister to others. Theology is important—as long as academic theologizing is not confused as Christian living!

What are the important theological issues in mission today? Before that question can be answered, we need to understand mission itself. In this chapter we explore some of the words used for mission. After that, we will look at some of the more important ideas used in the study and practice of mission today.

LAYING THE GROUNDWORK

Many organizations talk about their mission. There are missions to explore space,

military missions, diplomatic missions, mission statements of businesses, and fact-finding missions. All of these rely on the core idea of mission—the sending of someone or something to do a job. The basic idea of a mission is fairly clear. However, when it comes to defining the particular mission of the church, contradictory and competing agendas make the picture less than clear. This is precisely where much of today's debates over mission are centered (Moreau 2000b).

Within mission discussion since the 1950s terms have developed in such a way that it can be confusing to the uninitiated (for an overview, see Van Engen 1996, 127–56). Essentially, *mission* (without the *s*) and *missions* (with the *s*) are used to indicate different things. As if that were not confusing enough, another term, *missio Dei*, was coined to indicate a new way of thinking about mission.

To set the stage for our theological discussion in this chapter, then, we first return to some of the words introduced in chapter 1: *missions, mission, missio Dei,* and *missiology.* Here, we will take them on in greater depth.

Missions

In academic circles today *missions* (with the final *s*) is the word used for the specific task of making disciples of all nations. It is seen through the work of mission agencies, churches, and missionaries around the world. George Peters explains what he means by missions:

> *Missions* is a specialized term. By it I mean the sending forth of authorized persons beyond the borders of the New Testament church and her immediate gospel influence to proclaim the gospel of Jesus Christ in gospel-destitute areas, to win converts from other faiths or non-faiths to Jesus Christ, and to establish functioning, multiplying local congregations who will bear the fruit of Christianity in that community and to that country. (Peters 1972, 11)

In this sense it is the traditional term. More recently Southern Baptist mission leader Avery Willis and *Experiencing God* author Henry Blackaby explain missions as "the activity of God's people—the church—to proclaim and to demonstrate the kingdom of God cross-culturally in the world" (Willis and Blackaby 2002, 3).

Mission

Over the past several decades *mission* (without the final *s*) has been used more broadly than *missions*. It refers to everything the church does that points toward the kingdom of God. George Peters explains that it is

> the total biblical assignment of the church of Jesus Christ. It is a comprehensive term including the upward, inward and outward ministries of the church. It is the church as "sent" (a pilgrim, stranger, witness,

prophet, servant, as salt, as light, etc.) in this world. (Peters 1972, 11)

Thus, missions is a subset of mission, and mission combines the total assignment of the church while including the traditional idea of missions (Moreau 2000b).

DIAGRAM 5.1

However, in many mainline denominational circles, mission is not limited to evangelistic and church-planting tasks. There it includes additional elements such as addressing systemic injustice, enabling social or political liberation, and engaging in dialogue with people of other living faiths. In the words of Philip Potter, an ecumenical leader, "For some 25 years now, mission has been undertaken in terms of proclaiming the good news in word and costly deed to the poor and in liberation of the oppressed" (Potter 1991, 695).

Many evangelicals rightly note that the term has become so broadly defined in mainline discussion that everything the church has done is now seen as mission—which means, in effect, that nothing is truly mission (Van Engen 1996, 153–56; for more extended discussion on the terms *mission* and *missions,* see Moreau 2000b). At the same time, however, evangelical mission scholars have not come to agreement on what the terminology actually should be, and they use the same terms to mean different things. Thus, at least for now among evangelical writers, knowing how a particular person uses a term is more important than knowing what the term means in the larger discipline of missiology.

In most church settings, however, such fine-tuning makes little difference or even sense to the average person in the pew. In fact, it is not a point of discussion for the typical missionary. Our intention in this text is to introduce you to the flux in terms being used so that you may be a more discerning reader of mission materials, especially mission theology.

Missio Dei

Missio Dei, Latin for "the sending of God," is a relatively new term in mission circles. Over the course of the twentieth century mission scholars gained a new appreciation for the fact that mission originates in God, not in the church or in people. It was admitted that our traditional focus on mission was church-centered (what the church does) or people-centered (what the evangelist or missionary does) rather than God-centered (what God does).

In 1963, at the World Council of Churches conference in Mexico City, the term *missio Dei* was popularized to reflect that thinking. It was used to incorporate into mission theology the fact that mission is truly a God-centered enterprise in which the church is privileged to participate. God's mission, however, is broader than the church; it is everything God himself does in establishing his kingdom on earth. This is the foundation for the watchword used in ecumenical circles at the time: "Let the world set the agenda." This expression captured the idea that God's work is broader than the church, and the church can take

cues about God's work by looking outside of itself to the world, where God is actively reaching out.

Eventually, evangelicals also began to use the term *missio Dei*, though not with quite the same political or economic connotations. The simple fact is that mission is God's program, not simply that of the church. Additionally, God's work in the world is not limited to what the church is doing, though he has reserved a central role for the church in bringing the message of the gospel to unreached areas of the world. Diagram 5.2 illustrates the relationship among all three terms.

In sum, *missio Dei* is a comprehensive term encompassing everything God does in relation to the kingdom *and* everything the church is sent to do on earth (McIntosh 2000). The term *mission* represents something narrower: everything with redemptive purpose that the church is sent to do. Finally, *missions* is the most specialized of the terms, describing the activity of churches, agencies, and people in making disciples and planting churches.

DIAGRAM 5.2

Missio Dei:
All That God Does to Build the Kingdom

Mission:
What the Church Does for God in the World

Missions:
Evangelism, Discipleship, and Church Planting

Missiology

The term *missiology* is used of the formal, academic study of mission (Moreau 2001a). It draws on diverse areas such as biblical and theological studies and the social sciences. Because the task of missiology comes out of our role as Christ's ambassadors, however, it must go beyond these disciplines. They are tools to help Christians understand mission, but they are more than that. They also help Christians to chart ways to improve their work as missionaries seeking to bring Christ to a needy world. Missiology is an applied discipline, not an armchair one. Theory without practice cuts off the reason for thinking missiologically.

The foundations of missiology are grounded in biblical and theological studies. Missiologists build on these core areas with studies of the human contexts of missionary work. Thus, missiology includes the social, historical, and religious settings of people around the world. To understand these settings, the missiologist must engage social sciences such as anthropology, communication, economics, education, history, linguistics, political science, psychology, and sociology. Because all of these fields are constantly changing and growing, David Bosch is right to declare, "There is no such thing as missiology, period. There is only missiology in draft" (Bosch 1991, 498).

A THEOLOGICAL APPROACH TO MISSION

There is no more important question in encountering missions theology than this: How is a solid, biblically based foundation for mission theology constructed?

An architect, when beginning the process of designing a new house, faces many issues that parallel what is faced in building a theology of mission. Several questions are key in the design process. A good architect does not fail to address these questions, and neither should we. Thus, we will spend

the rest of this chapter focusing on four questions that help build a solid theology of mission.

TABLE 5.1
QUESTIONS FOR MISSION THEOLOGY

Architectural Questions	Mission Theology Questions
How does the proposed house fit into the larger neighborhood?	How does mission theology fit into theology as a whole?
What type of foundation will ensure long life for the house?	What is the appropriate foundation for our theology of mission?
What is the overarching theme that guides the construction of the house?	What guiding theme provides the orientation to our mission theology?
What motifs of the house complement the overarching theme?	What motifs in our mission theology complement our guiding theme?

Those who construct mission theology today have different answers to each of these questions. We do not have the space here to discuss or even show all the answers that have been offered. Those who are interested in a more comprehensive discussion may want to read chapters 12 and 13 of David Bosch's *Transforming Mission* (see also sidebar 5.1).

Question 1: How Does Mission Theology Fit into Theology as a Whole?

If you are in a college or seminary, you will recognize the theological topics presented in diagram 5.3. You may not recognize the connections among them all, which is what the diagram is intended to illustrate. Where, in this diagram, however, is the proper "place" for mission theology?

In North American colleges and seminaries, mission theology is a specialized

SIDEBAR 5.1
WHAT IS MISSION, ANYWAY?

Perhaps one of the best-known missiologists of the late twentieth century was David Bosch, a South African who is remembered as a brilliant advocate for and scholar of mission. He wrote,

> It is, in fact, theologically far more correct and practically far more realistic to regard the Church's missionary enterprise as something that, because of its very nature and being, will always be in dispute. . . .

> The practical missionary endeavors of the Church always remain, under all circumstances, ambivalent. Mission is never something self-evident, and nowhere—neither in the practice of mission nor in even our best theological reflections on mission—does it succeed in removing all confusions, misunderstandings, enigmas and temptations.

> In our theological reflections on mission it is, therefore,

a more serious matter than merely one of making a choice between the optimism of an earlier period and the pessimism of today. Neither is relevant here. Theology concerns itself with reflection on the nature of the gospel, and the theology of mission with the question of the way in which the Church spreads this gospel. Putting it differently: the theology of mission concerns itself with the relationship between God and the world in the light of the gospel. (Bosch 1980, 9–10)

In a later work, Bosch provided an analysis of the various paradigms, or approaches, to constructing a mission theology (Bosch 1991, 368–510). He discusses thirteen paradigms, each one centered on an organizing theme for mission:

1. Mission as the Church-with-others
2. Mission as *missio Dei*
3. Mission as mediating salvation
4. Mission as the quest for justice
5. Mission as evangelism
6. Mission as contextualization
7. Mission as liberation
8. Mission as inculturation
9. Mission as common witness
10. Mission as ministry by the whole people of God
11. Mission as witness to people of other living faiths
12. Mission as theology
13. Mission as action in hope

REFLECTION AND DISCUSSION

1. Why is the definition of mission so important? What is at stake?
2. As you look over Bosch's list of organizing themes, which ones strike you as more faithful to Scripture? Which ones do you think are less faithful to Scripture?
3. Choose one theme that interests you and read the relevant discussion in Bosch.

DIAGRAM 5.3

study usually confined to the mission departments. Is the current assignment of mission theology exclusively to specialized mission departments God's view of the place for theology of mission in the total theological spectrum? If God's concern is truly that all the nations be called to worship him (as seen in our previous discussion of the divine drama), then it is natural to build a theology of mission at the core of all theological studies (see diagram 5.4).

David Bosch explains that the early church did not have the luxury of constructing a theology. Rather, the exigencies of life and the desire to bring Christ to the world drove theology in such a way that "mission became the 'mother of theology'" (Bosch 1991, 489). Peters emphatically states, "Missionary theology is not an appendix to biblical theology; it belongs at its very core" (Peters 1972, 27). Others are in agreement:

> But mission lies at the core of theology—within the character and action of God himself. There is an impulse to give and share that springs from the very nature of God and that therefore characterized all his works. So all that theologians call fundamental theology is mission theology. (Dyrness 1983, 11)

> Missiology acts as the gadfly of theology. (Johnstone 1998, 177)

If Bosch, Peters, Dyrness, and Johnstone are correct, then mission is at the heart of who Christians are and what the church is to be and do. Mission theology, then, should be at the heart of the church's theology, serving as an anchor for the rest of the theological "house" (see diagram 5.4).

DIAGRAM 5.4

Question 2: What Is the Foundation for Our Theology of Mission?

The foundation establishes critical parameters for the building. Jesus' well-known warning in the Sermon on the Mount reminds Christians that building a strong house on a weak foundation is a foolish venture:

> Therefore everyone who hears these words of mine and puts them into practice is like a wise man who built his house on the rock. The rain came down, the streams rose, and the winds blew and beat against that house; yet it did not fall, because it had its foundation on the rock. But everyone who hears these words of mine and does not put them into practice is like a foolish man who built his house on sand. The rain came down, the streams rose, and the winds blew and beat against that house, and it fell with a great crash. (Matt. 7:24–27)

Thus, choosing a foundation that is strong and stable enough to support the theological superstructure is a crucial first step in encountering missions theology. What, then, is our "foundation" for mission?

In the most general sense, the only possible foundation is the Bible itself. The Bible alone has the authority to guide the church through the complex questions that face each new generation. It alone provides the general principles on which a theology of mission must be built and the specific instructions given to the church by God that inform our view of mission today.

Question 3: What Guiding Theme Provides the Orientation to Our Mission Theology?

Critical to any theology of mission is a guiding theme or metaphor. In our discussion of the divine drama of mission in the Bible several possibilities emerged that could stand as an organizing theme. These included the kingdom of God, Jesus Christ, the glory of God (or worship of God), and the Great Commission. Contemporary writers in mission studies add several more ideas, including contextualization, liberation, justice, *missio Dei*, and so on (see sidebar 5.1). Table 5.2 gives some examples of guiding themes and the implications of each for mission.

TABLE 5.2
SOME GUIDING THEMES FOR MISSION

If the guiding theme is:	Then mission is:
Missio Dei	Everything God is doing in the world to manifest his rule or reign
All that those sent by God are to do	Everything that the church does and should be doing on behalf of God's mission in the world
The central core of the "sent one's" responsibility	1. Glorifying God (worship or liberation), *or* 2. Proclaiming God's rule through evangelism and/or prophetic pronouncements, *or* 3. Manifesting (or demonstrating or signifying) God's call to the world through righteous living, *or* 4. Ushering in liberation through implementing social change
A single commissioned task that the "sent one" is uniquely to perform	1. Evangelism (the Great Commission) 2. Service (the Great Commandment) 3. Prophecy (against societal evils) 4. Justice (social restructuring)

Those who use biblical reflection as their foundation for mission theology range widely in this area but usually choose a single guiding theme. For example, those in ecumenical circles typically might choose *justice* or *liberation* for their organizing theme.

Evangelicals, on the other hand, traditionally have focused on God's concern for the world and human estrangement from God as the core issue that mission addresses, with *personal evangelism* and *church planting* being the core activities that address the human dilemma of separation from God. An example of a biblical reflection on mission following this core is the Frankfurt Declaration, in which Peter Beyerhaus identified seven "indispensable basic elements of mission," each of which specifically refuted a trend seen in more liberal church circles of the time (see sidebar 5.2 for a synopsis). While noting the need for the church to engage in social justice, Beyerhaus and those who signed the Frankfurt Declaration felt that the most appropriate organizing theme was the Great Commission emphasis on evangelism and discipleship:

> Through the Church's outreach, his name shall be glorified among all people, mankind shall be saved from his future wrath and led to a new life, and the lordship of his Son Jesus Christ shall be established in the expectation of his second coming. (Beyerhaus 1972, 111)

John Piper's concentration on God's supremacy and glory as his organizing theme, with *worship* of God as the primary lens for mission activities (Piper 1993), may be added to this focus. Such worship is not confined to Sunday morning services. It includes calling others to glorify God by acknowledging God's supremacy (through evangelism and church planting) as well as developing our own capacity to worship (through discipleship and church growth). Piper's clarion call has echoed throughout evangelical ranks:

Missions is not the ultimate goal of the church. Worship is. Missions exists because worship doesn't. Worship is ultimate, not missions, because God is ultimate, not man. When this age is over, and the countless millions of the redeemed fall on their faces before the throne of God, missions will be no more. It is a temporary necessity. But worship abides forever. (Piper 1993, 11)

In this book, and as noted in the very first act in the divine drama in chapter 2, we follow Piper's lead in placing God's glory and our reflection of his glory through worship as the guiding themes for mission theology. Those themes find their focus in the tasks that the church is commissioned by God to perform. Ultimately, as noted in the preface, the evangelistic mandate of winning people to Christ as the commissioned task of the church must be at the core of our theology of mission. Being sent by God, Christians are to call people to be reconciled to and come worship the King of kings while at the same time growing in their own ability to worship him by living lives that best reflect his glory. Around this core set of themes, which arises from a solid biblical foundation, can be constructed a coherent and godly theology of mission that will stand the test of time.

The core theme may be split into three concentric elements: (1) calling those who do not know Christ through the activities of evangelism and church planting; (2) growing in the capacity to live God-glorifying lives through the processes of discipleship and church growth; and (3) reflecting God's glory to a needy world through living lives of salt and light (see diagram 5.5). This model includes the ideas found in both missions and mission (see diagram 5.1) but prioritizes the former over the latter.

In choosing this guiding theme we are not saying that other elements of the ministry of the church are unimportant or disconnected from mission. We are saying that the core of our responsibility of reflecting God's glory through worship is (1) to engage in evangelism and church planting, as well as (2) discipling those who enter the kingdom and enabling local churches to thrive and grow, (3) while glorifying God by living lives that act as salt and light in a hurting world. Ministry that is oriented exclusively toward being salt and light in the world (e.g., social service, sociopolitical liberation or justice) is indeed a form of worshiping God, but if it does not include the invitation to the lost to turn to Christ, then it is not truly engaged mission. On the other hand, ministry that includes evangelism and discipleship but neglects salt-and-light living is at best truncated mission.

Question 4: What Motifs Are Important to Mission Theology?

A motif is a recurring pattern or element that reinforces the central guiding theme of the house. For our purposes, a motif can be thought of as a recurring idea that reinforces our central themes. With that in mind, we ask this question: What motifs in mission will support and supplement our guiding theme, bringing out the nuances of that theme and enabling a better understanding of a whole theology of mission? Contemporary scholars identify a number of such themes (see Van Engen 1996, 20; Cardoza-Orlandi 2002, 72–88). Two of those scholars offer insightful suggestions that will be useful for our discussion.

DIAGRAM 5.5

Salt-and-Light Living

Discipleship and Church Growth

Evangelism and Church Planting

Reflecting God's Glory through Worship

Biblical Revelation

DIAGRAM 5.6

The first scholar is South African missiologist David Bosch (1991). He proposed six motifs necessary for a comprehensive approach to mission theology. These motifs are shown in diagram 5.6 as arrows passing through and permeating theology of mission. Bosch included as his motifs: (1) incarnation, (2) cross, (3) resurrection, (4) ascension, (5) Pentecost, and (6) parousia (or the complex of events related to the return of Christ). Bosch thus systematically covers the life, work, and future return of Jesus, the person who is central to mission.

DIAGRAM 5.7

The second scholar is American missiologist Wilbert Shenk (1999), who also proposes six motifs: (1) reign (kingdom) of God, (2) Jesus, (3) Holy Spirit, (4) church, (5) world, and (6) eschaton (parallel to Bosch's parousia but more broadly focused on things related to the end of history). Thus,

while Bosch's motifs are focused on the centrality of Jesus Christ, Shenk chooses motifs that incorporate Christ and more broadly explore the world in which mission is to happen (see diagram 5.7). Neither is right or wrong; both seek to provide motifs of mission theology that enhance our understanding of God's approach to mission. Together, they illustrate how deep (Bosch) and broad (Shenk) mission thinking should be.

Like Bosch and Shenk, we choose six motifs integral to mission that build on our foundational theme of mission as rooted in evangelism, church planting, discipleship, church growth, and salt-and-light living: (1) the kingdom of God, (2) Jesus, (3) the Holy Spirit, (4) the church, (5) *shalom* (the Hebrew term for *peace*), and (6) the return of Jesus (as shown in diagram 5.8).

DIAGRAM 5.8

The diagram illustrates the relationships of the motifs to the core. The motifs permeate all areas of the core but do not replace it. They are ideas through which the core can better be explained and enhanced. In the discussion that follows we will limit our presentation to introducing selected basic elements of the motif and how the motif as a whole relates to each of the core areas of our theology of mission.

MOTIF 1: THE KINGDOM OF GOD

Visions of God's kingdom vary widely, and often they are linked to visions of the end times. In trying to understand the kingdom of God we come face-to-face with several paradoxes that describe it. It is in the world but not of it (John 18:36). It belongs to the little ones, but those in it are greater than the greatest ones (Matt. 11:11; 18:1–4). It comes as a free gift but demands all that we have (Luke 12:30–33), and only the truly righteous will enter it (Matt. 5:20). It is God's very reign but works in hidden ways (Matt. 13:33). It is already present (Luke 17:21) yet still coming in the future (Matt. 6:10). It does not consist of talk (1 Cor. 4:20), but it must be proclaimed (Luke 4:43; see also Rottenberg 1980, 16–19).

Mission and kingdom are inextricably intertwined. The kingdom is both the seat of operations and the goal for which Christians strive. The paradoxes of the kingdom are the paradoxes of mission as well. Mission is successful when God's rules are followed, which can appear topsy-turvy even to the missionaries themselves. Enemies of the kingdom are not conquered by force, but by loving concern. Mission, starting small, has become a large force in today's world. However, the loud splashes that missionaries and mission agencies sometimes make are not to be mistaken for the quiet, life-changing force of God's reign working through the lives of individuals around the world. It is the empowerment of the weak for tasks impossible even for the strong. It will make its ultimate mark on the world even if people refuse to respond to the call of Christ. It belongs to the poor and the persecuted.

Much more could be said about the kingdom as a motif for mission theology. Perhaps the most important consideration is that the kingdom, including its establishment and timing, is *God's*—and Christians are privileged to participate in the process.

The kingdom of God as a motif runs through every layer of the foundational mission focus. It grows or is increased by evangelistic and church-planting activities. It represents an attitude toward life that puts God first in all that Christians do, enabling personal and corporate growth. Finally, it is linked to acts of justice performed in the name of Christ as firstfruits of the everlasting kingdom that God will establish.

MOTIF 2: JESUS

The Christian faith is not centered on a book or a set of ideals. It is centered on a person—a person unique in the history of the world, a person who is so important that most of the world splits its reckoning of time around his coming.

Jesus is central not only to the Christian faith, but also to the mission that is integrated into that faith. The one who relinquished deity to be born as a baby in a feeding trough, who died on behalf of all humankind, who will return to gather his own, and who gave his followers their marching orders has established forever his priorities for the church that he birthed through his life, ministry, and death.

Having enabled mission through his sacrificial death, Jesus defined all mission-oriented Christians to be witnesses through the Spirit in their own Jerusalems, and Judeas and Samarias—to the very ends of the earth (Acts 1:8). In his compelling book *The Supremacy of Christ,* Sri Lankan Ajith Fernando states,

> The Creator of the world has indeed presented the complete solution to the human

predicament. As such it is supreme; it is unique; and it is absolute. So we have the audacity in this pluralistic age to say that Jesus as He is portrayed in the Bible is not only unique but also supreme. He is our message to the world. A Hindu once asked Dr. E. Stanley Jones, "What has Christianity to offer that our religion has not?" He replied, "Jesus Christ." (Fernando 1995, 262)

Christ, then, is the one to whom Christians turn for understanding mission in his name. Many have noted, however, that Christ's earthly ministry was focused on, though not exclusively limited to, a particular people: the house of Israel. Does

> *Have we forgotten that there is a Holy Ghost, that we must insist upon walking upon crutches when we might fly?*
> A. J. Gordon (Student Volunteer Movement for Foreign Missions [1891] 1979, 19)

this mean that Jesus in some way limited the extent of his interest in and desire to reach all of humankind?

Ultimately what answers this question is that Jesus strategically limited himself to a particular people while engaged in earthly ministry, but that his ultimate concern for the entire world is deeply embedded in what he taught and how he prepared his disciples to broaden their horizons. For example, certainly the Great Commission in its various forms (and as discussed in chapter 3) demonstrates that Jesus' concerns went far beyond the house of Israel. He came for all human beings and calls his followers to join his harvest work of bringing them into the kingdom of God.

Finally, we note that Jesus permeates all three levels of our missional foundation: (1) it is he who both calls people to himself and enjoins them to go and make disciples; (2) discipleship and growth, both individual and corporate, come through obeying all that he taught and through teaching others to do likewise; and (3) his example of salt-and-light living inspires Christians to keep their focus Godward as they live lives that cause people to glorify the King of kings.

MOTIF 3: THE HOLY SPIRIT

The Holy Spirit's role in mission is another crucial motif. He is the agent who empowers Christians for mission and makes mission work possible for the church (see Luke 24:45–49; Acts 1:8; see also Shenk 1999, 13). It is the Spirit who reverses Babel at Pentecost, confirming Jesus' teaching that the kingdom of God is not limited by language or ethnicity (Acts 2:1–11).

It is the Spirit who convicts the world of sin, righteousness, and judgment (John 16:8–11). He ripens fields for harvest (Peters 1972, 80), convicting those who do not know Christ, wooing them to commit themselves into his care (Rev. 22:17) and thereby paving the way for evangelistic fruit by means of his invisible work in the hearts of people around the world.

It is the Spirit who guides the church in all truth (John 16:13) and in its missionary labors (e.g., Acts 16:7). He works inside the human heart, empowering Christians for witness (Acts 1:8), motivating them to witness and giving them words to say (Matt. 10:17–20). The Spirit also gifts the church for the purpose of growth both in numbers (Acts 2:14–41) and in maturity toward Christlikeness (Eph. 4:7–13).

Wilbert Shenk unequivocally states,

God's redemptive mission cannot be understood apart from the role of the Holy Spirit. Jesus warned the disciples against attempting to engage in mission without the Holy Spirit ("but stay in the city, until . . ." [Lk 24:49]); he "charged them not to depart from Jerusalem, but to wait" (Acts 1:4) for the Holy Spirit, who is the Spirit of Jesus the Messiah, leader in mission, equipping and empowering for the arduous task of bearing witness in the world where there will assuredly be opposition and persecution (Mt 28:20; 2 Cor 3:8; 4:7–10). "The Anointed One becomes the Anointing One" . . . as the Spirit of Jesus the Messiah endows the disciple community with the spiritual gifts needed for witness in the world. (Shenk 1999, 14)

The Holy Spirit permeates all three levels of our core theology of mission: (1) he convicts those in the world of sin and woos them to come to Christ; (2) he empowers Christ's followers to witness and acts as the agent of change in the lives of those who have committed themselves to following Jesus; and (3) he prays for Christians with groanings too deep for words, guiding them in making wise decisions about the best way to live salty lives that shine the light of God into dark situations.

MOTIF 4: THE CHURCH

What is the church? Conventionally, the term *local church* is used of a group of gathered believers (see Acts 5:11; 11:26; 1 Cor. 11:18; 14:19, 28, 35). Keep in mind that at the time of the writing of the New Testament there were no church buildings. Jews who came to Christ initially used synagogues as places of worship, and many believers also gathered in homes (Rom. 16:23; 1 Cor. 16:19; Col. 4:15). Thus, the local churches of that time looked radically different from modern churches in suburban North America. In addition to the local church, Christians speak of the *universal church*. This is the whole body of believers, including all those who are still in the world (see 1 Cor. 10:32; 11:22; 12:28; Eph. 4:11–16) and all those who are in heaven (Eph. 1:22–23; 3:10, 21; 5:23–25, 27, 32; Col. 1:18, 24).

Every local church is both *organism* and *organized*. As an organism, the church is a communion of believers—community is the key. It is the "body of Christ" (Eph. 1:22–23; 1 Cor. 12:12–27) and "living stones of the temple of God" (1 Pet. 2:4–8). As an *organized* organism, local churches are the homes of all believers. They preach salvation and nurture Christians. They also need leaders and a system of formal organization for their earthly operation.

As we discussed previously, the church was long understood to be the exclusive place for God's work in mission. However, although God indeed works through the church, he also works where the church does not yet exist (see, e.g., Acts 14:17). This has important implications for mission. One is that mission is not confined to what the church does (*missio Dei;* see Van Engen 1996, 145–56). Another, say some, is that we should look at the world to see where God is already accomplishing his missionary work apart from the church.

What, then, is the purpose of the church? Essentially, the church submits to Christ (Eph. 5:23–24), who is its head (Col. 1:18). How this is done can be seen in terms of three relationships: (1) the church's relationship with God, (2) the church's relationship with itself, and (3) the church's relationship with the world.

In relation to God, the church is to send forth praise and glory to God for his merciful dealings with people (Eph. 3:20–21) and to make his wisdom known even in the heavenly realms (Eph. 3:10–11).

There are two components of the church's relation to itself. The first is edification. God gifts and appoints people in the church (1 Cor. 12:28). They lead the church in its responsibilities to build up the saints (1 Cor. 14:12, 26; Heb. 10:24), equip them for service (Eph. 4:11–16), and care for its own who are in need (Acts 12:5; James 1:27; 1 Tim. 5:1–16). The second is that of purification. The church is to allow Christ to cleanse it so as to be a spotless bride (Eph. 5:25b–27), morally (1 Cor. 5; Matt. 18:15–18) and doctrinally (Acts 15:22–29; 2 Tim. 2:16–18).

In relation to the world, the church is to call the peoples of the world to repentance by proclaiming the kingdom. Bought with Christ's blood (Acts 20:28), the church is the agent that God has chosen to call the world to repent and turn to Christ (Matt. 28:16–20) by sending people out into the world to preach the gospel (Acts 13:1–3). At the same time, the church is to live as a sign of the reality of the kingdom— being salt and light in a darkened world (Matt. 5:13–16) (adapted from Shenk 1999, 15).

A missionary theology of the church must have the purposes of the church in relation to the world as its driving focus. Questions about the polity of the church, the sacraments of the church, leadership and local organization of the church, roles in the church, and so on, while of great importance, must not detract from the missionary purpose of the church. The extent to which local churches fail in that task is the extent to which they run the risk of becoming fossilized institutions that distract the universal church from God's intended purpose.

MOTIF 5: SHALOM

The Hebrew term *shalom* expresses not only a sense of personal peace, but also a sense of community peace and wholeness. As we noted in chapter 1, *shalom* is concerned with the spiritual (salvation), the physical (healing), the psychological (wholeness), and the social (justice and freedom from war). Ultimately, this sense of peace is reflected not so much in the circumstances around us as it is in our ability to face them knowing that even in the valley of death God is walking with us and, when necessary, even carrying us. It is more than a passive response to circumstances, however. Perhaps no Old Testament verse captures the idea better than Mic. 6:8:

> He has showed you, O man, what is good.
> And what does the LORD require of you?
> To act justly
> and to love mercy
> and to walk humbly with your God.

The idea reflects more that Christians' lives have meaning and purpose than that they simply live peacefully, though obviously it includes the latter as well.

One critical thrust of mission is the reality of the kingdom conflict between Jesus and Satan (Matt. 4:23–24). This conflict is seen in Jesus' life when he resists Satan's temptations (Matt. 4:1–11; Luke 4:1–13; Matt. 16:21–23) and when he drives out demons (Matt. 4:23–24; Mark 1:39; Luke 6:18–19). It also is seen when he teaches that the kingdom is among us (Matt. 12:22–29; Mark 3:22–27; Luke 11:14–22) and when he proclaims that he came to earth to set the captives free (Luke 4:17–21).

Shalom in this sense relates to the fact that Christians have been set free and are called to participate in the kingdom conflict of setting others free through calling them to bond to Christ (Matt. 28:18–20; John 8:31–37).

Further, the spiritual warfare that Christians face requires that they be the salt of the earth and the light of the world (Matt. 5:13–16). As light, they are to live lives pleasing to God. They are to display kingdom ethics (i.e., ethics built on God's sovereignty over our lives) by following in the footsteps of Jesus, including taking up their crosses and following him daily (Matt. 16:24). They are to live such exemplary lives that others will see them and praise God as a result (Matt. 5:16). They are to expose Satan's kingdom of darkness by proclaiming the kingdom of God and the light of God's word so that the world may see God living through them.

As salt, they are to act as preservers of the societies in which they live by manifesting God's sovereignty to the world around them. Of great significance in this regard is the need to live their lives by God's rules rather than by those of people. This includes things such as turning the other cheek (Matt. 5:38–42), loving enemies (Matt. 5:43–48), forgiving others as Christ forgave them (Matt. 6:14; 18:21–35), and teaching others how to forgive as well (Matt. 28:18–20).

MOTIF 6: THE RETURN OF JESUS

Eschatology—the study of the events relating to the return of Christ and the end of history—has a deep impact on missionary theology and practice. One of the slogans that Scott Moreau heard early in his walk with Christ was "Don't take time to straighten out the pictures in a burning building." The implication was that he should not bother to fix social structures while people around him were going to hell.

After all, so the reasoning went, the world is only going to get worse before Christ returns. The picture painted by this slogan is chiefly an eschatological one—a vision of the future that determines responsibilities in the present. It is one of several illustrations that could be used to show how important eschatology is for mission.

As with the other motifs, eschatology relates to each of the three levels at the core of mission thinking. First, evangelism is God's response to the fact that people apart from Christ are destined to spend eternity separated from God in hell. The Christian's personal involvement in evangelism is an indication that he or she takes seriously both God's concern for humankind and the predicament of people separated from Christ.

Second, the certainty of Christ's return provides Christians with hope, enabling them to persevere in their own growth as followers of Christ. It also spurs the church on, providing security in the knowledge that it is the bride of Christ and the wedding awaits. It also motivates Christians to expose the world's darkness. The agony of those who will enter a Christless eternity impels Christians, with Paul, to urge people to respond to Jesus' call and be reconciled to God (2 Cor. 5:18).

Third, the coming of Christ motivates Christians to be preservers in a lost world. Their work to preserve is done not in the hope that what they build will enter eternity, but as a precursor of what eternity will bring after the old has passed away and the new has come.

PUTTING IT TOGETHER

No matter how broadly Christians may choose to define mission (or *missio Dei*), they must not lose sight of the eternal per-

---

SIDEBAR 5.3
CHURCH MODELS THAT WORK

Driving Theological Convictions at Bethlehem Baptist Church (Minneapolis, Minnesota)

This is a church that has made the biblical foundation for mission the cornerstone of their ministry. Their mission statement calls them as a church to "spread a passion for the supremacy of God in all things for the joy of all peoples." That foundation is spelled out in great detail by their senior pastor, John Piper, in his book *Let the Nations Be Glad!* It is also succinctly stated in the "Fourteen Convictions" that Telford calls "the driving convictions behind world missions at Bethlehem" (Telford 2001, 20):

Conviction 1: God's goal in creation and redemption is a missionary goal because our God is a missionary God.

Conviction 2: God is passionately committed to his fame. God's ultimate goal is that his name be known and praised by all the peoples of the earth. We believe that the central command of world missions is Isaiah 12:4: "Make known his deeds among the peoples, proclaim that his name is exalted."

Conviction 3: Worship is the fuel and the goal of missions. A God-centered theology must be a missionary theology. If you say that you love the glory of God, the test of your authenticity is whether you love the spread of that glory among all the peoples of the world. To worship him is to share that passion for his supremacy among the nations.

Conviction 4: God's passion to be known and praised by all the peoples of the earth is not selfish, but loving. God is the one being in the universe for whom self-exaltation is the ultimately loving act.

Conviction 5: God's purpose to be praised among all the nations cannot fail. It is an absolutely certain promise. It is going to happen.

---

spective. The central need of people is to be reestablished in a living relationship with a loving God—to love God with all their heart, soul, mind, and strength.

Loving God is the basis for being reestablished in relationships with each other and

> *How little chance the Holy Ghost has nowadays. The churches and missionary societies have so bound Him in red tape that they practically ask Him to sit in a corner while they do the work themselves.*
> C. T. Studd (Walker 1980, 120)

loving our neighbors as we love ourselves. Biblically speaking, the latter cannot be fully accomplished until the former is settled. Thus,

as explained above, the evangelistic mandate of winning people to Christ must be at the core of any theology of mission that hopes to remain true to the biblical orientation.

In summary, we define the mission of the church centrally in terms of the Great Commission (Matt. 28:18–20; cf. Luke 24:47; John 20:21; Acts 1:8) and the priestly purpose of the church in the world. As "priests of God" (see Rev. 1:6), the mission of the members of the body of Christ is mediatorial in nature. Mediators serve with one overall purpose: reconciliation between two estranged parties. That is their mediatorial role. In performing that mediatorial role, however, they may serve in what may be called three phases.

The first phase is bearing witness that reconciliation is possible (Acts 1:8). Chris-

Conviction 6: Only in God will our souls be at rest. The one transcultural reality that unites every person of every culture is that God has set eternity in our hearts (Eccles. 3:11).

Conviction 7: Domestic ministries are the goal of frontier missions. What this means is that frontier missions is the exportation of the possibility and practice of domestic ministries in the name of Jesus to unreached people groups.

Conviction 8: The missionary task is focused on peoples, not just individual people, and is therefore finishable.... The task of missions is planting the church among all the peoples, not necessarily winning all the people.

Conviction 9: The need of the hour is for thousands of new Paul-type missionaries—a fact which is sometimes obscured by the quantity of Timothy-type missionaries. Our prayer for Bethlehem is that we put a very high priority on raising up and sending frontier missionaries—Paul-type missionaries.

Conviction 10: It is the joyful duty and the awesome privilege of every local church to send out missionaries "in a manner worthy of God" (3 John 6).

Conviction 11: We are called to a wartime lifestyle for the sake of going and sending. To send in a manner worthy of God and to go for the sake of the Name, we must constantly fight the deception that we are living in peacetime where we think that the luxury of self-indulgence is the only power that can break the boredom.

Conviction 12: Prayer is a wartime walkie-talkie and not a domestic intercom. In wartime, prayer takes on a different significance.... John 15:16 . . . means that prayer is for mission. It is designed to advance the kingdom.

Conviction 13: Our aim is not to persuade everyone to become a missionary, but to help everyone become a World Christian. Those who are not called to go out for the sake of the Name are called to stay for the sake of the Name.

Conviction 14: God is most glorified in us when we are most satisfied in him; and our satisfaction in him is greatest when it expands to embrace others—even when this involves suffering.

tians bear personal verbal testimony of the salvation wrought in Christ. They also live lives that demonstrate that reconciliation with God has been accomplished. Additionally, they call on those who are not living under the rule of God to repent of their attitudes and deeds, to give their lives to Christ and come worship him. It is the privilege of Christians to be used by God as instruments in effecting the actual reconciliation wrought by Christ (1 Cor. 5:18–21). They invite people to personally commit themselves to the saving work of Christ and, when appropriate, provide them with a biblically appropriate and contextually relevant ritual or method by which they express their commitment.

The second phase is that of building up those who have entered God's kingdom through discipleship and appropriate enfolding in local groups of believers collectively known as the church. These local bodies are where people are nurtured, strengthened, and encouraged, and are the places from which they are thrust out into the harvest field to continue with the first phase of the missionary task. While doing this, they should lead a life that shows, in word and in deed, a love of God with heart, soul, mind, and strength. Integrally related to this is a life that shows, in word and in deed, a love of neighbor as exemplified by Jesus in the parable of the good Samaritan (Luke 10:25–37).

The third phase is that of living lives that shine light into dark places, acting as preservatives in the world to effect healing of hearts, minds, souls, and bodies. This

---

CASE STUDY:
BAN ON EVANGELISM

A. Scott Moreau

John and Ben, exhausted from the long journey back home, collapsed on the beds in John's apartment. The tense driving on dusty dirt roads, having to hang on tightly to the steering wheel just to keep the car from swerving off the road, always left John feeling drained when he returned home from his trips around the country visiting the "For the Least of These" (FLT) workers on location. John was the country director of FLT, and Ben was the regional director and John's immediate supervisor. Though Ben was accustomed to the realities of transportation in developing countries, he too was drained. They could have taken public transportation, but the cramped space (there was always room for one more!), the long stares of other passengers, and endless waiting for the next bus took their own toll. That did not even count the tripling of time it would have taken to visit the twelve FLT small staff teams in Arkenasia. After this most recent trip, however, Ben's mind was churning over the issues that his agency faced. Physically ready for a nap, he was mentally in turmoil over how to proceed from here. He began to rehearse the events of the past several months.

Arkenasia had been plunged into economic chaos. It was a small country not considered important in geopolitics, and literally off the mental maps of most people in the rest of the world, too insignificant to matter. With the local banks in disarray, the inflation rates so high that wages paid one day were worth half their value the next, a work force depleted because of the AIDS epidemic, and government officials salting away whatever they could in foreign banks, even the basic necessities of life were hard to secure. Everywhere John looked, the picture was bleak at best. Literally thousands faced starvation unless drastic measures were taken, and millions were threatened by AIDS. Educational opportunities were almost nonexistent, as the country focused its energy on surviving the present rather than on preparing for the future. Medical care was virtually unavailable, except to those who could afford to leave the country. Added to all of this, a recent drought had put strains even on the normally self-sufficient farmers.

FLT was committed to holistic mission, and their workers concentrated on relief and development in the country while also quietly carrying on an effective evangelistic work. Several small but energetic churches had been planted even though church planting was not FLT's primary focus. Their unanticipated success in church planting, however, had given rise to the current dilemma.

---

healing is to take place both individually and corporately. Light needs to be brought to bear wherever injustice prevails, and salt needs to be applied when justice has made its mark.

CONCLUSION

The mission of the church is that it be used by God (1) to witness to people about the reconciliation offered in Christ; (2) to invite people to worship their creator by leading them to Christ; (3) to incorporate those led to Christ into local church contexts; and (4) to teach them, as people reconciled to God, to obey all that Christ commanded in being salt and light in the world. All four components are necessary and integral to the mission of the church.

Although all four components are necessary and integral to mission, they are not all equal in priority. Evangelism is to be given a

The government was strongly committed to an anti-Christian stance. The authorities were willing to tolerate Christian groups entering the country because they offered relief and development work, but explicitly had warned FLT not to get involved in "proselytism" when FLT first signed the contract enabling entry into Arkenasia. They were notified in no uncertain terms that Arkenasians had a rich religious history and identity, and challenges to that identity would be considered threats not only to the culture, but also to the government.

Two months prior to Ben's visit FLT had received a harsh letter from the Ministry of Development. Although FLT's exemplary work in helping the poor of the country was noted, the letter also included a sharp warning that all proselytism was to be curtailed immediately and that the FLT staff was to be monitored closely for compliance in the future. The letter not only demanded that FLT workers stop their low-key evangelism, but

also forbade them even to talk about the Christian faith with nationals. Anyone caught in such activities would be expelled.

To demonstrate their seriousness, the authorities, one month after sending the first letter, issued a forty-eight-hour notice of expulsion to Fred Aleb, a veterinarian working with domestic livestock. In the hectic twenty-four hours before Fred left, he and John wrestled through every issue that could have brought about the notice. Fred could not remember any explicitly Christian conversations since FLT had received the warning, but when John and Fred went to appeal the expulsion, the local officials insisted that he had been overheard discussing spiritual matters in an inappropriate way with the local farmers while he examined their animals. The fact that Fred's work already had resulted in several small house congregations in the rural areas was not lost on John as a possible reason for his expulsion. Was it possible that Fred was simply a scapegoat

that the government was using to ensure FLT's compliance? It seemed likely, as it was a commonly used technique to keep stability among the masses, and perhaps Fred was nothing more than the unlucky choice.

With Fred now gone, the rest of the FLT people were discouraged. John had arranged for an emergency visit from Ben, who was charged with the responsibility of keeping FLT in the country and true to its organizational calling. As the local director, John faced the responsibility not just of maintaining their morale, but also of developing an appropriate plan to help the ministry continue to operate.

After they both had rested, they sat down at the simple table to develop a long-term plan that would take into account the present realities. After much prayer and discussion over the next several days, they decided that the best approach to the whole situation was to ...

logical (not necessarily a temporal) priority in the total mission of the church. Mission that does not include evangelism is missing the core. Christ commanded the disciples to preach the kingdom, not to establish it, as the latter act belongs to God alone. Our case study for this chapter explores this in a challenging situation that forces two missionaries to consider what it is they are called to do.

At the same time, however, mission is more than evangelism. Mission that does not include incorporating those led to Christ into a local body of believers or teaching them to obey all that Christ commanded his followers to be as salt and light is, at best, truncated mission. God's desire is that Christians not separate these elements of mission as they pursue the path of reflecting his glory to a world estranged from its creator.

PART 2

Encountering Missions in History

The story of mission does not end with the close of the New Testament. That story has continued for almost two thousand years until Christ's church now has a presence in almost every nook and cranny of the earth.

Encountering the story of the expansion of the church through history is also an important part of introducing mission. This part tells that story in three chapters. In chapter 6 we explore missions and evangelization from the day of Pentecost to the rise of Christendom early in the fourth century on through to the conquest of Constantinople (now Istanbul) in 1453 and also beyond the walls of Christendom to the East. In chapter 7 we trace the encounter with Christian missions in the age of discovery and colonial expansion during the early modern era (1500–1800) through most of the "Great Century" in missions (1800–1914). In chapter 8 we look at the twentieth century in missions, a phenomenal century by any account.

6

Expansion in the Premodern Era, A.D. 30–1500

INTRODUCTION

At a construction site in northern China in 1625 workers were surprised to uncover a large black stone tablet over nine feet high and three feet wide. Engraved with Chinese characters, the title read, "A Monument Commemorating the Propagation of the Luminous Religion in China." It not only told the story of Alopen, the first known Christian missionary to enter China almost a thousand years earlier, but also opened a long-lost chapter in the history of Christian mission. Though far removed in time, the stories of missionaries such as Alopen provide valuable insights into how Christianity developed and how present-day mission should or should not be conducted. They also remind contemporary Christians of the accomplishments of earlier missionaries who struggled to overcome enormous difficulties not faced by missionaries today.

Before the day of Pentecost Jesus promised the disciples, "You will receive power when the Holy Spirit comes on you; and you will be my witnesses in Jerusalem, and in all Judea and Samaria, and to the ends of the earth" (Acts 1:8). As we saw previously,

Acts records the persecution that drove the early Christians from Jerusalem to the surrounding regions and closes with Paul's testimony for Christ in Rome. In the millennium that followed, Christianity spread in an ever-widening circle westward as far as Spain and Ireland, northward to Scandinavia and Russia, southward to Ethiopia, and eastward to India and China. Given the primitive means of travel and communication, political upheavals, and the opposition of non-Christians, this expansion represented a remarkable achievement. Nevertheless, even after missionaries accompanied Christopher Columbus on his second voyage to the West Indies in 1493 and Francis Xavier preached in Japan in 1549, the "Luminous Religion" had yet to reach the "ends of the earth."

The expansion of Christianity never followed a single prescribed strategy. Indeed, the motives that drove believers to risk their lives to proclaim the good news, their methods of persuasion, and the forms of the faith that developed varied widely. Whereas early Christians simply had prayed for their neighbors and humbly shared the gospel with them, the tenth-century king Olav of

Norway threatened peasants to either receive baptism or be killed. Although quickly seeing the wisdom of conversion, they still had to provide Olav with hostages "to guarantee that they would keep the faith" (Barry 1985, 278). Despite the questionable sincerity of their conversion, others discovered the true meaning. Thousands of miles away in south India a believer erected a stone cross with the inscription "Let me not glory save in the cross of our Lord Jesus Christ" (Kuriakose 1982, 9).

In some places Christianity grew to the point where nations became officially Christian, as happened in Armenia and the Roman Empire. This resulted in the emergence of Christendom, a scenario that produced an ill-fated marriage of church and state. Wilbert Shenk observes that "rather than being the faith of those who voluntarily responded to the call to follow Jesus Christ as Lord, Christianity was now identified with the political power structures and struggles of the world" (Shenk 1984, 159). Elsewhere it remained a minority faith without state support, leaving its adherents to brave the uncertain winds of toleration.

In this chapter we explore mission and evangelization from the day of Pentecost to the rise of Christendom early in the fourth century, then afterward in territories where church and state joined forces, and finally beyond the walls of Christendom. The chapter closes with the conquest of Constantinople (now Istanbul) in 1453 that marked the ultimate triumph of Islam in the Middle East, the birthplace of Christianity. This event took place just thirty years before the Portuguese discovered the mouth of the Congo River in central Africa and forty years before small Spanish ships began to drop anchor in the western hemisphere, new worlds in which to introduce the Christian faith.

MISSION BEFORE CHRISTENDOM (A.D. 30–313)

Jesus commissioned his disciples to preach the message of "repentance and forgiveness of sins . . . beginning at Jerusalem" (Luke 24:47). Thus, on the day of Pentecost, Jewish pilgrims from Rome, North Africa, Asia Minor, Arabia, Parthia, and elsewhere miraculously heard the "wonders of God" in their own languages and listened as Peter told them about the risen Christ. His reference to Joel's prophecy—"I will pour out my Spirit on all people" (Joel 2:28)—had far-ranging implications for mission. As New Testament scholar Josephine Ford notes, "The passage from Joel which Peter sees as fulfilled at Pentecost speaks of the Spirit coming to all classes of people—young and old, slave and free, men and women, saint and repentant sinner" (Ford 1988, 148).

Instead of taking the usual course of human institutions that become ever more exclusive over time, the Christian church grew as a fellowship of Spirit-filled believers by welcoming persons of all cultures and backgrounds, though not without some difficulty at times. Opponents grumbled that "only foolish and low individuals, and persons devoid of perception, and slaves, and women, and children" became converts (Origen 1972, 484). But in fact, from the beginning all classes of people could be found among them, with the majority being common folk. The good news had a transforming effect through bringing love and reconciliation into human relationships (Acts 2:42–47). "It is our care for the helpless, our practice of lovingkindness, that brands us in the eyes of many of our op-

94

ponents," wrote the second-century church father Tertullian to explain what made the faith attractive. "'See,' they say, 'how they love one another!'" (Barry 1985, 57).

Physical healings and deliverances from demonic power also convinced unbelievers of the power of the gospel. From Peter's healing of the crippled beggar at the Jerusalem temple to Paul's exorcism of a demon from a slave girl in Philippi, they saw the power of the Christian God overcome the pagan deities. Demonstrations of supernatural power—"power encounters"—continued in some quarters with the activities of Gregory the Wonderworker becoming especially well known. His ministry resulted in the conversion of nearly the entire city of Neocaesarea in Asia Minor, prompting another church father, Basil the Great, to remark, "By the superabundance of gifts, wrought in him by the Spirit in all power and in signs and in marvels, he was styled a second Moses by the very enemies of the Church" (Basil the Great 1968, 74).

You Will Be My Witnesses

Who were the first missionaries? Although the Book of Acts largely records the evangelistic activities of the apostles Peter and Paul, it also tells of Barnabas, Timothy, and Philip and his "four unmarried daughters who prophesied" (Acts 21:9). Ordinary Christians composed the rank and file of witnesses, people such as Paul's friend Lydia, who was a cloth merchant in Thyatira, and Aquila and Priscilla, who were tentmakers in Corinth. "Christians cannot be distinguished from the rest of the human race by country or language or customs," wrote one observer, since "they do not live in cities of their own; they do not use a peculiar form of speech; [and] they do not follow an eccentric manner of life." Their values set them apart from their neighbors: "Christians dwell in the world, but do not belong to the world" (Richardson 1970, 216, 218).

Early Christians had looked for the return of Jesus Christ in their lifetimes, but by the end of the first century the organization of their churches took on more permanent and complex forms. A chain of command headed by one bishop, several presbyters (priests/pastors), and numerous deacons and other minor officers gradually became typical in large urban centers. In an early Christian writing, *The Didache* (also called *The Teaching of the Twelve Apostles*), reference is made to the continuing activities of traveling charismatic "apostles and prophets." Still, it encourages believers to give equal honor to leaders they have chosen (Richardson 1970, 178). Along with the work of bishops and pastors who shared the

> *[Christians] busy themselves on earth, but their citizenship is in heaven. They obey the established laws, but in their own lives they go far beyond what the laws require. They love all men, and by all men are persecuted.*
>
> Epistle to Diognetus 5:9–11
> (Petry 1962, 19)

gospel, evangelization continued through the witness of local church members as well as the efforts of itinerant evangelists. Around A.D. 250 the Alexandrian theologian Origen referred to an increasing number of Christians who spent their time chiefly in evangelism.

Christians used every opportunity to share the good news. Since they met in homes for worship, evangelism took place in part through these "cell groups." Other practices included open-air evangelism, visiting the sick, and caring for the needy. Christian writers explained the faith to non-Christians and also challenged the teachings of those who sought to distort it (Green 1970, 194–235). The interaction with non-Christians prompted theologians such as Justin Martyr to find elements in the writings of the pagan philosophers that could be used to help them see the truth of Christ.

Everyone needed to hear the gospel regardless of his or her cultural background or social standing. Paul, in his apostolic ministry, worked to make it understandable to all who heard him. When preaching to Jews, he focused on their knowledge of the long-awaited messiah spoken of in the Scriptures, "explaining and proving that the Christ had to suffer and rise from the dead." "This Jesus I am proclaiming to you is the Christ," he announced at the synagogue in Thessalonica (Acts 17:3). When Gentiles formed the audience, he used other approaches. At Lystra the miraculous healing of a crippled man captured the attention of the crowd and the priest of the temple of Zeus (Acts 14:8–18). Speaking to the philosophers in Athens, he began with familiar religious truth before telling them about the revelation of Jesus Christ (Acts 17:16–34). Paul had the ability to communicate the gospel to a wide range of audiences, whether members of a synagogue, people on the street, or the intellectual elite.

In all these endeavors Christians saw how the power of the Holy Spirit and the preaching of the gospel brought persons to faith. They also recognized the absolute necessity of prayer. Ignatius, an early bishop in Antioch, sent a letter to the Ephesian Christians telling them to "'keep on praying' for others too, for there is a chance of

their being converted and getting to God. Let them . . . learn from you at least by your actions. Return their bad temper with gentleness; their boasts with humility; their abuse with prayer" (Richardson 1970, 91). Such testimony, however, sometimes came at great price, as Ignatius's martyrdom and those of Stephen, James the brother of John, Polycarp, Perpetua, and other Christians demonstrated.

Into All the World

American and European Christians often have thought of the church extending to the West, due in part to Luke's tracing events from Jerusalem to Rome, but more likely because the story of Christianity in the East was lost as believers separated from each other. While Paul was directed westward by the vision of a man begging him, "Come over to Macedonia and help us" (Acts 16:9), others went elsewhere. An angel of the Lord instructed Philip to take the desert road from Jerusalem to Gaza to witness to a royal official on his way home to Ethiopia after worshiping in Jerusalem (Acts 8:26–39). Eusebius Pamphilus, a later church historian, said that Mark first preached the gospel in Alexandria, John went to Ephesus, and Thomas and Andrew ventured east of the Mesopotamian river valley (Eusebius Pamphilus 1955, 65, 82). Other influential witnesses included Pantaenus, who reportedly visited India (Mundadan 1989, 117).

By the year 180, Christians could be found in all the provinces of the empire. Just as members of the palace guard in Rome had whispered the gospel among themselves in Paul's day (Phil. 1:13), so now soldiers carried the faith to the farthest imperial outposts in Roman Britain, Germany, and Romania, while merchants built churches where they located new markets. How far they traveled southward into Africa and eastward into Asia and how many Christians lived in these regions remain unknown. But in any event, the number of Christians within the empire may have grown to several million by the year 313, when the Edict of Toleration (Treaty of Milan) was published. Notable centers for

> *Most of the disciples . . . first fulfilled the Savior's command . . . and distributed their goods among the needy (Mt. 19:21), and then, entering upon long journeys, performed the work of evangelists (Rom. 15:20, 21), being eager to preach everywhere to those who had not yet the word of faith and to pass on the writing of the divine Gospels (Eph. 9:19, 20). As soon as they had only laid the foundations of the faith in some foreign lands, they appointed others as pastors and entrusted to them the nurture of those who had recently been brought in, but they themselves went on to other lands and peoples with the grace and co-operation of God, for a great many marvelous miracles of the divine spirit were still being worked by them at that time, so that whole multitudes . . . at the first hearing eagerly received within their souls the religion of the Creator of the universe.*
>
> Eusebius of Caesarea
> (Thomas 1995, 7–8)

Christian training and mission inside the empire arose in Alexandria, Antioch, Ephesus, Rome, and later Constantinople. To the east of Syria, Edessa, the capital city of the kingdom of Osrhoene, and later Nisibis, in upper Mesopotamia, became launchpads for sending forth Syriac-speaking Christians intent on sharing the gospel, some of whom would trek across the rugged mountains of Afghanistan to the deserts of central Asia and ultimately to China.

Christians benefited from the *Pax Romana* (the enforced "Roman Peace") and the protected system of roads that connected all parts of the empire. The Greek language also helped because it was the common language of persons engaged in commerce and government. Christianity thrived in urban centers linked to the roads. Villagers from conservative rural areas, however, resisted surrendering their confidence in the local gods. Consequently, a non-Christian came to be known as a *paganus*, a "pagan" or "heathen" in contrast to a Christian or a Jew.

Troublemakers Everywhere

News about Christianity had already reached the city of Thessalonica by the time Paul and his party arrived. Opponents warned the city fathers of "these men who have caused trouble all over the world" (Acts 17:6). The good news, with its message of love and equality in Christ, challenged cultures founded on distinctions between races and between the rich and the poor. Later, when Paul urged Philemon to receive back his penitent slave Onesimus "no longer as a slave, but better than a slave, as a dear brother" (Philem. 16), he knew that Christian love could break the chains of slavery.

The first indication of the gospel's blockbuster effect arose over the question of how the gospel should be "contextualized"—made understandable and applied to the culture of the Gentiles. Peter's baptism of the Roman centurion Cornelius and his family and friends sparked controversy among Jewish Christians because it appeared to discount the value that the Old Testament law placed on circumcision and ceremonial laws that included regulations on the kinds of food that could be eaten and their preparation. Nevertheless, the "Gentile Pentecost" at the home of Cornelius—"The Holy Spirit came on all who heard the message. . . . For they heard them speaking in tongues and praising God" (Acts 10:44, 46)—symbolized the entrance of the Gentiles into the community of the redeemed. Arriving in Jerusalem to explain his actions, Peter found that his critics—"Judaizing Christians"—could not see beyond the cultural issue: "You went into the house of uncircumcised men and ate with them," they told him scornfully (Acts 11:3).

The seriousness of the dispute eventually led to the convening of the first council of the Christian church in Jerusalem, since the very meaning of the gospel was at stake. To his opponents Peter declared, "God, who knows the heart, showed that he accepted them by giving the Holy Spirit to them, just as he did to us. He made no distinction between us and them, for he purified their hearts by faith. . . . We believe it is through the grace of our Lord Jesus that we are saved, just as they are" (Acts 15:8–9, 11). Therefore, the Gentiles did not need to be circumcised or burdened with other Judaizing applications of the law, although James advised them to follow certain Mosaic prescriptions to avoid offending Jewish Christians (Acts 15:19–21). This "Magna Carta" of Christian liberty made possible the unhampered development of Gentile churches within their cultural contexts. The council affirmed that Jesus, through his incarnation, death, and resurrection, had become the means of salvation for all peoples. The

Christian faith never could become the exclusive property of a particular culture and remain true to its nature. According to missiologist Julian Saldanha, "The all-inclusive nature of the Church welcomed all races and classes, learned and ignorant, rich and poor, so that no other [religion] took in so many groups and strata of society" (Saldanha 1988, 21).

Christianity arose at a pivotal time when the older religions had begun to fall into disrepute as superstitions, creating a spiritual vacuum that the cold teachings of the philosophers could not fill. Mystery religions such as the Persian cult of Mithras tried to fill this void (Barrett 1987, 125–27, 132–34). However, faith in Jesus Christ appealed to persons of all classes who struggled with spiritual emptiness, bringing them not only a saving relationship with God, but also membership in a loving community of fellow believers. In the middle of the fourth century the emperor Julian the Apostate grumbled, "The Galilaeans [Christians] care not only for their own poor but for ours as well; while those who belong to us look in vain for the help that we should render them" (Neill 1986, 38). No one accused Christians of "buying converts."

The joy and fulfillment of the Christian faith came at great risk. Without legal recognition, Christians faced the danger of meeting together for worship without public sanction, and their close fellowship often sparked misunderstanding among neighbors who spread malicious rumors about them (e.g., sexual immorality, cannibalism, and even atheism, since people could not see their god [Bush 1983, 1–61]). Their actions also appeared hostile to traditional values. For instance, Christians shunned public office because they refused to "pledge allegiance" to the emperor by throwing incense on an altar in honor of his divinity. Many, but not all, Christians were pacifists, often choosing to avoid military service because of the possibility of having to kill. Not surprisingly, believers suffered during persecutions and sometimes died from torture or were torn to death by animals in coliseums, the sports arenas of the time. Tertullian contended that "the blood of the martyrs was the seed of the church," a comforting hope and frequently true, but one not always confirmed by history.

MISSION AND CHRISTENDOM (A.D. 313–1500)

The status of Christians in the Roman Empire took a dramatic turn for the better in 312. On the day before the battle of Milvian Bridge, near Rome, the emperor Constantine saw a cross of light in the sky, superimposed over the sun, and the words "In this, conquer." To him this meant that Christ, the Lord of the cross, would protect him and grant him victory over his enemies. He then placed an emblem made by combining the Greek letters X (chi) and P (rho) to signify "Christ" on his helmet and on the shields of his soldiers. On the next day they marched into battle and slaughtered much of the opposing army (Jones 1978, 84–86).

Gratitude to the Christian God prompted Constantine a year later to proclaim the Edict of Toleration, which announced, "Every man may have complete toleration in the practice of whatever worship he has chosen" (Hastings 1999, 36). For Christians this meant an end to persecution and the return of confiscated property. Several years later he granted them legal and economic privileges, including the right to leave property and monies to the churches in their wills. In 325 he convened the Council of Nicea, the

first ecumenical (universal) council of Christian bishops, to resolve a serious doctrinal dispute known as Arianism, a belief that viewed Jesus as neither eternal nor equal with God the Father (Davis 1987, 51–77). Although not baptized as a Christian until shortly before his death in 337, Constantine supported the faith throughout his reign, built many churches, encouraged charitable endeavors, abolished cruel practices (e.g., punishment by crucifixion), and became a model for later Christian rulers.

In 380 the emperor Theodosius made Christianity the official religion of the empire. Eleven years later he ended the toleration of non-Christian religions and outlawed pagan sacrifices (Judaism, however, remained legally protected). In the new order political, cultural, and religious factors joined forces. Before long the empire divided into the Western Roman Empire,

> *The priesthood and the Empire are the two greatest gifts which God ... has bestowed upon mortals; the former has reference to Divine matters, the latter presides over and directs human affairs, and both, proceeding from the same principle, adorn the life of mankind.*
>
> Emperor Justinian (Petry 1962, 75)

with Rome as its capital, and the Eastern Roman or Byzantine Empire, with its capital at Constantinople (prior to being rebuilt as "Constantine's city," it had been known as Byzantium.) The sixth-century emperor Justinian, who managed to briefly reunite the two halves, went further in stamping out paganism (Cunningham 1999, 69).

With the end of persecution, masses of

99

people joined the church for a variety of reasons. Some simply heard the gospel and repented of their sins. Others saw an opportunity for social advancement. Bishop Cyril of Jerusalem told a group of new converts, "You become Christians, one to win a friend and another to marry a rich wife. However, by all means come, for it is Christ who casts the bait" (Schmidlin 1933, 119). Despite his positive spin on the awkwardness of such "conversions," the lack of deeply felt commitment often resulted in a superficial form of Christian living. Little wonder that Bishop Ambrose of Milan lamented, "How many made external profession of faith and denied it interiorly!" (Saldanha 1988, 113 n. 37).

The movement of people into the church continued in the succeeding centuries, with entire tribes converting on the command of their leaders. Immediate baptism without appropriate teaching about its meaning led many to view it in magical terms—in some places people used it as a remedy for sickness. The Burgundians, a Germanic tribe west of the Rhine River, became Christians as a group, as did the Franks in Gaul (now France) and Arab tribes that entered Roman territory. When Lithuanian rulers established Christianity as the state religion, the people "were driven in droves to the banks of the rivers and into the water" for baptism (Schmidlin 1933, 220).

By the year 1500 the entire region from Europe to Russia had been Christianized. Though divided politically, the various territorial states had affirmed the Christian faith, boasted Christian rulers, and promoted Christian culture. Yet the outward "victory" of Christianity masked the persistent endurance of non-Christian practices that remained hidden from public view. The formation of Christian states, together comprising Christendom, ushered in a territorial and cultural understanding of Christianity that lasted into the twentieth century. Although this positively imprinted Christian values into various cultures, with it also came the crusades against the Muslims, the hunting down of heretics, and the persecutions of Jewish communities—all, unfortunately, done in the name of Christ.

The Plow of Apostolic Preaching

The call to mission came in many ways, from simple obedience to Christ's commands, to the missionary vision of church and civil leaders, to unusual happenings. Pope Gregory the Great, stirred by the need to evangelize the Anglo-Saxon invaders in

> Let us not return evil for evil, the long expected day has come, and the time of our departure is at hand. Strengthen yourselves in the Lord, and He will redeem your souls. Be not afraid of those who can only kill the body, but put your trust in God, Who will speedily give you His eternal reward, and an entrance into His heavenly kingdom.
>
> Boniface, before his martyrdom
> (Moister 1885, 43)

Britain, became the first bishop of Rome to initiate a mission to non-Christians. He sent the monk Augustine (later known as Augustine of Canterbury) and thirty or forty other monks to Britain in 596. Within a relatively short time, they baptized ten thousand Saxons. Almost three centuries later the Byzantine emperor Michael III and Photios, the "Ecumenical Patriarch" of Constantinople, sent the brothers Cyril and Methodius as missionaries to the Slavs in Moravia in central Europe. They are remembered as the apostles to the Slavic peoples. With far less fanfare, a woman named Lioba accepted the invitation of her cousin Boniface to assist him as he evangelized in Germany; she, with five other nuns, left England to face a dangerous life among hostile peoples (Tucker and Liefeld 1987, 136).

Sometimes, captured slaves sowed the gospel seed in distant places where, according to the fourth-century historian Rufinus, "the plow of the apostolic preaching had made no furrow" (Rufinus of Aquileia 1997, 10.9). In the Caucasus region of Georgia the slave woman Nino prayed for the healing of Queen Nana, whose subsequent recovery eventually led to the conversion of her husband, King Mirian, and the nation (Rufinus of Aquileia 1997, 10.11). The Orthodox Church of Georgia later canonized Nino as a saint with the title "Equal to the Apostles." A British youth, Patrick, captured by Irish pirates, spent six years working as a slave, an experience that led to his spiritual transformation. After his return home, Patrick received the call in a dream. Similar to Paul's vision of the Macedonian man, he heard the Irish people shout with one voice, "We ask you, boy, come and walk once more among us." "I was cut to the very heart," remembered Patrick, who then added, "Thank God, after many years the Lord answered their cry" (Duffy 1985, 22).

Businessmen also shared their faith. Frumentius and Aedesius, two young Syrian merchants from Tyre, had been shipwrecked in the Red Sea on their way home from India. Finding refuge in the kingdom of Axum (later known as Ethiopia), they became the tutors of Crown Prince Aeizanes. When Aeizanes ascended the throne, he made Christianity the state religion. His tutors then returned to the Roman Empire.

During a visit to Alexandria, Bishop Athanasius consecrated Frumentius as a bishop and sent him back to Ethiopia (Meyendorff 1989, 117–18).

In other instances people felt called to return to the homelands from which they had been expelled. Although tradition holds that the apostles Thaddeus and Bartholomew first preached the gospel in Armenia, the ministry of Gregory the Illuminator, known as the "Apostle to the Armenians," cannot be underestimated. He returned to Armenia as a Christian, only to be arrested by King Trdat and to spend fifteen miserable years in prison. In the meantime, the small Christian population suffered through a severe persecution. When Trdat's sister saw the face of Gregory in a dream pleading for an end to the persecution, she arranged for his release. His prayers led to the restoration of Trdat's health and sanity. This brought about Trdat's conversion and that of the Armenian nation, the first to declare itself Christian, ca. 301 (Fortescue 1913, 396–400 [nevertheless, this credit may actually belong to the kingdom of Osrhoene]).

The Sword and the Cross

Demonstrations of supernatural power, whether through the exorcism of demons, physical healings, or other miraculous happenings, continued to attract non-Christians (Kydd 1998, 20–33). Augustine, the famous theologian who lived in North Africa, told of miracles such as the healing of a blind man in Milan (Augustine 1972, 22:8; Burgess 1993, 282–84). In Britain an eighth-century monk, the Venerable Bede, recorded miracles that took place during the evangelization of England. Stories of healings, exorcisms, calming of the sea, raising the dead, signs in the heavens, and other unusual occurrences are sprinkled throughout his *History of the English Church and People.* Though many of the stories sound fantastic, others parallel those found in the New Testament (Allen 1994, 34–38). Gregory the Great praised the achievements of Augustine and his monks, saying that they stood "resplendent with such great miracles . . . that they seem to imitate the powers of the apostles in the signs which they display" (Gregory the Great 1969, 7, 12, 30). In Germany Boniface courageously cut down the sacred oak of Thor, a feat that demonstrated the superior power of the Christian God to the peoples of that area.

Yet, it was the power of the sword that often persuaded the obstinate. Conversion "from the top down" appeared to have great benefits and worked in cultures where individuality ranked second to the well-being of the group. Sometimes, political marriages resulted in the conversion of a king, thus requiring the conversion of an entire people group. The marriage of the Christian princess Clotilda to Clovis, king of the Franks, contributed to his conversion (ca. 496), an event that secured the position of Nicene Christianity in Gaul over peoples that had embraced Arian Christianity (Gregory, Bishop of Tours 1969, 38).

Farther to the east, the conversion of Prince Vladimir of Kievan Rus in 988 immediately led to the conversion of the Russian and Ukrainian peoples in his domain. Though some of the circumstances surrounding this event remain obscure, the prior conversion of his grandmother Princess Olga and his marriage to the sister of the Byzantine emperor, as well as other contacts with Constantinople, proved influential (Knowles and Obolensky 1969, 312–14). According to the traditional account in the *Russian Primary Chronicle,* Vladimir had sent emissaries to different faith groups—Khazars (Jews), Bulgars (Muslims), Germans (Roman Catholics), and Greeks (Orthodox)—to determine which faith he should adopt. Arriving in Constantinople, they visited the magnificent cathedral Church of Hagia Sophia ("Holy Wisdom"). "We knew not whether we were in heaven or on earth," they reported. "For on earth there is no such splendour or such beauty and we are at a loss how to describe it. We know only that God dwells there among men, and their service is fairer than the ceremonies of other nations" (Geanakoplos 1984, 190). In their estimation, nothing could compare with the Greek Church and its resplendent worship (liturgy), which seemed to reveal the presence of heaven on earth. Vladimir accepted their account and was baptized in the Dneiper River, which flows past Kiev.

But whether non-Christian Romans during the reign of Theodosius, the Franks under Clovis, the subjects of King Ethelbert in England, the Slavs under Vladimir, or the Georgians and Armenians, all were expected to embrace Christianity or be labeled as enemies of the state. The hostile Saxons in Germany observed that every Christian community became a Frankish military base. When they refused to be subject to the Frankish king Charlemagne (crowned Roman emperor on Christmas Day in 800), he brutally conquered them by force, putting to death 4,500 on a single day. Nevertheless, it took thirty years to finally subdue them. The peace treaty specified the requirement of their conversion (Neill 1986, 68). Such circumstances could place missionaries in danger: Frisian pagans in the Netherlands killed Boniface and his companions as they prepared new converts for confirmation (Water 2001, 526–32).

Forced conversions often resulted in merely verbal pledges to the faith. For a century after Vladimir's conversion the ruling classes practiced the Christian faith, while the larger population only paid it lip service. Whole populations occasionally reverted back to the old religions, as in the cases of the Prussians and Wends who rebelled against their German overlords and the Finns who revolted against their Swedish masters. In all these instances the rebels destroyed churches and monasteries and either killed or drove out the priests to eliminate Christian institutions. Reprisals could be just as cruel. In 1217 Pope Honorius III authorized a crusade against the Prussians;

> (The Holy Roman Church) firmly believes . . . that "no one remaining outside the Catholic Church, not only pagans," but also Jews, heretics or schismatics, can become partakers of eternal life; but that they will go to the "eternal life prepared for the devil and his angels" (Mt. 25.41). . . . And no one can be saved, no matter how much alms he has given, even if he sheds his blood for the name of Christ, unless he remains in the bosom and unity of the Catholic Church.
>
> Decree for the Jacobites (1442), Council of Florence (Neuner and Dupuis 1991, 305)

for their taking up of the sword, crusaders were promised spiritual rewards equal to that of a Holy Land pilgrimage (Saldanha 1988, 45–46). Needless to say, the Christianization of Europe progressed slowly.

Until the eleventh century the Christian church had remained formally united despite the existence of numerous Christian kingdoms in the West and the Byzantine Empire in the eastern Mediterranean basin. However, differences in doctrine, practice, and culture between the Western Latin ("Roman" Catholic) and the Eastern Greek ("Orthodox") churches had been slowly tearing the "seamless robe of Christ" apart for some time (Ware 1963, 51–67). The final break came in 1054 when the pope and the ecumenical patriarch of Constantinople excommunicated each other, a schism partially triggered by rivalry among missionaries. Centuries later, Pope Paul VI and Patriarch Athenagoras of Constantinople rescinded the mutual excommunications in a common declaration issued on December 7, 1965 (for further information, see Stormon 1987, 126–28).

Monks, Nuns, and Friars

The work of monks and nuns proved to be exceptionally important in evangelization, with the foundational leadership of two monks in particular deserving mention: the fourth-century Basil the Great, who profoundly influenced the course of Eastern Orthodox monasticism, and Benedict of Nursia, who wrote the "Rule" for monastic living in 530 that guided the daily lives of Western monks. Towns grew up around monasteries as tribes left the nomadic lifestyle for the agrarian, a transition that added dignity to manual labor. These centers aided in the civilization of vast parts of Europe until the "Dark Ages" of the barbarian invasions came to an end in the tenth century, concluding the earlier part of the "Middle Ages" (ca. 500–1500). Without the labors of these dedicated men and women, Christianity might have remained superficial among the common people.

Much of the evangelization of Ireland, England, Scotland, and continental Europe came about through the itinerant ministry of Celtic monks moving eastward from Ireland to the continent. However, the Roman Christian tradition that Augustine of Canterbury brought to England eventually clashed with the Celtic tradition over a variety of issues. The victory over Celtic church leaders by Roman representatives at the Synod of Whitby in 664 ensured that Roman Christianity would dominate not only Britain and Ireland, but also much of Europe and Scandinavia as the barbarian tribes were evangelized (Edwards 1980, 56–57). Indeed, conversion meant not only giving up the traditional gods, but also adopting Roman culture. Becoming Christian meant, in many contexts, rejecting one's culture for another, thus reversing the achievement of the council of Jerusalem (Acts 15) that opened the door for the gospel to be planted in all cultures. "It is the mission of the church," writes Saldanha, "to break out, with her risen Lord, from the tomb of fixed external [cultural] forms in order to belong to all peoples in all ages" (Saldanha 1988, 31).

Monasteries or abbeys, such as the one founded on the island of Iona off the western coast of Scotland by the Irish monk Columba in 526, became training centers for missionaries. Hilda, the abbess of Whitby in England, trained future bishops. Others established them on the continent, such as the British missionary Willibrord, who worked to convert the wild Frisians. The Benedictine monk Ansgar journeyed to Denmark and Sweden early in the ninth century, evangelizing the populations and attempting to break the Viking slave trade.

In their desire for solitude Russian monks traveled north to the forests beyond Moscow into the Arctic Circle. Much to their surprise, they discovered tribal groups. Like monks in the West whose communities attracted the interest of local peoples, they taught a new way of life (Meyendorff 1960, 103–4).

Over time monastic communities lost their involvement in mission, perhaps victims of their own success as nomadic peoples adopted a settled way of life. New movements of renewal arose that increased the level of spiritual vitality, including the Cistercians and Carmelites. However, the

> *Through [Bertilla, Abbess at Chelles near Paris], the Lord collected such great fruits for the salvation of souls that even from over the seas, the faithful kings of the Saxons . . . asked her to send some of her disciples for the learning and holy instruction they heard were wonderful in her, that they might build convents of men and nuns in their land. . . . That the harvest of souls in that nation might increase through her and be multiplied by God's grace, she sent chosen women and devout men.*
>
> Jo Ann McNamara (McNamara, Halborg, and Whatley 1992, 286)

coming of the "friars" ("brothers")—the "Mendicant orders"—in the thirteenth century brought new interest in traveling and preaching. The followers of Francis of Assisi chose a life of "apostolic poverty," a simple lifestyle reminiscent of Jesus and his disciples. Going from place to place to preach and help people in their needs, the "Fran-

MAP 6.1
IRISH/CELTIC AND BRITISH MISSIONS
TO EUROPE, SIXTH TO EIGHTH CENTURIES

(Copyright Angus Hudson Ltd./Three's Company)

ciscans," along with the Order of Preachers (the "Dominicans," founded by Dominic), depended on the charitable contributions of people they met. The subsequent Franciscan missionary dispersion included friars who went to North Africa, where many suffered martyrdom, and others who journeyed to China (Moorman 1968, 226–32).

Islam, the religion of the seventh-century prophet Muhammad, had swept like a firestorm across Arabia, North Africa, and much of the Middle East before extending into central Asia, India, and finally to Indonesia and the Philippines in the millennium that followed (Brockelmann, Perlmann, and Carmichael 1973, 45–70). When the Arabs ("Saracens") gained control of the Holy Land with its pilgrimage sites, this prompted the crusades that occurred between 1095 and 1291. Western Christians

105

saw regaining control of the holy places in Palestine as a sacred duty. Although the crusaders believed that by fighting the Muslim "infidels" they would store up for themselves treasures in heaven, they proved to be more adept at looting on earth. Destruction came to all who crossed their path: Muslims, Jews, and even Greek Christians on occasion. The Fourth Crusade (1202–4), tyrannically diverted from its original destination by the Venetians, proceeded with the plundering of Constantinople, a tragedy that earned the enduring enmity of Greek Christians (Runciman 1955, 150). "Even the Saracens are merciful and kind," said one writer who described the pillage, "compared with these men who bear the Cross of Christ on their shoulders" (Ware 1963, 69). Though ultimately unsuccessful, the crusades succeeded in creating a legacy of suspicion and bitterness between Muslims and Christians, and among Christians themselves, that exists to the present day.

By the thirteenth century some recognized that countering Islam required dialogue and persuasion. Francis himself tried unsuccessfully to convert the sultan of Egypt. Nevertheless, it was the Franciscan Raymond Lull who proved to be among the most visionary strategists of mission. Born on the island of Majorca in the western Mediterranean in 1235, just nine years after the death of Francis, Lull found his call to mission through a vision of the crucified Savior. He dedicated his life to preaching to non-Christians, especially Muslims. Lull wrote books in Arabic and personally dialogued with Muslim and Jewish scholars. He also encouraged missionaries to master the Arabic language and Arabic philosophy, and he appealed to Christian rulers to establish special schools for the training of missionaries. That church leaders listened

to his advice became evident at the Council of Vienna (1311–12): "The holy Church should have an abundant number of Catho-

> *One will first draw up a list of various sects throughout the world that resist the Catholic faith, and he will apply himself by numerous studies to learn the language of the infidels. Such work will be entrusted only to the noblest and most devoted men, those ready to die for Christ, learned in philosophy and theology, and of well regulated habits. These will then be sent to preach and debate with the infidels. Let their practice of disputation display the requisite grounding together with the necessary arguments and it will be of such stature as to [crush] the positions of the infidels as well as to counter their objections; sufficient also to buttress the appropriate doctrines and retorts of the faithful. These rudiments of argumentation are scattered throughout the passages of Holy Scripture and in many learned authors. It will be necessary that competent men compose treatises based on arguments of this kind and translate them into various [languages], so that the infidels may be able to study them and take cognizance of their errors.*
>
> Raymond Lull (Petry 1962, 369)

lics well versed in all languages, especially those of the infidels [Muslims]," the council decreed. "Once they have learned and are sufficiently proficient in those languages

. . . they will be able by God's grace to bear the fruit which is hoped for and to present the faith adequately" (Neuner and Dupuis 1991, 340–41).

Despite such novel ideas for missionary preparation, the spirit of the times remained confrontational. On several occasions when Lull traveled to North Africa to evangelize, one of his tactics included holding up a copy of the Ten Commandments and then announcing that the prophet Muhammad had broken every one of them. Though he gained several converts, this method failed to win the applause of other Muslims, and a mob stoned him to death in 1315 (Zwemer 1902, 108). But in another part of Africa the monk Takla-Haymanot, known for piety and miracles in his ministry, preached with success among pagan peoples. He reversed the Muslim expansion and helped to ensure the survival of Ethiopia as a Christian kingdom (Budge 1928, 911, 1241–46).

The Heresy of the Three Languages

Another significant strategy came with the preparation of Bible translations. The fact that Christianity had thrived among the educated Latin-speaking Roman classes in North Africa, but not among the native Berber peasants, indicates that the faith may not have been sufficiently translated into the latter's language. This partly explains why Christianity collapsed there in the Islamic conquest that began after Muhammad's death in 632. In central Europe Irish and German missionaries working in Moravia before the arrival of Cyril and Methodius considered only three languages to be suitable for sacred purposes: Hebrew, Greek, and Latin—justified by their use on Pilate's inscription on Jesus' cross (John 19:20). Hence, as Christianity advanced in Europe,

church officials required Latin for worship and Bible reading, a policy that required explanation in the vernacular language. This policy made the effective discipling of new converts more difficult but provided a common means of communication for church leaders and missionaries working across great distances in a variety of cultural contexts. Greek Christians branded this practice as the "heresy of the three languages" (Meyendorff 1960, 102).

More productively for grassroots believers, the Arian missionary bishop Ulfilas translated a large portion of the Bible from Greek into the Gothic language. This feat required him to devise an alphabet for the Goths, tribal peoples that roamed across Europe and later entered Roman territory. Also among the greatest of Christian missionaries, Cyril and Methodius envisioned the creation of an alphabet for translating the Scriptures and liturgical texts from Greek into Slavonic, the mother language of the Slavic peoples. Natives of the bilingual city of Thessalonica, they were fluent in both Greek and the Slavonic dialect of nearby Macedonia. A gifted philologist, Cyril created the first letters in 862 to form the "Glagolithic" alphabet. Along with the later "Cyrillic" alphabet developed by his disciples, it profoundly influenced the language and literature of the Russian, Ukrainian, Serbian, and Bulgarian peoples.

With this invention he translated selected readings from the Gospels used in Orthodox church services in addition to Psalms, portions of Acts, and the Pauline and General Epistles, as well as the Byzantine liturgy into "Old Church Slavonic" (Veronis 1994, 45). Historian Dimitri Obolensky notes that the development of Old Church Slavonic represented a new literary language "based on the spoken dialect of the Macedonian Slavs,

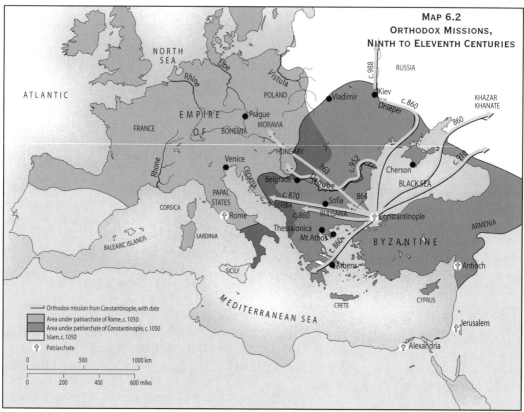

modeled on Greek, largely ecclesiastical in character, and—in view of the close similarity between the different Slavonic languages in this period—intelligible to all the Slav peoples" (Knowles and Obolensky 1969, 21–22). That the Slavic peoples of eastern Europe, Ukraine, and Russia owed much of their religion and culture to Byzantium never could be doubted.

To a certain extent the problems encountered by Cyril and Methodius occurred because of the value they placed on the vernacular language. Though their mission in Moravia ultimately failed, their methods and linguistic achievements found success elsewhere and encouraged other missionar-

ies. In northwest Siberia the Orthodox monk Stephen of Perm, inspired by the lives of the two brothers, studied Greek and began mission work among the Zyrian tribes. By the time of his death, in 1396, he had formulated an alphabet and translated the Scriptures and the liturgy into their language (Komi) without using either Greek or Cyrillic letters. He also established parishes and monasteries, taught children how to read their own language, and ordained his best students to the priesthood in order to build a native church. Nonetheless, Russian Orthodox churchmen, desiring the "Russification" of the Zyrian tribes, ironically criticized his translation work because they felt that only four languages should be used in the church: Hebrew, Greek, Latin, and Slavonic (Veronis 1994, 59)!

Applying the Faith

Missionaries applied the faith in many ways. The use of pictures made with bright colors, called "icons," painted on the walls of churches and also on pieces of wood, represented a distinctive element in the Orthodox tradition that effectively tied converts and their children into the church (beautiful churches and Christian art often attracted non-Christians). For millions of illiterate believers in Greece, eastern Europe, Russia, and Georgia, pictures of biblical events and personalities, as well as the saints, visually taught them the great stories of the Christian faith (Zernov 1968, 107).

At Sunday worship Christian education for the faithful consisted of learning through all five senses: they saw the story of redemption in the icons; they heard (and memorized) Scripture readings and doctrinal teachings in the liturgy; they kissed (touched) certain icons to honor the persons portrayed and the spiritual insights they championed; they tasted the faith by consuming the bread and wine of the Lord's Supper; and they smelled the burning incense that symbolized the prayers of the saints (Rev. 8:3–4)—the "sweet odor of the Kingdom" (Quenot 1991, 47). Hence, the Christian faith came to permeate the life and cultures of the Greek, Slavic, Romanian, and Georgian peoples and partially accounts for the long-term survival of Eastern Orthodox Christianity under Islam and later communism (Ugolnik 1989, 42–68).

Contextualization in western Europe also faced challenges: What should a missionary do with the temple of a heathen god

after the people had accepted the Christian faith? What about their religious customs and annual celebrations? In earlier times, missionaries such as Martin of Tours had destroyed such temples in Gaul and replaced them by building churches and monasteries (DuBose 1979, 122). Nevertheless, Gregory the Great advised Augustine of Canterbury to convert the temples into churches and to substitute events on the Christian calendar in the place of their festivals. "If temples are well built," he wrote from a practical bent, "it is a good idea to detach them from the service of the devil, and to adapt them for the worship of the true God" (Thomas 1995, 22).

With other issues the Scriptures provided a clear-cut answer, as when Boniface asked Pope Gregory II if believers could eat meat previously offered in sacrifice to idols if they first made the sign of the cross over it (Talbot 1954, 82). Gregory simply told him to follow the instructions given by Paul in 1 Cor. 10:28: "But if anyone says to you, 'This has been offered in sacrifice,' then do not eat it, both for the sake of the man who told you and for conscience' sake." Nevertheless, the limits to contextualizing Christianity without jeopardizing the integrity of the faith would vex church leaders for centuries to come.

MISSION BEYOND CHRISTENDOM (A.D. 33–1500)

That Christianity grew outside of Christendom in Mesopotamia, Persia, India, Sri Lanka, and all the way to Afghanistan, Tajikistan, Tibet, and China comes as a surprise to many who are accustomed to thinking of it only as a Western religion. Yet tradition says that the apostle Thomas journeyed eastward, arriving on the Malabar

Coast of south India in A.D. 50 (Kuriakose 1982, 2–3). The sixth-century Alexandrian merchant Cosmas the Indian Navigator discovered that "even in [Sri Lanka], an island in Further India, where the Indian sea is, there is a church of Christians, with clergy and a body of believers" (Kuriakose 1982, 8). And upon his return to Italy in 1295, Marco Polo, who had traveled to the court of the Mongol ruler Kublai Khan, described breathtaking adventures and unexpected encounters with Christians in far-off China to his wide-eyed hearers (Komroff 1930, 102, 119–20).

Looking back again to the day of Pentecost, "Jews from every nation under heaven" heard the praises of God in their languages. Luke records that the crowd included "Parthians, Medes and Elamites" and "residents of Mesopotamia" (Acts 2:5–12)—all from territories east of Roman Syria. Those who accepted Christ as Messiah returned to their homes as witnesses. Believers also traveled to Phoenicia, Cyprus, and Antioch to share the gospel with local Jewish communities. Others from Cyprus and Cyrene "went to Antioch and began to speak to Greeks also, telling them the good news about the Lord Jesus" (Acts 11:19–21). At Antioch, the major city of the region, believers were first called "Christians" to distinguish them from Jews.

As time passed, Antioch became an important center for Christianity that would impact the eastward advance. By the fourth century it ranked among the famous "pentarchy" of churches (Rome, Constantinople, Alexandria, Antioch, and Jerusalem), whose archbishops later received the title "patriarch" ("chief father," highest-ranking bishop) because of the historical origins of the churches and their influence (Prokurat, Golitzin, and Peterson 1996, 257–59). With the division of the empire at the end of the fourth century, the latter four "patriarchates" remained within the sphere of Byzantine power, including Antioch and the Syrians living west of the Euphrates River—the "West Syrians." The "East Syrians" on the other side lived under the rule of the Persian Empire, an avowed enemy of the Byzantines. Historian Samuel Moffett notes that the fourth-century Persian persecution of Christians "surpassed in number of martyrs and in intensity of religious hatred anything suffered in the West under three hundred years of pagan Roman emperors" (Moffett 1992, 504).

Syrian Christianity Divides

Serious doctrinal disputes arose from the fourth to the seventh centuries. As with many other Christians, Syriac-speaking Christians loyally held to the teachings of the Nicene Creed, produced by the Councils of Nicea (325) and Constantinople (381), which declared the true divinity of Christ—that he was begotten and not created by God the Father and was of the "same substance" with the Father. Eventually disagreements about the human and divine natures of Christ rocked the churches, requiring the convening of the Councils of Ephesus (431) and Chalcedon (451). Since the council fathers did their work in Greek—a language particularly suited for making extremely refined and complex arguments within the Greek philosophical context—it sometimes proved difficult to explain them accurately in other languages. Certain terms could not be translated easily into Syriac words because the latter might not carry the same technical meaning. According to historians Dale Irvin and Scott Sunquist, "While the process of translation could add depth to the meaning of various biblical terms or extend insights from the Bible into new theological directions, it could also set communities at odds with one another as they no longer found common words to carry similar cultural meanings" (Irvin and Sunquist 2001, 201). For their part, Syrian believers had biblical and theological insights neither fully appreciated nor known by Greek and Latin Christians (Burgess 1989, 85–109).

Unhappiness with the doctrinal pronouncements of Ephesus and Chalcedon led many Syrians to embrace teachings known as Monophysitism (the incarnate Christ had a single [divine] nature) and Nestorianism (two persons [human and divine] in the incarnate Christ), the latter being attributed to Nestorius, sometime patriarch of Constantinople. Many West Syrians adopted Monophysitism, while the East Syrians formed the Nestorian Church of the East. To complicate the picture, the Byzantines fiercely persecuted both Monophysites and Nestorians because of their differences with the decrees of Chalcedon (church and state—doctrine and politics—often danced together in the Byzantine empire). At the same time, Persian rulers (devout Zoroastrians) persecuted the East Syrians because their Christian beliefs made them appear loyal to Byzantium.

According to tradition, Christianity among the East Syrians in upper Mesopotamia had begun when the apostle Thomas sent his disciple Addai (Thaddaeus) to the city of Edessa, making him the first known Christian missionary to cross the Roman imperial boundary into the kingdom of Osrhoene. This significantly linked Christianity there directly to Jerusalem and to Jesus, not to Antioch. Edessa, located on the Silk Road—a four-thousand-mile trade route from the Mediterranean to China—became famous

for its theological school, teachers such as Ephrem the Syrian (who wrote his theology in poetry like the ancient Hebrew prophets), bishops, and missionary monks. Other key Nestorian centers included Nisibis and the Persian royal capital of Seleucia-Ctesiphon (south of Baghdad). "Nestorian" became synonymous with "Christian" in the East, seldom "[carrying] a doctrinal reference to the teachings of Nestorius" (England 1996, 4; see also Moffett 1992, 507).

Mission to Asia

Monophysite Christians outside of Syria lived in Armenia, Egypt, Ethiopia, and India. However, the greater missionary thrust into Asia came through the efforts of laypersons and clergy of the Church of the East. Unlike many Western and Greek missionaries, the Nestorians could not rely on the protection of the sword, but simply on persuasion and the power of the gospel. By the year 1300 they had crossed central Asia to the Pacific Rim and also ventured into southern and Southeast Asia. For the most part they kept Syriac for worship, but they translated the Scriptures and other religious materials into the local languages. These "missionaries" ranged from monks trained in Mesopotamia and Persia, to physicians, to merchants who traded in perfumes, textiles, and precious metals and stones. Their work often required traveling long distances, sometimes yearlong treks by camel, donkey, or on foot along the Silk Road as it snaked through mountain ranges and across deserts. Monks journeyed wearing sandals, walking with a staff in their hands, and carrying a basket on their backs containing copies of the Scriptures and other Christian literature. Others traveled by sea with Persian, Arabian, and Indian traders in small ships that hugged

111

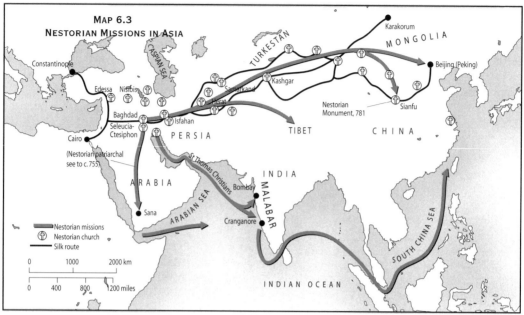

MAP 6.3
NESTORIAN MISSIONS IN ASIA

Karakorum
MONGOLIA
Beijing (Peking)
TURKESTAN
Constantinople
CASPIAN SEA
Kashgar
Edessa Nisibis
Samarkand
Herat
Nestorian
Monument, 781
Sianfu
Baghdad
Seleucia-
Ctesiphon
Isfahan
Cairo
PERSIA
TIBET
CHINA
(Nestorian patriarchal
see to c. 755)
St Thomas Christians
ARABIA
Bombay
INDIA
MALABAR
Sana
ARABIAN SEA
Cranganore
SOUTH CHINA SEA

Nestorian missions
Nestorian church
Silk route

0   1000   2000 km
0   400   800   1200 miles

INDIAN OCEAN

(Copyright Angus Hudson Ltd./Three's Company)

the coastline all the way past India to the Strait of Malacca.

Moving to Turkestan in central Asia, laymen John of Resh-aina and Thomas the Tanner testified to their faith along with the assistance of priests and bishops. In addition to preaching, baptizing many Turks into the faith, and engaging in works of compassion, they shared agricultural skills (England 1996, 43). Other believers included a Persian Christian in the employ of the emperor of China serving as the governor of Tibetan tribes in the mid-seventh century. As Mongol tribes migrated across Asia in their yurts (tents on wheels and pulled by teams of oxen), Nestorians built their own yurts with chapels to accompany them (Cameron 1970, 34–35). Women also contributed to the vitality and expansion of the faith, among them Alaghai Beki, a daughter of the Mongol conqueror Genghis Khan, and Sorghaqtani

Beki, the Christian mother of the emperor Kublai Khan.

Bishop Alopen, whose story unfolds in the famous Nestorian Stone (see the introduction to this chapter), arrived in 635 at Chang'an (now Xi'an), then the largest city in the world, at a time when various religions received toleration. After the emperor T'ai-tsung discovered that his religion came from a book, he welcomed him, took him into his library, and asked him to begin translating the Scriptures, presumably with the aid of Chinese scholars. According to the stone monument, the emperor "investigated 'the Way' in his own forbidden apartments, and being deeply convinced of its correctness and truth, he gave special orders for its propagation" (Moffett 1992, 291). Even so, this signaled his interest in learning, not in conversion. Interestingly, information on the stone reveals that the Nestorians did not hesitate to use Confucian, Taoist, and

Buddhist terminology to clarify their faith. Another document portrayed salvation as "'the Great Sanctifying Transformation' which the Holy Wind of God brings to all, through the life, death and resurrection of Jesus" (England 1996, 134).

Roman Catholic missionaries also traveled to Asia, with the Italian John of Montecorvino reaching Beijing in 1294. There he built a church—the first Catholic church in China—complete with a belfry (adopting indigenous architecture for church construction generally did not occur until the twentieth century)! With the help of other Franciscans, he built churches, baptized thousands of converts, extended their mission into the Fujian province in the south, and translated the New Testament and Psalms into the Mongolian language. Bishop John conducted the Catholic Mass in the Mongol language, although in accordance with the Latin liturgy (England 1996, 141; Barry 1985, 592). He also converted the Nestorian prince George of Tenduc (now Inner Mongolia). Needless to say, the Franciscans and the Nestorians clashed, a development that weakened their Christian witness.

Unfortunately, Christianity in China and much of Asia had collapsed by the fifteenth century due to its isolation, unstable political conditions, and the fall of the Mongol dynasty in 1368. Especially devastating were the brutal conquests of the fiercely Muslim conqueror Tamerlane that destroyed churches, synagogues, and temples on an unprecedented scale from the western edge of China to Asia Minor and southward to Delhi, India (Moffett 1992, 480–88). Reports from the Franciscans cease after 1360. Although historians still ponder the reasons for the decline of Christianity in Asia, they agree that among the chief reasons were the Muslim conquests that began in the seventh century. The subsequent persecutions and forced conversions paralyzed the life of the churches. Tamerlane's attacks on the Nestorians in Persia and Mesopotamia—the "home base" for the mission endeavors of the Church of the East—spelled disaster for the great missionary enterprise that stretched across the Asian landmass.

Though the Muslim advance westward had been halted by the army of Charles Martel at the battle of Tours in France in 732, Islam came to dominate the Middle East, North Africa, and much of central Asia. In 1453 the Turks breached the walls of Constantinople, the last great fortress of Christendom facing Asia. The Byzantine emperor died with his troops defending the city. In the Church of Hagia Sophia the liturgy abruptly stopped. Now a museum, its quiet atmosphere symbolizes the silence that today shrouds once great churches that commissioned missionaries such as Paul and Barnabas, Cyril and Methodius, and Alopen to preach the good news in the "regions beyond."

7

Expansion in the Era of Discovery and Colonialism, A.D. 1500–1900

INTRODUCTION

'Twas an ill wind that blew Columbus's ships off course on their way home from the West Indies, forcing them to dock for repairs at Lisbon, the capital of Portugal. Seizing the opportunity, King John II announced that by treaty right all the territorial claims made by Columbus now belonged to Portugal instead of Spain. Both countries hoped to find new routes to the East Indies to gain access to the lucrative spice trade. If they could circumvent the Muslim nations that controlled it, they might also locate long-isolated Christian communities with whom they could fight against the "infidels." Since European nations viewed the papacy as an international arbiter, King Ferdinand and Queen Isabella of Spain immediately sent ambassadors to Rome to gain a ruling from Pope Alexander VI, a Renaissance pope better known for other pursuits than piety.

At Columbus's suggestion, the ambassadors lobbied for a line of demarcation running longitudinally "one hundred leagues towards the west and south" from the Azores and Cape Verde Islands (Barry 1985, 596).

Everything west of the line would go to Spain, while Portugal would receive all to the east of it. Without any of the parties involved understanding the geographical magnitude of the decision, Alexander decided in favor of Spain on May 4, 1493. A year later the two countries signed the Treaty of Tordesillas and extended the line to 370 leagues west of the Cape Verde Islands, a move that soon would enable the Portuguese to colonize Brazil. Missionaries from Spain then traveled to the western hemisphere and eventually to the Philippines by way of the Pacific Ocean, while the Portuguese evangelized along the coasts of Brazil, Africa, and Asia. For the first time, Christian mission encircled the globe, facing challenges both old and new.

Given the vigorous new mission thrust of the Catholic Church in the sixteenth century, it might have been remembered as a new era in Catholic mission. Instead, the mischief of the "wild boar" trampling the vineyard of the Lord (Pope Leo X's description of Martin Luther) guaranteed that historians would call it the period of the Reformation (Barry 1985, 635). The ensuing division of Western Christianity between Catholics and Protestants, their respective mission endeavors, and the widening influence of European culture transformed the world scene in the centuries that followed. This chapter explores Christian mission in the age of discovery and colonial expansion during the early modern era (1500–1800) and most of the "Great Century" in mission (1800–1914).

THE GLORY OF ALL CHRISTENDOM

Ferdinand and Isabella and their neighbor King John genuinely desired the evangelization of the peoples that came under their dominion. Indeed, Columbus's log book for December 12, 1492, has this entry, written after setting foot on the coast of northern Haiti: "So I went on shore and at the entrance to the harbour, on a clearly visible eminence situated to the west, I erected a large cross, to show that this land belonged to your [Spanish] Majesties, under the banner of Jesus Christ our Lord, and to the glory of all Christendom" (Meier 1992, 55). The cross symbolized the political and religious unity of Spain. Having recently defeated the Moors, its "holy war" against these Muslims produced a crusading mentality that also brought an end to religious tolerance in the country. Portugal earlier had expelled the Moors and shared the same driving temperament. The Spanish and Portuguese then looked at their conquests from Mexico to India in crusading terms. Crusading terminology has peppered missionary sermons and publications to the present day.

Yet nothing prepared them for what they discovered: millions of people who seemed to lack any knowledge of the faith. Europeans had viewed the world as largely coextensive with Europe—Christendom. Outside peoples such as the Muslims knew enough about Christian truth to be guilty for having rejected it; hence, they were doomed for hell. Catholic theologians now began to wonder about people who had had no opportunity to hear the gospel (Sullivan 1992, 63–69). Some colonists used this as evidence of the subhuman nature of indigenous American peoples in order to justify their subjection. Nevertheless, the Catholic rulers of Spain and Portugal pressed for their evangelization, though their motives when mixed together percolated a wicked brew of "gold, glory, and the gospel."

Royal Patronage

In view of the discoveries, the papacy conferred on each king the "Right of Royal Patronage" (Barry 1985, 598–99). This gave the monarchs and their successors control of the church in their colonies by conferring on them the right to create new dioceses and nominate persons for all church offices. In turn, they promised to finance the construction of churches and pay the salaries of the clergy.

Unfortunately, the Spanish conquests brought cruel forms of exploitation and the introduction of European diseases, particularly smallpox, leading to the decimation of the native populations. In central Mexico the population dropped from about 25 million to 16.8 million within ten years of the arrival of the Spanish (Crosby 1972, 53). The *encomienda* system allowed those Spaniards who had received land grants from the Spanish crown to demand tribute from the Native Americans living thereon. However, the abuse of the arrangement led to their virtual enslavement.

The insatiable demand for gold set no limits on attempts to meet it. When the Spaniards entered Cuba in 1511, they encountered chief Hatuey, who had fled with his people from Hispaniola to avoid them. Describing them to his people, he held up a basket of gold and jewels and said, "Behold, here is the God of the Christians." Finally captured, he was tied to a stake to be burned to death. When a Franciscan friar told him that if he became a Christian he would go to heaven—a place of glory and eternal rest—and thus avoid hell, Hatuey inquired as to the destination of the Christians. Hearing that they too would be in heaven, "the [chief] at once said, without any more thought, that he did not wish to go there, but rather to hell so as not to be where Spaniards were, nor to see such cruel people" (Sanderlin 1992, 147).

By the sixteenth century Catholic missionaries came exclusively from the religious orders. The first to the western hemisphere included the Augustinians, Dominicans, Franciscans, and later the Society of Jesus (the "Jesuits"). Although mass baptisms occurred, the Dominicans sought to improve religious instruction. They endeavored to understand the local languages and religious beliefs, teach through the use of stories, preach frequently from the Scriptures, and witness by their own disinterest in material gain. As historian Mario Rodríguez León observed, "Not everything in the conquest and evangelization of the New World should be seen as negative. . . . Alongside cruel and unjust conquistadors came good Christians too, men and women of upright conscience who made [it] their second homeland" (Rodríguez León 1992, 53).

One of these upright persons became the Spanish voice of conscience: the Dominican Bartolomé de Las Casas, the "Apostle of the Indies," who worked tirelessly to alleviate the sufferings of the indigenous populations (Sanderlin 1992, 1–17). His *Brief Account of the Destruction of the Indies* (1552) and influence at the Spanish court eventually brought about new laws to curb abuses. Unfortunately, his concern for the local peoples initially led him to support the importation of black slaves to replace them as workers in certain areas of labor.

Help also came from Rome. To condemn the notion of the indigenes as "dumb brutes created for our service, pretending that they are incapable of receiving the catholic faith," Pope Paul III declared in 1537 that the "Indians are truly men," capable of conversion and instruction (Barry 1985, 599). Such notable strides in promoting human rights, however, made little difference in the lives of African slaves, since both colonialists and clergy purchased them to work on their sugar and tobacco plantations. The religious orders, including the Jesuits who worked strenuously to combat the slavery of the locals, generally exhibited little interest in evangelizing them (Lippy, Choquette, and Poole 1992, 70). Exceptions included the Jesuit Peter Claver, who worked in the coastal port of Cartagena, Colombia, feeding and providing health care for newly arriving Africans.

The Royal Patronages of Spain and Portugal brought the larger part of the western hemisphere under the umbrella of Christendom. Populations scattered across vast areas separated by steep mountain ranges and rain forests, combined with the continuing shortage of missionaries and the general refusal to ordain a native clergy, ensured that Christianity would be only a surface-level phenomenon in many places. The traditional religions still thrived in remote places and in modified forms under a Christian veneer, a state of affairs illustrated by the significantly different meanings attached by Spaniards and Mexican indigenes to the reported apparition of the Virgin Mary at Guadalupe in 1531 (Lippy, Choquette, and Poole 1992, 46).

East of the line of demarcation, the Portuguese admiral Vasco da Gama reached the western coast of India in May 1498 after a long passage around Africa that outflanked the Muslim traders. The colony of Goa became the command center for the Portuguese Empire in the East. Home to magnificent churches, the city of Goa became known as the "Rome of the East" (Mundadan 1989, 436), with its archbishop assigned a diocese that stretched from Mozambique on the southeast coast of Africa to India, China, and Japan.

Since Portugal preferred trade to empire building, the extent of its territories in Asia remained small, with the most important settlements being Goa, the Malaysian port of Malacca, the Chinese port of Macau, and the island of Timor. Not surprisingly, conflict in gaining access to markets and repulsing the attacks of unfriendly local rulers often required the use of force. "The two swords of the civil and the ecclesiastical power were always . . . close together in the conquest of the East," wrote a Portuguese Franciscan in 1638. "For the weapons only conquered through the right that the preaching of the Gospel gave them, and the preaching was only of some use when it was accompanied and protected by the weapons" (Boxer 1978, 75). These colonies, along with the Philippines, represented the small-scale planting of Christendom in Asia.

The Hindus and Muslims living in Goa either left, accepted second-class citizenship, or converted to the faith. The methods of Christianizing the colony included preaching, works of charity, and the encouragement of interracial marriages, as Portuguese women seldom received permission to sail

to India. The first provincial (church) council of Goa in 1567 forbade coercive measures of conversion and declared, "No one comes to Christ by faith, unless he is drawn by the heavenly Father with voluntary love and prevenient grace" (Thekkedath 1988, 349). Nevertheless, to prod people in the right direction, Portuguese officials blended social and economic pressures with deprivation of rights, destruction of temples, and the outlawing of publicly celebrated Hindu festivals. As a result, the colony became predominantly Catholic.

Conversion meant the adoption of Portuguese culture and a Portuguese name, thus compelling believers to embrace European customs. This was repulsive to high-caste Brahmins because the Portuguese did not frequently bathe, ate meat, drank liquor, and associated with people of the despised lower castes. Because converts faced the total rejection of their families, Goa celebrated baptisms, especially those of high-caste people, with great pomp and ceremony to put conversion in an appealing light. Candidates wore special clothes and marched in procession to the church through decorated streets accompanied by the governor, prominent citizens, and church officers (Thekkedath 1988, 317–18).

Beyond the Royal Patronage in Asia

"I began to go through all the villages of the coast, calling around me by the sound of a bell as many as I could, children and men," wrote Francis Xavier, the most famous missionary of the sixteenth century. "I assembled them twice a day and taught them the Christian doctrine" (Kuriakose 1982, 27). A founding member of the Society of Jesus (1540) led by Ignatius Loyola, Xavier and his associates were the marines

117

of the Counter-Reformation, the response of the Catholic Church to the Protestant Reformation (Schurhammer 1973, 475–509; Evennett 1970, 43–45).

Arriving in Goa in 1542, he worked to improve the spiritual and moral climate of the city before evangelizing down the coast. His methods included "singing the lessons which he had rhymed and then [making] the children sing them so that they might become . . . better fixed in their memories. Afterward he explained each point in the simplest way, using only such words as his young audience could readily understand" (Rayanna 1989, 67). In one region, he baptized ten thousand people within a month.

Sailing on a Portuguese merchant ship, Xavier and his party arrived in Japan in 1549. Recognizing that the "apostolic poverty" that he practiced in India would discredit him before the Japanese, he changed tactics. To meet the governor of Yamaguchi, he wore the finest clothes available and took expensive gifts, including a large clock and a three-barreled musket. Impressed with the visitors and their gifts, the governor gave them permission to preach in his territory (Ross 1994, 26–27). Xavier recognized that Christianity had to be presented in the Japanese language and that becoming a believer should not require a change of culture. Although he left Japan in 1551 and died a year later after unsuccessfully trying to enter China, he set in motion a strategy for the contextualization of the gospel that would bear fruit as well as controversy.

Not as well known as Xavier, the Italian Allesandro Valignano guided the mission enterprise in the latter half of the century as the Jesuit "Visitor to the East." Since his missionaries worked in countries where the Royal Patronage had little authority, they enjoyed more freedom. With Xavier as his model, he encouraged missionaries to learn the language, practice Japanese etiquette, and eat local foods (Schütte 1980, 240–46). He also supported the training of native church leaders. The implementation of his mission principles led to dramatic success in Japan, with Nagasaki virtually becoming a Christian city. When great persecution began in 1614, there were approximately three hundred thousand Christians in Japan (Ross 1994, 87). Fears of a Spanish invasion from the Philippines caused the drastic turn of events. The brutal persecutions that followed, thousands of martyrdoms, and the survival of an underground church testify to their deep faith (Jennes 1973, 216–24).

Valignano encouraged Matteo Ricci, who entered China in 1583, to learn the Chinese language, translate and study Confucian philosophy texts, and wear the garb of a Chinese scholar. The high level of education of Ricci and his Jesuit colleagues impressed the Chinese, particularly their skills in geometry, astronomy, and increasing knowledge of Chinese culture (MacDonnell 1989, 62–67). According to historian Jean-Paul Wiest, "The Jesuits saw in Confucian culture an expression of the human spirit worthy of respect, and they searched for ways to adapt Christianity within that context" (Wiest 1993, 183). Just as the late medieval theologian Thomas Aquinas had used Aristotelian thought to express his theology, so also these Jesuits could use Confucian ideas to assist in making the Christian faith acceptable to the educated classes (Ross 1994, 126–28). With close contact to imperial officials in Beijing and the educated elite, they hoped to convert "from the top down," and in this they partially succeeded (Peterson 1988, 129–52).

Other religious orders strongly criticized this approach as syncretistic and used different methods. Following the example of Francis of Assisi, the Franciscans ministered to the poor, a strategy that alienated them from the upper classes. When some Dominicans preached, they held up the crucifix and announced that Confucius and his disciples were in hell (Saldanha 1988, 68). Regardless of the methods employed, some two hundred thousand to more than

> *In China intellectual activity is highly prized. . . . Since this is so, I think it will be easy to persuade the elite of the kingdom of the truths of our holy faith which are confirmed with so much reasonable evidence. For if the intelligentsia agrees with us, it will be far easier to convert the masses.*
>
> Matteo Ricci (Barry 1985, 803)

half a million Christians could be found in the country by 1700. Rome also had given permission for Chinese priests to celebrate the mass in Chinese.

A French Jesuit, Alexandre de Rhodes, successfully adapted the faith into Vietnamese culture. As the language had been written with Chinese characters, he invented a system employing the Roman alphabet still used today. A brilliant linguist who could converse in twelve languages, he wrote the first books in the new alphabet: a catechism, a grammar, and a French-Vietnamese dictionary. Sharing the perspective of his contemporaries, explains biographer Peter Phan, "de Rhodes's theology of revelation and religions [did] not allow him to acknowledge the presence of God and God's

self-communication anywhere other than in Christianity." Indeed, "he [made] conversion to Christ the King the goal and cornerstone of his mission and catechesis" (Phan 1998, 198). With his colleagues, he trained a native clergy and brought one hundred thousand Vietnamese into the church by 1640.

After Ricci's death, in 1610, controversy exploded between the Jesuits and the other religious orders working in China over the extent to which the gospel could be contextualized. Were Confucianism and Christianity really compatible? Could Chinese Christians perform traditional rites that honored their ancestors (to the Chinese, Koreans, and other Asians, rejection of ancestor veneration seemed to undermine the foundation of morality and society)? Although the Jesuits described the rites as civil acts, Rome finally condemned them as religious practices, and the "Valignano-Ricci tradition" failed (Ross 1994, 190–99). The Chinese "Rites Controversy" created one of the most bitter and prolonged debates in mission history. It dragged on until 1939, when Rome reversed the policy.

New Developments in Catholic Mission

By the seventeenth century Spain and Portugal had fallen into economic and military decline. Three powerful maritime nations now began to challenge their trading monopolies and rule the seas: the Protestant states of England and the Netherlands, and Catholic France. Though no longer capable of fulfilling the financial promises of the Patronage agreements, the kings of Spain and Portugal refused to renegotiate the terms with Rome. Recognizing the need for change in the supervision of the missions and to expedite activities beyond the Patronage lands, Pope Gregory XV established the Sacred Congregation for the Propagation of the Faith ("Propaganda Fide") in 1622 (Schmidlin 1933, 257–58).

As France became a naval power, its missionaries went to North America, India, China, and Indochina. Those who sailed to Canada included Marie Guyart, the first woman missionary to the New World. Bet-

> *Do not in any way attempt, and do not on any pretext persuade these people to change their rites, habits and customs, unless they are openly opposed to religion and good morals. For what could be more absurd than to bring France, Spain, Italy or any other European country over to China? It is not your country but the faith you must bring, that faith which does not reject or belittle the rites or customs of any nation as long as these rites are not evil, but rather desires that they be preserved in their integrity and fostered.*
>
> Instructions for missionaries from the Sacred Congregation for the Propagation of the Faith (1659) (Neuner and Dupuis 1991, 343)

ter known as "Marie of the Incarnation," she heard the call to mission in a dream. With several other Ursuline sisters, she sailed to Quebec and opened a boarding school for French and indigenous girls in 1639 that demonstrated to a critical audience how effective Catholic women could be in mission (Lippy, Choquette, and Poole 1992, 167–69). It survived despite scarcity of money, sickness, and the hostility of the Native Ameri-

cans. Other notable French missionaries served in North America, including Isaac Jogues, who died at the hands of Mohawk tribesmen, and Jacques Marquette, who explored the Mississippi River Valley (Barry 1985, 806–13).

In South America, in eastern Paraguay, Jesuit missionaries created more than thirty missions or "reductions," experimental communities for the welfare and protection of the Guarani people (Goodpasture 1989, 90–93). Although other orders founded such missions elsewhere in Latin America, the Jesuits in particular incurred the wrath of the Spanish and Portuguese governments. Finally, the latter succeeded in persuading Rome to dissolve the Jesuit order in 1773, a decision that created one of the worst disasters in Catholic mission history.

REFORMERS AND MISSION

How could anyone doubt that the Great Commission already had been completed when three decades after the day of Pentecost, Paul informed the Colossians, "All over the world this gospel is bearing fruit and growing, just as it has been doing among you since the day you heard it and understood God's grace in all its truth" (Col. 1:6)? Such Scripture passages seemed to indicate that the early church had accomplished the initial apostolic task. Protestants, therefore, addressed other issues and did not preach the gospel beyond the fence lines of Christendom. Nontheological factors also hampered their involvement: the struggle to survive Roman Catholic opposition, the landlocked status of some Protestant states, and the lack of missionary orders to provide personnel.

The Protestant Reformers Martin Luther, Huldrych Zwingli, and John Calvin said little about foreign mission. Believing that the world had been evangelized centuries before, they focused their energies on reforming Christian life within the Western church. Nevertheless, as missiologist James Scherer contends, "Luther's obedience to mission meant reestablishing the church on its one true foundation in Jesus Christ and the gospel" (Scherer 1987, 55). Genuine church reform required a return to a more biblically based faith than that of the late medieval church. The Reformation principle of "Scripture alone" as the final authority for doctrine and practice inspired later Protestant missionaries to engage in Bible translation, a mission strategy pioneered by earlier missionaries, especially Orthodox ones.

Outside Lutheran and Reformed circles, Anabaptists exhibited considerable enthusiasm for evangelism. Infant baptism, the standard practice in every Christian country, had no spiritual validity in their estimation, whereas genuine baptism—"believer's baptism"—demanded a conscious decision to follow Christ (Estep 1975, 150–54, 171–75). Therefore, most "Christians" were "nominal" in their faith and devoid of salvation. Missiologist Hans Kasdorf says that Anabaptists desired "to restore the primitive-apostolic model of the believer's church with its implicit theology of discipleship under Christ's lordship and explicit evangelistic witness in the power of the Holy Spirit" (Kasdorf 1984, 51). But despite the first Anabaptist missionary conference in 1527 and the sending out of "apostles" to many parts of Europe, fierce persecution hampered their efforts, and in the end they too failed to move outside the walls of Christendom.

Pioneer Protestant Missionaries

Few mission societies existed before the late eighteenth century. With no infrastructure, the commissioning of missionaries initially coincided with trade in faraway lands, with chartered trading companies providing chaplains for their personnel. In certain places the merchants forbade any Christian witness to the native peoples. Thus, the Dutch East Indies Company issued its Japan Edict of 1648, warning its sailors and traders not to display any Christian sign or symbol while visiting the country. Ironically, the first Protestant (Reformed) mission seminary had been founded in the Netherlands twenty-six years earlier with the company's support (Jongeneel 1995, 224).

Lutheran participation in mission emerged with Justinian von Welz, an Austrian nobleman who devoted his life to evangelism, much to the annoyance of orthodox Lutherans in Germany. Unable to secure approval for a mission society, he went as a freelance missionary to Dutch Guiana (now Suriname), where he died. His dedication inspired others to follow the call to mission. "Is it right," he asked Protestants in a treatise written in 1664, "that we evangelical Christians spend so much money on . . . [expensive clothes], luxuries of food and drink, many unnecessary amusements and expensive habits, but until now have given no thought to . . . spreading the gospel?" (Scherer 1969, 59).

After several months observing conditions in the colony of Maryland, the Anglican Thomas Bray organized the Society for Promoting Christian Knowledge (SPCK) in 1699 to distribute Christian literature in North America. Two years later, he founded the Society for the Propagation of the Gos-

121

pel in Foreign Parts (SPG) to send missionaries to English settlers and natives. Local missions usually depended on the interest of individuals. In the colony of Massachusetts, whose charter stipulated the evangelization of the natives, the Puritan John Eliot, who pastored in Roxbury, preached twice a week to the Narragansetts and other nearby tribes. In his long ministry

> I never saw the work of God appear so independent of means as at this time. I discoursed to the [Native Americans], and spoke what, I suppose, had a proper tendency to promote convictions. But God's manner of working upon them appeared so entirely supernatural and above [human] means that I could scarce believe He used me as an instrument, or what I spake as means of carrying His work. . . . I seemed to do nothing, and indeed to have nothing to do, but to "stand still and see the salvation of God." I found myself obliged and delighted to say, "Not unto us," not unto instruments and means, "but to thy name be glory."
>
> David Brainerd (DuBose 1979, 183)

he organized converts into fourteen villages known as "Praying Towns," fought to protect them against white settlers and traders, established schools, trained evangelists, and translated the Bible.

Decades later young David Brainerd died of tuberculosis after a short but strenuous career of evangelizing Native Americans in New England and the Middle Atlantic colonies. Touched by the Great Awakening (1740–42), he had been expelled from Yale

College for his convictions, and he set his course for mission. After Brainerd died, Jonathan Edwards edited his diaries, added his own commentary, and published them in 1749 as *An Account of the Life of the Late Reverend Mr. David Brainerd*. Through innumerable printings this book gave Brainerd celebrity status, portrayed his saintliness, made him a larger-than-life missionary hero, and inspired countless persons, such as William Carey and Henry Martyn, to become missionaries. Becoming a model for later missionary biographies, the book highlighted the inspirational aspects of Brainerd's ministry but failed to mention his human shortcomings, thus limiting what could be learned from his life (Neely 1999, 441–47.

Hope for the World

The roots of Protestant mission in the "Great Century" lie in the revivals (spiritual awakenings) of the preceding century. Building on the teachings of the Reformers, revival leaders such as Philipp Jakob Spener and August Hermann Francke in Germany and John Wesley in England addressed the nature of regeneration—what it really means to live the Christian life. Pietism—the revivalism in the Lutheran and Reformed churches in continental Europe, the evangelical and Methodist revivals in the United Kingdom, and the Great Awakening in the North American English colonies—brought new life to the churches. The core values of these movements included the reformation of the church, devotional study of the Bible to improve Christian behavior, the "heartfelt" experience of conversion (receiving Christ as one's "personal Savior"), and "hope for the world" through mission and the transformation of society (Brown 1978, 27–28).

Spiritual renewal in the churches came none too soon, because the religious skepticism of the eighteenth-century Enlightenment contested the traditional claims of Christianity. Increasing knowledge in the West about the religions and the advanced culture of China sparked interest in comparative religion, which prompted some to place Confucius and Buddha on the same pedestal with Jesus. Virtuous pagans, therefore, could enter heaven through the mercy of God without having heard the gospel (Jongeneel 1995, 226).

Recruiting missionaries from Francke's pietist University of Halle in Germany, and with the financial backing of the Danish king, the Danish-Halle Mission sent Bartholomäus Ziegenbalg and Heinrich Plütschau to the Danish trading colony on the Tranquebar coast of southern India, where they arrived in 1706. Ziegenbalg became fluent in the Tamil language and translated a large part of the Old Testament and the entire New Testament. However, their burden to evangelize the Tamil people, build an indigenous Indian Lutheran church, and minister to the lower castes met with strong resistance from the governor, who feared that this might jeopardize commerce (Beyreuther 1955, 29–42).

The work of the Holy Spirit became evident at the "Moravian Pentecost" on August 13, 1727. This event galvanized the world mission of the Moravian refugees who had found a home on the Saxon estate of the pietist German nobleman Count Nikolaus Ludwig von Zinzendorf. Known as the Renewed Unitas Fratrum (the "United Brethren"), they had fled from persecution in Moravia and built the village of Herrnhut ("The Lord's Watch"). Unfortunately, dissen-

sion had torn their unity apart. After they had spent weeks in prayer and fasting, "the Holy Ghost came upon us and in those days great signs and wonders took place in our midst," according to one eyewitness. "Self-love and self-will as well as all disobedience disappeared and an overwhelming flood of grace swept us all out into the great ocean of Divine Love" (Greenfield 1928, 10).

Determined to "reach souls for the Lamb," the Moravians became devoted to mission and were far ahead of their time in strategy and conception of Christian unity. To uphold their missionaries in prayer, twenty-six Moravians at Herrnhut made a covenant to pray and began an around-the-clock prayer meeting that lasted for one hundred years. Zinzendorf led the community, spending his considerable fortune on mission and devoting substantial time to mentoring leaders and missionaries. To minimize the difference between clergy and laity, all those sent abroad enjoyed the status of missionaries. Since many had skills as craftsmen, they often engaged in business activities to support themselves. Some worked at a trade, while others evangelized and did pastoral work. In Dutch Guiana a tailor shop, bakery, and watchmaker's business provided opportunities for evangelizing their customers (Danker 1971, 51–56). When denied access to African slaves in the West Indies, Moravians purchased plantations of their own, complete with slaves, in order to freely lead them to Christ and treat them humanely (Danker 1971, 36).

An important new chapter in mission opened through the efforts of William Carey, a shoemaker and lay preacher in Northampton, England. On one occasion he asked the leaders of the Northampton Baptist Association to consider "whether the command given to the apostles to teach all nations was not binding on all succeeding ministers to the end of the world, seeing that the accompanying promise was of equal extent." A sharp rebuke followed: "Young man, sit down. . . . When God pleases to convert the heathen, He will do it without consulting you or me. Besides, there must first be another Pentecostal gift of tongues!" (Carey 1923, 50) Not easily discouraged, Carey published a lengthy tract entitled *An Enquiry into the Obligations of Christians to*

> *I have, through the good hand of my God upon me, now nearly translated all the New Testament [into the Bengali language]. . . . I have a pundit [a learned person in India], who has, with me, examined and corrected all the Epistles, to the second of Peter; we go through a chapter every day. The natives, who can read and write, understand it perfectly; and as it is corrected by a learned native, the style and syntax cannot be very bad. I intend to go through it again, and, as critically as I can, compare it with the Greek New Testament.*
>
> William Carey
> (Manschreck 1981, 475)

Use Means for the Conversion of the Heathens (1792), which justified overseas evangelism and became the first manifesto of the modern missionary movement.

Carey and like-minded friends founded the Baptist Missionary Society in 1792; he became its first missionary and spent the rest of his life in India. Other new agencies appeared: the London Missionary Society (1795), Church Missionary Society (1799), and Netherlands Missionary Society (1797).

In Germany the Lutheran pastor Johann Jänicke and Baron von Schirding, products of the "Berlin Awakening," started a mission seminary that trained over eighty missionaries.

THE GREAT CENTURY

Historian Kenneth Scott Latourette described the unprecedented nineteenth-century advance of Christianity around the world as the "Great Century" in Christian mission (Latourette 1941, 1–8). In the same period the economic and technological advantages of the North Atlantic nations enabled them to gain control of the larger part of the world's landmass. With the exception of a few countries, all others became politically subject to peoples of European heritage. The descendants of European settlers ruled Latin America. England, France, Belgium, Spain, Portugal, and Germany governed most of Africa. Russia consolidated its interests across central Asia and Siberia. England considered British India (India, Sri Lanka, Pakistan, Bangladesh, Nepal, and Burma [now Myanmar]) to be the "jewel" of its imperial crown. The Netherlands owned the Dutch East Indies (present-day Indonesia), and France ruled Indochina. Victorious in the Spanish-American War of 1898, the United States joined the imperial stampede and took Cuba, Puerto Rico, Guam, and the Philippines from Spain, and annexed the Hawaiian Islands in the same year (Anderson 1969, 279–300). China, the most populous nation in the world, found itself carved up into trade zones managed by the Western powers.

Colonialism meant legal standing and protection for missionaries. Hence, in British India they could evangelize Muslims and Hindus, populations often intensely hostile

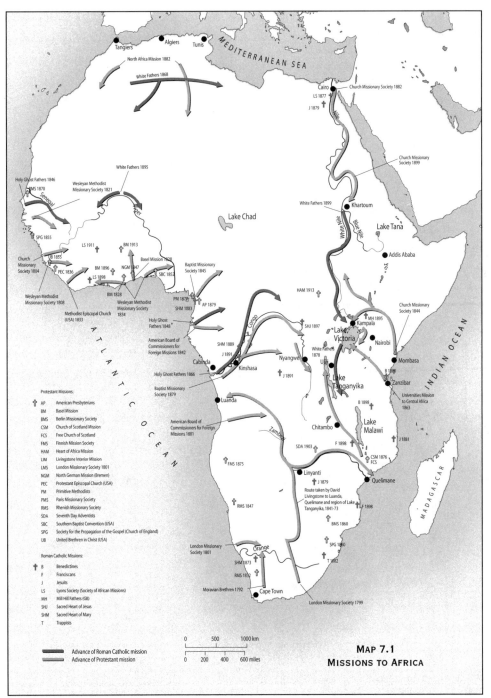

MAP 7.1
MISSIONS TO AFRICA

(Copyright Angus Hudson Ltd./Three's Company)

to the gospel. Many missionaries believed that God had sovereignly given the subcontinent to England for its Christianization. For businessmen, colonialism gave unrestricted access to natural resources, cheap labor, and sizable profits. The close connection of colonialism and mission appeared to serve the common good, as evident in the explorations

> My object is to open up traffic along the banks of the Zambesi, and also to preach the Gospel. The natives of Central Africa are very desirous of trading, but their only traffic is at present in slaves, of which the poorer people have an unmitigated horror; it is therefore most desirable to encourage the former principle, and thus open a way for the consumption of free productions, and the introduction of Christianity and commerce. By encouraging the native propensity for trade, the advantages that might be derived in a commercial point of view are incalculable; nor should we lose sight of the inestimable blessings it is in our power to bestow upon the unenlightened African, by giving him the light of Christianity. Those two pioneers of civilization—Christianity and commerce—should ever be inseparable.
>
> David Livingstone
> (Thomas 1995, 67–68)

of missionary David Livingstone in central Africa. He believed that with opening the region to trade, "commerce and Christianity" would break the Arab and Portuguese slave trades (Walls 1994a, 142).

Naturally, lust for gold, diamonds, ivory, rubber, and other commodities usually sidetracked Christian values. Missionaries sometimes found themselves as the only advocates for the protection of indigenous peoples. Greed at its worst became evident in the Belgian Congo, originally the private property of King Leopold II, a monarch not easily troubled by conscience. From 1878 until after Leopold's death in 1909, ten million people—half the population of this vast land—perished, victims of the outrageous cruelties of the ivory and rubber trades (Hochschild 1998, 233).

Great Britain forced the sale of Indian-grown opium in China, engendering a conflict that led to the First Opium War (1839–42). The humiliating terms of surrender forced the Chinese government to allow the sale of imported opium, open five ports to foreign commerce, and lease the coastal island of Hong Kong to Britain. France joined Britain in the Second Opium War (1856–60) to bolster its own interests (Stanley 1990, 104–9). The "unequal treaties" that came about from these wars embittered Chinese patriots.

Since the North Atlantic countries viewed themselves as Christian, they carried a responsibility—the "White Man's Burden"—to enlighten the dark "heathen" regions of the world with the light of Western civilization (Gollwitzer 1969, 51–3). Isaiah had promised, "The earth will be full of the knowledge of the LORD as the waters cover the sea" (Isa. 11:9b). But as Shenk observes, "Missionaries tended to believe that 'knowledge of the Lord' came clothed in the language and forms of their own culture. Only gradually did they perceive their own provincialism and admit to the relativity of all cultures" (Shenk 1984, 163). In the first noteworthy hymn written on the theme of mission,

Isaac Watts captured the outlook in "Jesus Shall Reign" (1719), in which he crowed that "Western empires own their Lord, and savage tribes attend His word."

The Command of Christ

"It was during a solitary walk in the woods behind the college, while meditating and praying on the subject, and feeling half inclined to give it up," wrote pioneer missionary Adoniram Judson, "that the command of Christ, 'Go into all the world, and preach the gospel to every creature,' was presented to my mind with such clearness and power, that I came to a full decision, and though great difficulties appeared in my way, resolved to obey the command at all events" (Thomas 1995, 65). Motivations for mission ranged, with some overlapping, from Judson's love for Christ through obedience to the Great Commission, to promoting the glory of God through "disinterested benevolence"—selfless love expressed through sharing the gospel and sponsoring humanitarian projects to prepare for the coming kingdom of God on earth—to saving souls from hell by "plucking brands from the burning" (Beaver 1968, 121–26). In a tract published in 1818, missionaries Gordon Hall and Samuel Newell lamented the colossal number of people in the world, more than half a billion, perishing without Christ. Those "who have never heard of the name of Jesus, who know not that a Saviour has bled for sinners, are rushing through pagan darkness, by millions, down to hopeless death" (Beaver 1968, 127). Calculations of those who died without Christ were determined by year, month, day, hour, and minute—a remarkable feat given the paucity of census data.

Missionaries risked their lives to fulfill their calling, with many dying from malaria and other diseases, killed for their Christian witness, or suffering when caught up in the whirlwind of political upheavals. In Burma Judson suffered through the death of his first wife and child, the death of his sec-

> *The motto of every missionary, whether preacher, printer, or schoolmaster, ought to be "Devoted for life."*
>
> Adoniram Judson
> (Anderson 1956, 409)

ond wife, imprisonment, and poor health. Within twenty years fifty Church Missionary Society missionaries died in Sierra Leone. During the first two decades of its work in India, the number of missionaries of the American Board of Commissioners for Foreign Missions (ABCFM) who died outstripped the number of converts (Robert 1996, 81). Cannibals took the lives of John Williams in the New Hebrides and James Chalmers in New Guinea. Fears of a French invasion caused the Vietnamese emperor to execute Jean Théophane Vénard and other Catholic missionaries. Vietnamese believers hid some missionaries underground during the persecution; one report told of a missionary who "[had] not seen the sun for eighteen months and his letter is dated from the kingdom of the moles, ten feet underground" (Simonnet 1988, 139). In one of the most tragic episodes approximately 225 missionaries and thirty thousand Chinese Christians were brutally killed in the Boxer uprising in China in 1900.

Remarkable deliverances also dot the record, with one of the most unusual occurring in a Bantu-speaking part of South

Africa in the late 1840s during a severe drought. Fears of famine led the local chief to call in the rainmakers. When unsuccessful, they blamed their failure on the presence of missionaries. Realizing the danger to his family, since they were the only missionaries in the area, Methodist missionary W. J. Davis knew that he had to act quickly. Riding on his horse into the chief's village and interrupting ceremonies in progress, he boldly announced that the rainmakers and the sins of the people were the real culprits. Emulating the prophet Elijah, who challenged the prophets of Baal to a test on Mount Carmel (1 Kings 18:16–46), he proposed to his startled hearers, "Come to chapel next Sabbath, and we will pray to God, who made the heavens and the earth, to give us rain, and we will see who is the true God, and who are His true servants, and your best friends." After the chief accepted his offer, Davis and his fellow believers spent the next day in fasting and prayer. On Sunday, without a cloud in the sky, not even "a cloud as small as a man's hand," the chief and his retinue entered the church. At the moment when Davis and the congregation knelt in prayer, "they heard the big rain drops begin to patter on the zinc roof of the chapel. . . . The whole region was so saturated with water that the river nearby became so swollen that the chief . . . could not cross it that night" (Taylor 1880, 275–76).

Woman's Work for Woman

The extensive activities of women missionaries caught the attention of the Centenary Conference on Protestant Missions held at London in 1888. "We must not allow . . . the ability and efficiency of so many of our female helpers, nor even the exceptional faculty for leadership and organization which some of them have displayed in their work to discredit the natural and predestined headship of man in Missions," charged J. N. Murdock, secretary of the American Baptist Missionary Union (Murdock 1888, 167). His unwitting tribute confirmed the significant presence of women in the mission lands. Reports two years later listed thirty-four women's societies supporting 926 women, and when combined with single and married women from the general missionary boards, they constituted 60 percent of the American missionary force (Hunter 1984, xiii). Their work had become crucial in education, evangelism, medical missions, and benevolent ministries.

Opportunities for women in ministry had declined since the Reformation. The Reformers had strongly criticized the Roman Catholic ideal of clerical celibacy and the function of the religious orders. Women had to be satisfied with responsibilities in the home because the churches offered them few avenues of ministry. But the call of God could not be so easily denied in the nineteenth century. Whether venturing abroad as the wives of missionaries or sent to care for the children of missionaries, women found exciting doors of service being opened to them. As a single woman, Cynthia Farrar left for India in 1827 under ABCFM appointment to supervise schools for girls. Charlotte ("Lottie") Moon went to China in 1872 and devoted her life to teaching and evangelism. Her personal sacrifices and letters home asking Southern Baptist women to support mission, as well as her challenges to church leaders, profoundly influenced the course of Southern Baptist missions (Allen 1994, 205–15). On the home front, Mary Lyon founded Mount Holyoke Female Seminary at South Hadley, Massachusetts, for training women missionaries. One of its most illustrious graduates, Fidelia Fiske, established a boarding school for Nestorian girls at Urmia in present-day Iran. Sarah Doremus, a wealthy Presbyterian who lived in New York City and had nine children, overcame opposition to found the Woman's Union Missionary Society of America in 1861, the first board to send women abroad. This event marked the emergence of the women's missionary movement. Women continued to organize and fund their own societies after the Civil War, since male-dominated boards frequently hesitated to send them. The "Woman's Work for Woman" missiology, devoted to taking the gospel to women and advancing their status through education, offered a vital ministry to thousands of women (Robert 1996, 130).

Revivalism as promoted by the Wesleyan-Holiness and Higher Life movements highlighted the "outpouring of the Holy Spirit" (Joel 2:28–29) on both men and women in the "last days" (Palmer 1859, 21–33). Hence, periods of revival enlarge the horizons of ministry for women. New Testament scholar Janet Powers notes that at such times "spiritual power reigns and social patterns are disrupted, so women who have spiritual power can operate autonomously. But when revival wanes, the original social and religious patterns are restored" (Powers 1999, 332). This spiritual emancipation of women was illustrated in the highly acclaimed ministry of the ex-slave Amanda Berry Smith, who served as a missionary in both India and Africa (Hardesty and Israel 1993, 61–79).

Mission Societies

Mission societies mushroomed in North America. In the United States they included the ABCFM (1810), African Baptist Missionary Society (1815), Presbyterian Board of Foreign Missions (1831), Seventh-Day Adventist Mission Board (1863), American Mission to Lepers (1874), and Board of Foreign Missions of the General Conference of the Mennonites of North America (1880); in Canada, the Board of Foreign Missions of the Presbyterian Church of Canada (1843), Canada Congregational Foreign Missionary Society (1881), and others. Women's agencies included the Women's Home and Foreign Missionary Society of the African Methodist Episcopal Church (1892) and Women's Baptist Foreign Missionary Society of Ontario (1876), the latter devoted "to give the Gospel to the women and children of India, chiefly to those among the Telugus, and also to the Indians of Bolivia" (Beach and Fahs 1925, 17).

The mission program of the Methodist Church in the United States (1819) can be traced partially to the calling of John Stewart, an American of mixed European and African descent. While living in Virginia, he heard the voice of a man and then of a woman "from the sky" say to him, "Thou shalt go to the northwest and declare my counsel plainly." Afterward, a "peculiar halo" became visible and filled the western horizon (Love n.d., 5). Traveling to the northwest region of Ohio, he began preaching to the Wyandots with great success in 1816. Stewart's example inspired other Methodists to action.

European agencies also sharply increased in number. In Great Britain early societies included the British and Foreign Bible Society (1804) and Church Missions to Jews (1809). In Norway was formed the Society for Preaching the Gospel to Scandinavian Seamen in Foreign Ports (1863). Continental societies ranged from the Rhenish Missionary Society (1828) in Germany, to the Basel Mission Trading Company (1815) headquartered in Switzerland, to the Swedish Mongol Mission (1897). Growing cooperation led to "comity" agreements—the assignment of regions in countries to different mission agencies—to eliminate unnecessary duplication of effort (Beaver 1962, 42–68). To advance such endeavors and address issues, regional and international mission conferences were convened. The last such gathering of the century, the Ecumenical Missionary Conference, met in New York City in 1900 and attracted an estimated two hundred thousand supporters and missionaries (Askew 2000, 146–54).

Catholic mission also experienced an upsurge with the renewed vigor of the Paris Foreign Mission Society (1663) and the restoration of the Jesuit Order in 1814. New organizations included the Society of the Divine Word in the Netherlands (1875), and in America the Sisters of the Blessed Sacrament for Indians and Colored People (1879), the latter founded "to lead the Indian & Colored Races to the knowledge & love of God, & so make of them living temples of Our Lord's Divinity" (Dries 1998, 31). French cardinal Charles Lavigerie founded the White Fathers (1868) and White Sisters (1869) (so-called for the Arab-style white robes they wore) and worked against the slave trade in central Africa (de Vaulx 1961, 137–43).

Unlike the Orthodox churches existing in Muslim-controlled countries for which the extent of formal witness centered on the Sunday celebration of the liturgy, the Russian Orthodox Church experienced a revival of mission in the nineteenth century. In 1830 Macarius Glukharev ventured into the Altai Mountains in Siberia, where he preached to the Kalmyk people and trans-

lated the Scriptures, the Nicene Creed, and other church materials into their language. To keep converts from reverting back to Tibetan Buddhism, he organized them into Christian villages governed by missionaries

> No matter what stories [I heard] about America in general or about the Aleuts in particular, no matter how he [an old Russian adventurer] tried to persuade me to go to Unalaska [one of the Aleutian Islands], I remained deaf; none of his persuasion even touched me. Indeed, how could I—why should I (humanly speaking) have traveled God-knows-where when I had one of the best parishes in the city, when I enjoyed the love of my parishioners . . . when I already owned my own home and had a larger income than the salary being offered to whomever was assigned to Unalaska?
>
> Blessed be the Name of the Lord! I began to burn with desire to go to such a people!
>
> May my own example serve as a new proof of the truth that the "Lord guides a man safely in the way he should go," and that each of us servants of His Church is no more than an instrument in His hands. He saw fit to establish my field of ministry in America—and that despite my opposition.
>
> Innocent Veniaminov
> (Garrett 1979, 34, 36)

(Veronis 1994, 86–93). Innocent Veniaminov ("St. Innocent of Alaska") evangelized the indigenous populations of the Aleutian Islands and Alaska and later founded the Russian Orthodox Missionary Society in 1870 (Veronis 1994, 94–106). One of the most significant achievements occurred in Japan under another Orthodox missionary, Nicholas Kasatkin. Inspired by Stephen of Perm and Innocent, he worked to build a strong Japanese church. By 1896 there were twenty-seven thousand baptized Christians, thirty Japanese priests, and eighty-nine translated theological works in a country generally resistant to Christianity (Stamoolis 1986, 35–40; Struve 1960, 113–15).

In the latter half of the century independent "faith missions" garnered considerable support. They advocated a return to simpler "apostolic methods," taking their cue in part from the "faith principle" advocated in Anthony Norris Groves's *Christian Devotedness* (1825) and Edward Irving's *Missionaries after the Apostolic School* (1825). No one exemplified the "faith life" better than the Christian philanthropist George Müller, who trusted God to supply the needs of his orphanage in Bristol, England. The faith life focused on dependence on God's provision rather than on human techniques in fundraising. Faith missions and missionaries frequently refused to publicly share their financial needs, praying instead that God's people would be divinely inspired to send monies (Fiedler 1994, 55).

Faith missionaries often sought to go beyond the protected coastal ports where missionaries usually clustered and move inland to potentially dangerous unevangelized areas. Hence, the China Inland Mission (1865), founded by J. Hudson Taylor, pressed its missionaries to work in the interior as well as to learn the language, eat local food, wear customary clothes, and observe Chinese etiquette. The Sudan Interior Mission (1893) and the Africa Inland Mission (1895) followed suit in Africa. Another such

> *On Sunday, June 25th, 1865, unable to bear the sight of a congregation of a thousand or more Christian people rejoicing in their own security, while millions were perishing for lack of knowledge, I wandered out on the sands alone, in great spiritual agony; and there the Lord conquered my unbelief, and I surrendered myself to God for this service. I told Him that all the responsibility as to issues and consequences must rest with Him; that as His servant, it was mine to obey and follow Him—His, to direct, to care for, and to guide me and those who might labour with me. Need I say that peace at once flowed into my burdened heart? There and then I asked Him for twenty-four fellow-workers, two for each of eleven inland provinces which were without a missionary, and two for Mongolia. . . . I returned home with a heart enjoying rest such as it had been a stranger to for months. . . . I had previously prayed, and asked prayer, that workers might be raised up for the eleven then unoccupied provinces, and thrust forth and provided for, but had not surrendered myself to be their leader.*
>
> J. Hudson Taylor (n.d., 108)

agency, the Christian and Missionary Alliance (1887), founded by A. B. Simpson, sent missionaries to many countries.

Although the personnel of the denominational boards often received their education in colleges, universities, and seminaries, those of the faith missions usually had little formal training, but they did carry a strong sense of calling. Increasingly, the new "Bible institutes" provided recruits. As the century drew to a close, some missionaries called for Christians to better understand the non-Christian religions, discern their best values, and work with them to build a better world. Their interest in evangelizing non-Christians declined as they concentrated on humanitarian endeavors (Hutchison 1987, 102–4). In contrast, the theologically conservative faith missions became a strong new force in evangelism (Frizen 1992, 30–32).

Faith missions and Bible institutes reflected the steadily growing influence of dispensational premillennialism, an outlook on the end times that negatively viewed the future course of human history (Fiedler 1994, 272–79). Originating with the Plymouth Brethren, this pattern of biblical interpretation looked for the imminent return of Christ to be followed by seven years of tribulation and then a literal one-thousand-year period (millennium) of peace (Erickson 1998, 91–106). Inspired by the words of Jesus in Matt. 24:14, premillennialists believed that the world had to be speedily evangelized in the "last days" (Robert 1990, 29–37). Despite the growing popularity of this view, many missionaries followed a postmillennial calendar, one that optimistically looked forward to a long period of time (symbolically a millennium) in which the world would be Christianized.

Mission Strategies

Missionaries engaged in a wide range of activities, from preaching, teaching, and coordinating the ministries of national evangelists and "Bible women," to other tasks (Tucker 1988, 119–25). William Carey translated the Scriptures into dozens of languages; his friend Henry Martyn did translations in Urdu, Arabic, and Persian. Ann Judson pioneered Bible translation into Thai, while Robert Morrison and William Milne produced the Bible in Chinese. Reflecting how the eighteenth-century Enlightenment notion of human progress influenced mission, Alexander Duff established the first English-speaking school of higher education in India (Stanley 2001, 12). Instruction in Western learning, it was hoped, would inspire students to see the superiority of the Christian religion and become converts— "civilizing" would precede "evangelizing." Taking that notion farther, W. A. P. Martin contended that mission should make Western science and political theory available to the Chinese people; to accomplish this, he spent his life as a teacher, interpreter, translator, and author, but not as an evangelist (Covell 1986, 99–106).

Medical missions called attention to the physical plight of people and served to express the compassion of Christ (Grundmann 1990). Granddaughter of the first American medical missionary to India, Ida Scudder received her call to medical missions in 1894. While she was staying with her missionary parents (her father was also a physician), three visitors came at different times during one night to plead for a woman doctor to deliver the babies of three women in labor. Since custom prevented the assistance of a male doctor, the lack of an available woman doctor resulted in all three women dying in childbirth (Wilson 1959, 29–43). Deeply troubled by her inability to help, Scudder found her vocation and enrolled at Cornell University Medical School in the first class to admit women. After graduation she returned to Vellore in South India and became one of the foremost leaders in the advancement of health care in India.

Calls for establishing indigenous churches—culturally relevant in their contexts and self-governing, self-supporting, and self-propagating—could be heard

> *Such is the simple structure of our foreign missions, as the combined result of experience, and of the apostolic example; in all which the grand object is to plant and multiply self-reliant, efficient churches, composed wholly of native converts, each church complete in itself, with pastors of the same race with the people. And when the unevangelized world shall be dotted over with such churches, so that all men have it within their power to learn what they must do to be saved, then may we expect the promised advent of the Spirit, and the conversion of the world.*
>
> Rufus Anderson (1869, 117)

throughout most of the century. However, implementing the Pauline model of church planting, summed up at the time in the "three self's," proved to be elusive because missionaries paternally controlled virtually all mission activities and believed that the preparation of indigenous leadership would require many years. Nonetheless, some strategists opposed delaying what they knew to be inevitable, most notably Rufus Anderson of the ABCFM, who penned *Outline of Missionary Practice* (1856), and Henry Venn of the Church Missionary Society in England. Late in the century John Nevius, a Presbyterian missionary to China, wrote *Planting and Development of Missionary Churches* (1889), a book that called for the "three self's" and Bible study groups. It is noteworthy that the "Nevius Plan" shaped the course of Korean Protestantism.

REVIVALS AND THEIR IMPACT

The impact of the Second Great Awakening in America (1776–1810) became evident as students of Williams College in Massachusetts met in a grove of trees near the campus for prayer and discussion about the need of foreign mission. On one occasion, during a violent thunderstorm, they found shelter in a nearby haystack. After a time of intense prayer they pledged themselves to become missionaries. From the "Haystack Prayer Meeting" came the founding of the American Board of Commissioners for Foreign Missions.

After mid-century, revivalist Dwight Moody challenged students in North America and Great Britain to dedicate their lives to evangelism and mission. "I look upon this world as a wrecked vessel," he told his audiences. "God has given me a lifeboat and said to me, 'Moody, save all you can.'" His annual student conferences at Northfield, Massachusetts, proved to be particularly influential. In 1886 the well-known promoter of mission and later editor of the *Missionary Review of the World*, Arthur Pierson, challenged the students to "the evangelization of the world in this generation." One hundred dedicated themselves to mission. Two years later they organized themselves as the Student Volunteer Movement for Foreign Missions under the leadership of John Mott and Robert Wilder (Hopkins 1979, 24–30). Each year thousands of students signed the Student Volunteer Movement pledge: "It is my purpose, if God permit, to become a foreign missionary." Though not a mission agency, it received the strong support of mission leaders. Moody's ministry also inspired several nationally known student athletes in England—the famous "Cambridge Seven"—to join the China Inland Mission (Pollock 1955, 38–44). Finally, his influence extended to the Young Men's Christian Association (1844) and the Young Women's Christian Association (1855), each of which provided an evangelistic witness at its hostels around the world.

Revivalism led to the advance of theological insights such as the Wesleyan-Holiness and Higher Life understandings of the Holy Spirit's work, both of which taught that every believer should experience a work of grace separable from conversion (Dayton 1987, 87–113). Holiness leaders such as Phoebe Palmer and William Taylor, Methodist missionary bishop for Africa, taught that the "second blessing" would remove the sinful disposition and lift the believer to a higher plateau of Christian living. Higher Life advocates such as Moody and Reuben Torrey spoke of a "full consecration" that empowered Christians for evangelism.

The revivals from 1857 to 1860 in North America and the British Isles emphasized the ministry of the Holy Spirit and triggered similar movements elsewhere. Historian Klaus Fiedler observes, "Each revival decreases the uniformity of the church and, inevitably, increases its pluralism, as new spiritual truths and experiences express themselves in new initiatives and organizations" (Fiedler 1994, 113). Furthermore, they inspire individuals who may not meet the qualifications of established denominations and mission agencies to venture into ministry themselves, whether men or women, and perhaps start their own organizations.

On the mission lands revivals brought demonstrations of supernatural power that led people to become Christians, adopt indigenous forms of worship, and choose their own leaders. In the Dutch East Indies, Rhenish missionary Johannes Warneck reported that from the 1860s the Christian community increased after the coming of sensational phenomena, including dreams, visions, signs in the heavens, and several instances in which missionaries (e.g., Ludwig Nommensen) unwittingly consumed poison in food given by their enemies and remained unharmed (see Mark 16:18) (Warneck 1909, 175–82; Lehmann 1996, 105–40).

On the other side of the world, in Jamaica, "a very remarkable revival of religion" took place in 1860. Lengthy prayer services that set aside fixed liturgical practices; seekers being "stricken" or prostrated on the ground, presumably by the might of God; and public confessions of sin marked the awakening. Impressive results followed: Many "rum shops" and gambling houses closed, separated spouses reconciled, wayward children returned to their parents, ministers grew in spiritual zeal, sinners were converted, churches became crowded, and the demand for Bibles exceeded supplies. According to historian Richard Lovett, "The testimony of men of sober judgment is that at least 20,000 souls were savingly awakened at this period. The missionaries . . . believed it to be a special outpouring of the Holy Spirit in response to prayer" (Lovett 1899, 2:385).

Yet, while some missionaries rejoiced at the evident fruit, others viewed such movements with alarm because of the problems they created and their rejection of Western forms of worship and leadership. Missionaries in southern India found the claims of new apostles and prophets to be especially galling (Lang 1939, 199). Not until the twentieth century would such movements gain the attention they deserved.

When the first missionaries crossed the Atlantic to the New World with Columbus on his second journey in 1493, the journey by sea lasted three weeks. In the twentieth century, however, air travel reduced that time to a few hours. Faster means of transportation made the world seem smaller, the migration of peoples turned the world into a global village, the battlements of Christendom collapsed like the walls of Jericho, and the center of gravity of Christianity shifted to the southern hemisphere. Missions would face unprecedented changes. A "Greater Century" had dawned.

8

Expansion to and from Every Continent, A.D. 1900–2000

INTRODUCTION

In a little-noticed publishing event in 1910 May Agnew Stephens produced a songbook entitled *Missionary Messages in Song*. The 113 selections included traditional favorites such as "O Zion, Haste" and "From Greenland's Icy Mountains," along with new songs featuring different parts of the world. Written for North American audiences, it contained songs such as "The Neglected Continent" (South America), "We're Bound to Take the Congo," "India's Saviour," and "Christ for the Philippines." One noteworthy composition, "Bringing in Chinese" (sung to the tune of "Bringing in the Sheaves"), mentions all the provinces of China, as well as Mongolia and Tibet. *Missionary Messages in Song* provided a prism through which Christians in the homeland could see the whole world and reflect on the imperative of mission (Stephens 1910, ii). In response to such promotional efforts they gave millions of dollars and spent countless hours in prayer to enable thousands of missionaries to effectively preach the gospel, translate the Bible, start schools, and care for the needy.

In the same year the World Missionary Conference convened in Edinburgh, Scotland, attended largely by members of the Western missionary establishment. Conference chairman John Mott dubbed it "the most significant gathering ever held in the interest of the world's evangelization" (Mott 1910, v). Greetings were read from representatives of the leading Protestant nations: "King-Emperor" George V of the British Empire; the German Imperial Colonial Office on behalf of Kaiser Wilhelm II; and Theodore Roosevelt, former president of the United States. Sharing the sentiments of the others, the German letter acknowledged "with satisfaction and gratitude that the endeavors for the spread of the Gospel are followed by the blessings of civilization and culture in all countries" (Gairdner 1910, 45).

Although Christianity by now had become the first religious faith to become a world religion, the center of gravity remained in the northern hemisphere, missionaries traveled on a one-way street from Europe and America to the non-Christian world, and paternalism (the practice of controlling others by acting like a parent without giving

them responsibility for themselves) too frequently marked their posture toward indigenous church leaders (Azariah 1910, 315).
The Edinburgh conference, a landmark in
many ways, including its recognition of the
growing maturity of the "younger churches,"
still fenced Christendom off from the non-
Christian world.

As the delegates listened to the speeches
in the assembly hall of the United Free
Church of Scotland, they could hardly
imagine how much the world scene and
mission soon would change. Although

> *I go to Africa not for fame or prominence,
> but because I am attached to Jesus Christ
> in a love that knows no sacrifice too
> great to be made, that men and women
> everywhere throughout Africa may know
> of and come to possess the wonderful
> inheritance He has won for them on the
> cross of Calvary. I go to Africa because
> I believe the Africans to be worthy of the
> most heroic effort that can be put forth
> to save them. I believe this because Jesus
> Christ believed and proved to the world
> that it was true.*
>
> Helen Virginia Blakeslee, D.O.
> (Robert 1996, 214)

"cultural optimism, the West's sense of superiority, and the expectation of a speedy
Christianization of the whole world still
prevailed," writes missiologist Anne Wind,
"the end of the Vasco da Gama era had already announced itself with Japan's victory
over Russia in 1905" (Wind 1995, 243). The
coming world wars, nationalism, secularism, the renaissance of the non-Christian

religions, and internal doubts about the ultimate claims of Christianity (i.e., salvation
solely through Jesus Christ) would severely
test the missions enterprise.

The second day of the conference opened
with Isaac Watts's hymn "Jesus Shall Reign."
As the audience sang its triumphant line,
"While Western empires own their Lord, and
savage tribes attend His word," the pillars
of Christendom appeared to stand firm.
In a short time the "Great War" (1914–18)
between the Western powers, with its years
of sustained horror in the trenches of Europe, would discolor the moral image of the
"Christian" nations. Observers wondered
how the Western empires could still "own
their Lord" and display such savagery.

This chapter briefly introduces six significant developments in twentieth-century
mission: (1) the growth of Christianity outside North Atlantic countries, (2) mainline
Protestant missions, (3) the ascendancy of
conservative evangelical missions, (4) Pentecostalism, (5) Vatican Council II and liberation theology, and (6) the unparalleled global
mission advance at the century's end, to and
from every continent. Though not strictly
chronological, the topical sequence follows
the general historical order of events.

VOICES CALLING IN THE DESERT

The customary course in tracing the
history of Christian mission is to progress
from the 1910 Edinburgh conference to the
institutions that came in its wake. However,
this approach perpetuates a Western interpretation of events. It also draws attention
away from the rise of indigenous Christian
leaders and movements, a maturation that
always had been the goal of mission. But
just as John the Baptist preached in the
desert to the common people who came

to hear him beyond the reach of the religious authorities in Jerusalem, so also new voices began to call for revolutionary applications of the faith in their cultural contexts, sometimes without the blessing of the missionary establishment. Another factor figured prominently into the changing scene: beginning early in the twentieth century, revivals in many countries contributed to the further development of indigenous churches, adding new voices to those already being heard.

Even as missionaries dominated the churches in the nineteenth century, important leaders emerged. Some remained within the mission churches, others worked in association with mission agencies, while an increasing number demanded more freedom and left to form independent ministries. Reflecting on the legacy of paternalism, North China missionary Roland Allen lamented in 1912, "We have simply transplanted abroad the [church] organization with which we are familiar at home." He added, "We have maintained it by supplying a large number of European officials who can carry it on." When native leaders finally are ready to take charge, Allen argued, "the system will proceed precisely as it did before, natives simply doing exactly what we are now doing" (Allen [1912] 1962, 135–36). But four decades later, major changes did come when devout and gifted indigenous leaders took the reins of leadership in churches around the world.

Notable Indigenous Leaders

In the nineteenth century distinguished leaders such as the Nigerian Samuel Adjai Crowther worked within the mission churches. Fulani and Yoruba Muslim raiders had sold Crowther into slavery as a youth. As Crowther and other slaves crossed the Atlantic, the Portuguese ship on which they were imprisoned was intercepted by a British warship, and the slaves were liberated in Sierra Leone. Converted three years later, he remembered becoming "convinced of another worse state of slavery, namely, that of sin and Satan. It pleased the Lord to open my heart" (Walls 1994b, 133). The Church of England ordained him in 1843, and later he became its first African bishop. Crowther worked to produce the Yoruba Bible, superintended the Niger Mission, and modeled church leadership for other Africans.

The value of translations such as the Yoruba Bible cannot be overestimated. The preservation of languages through translations saved valuable facets of cultures. They also provided an independent frame of reference for the faithful to evaluate the form of Christianity brought by the missionaries. "But even more important was the discovery that many things in the Bible seemed to correspond with the worldview and aspirations of . . . indigenous leaders," writes missiologist Frans Verstraelen. This was especially the case in the "recognition of the influence of spirits and the central place of Jesus' healing power" (Verstraelen 1995, 80).

Associated with the China Inland Mission (CIM), Pastor Hsi had been a Confucian scholar who became addicted to opium. At his conversion in 1879 he changed his name to Hsi "Shengmo"—"Demon Overcomer"—as testimony to his deliverance from satanic power (Taylor 1949, 58). He engaged in evangelism in Shansi province and established more than fifty opium refuges for addicts, which also served as beachheads for church planting.

With links to the CIM as well, Dora Yu became the foremost Chinese evangelist in the early decades of the twentieth century. Historian Silas Wu credits her as being "the first cross-cultural Chinese missionary in modern times" and "the first to establish a Bible institute for women workers in China" (Wu 2002, 85). Her ministry as a revivalist bore fruit in the ministry of Watchman Nee and other leaders of the next generation.

At the turn of the century Christians around the world recognized the name of Pandita Ramabai, one of the best-known Christians in India and widely respected for her life of faith. Her independent Mukti ("Salvation") Mission near Kedgaon in Maharastra State cared for thousands of child widows, orphans, and famine victims (Dyer

> *Christ came to give different gifts to different people. Some He made prophets; some He made preachers; some He made teachers. Since I have become a Christian I have thought He has given me the gift of being a sweeper. I want to sweep away some of the old difficulties that lie before the missionaries in their efforts to reach our Hindu widows.*
>
> Pandita Ramabai
> (*Heroes of the Cross* 1933, 22)

1923, 9–17). Missionaries from England and the United States assisted in her charitable endeavors. As a social reformer, Ramabai worked to elevate the status of women and improve their quality of life. In addition, she gained recognition for her translation of the Bible into the Marathi language. A friend of Ramabai, Narayan Tilak, tried to develop a radical Indian expression of the Christian faith that would attract Hindus; eventually this led him to disassociate himself from the missionary establishment (Richard 1998, 72–81). Part of his legacy appears in his more than 254 songs (out of seven hundred) in the Marathi hymnal.

Unlike Ramabai, who retained membership in the Church of England, Kanzo Uchimura rejected Western church organizations altogether. In his estimation, the evangelization of Japan required a completely indigenized faith, one free of the disunity that marked Protestantism. With "seven brothers," he founded an independent congregation that became the model for his later "Mukyokai" or "Non-church Movement," a network of assemblies free of human hierarchy. "The Bible produced the Lutheran Church in Germany and the Methodist Church in England," Uchimura observed. "Cannot the Bible with the same capability produce the genuine Japanese Church?" (Miura 1996, 99). The movement thrived, and his work helped to shape Japanese Christianity before his death in 1930.

Prophets by Divine Commission

Radical movements, dating back to the earlier part of the nineteenth century, continued to multiply, complete with prophets, apostles, and faith healers. Their adaptation of the faith, practices, and spiritual gifts of the early church (1 Cor. 12:7–11; Eph. 4:11) to their own cultural contexts usually triggered condemnation by missionaries and sometimes engendered the hostility of colonial authorities. Blending Christian doctrines with traditional religious beliefs often prompted charges of syncretism and spiritual compromise. Nevertheless, indigenous leaders such as William Wadé Harris and Simon Kimbangu in Africa cut a path that many others followed.

Possessing the appearance of an Old Testament prophet, Harris began a preaching ministry across Liberia, Ivory Coast, and Gold Coast (now Ghana) in West Africa. Born in Liberia and converted in the Methodist Church at Cape Palmas, his call to the ministry came in 1910 while he was imprisoned for political activities. Through a visitation of the angel Gabriel he was informed that God would anoint him as the prophet of the "last times" to preach the gospel, command the destruction of fetishes, and baptize new believers (Shank 1994, 115). Harris said that he experienced the same spiritual empowerment as that of the first disciples on the day of Pentecost.

After release from prison, his astonishing ministry began. Walking barefoot, the white-bearded Harris proved to be an imposing figure with his round white turban and white calico robe. Accompanied by two women disciples who were excellent singers, he traveled from village to village carrying a Bible, a staff shaped like a cross, a calabash rattle, and a gourd bowl. They entered villages singing and shaking their rattles. When a crowd gathered, Harris would begin preaching and challenge the people to abandon their traditional religious practices. He also cast out demons and prayed for the sick. Converts received Trinitarian baptism with water poured from his gourd bowl (Anderson 2001, 71). Reports indicate that between 1913 and 1915 he made some sixty thousand to one hundred thousand converts. After their baptisms, he sent them to Catholic and Protestant missionaries for instruction.

Little wonder that Harris became known as "the father of Christianity in the Ivory Coast" and that the Methodists respectfully date their beginnings to his ministry there. However, the majority of his followers joined independent "prophet-led" churches. According to historian Lamin Sanneh, Harris left an "indelible impression . . . after only a few years of preaching in what was no more than a once-and-for-all visit in most places" (Sanneh 1983, 125). His recognition of the African spirit world and belief that spirits, satanic in nature, should be exorcised won him vast popularity. This approach, in sharp contrast to the limited outlook on the spirit world held by most Euramerican missionaries, established him as a model for other African prophets.

Another such prophet appeared in central Africa. Baptized in 1915 at a mission of the Baptist Missionary Society, Simon Kimbangu heard the call to ministry during the flu epidemic of 1918 when thousands were dying in the Belgian Congo. He heard a voice say, "I am Christ. My servants are unfaithful. I have chosen you to bear witness before your brethren and to convert them. Tend My flock" (Martin 1975, 44). During his six-month ministry thousands of people came to hear him preach. Miracles followed, and many believed that an African Pentecost had begun through his obedience to the Holy Spirit. Threatened by the potential political force of his popularity, the Belgian authorities imprisoned him for the rest of his life. At the end of the twentieth century several million people belonged to the Church of Jesus Christ on Earth because of Prophet Simon Kimbangu. His followers considered him to be the Black Messiah and placed him on what appears to be an equal footing with Jesus Christ as an authority figure (Anderson 2001, 128–29).

Looking at the impact of such movements in Africa, missiologist Allan Anderson suggests that the contextualization of the faith by indigenous leaders such as Harris and Kimbangu has resulted in a transformation of Christianity "of at least the magnitude of the Protestant Reformation in Europe, and we may be excused for concluding that this was perhaps a more profound Reformation than the European one ever was" (Anderson 2001, 10). The appearance of non-Western forms of the faith certainly has altered the landscape of world Christianity.

The Fruit of Revivals

Revivals and mission always have been closely related. Eighteenth-century awakenings laid the foundation for the modern missions movement. In the next century they brought renewed zeal among the faithful, inspired believers to enter the ministry or become missionaries, and influenced non-Christians to convert (F. Hale 1993, 109–14). Many evangelicals prayed for the "outpouring" of the Holy Spirit (Joel 2:28–29) to enable the church to complete the Great Commission. Each revival then represented a new measure of the Spirit's work. Arthur Pierson listed twenty-five revivals, beginning with an awakening in Tahiti (1815–16) to one in Uganda (1893–98) near the end of the century, all of which represented the "most indisputable . . . sanction and seal of God on modern missions" (Pierson 1917, 332).

Revivals in the first decade of the twentieth century had long-term effects. When revival fires burned in Wales in 1904, many interpreted this as the commencement of the promised worldwide outpouring of the Spirit. It immediately gained notoriety for public confessions of sin, prayer in concert, vibrant singing, seeking for Holy Spirit baptism, and significant changes in the moral behavior of thousands of converts. Wales then became the inspiration for similar awakenings in Africa, Australia, India, Korea, Manchuria, Chile, North America, and elsewhere (Orr 1975, 7–28). Missionaries told of even more unusual phenomena. In the 1905–6 revival in India, American Presbyterian missionary A. L. Wiley announced that during services at Ratnagiri "the Spirit worked marvelously." In the intense revival atmosphere, with its accent on confession of sins and repentance, not only did believers fall down, sway, shout, and weep, but also "many have seen visions of various kinds—Christ on the Cross, angels with drawn swords, fire, etc. Many have experienced inward burning, marking the cleansing by the Spirit of burning (Isaiah iv:4) and his empowering for service" (Wiley 1906, 21).

Such happenings transformed indigenous workers into key players in the churches. "The fact that over three hundred of the choicest young men in our educational institutions have consecrated their lives to the work of the ministry, believing that they are called by the Holy Spirit, and that even a larger number of the young women have pledged themselves to Christian work," noted Methodist bishop Frank Warne in India, "is one fruit of the revival that has given us great joy" (Warne 1907, 29–30). In colonies such as British India revivals further contextualized the faith and prepared the churches for national independence.

As the Edinburgh delegates enthusiastically sang "Jesus Shall Reign" and pondered the future, the pillars of Christendom already had begun to tilt as the gravity of Christianity steadily shifted to the southern hemisphere. The demise of colonialism after mid-century and the independence of mission-founded churches in Africa and Asia, now shorn of Western financial support, also began to challenge the equation of Christianity with Western culture.

MISSION AND CHRISTIAN UNITY

Though the Western nations soon would draw their sabers, the Edinburgh conference unveiled the potential of what international Christian cooperation might accomplish in bringing about the kingdom of God on earth. To plant the church—seen in this light as virtually identical in nature to the kingdom—in all the non-Christian lands, the conference emphasized planning and strategy. In his closing speech Mott declared, "The end of the Conference is the beginning of the conquest. The end of the planning is the beginning of the doing" (Latourette 1967, 362).

To carry their plans forward, the delegates approved the formation of the Continuation Committee that in 1921 became the International Missionary Council (IMC). The Edinburgh conference birthed not only international missionary cooperation, but also the ecumenical movement, with the IMC bringing together national and regional interdenominational mission organizations, as well as councils of churches, from around the world (Hogg 1952, 202–43).

Heralding the news of the kingdom of God now involved more than simply preaching the gospel; the responsibilities of Christians in the marketplace had to be addressed. "Given the missionary focus and international connections of the student Christian movements before World War I," writes historian Dana Robert, "it was a logical though not uncontested step for the younger generation to merge the missionary agenda into the internationalism of the postwar period" (Robert 2002, 50–51). The notion of churches working together for peace and justice between the nations led to the formation of the Universal Christian Conference on Life and Work in Stockholm in 1925, commonly known as "Life and Work" (Ehrenström 1967, 545–52). Two years later the first conference of "Faith and Order" met in Lausanne to encourage churches to engage in theological discussions to resolve conflicts in the pursuit of unity in Christ (Tatlow 1967, 420–25). Envisioning a global council of churches that would include the younger churches, Faith and Order merged with Life and Work to form the World Council of Churches in Amsterdam in 1948. The IMC got on board in 1961.

Mainline Mission

Two missionary streams flowed through Edinburgh: mainline Protestant mission and conservative evangelical mission. Mainline mission at the time still generally held an evangelical theological consensus. Among its best-known missionaries stood Samuel Zwemer of the Reformed Church in America and E. Stanley Jones of the Methodist Church. Stationed at Bahrain in the Persian Gulf, Zwemer evangelized from Basra to Muscat. He spent a lifetime energetically promoting the evangelization of Muslims—being a veritable "steam engine in breeches," according to his friends. He helped to establish the American Arabian Mission, organized conferences on Muslim evangelism, wrote many books, and founded the journal *The Moslem World*. Late in life, in 1949, he visited the graves of his two daughters in Bahrain and remarked, "If we should hold our peace, these very [tomb] stones would cry out for evangelization of Arabia!" (Wilson 1986, 120).

Jones sailed to India in 1907. Discovering the need to evangelize high-caste intellectuals, he used methods familiar to Indian society, especially roundtable conferences and Christian ashrams where he participated in discussions with Hindu intellectuals on religious experience and understanding. "Christianity must be defined as Christ, not the Old Testament," he contended, "not Western civilization, not even the civilization built around him in the West, but Christ himself, and to be a Christian is to follow him. . . . Christ must be in the Indian setting. It must be the Christ of the Indian Road" (Taylor 1994, 340). Jones's legacy includes many books, but most importantly his means of contextualizing the gospel in Indian culture.

In the years after the Edinburgh conference liberal theology and the social gospel in the mainline churches, along with the enthusiasm for Christian internationalism, steadily moved their mission focus in the direction of humanitarianism and away from evangelism. Social action, or meeting social needs, rose above evangelism as a priority. Having replaced its theological focus with doubts about the legitimacy of world evangelization, the Student Volunteer Movement became a casualty of the transition when interest in its program dropped sharply in the 1920s.

Cracks in the Unity

Serious cracks in the unity of the mission movement already had surfaced in the pavement leading to Edinburgh. For example, when the organizers determined to include the Anglo-Catholic party in the Church of England and continental Lutherans, they bowed to their sensitivities and invited only representatives from agencies that sent missionaries to the non-Christian world (Pierson 1910, 561–63). This rankled many evangelicals because organizations that worked in Latin America were excluded. A significant group of evangelicals, primarily from North America, then organized the Panama Congress in 1916. Chaired by Presbyterian mission leader Robert Speer, it became a watershed in the advancement of mission in the region (Speer 1916, 249–59).

Protestant missionaries began to divide over doctrine and strategy, most bitterly in China during the 1920s and 1930s. (China represented the largest investment in personnel and funds in the history of Protestant mission, with over five thousand missionaries serving there by the mid-1920s.) A new generation of mainline missionaries embraced the liberal theology of the day, doubted the ultimate claims of Christianity and the infallibility of Scripture, and envisioned an alliance with the religions of the East. They preferred educational, medical, and charitable endeavors to evangelism (Xi 1997, 14). Some saw the answer to China's needs in socialism, even communism. The response of conservatives in the mainline mission and those in the interdenominational agencies came with the establishment of the Bible Union in 1920 (Hutchison 1987, 138–41). These and other events added to the fire of the Fundamentalist/Modernist controversy that raged through American Protestant denominations in the 1920s.

Tensions over the necessity of evangelism, as well as the issue of syncretism, boiled over again in 1932 with the report of the "Laymen's Foreign Missions Inquiry." Conducted by the Institute of Social and Religious Research in New York City, funded by the liberal Baptist John D. Rockefeller, and chaired by Harvard University philosophy professor William Hocking, the project examined missionary activities in India, Burma, China, and Japan (Xi 1997, 191–96). Evangelicals, both within and outside the mainline mission, expressed strong objections to the conclusions, which were published in condensed form in the widely read *Re-Thinking Missions* (1932). They complained about its call for an "overhaul" in missionary thinking, accommodation of Christianity with the Eastern religions, and de-emphasis on conversionary evangelism.

The inquiry's commission had sighed with relief that "Christianity has in the main shifted its stress from the negative to the affirmative side of its message; it is less a religion of fear and more a religion of beneficence." Furthermore, "there is little disposition to believe that sincere and aspiring seekers after God in other religions are to be damned" (Hocking 1932, 19). Controversy exploded not only in North America, but also in the corridors of the IMC. Professor Hendrik Kraemer of the University of Leiden in the Netherlands provided the IMC's response with his *Christian Message in a Non-Christian World* (1938).

Despite the decline of mainline mission, it had notably recognized the younger churches as equal partners, promoted indigenization, called attention to the importance of justice and human rights as they relate to mission, and pointed to the need for Christian unity as a witness before non-Christians (Neill 1986, 400–413).

ASCENDANCY OF EVANGELICAL MISSION

Although many of the mainline missionaries remained evangelical, their movement as a whole ran out of energy after mid-century. In contrast, conservative evangeli- cal missions surged forward in scope of operations and number of personnel. For example, in Africa they "leapfrogged" over the mainline missions concentrated on the coastal areas and successfully evangelized interior regions (Taber 1991, 123). Many of these missions adhered to premillennialism, an eschatological scenario that ticked with intense expectancy of Christ's return. As a result, they maintained a particularly strong concern for evangelism and church planting in their missionary work.

Innovative Methods

The determination and creativity of evangelical missionaries led many to experiment in methodology. William Cameron Townsend, on a visit to Guatemala selling Bibles, was challenged by a national who had only a limited knowledge of Spanish: "Why, if your God is so smart, hasn't he learned our language?" (Tucker 1983, 352). Recognizing the need for more translations, he cofounded the Summer Institute of Linguistics in 1936 and Wycliffe Bible Translators six years later. By the end of 2000 Wycliffe personnel had translated Scripture into more than twelve hundred languages. Convinced of the potential of radio evangelism, Clarence Jones started World Radio Missionary Fellowship and radio station HCJB ("Heralding Christ Jesus' Blessings") in Quito, Ecuador. The inaugural broadcast took place on Christmas Day in 1931. His vision of establishing a radio station in Latin America—called "Jones's folly" by skeptics—bore fruit in reaching a worldwide audience.

Another successful venture came with Mission Aviation Fellowship (MAF). Betty Greene, who had served during World War II with the Women's Air Service Pilots, cofounded MAF and became its first field pilot in 1945 (Tucker 1983, 395–98). It offered valuable services for missionaries, native church workers, and medical patients in need of air transportation. On the ground in Central America Kenneth Strachan developed "Evangelism-in-Depth," a strategy for "saturation evangelism" based on the mobilization of all Christians in a country to witness for Christ.

Guatemala missionaries Ralph Winter and James Emery launched a new program in ministerial training in 1963 when they conceived a plan to provide church leaders with instructional materials where they lived. It became known as Theological Education by Extension (TEE). The combination of personal study and weekly seminars with tutors proved to be immensely popular around the world.

Cooperation in Mission

In some places the Edinburgh conference's call for cooperation fell on deaf ears. When the denominational representatives in the Foreign Missions Conference of North America refused to give full membership to the interdenominational and faith mission societies, the latter founded the Interdenominational Foreign Mission Association (IFMA) in 1917 (Frizen 1992, 103–10). Strongly critical of the liberal theology evident in the Foreign Missions Conference, the IFMA included conservative agencies such as the China Inland Mission, Central American Mission, Inland South America Missionary Union, Sudan Interior Mission, and Woman's Union Missionary Society, among others.

The National Association of Evangelicals (1943) created a mission affiliate for its constituent members in 1945: the Evangelical Fellowship of Mission Agencies (EFMA). More inclusive than the IFMA, it welcomed both denominational and nondenominational boards and pulled together a broader variety of traditions: Baptist, Reformed, Mennonite, Wesleyan, and Pentecostal (Coggins 1984, 1–7). In the ensuing years the IFMA and EFMA worked together on projects such as founding the Evangelical Missions Information Service ([EMIS] publishers of *Evangelical Missions Quarterly* and *World Pulse*). The Billy Graham Evangelistic Association, in cooperation with a wide range of evangelical organizations, initiated and organized the Congress on the Church's Worldwide Mission, held at Wheaton College in 1966; the World Congress on Evangelism at Berlin in 1966; the Lausanne Congress on World Evangelization in Switzerland in 1974; and the International Conference for Itinerant Evangelists in Amsterdam in 1983. Another association, the World Evangelical Alliance (formerly World Evangelical Fellowship), has also strongly promoted mission since its beginning in 1951 (Fuller 1996, 25–37).

Though fundamentalist organizations joined the IFMA, others with a stronger separatist orientation remained aloof from both the IFMA and the EFMA. Agencies such as the Independent Board for Presbyterian Foreign Missions, established in 1933 at the height of the Fundamentalist/Modernist controversy by conservative Presbyterians including theologian J. Gresham Machen, and Baptist Mid-Missions aligned with The Associated Missions. This agency works with the International Council of Christian Churches founded by Carl T. McIntire and other fundamentalists at Amsterdam in 1948 (Dollar 1973, 179–80).

Parachurch Ministries

Signs of evangelical vigor appeared in the founding of more parachurch organizations. InterVarsity Christian Fellowship originated in Great Britain, with college chapters devoted to advancing evangelism and mission. From there its influence spread to Canada and then the United States in 1941. Just as the Student Volunteer Movement once had inspired college and university students to become missionaries, InterVarsity continued that tradition through its triennial Urbana Missionary Conferences at the Urbana campus of the University of Illinois, which have attracted altogether hundreds

> *The way I see it, we ought to be willing to die. In the military, we were taught that to obtain our objectives we had to be willing to be expendable. Missionaries must face that same expendability.*
>
> Nate Saint
> (Hefley and Hefley 1981, 17)

of thousands of students. Its work has been augmented by the International Fellowship of Evangelical Students founded in 1947. Other organizations centering on youth have included Campus Crusade for Christ, The Navigators, Operation Mobilization, and Youth With a Mission, with all having international ministries.

One of the largest parachurch endeavors, World Vision, came into existence in 1950. Deeply affected by the spiritual and physical needs of the people that he encountered in post–World War II China and Korea, Bob Pierce founded the agency to promote evangelism, sponsor orphans, build hospitals, aid refugees, and provide relief to war

and disaster victims (Graham and Lockerbie 1983, 68–77). In the area of education, the International Council for Evangelical Theological Education was born in 1980 to raise institutional standards for Bible institutes, Bible colleges, and seminaries outside North Atlantic countries.

Dying for Christ

Mission never has progressed without suffering and martyrdom. One of the most dramatic episodes occurred in Ecuador. Five missionaries from the United States (Nate Saint, Ed McCully, Jim Elliot, Peter Fleming, and Roger Youderian) who had been working with other indigenous peoples decided to reach the Auca with the gospel. Initial contacts appeared to be friendly, but on Sunday, January 8, 1956, the missionaries were speared to death at their encampment. Fortunately, the story did not end there. When news of the tragedy reached North America, over one thousand collegians volunteered for mission service (Water 2001, 901). Missionary efforts continued with the help of Rachel Saint (sister of Nate Saint) and Elizabeth Elliot (widow of Jim Elliot); the Aucas eventually accepted the gospel message.

Martyrs in other countries included medical doctor Paul Carlson, who died during the Congo uprising in the early 1960s. At the height of the turmoil in 1964 he was tortured and then fatally shot while trying to escape from the Simba rebels (Tucker 1983, 425–29). In another area of the Congo they clubbed to death missionary J. W. Tucker and threw his body into the crocodile-infested Bomokandi River. Sometime later, when a convert of Tucker's told the Mangbetu of Nganga—a people previously unresponsive to the gospel—that his body "had

146

been thrown into 'their' river" and his "blood had flowed through 'their' waters," the news troubled them deeply. "The Holy Spirit used this belief in the Mangbetu culture which considers the land and rivers where they live to be theirs personally," wrote missionary Derrill Sturgeon. "Now they *must* listen to the message of the one who had been thrown into their water. This proved to be the key to their hearts" (Sturgeon 1986, 11).

PENTECOSTALISM

In the last decades of the nineteenth century "radical evangelicals"—Christians aligned with the Wesleyan-Holiness and Higher Life movements—prayed for unusual manifestations of supernatural power to accomplish the evangelization of the world. Frustrated by the slow pace of

> *Since the church has lost her faith in a great measure in the supernatural signs and workings of the Holy Ghost, she has lost the signs also, and the result is that she is compelled to produce conviction upon the minds of the heathen very largely by purely rational and moral considerations and influences, and the direct appeal to the supernatural power of God, which the apostles ever made, is rarely witnessed.*
>
> A. B. Simpson (1892, 389)

conversions in the mission lands—only 3.6 million Protestant Christians were counted in 1900—and the seemingly ineffective mission practices of the day, they prayed for the return of the "signs and wonders" (Acts 5:12) that had characterized the expansion of the

early church (Beach 1906, 19). For some, this meant that missionaries should pray for the sick; miracles of healing would then be a witness of God's power to non-Christians (Simpson 1915, 54–58). They also looked to intercessory prayer for spiritual victory in the cosmic realm to pin down satanic forces that resist the evangelization of the nations. Others believed that if they had sufficient faith, God might bestow on missionaries the "gift of tongues" (unlearned languages). This would enable them to bypass the nuisance of language school and begin preaching as soon as they reached their destination, reflecting the urgency of premillennialists since little time remained to preach the gospel (McGee 2001b, 118–23).

Pentecostal Beginnings

In a noteworthy development, Kansas Holiness preacher Charles Parham became convinced in the fall of 1900 that Holy Spirit baptism with the gift of tongues—an experience of grace after conversion—would bring spiritual empowerment and linguistic expertise. This then would remove the last barrier for the speedy evangelization of the world (Goff 1988, 62–79). When revival began at his Bethel Bible School in Topeka, Kansas, in January 1901, students testified that God had given them the languages of the world (e.g., Swahili and Hindi). Other influential revivals occurred several years later in California, India, Norway, South Africa, and Chile. At the multicultural Azusa Street Revival (1906–9) in Los Angeles led by the African-American William Seymour, whites, blacks, and Hispanics all worshiped together, a novelty in a largely segregated culture (Bartleman 1980, 54). Azusa Street highlighted not only power to witness, but also reconciliation and the Spirit's conferral of dignity on the downtrodden. Years later it became an inspiration to Christians living under various forms of oppression (LaPoorta 1999, 151–69).

As a movement within the broader evangelical tradition, Pentecostalism not only held firmly to historic Christian doctrine, but also pressed to recapture the apostolic dimension of the New Testament church. Other movements also had emphasized the

> *The power of God now has [Los Angeles] agitated as never before. Pentecost has surely come and with it the Bible evidences are following, many being converted and sanctified and filled with the Holy Ghost, speaking in tongues as they did on the day of Pentecost. The scenes that are daily enacted in the building on Azusa street and at Missions and churches in other parts of the city are beyond description, and the real revival is only started, as God has been working with His children mostly, getting them through to Pentecost, and laying the foundation for a mighty wave of salvation among the unconverted.*
>
> *Apostolic Faith*
> ("Pentecost Has Come" 1906, 1)

ministry of the Holy Spirit, especially the Wesleyan-Holiness and Higher Life movements, from which Pentecostalism emerged. However, they did not anticipate the restoration of speaking in tongues for every believer or the full-scale return of the gifts of the Spirit (Dayton 1987, 87–113). Linking the work of the Holy Spirit to mission in an unprecedented fashion, Pentecostals expected

that as Spirit-filled believers preached the gospel and prayed for the sick, demonstrations of miraculous power would follow and liberate people from the bondage of evil. Not surprisingly, Pentecostal periodicals carried thousands of stories of conversions, healings, exorcisms, and deliverances from chemical addictions at home and abroad (McGee 2001a, 71).

Lightning in a Bottle

Over the century, Pentecostalism in its various forms produced the second largest family of Christians after the Roman Catholic Church, one that transcends traditional walls of separation between Christians. What accounts for this dramatic growth? According to historian Grant Wacker, "The genius of the Pentecostal movement lay in its ability to hold two seemingly incompatible impulses in productive tension": New Testament restorationism and pragmatism. This "enabled them to capture lightning in a bottle and, more important, to keep it there, decade after decade, without stilling the fire or cracking the vessel" (Wacker 2001, 10). The focus on human encounter with the Holy Spirit and a remarkable willingness to use every possible means to spread the gospel has distinguished the movement. When Pentecostal missionaries experienced disappointment with their newfound languages, they persevered in the belief that speaking in tongues—now understood as prayer in the Spirit (1 Cor. 14:14)—brought spiritual power. This modification denoted their confidence in the transforming nature of the experience, fundamental zeal for evangelism and missions, and pragmatism about the means to accomplish their objective of evangelization.

The story of the Swedish-American missionaries Daniel Berg and Adolf Gunnar Vingren further illustrates the relationship of Pentecostal spirituality with mission. During a Saturday night prayer service in South Bend, Indiana, an elder prophesied over Vingren and later over Berg the same message: God wanted them to go to "Para" and preach the gospel. Convinced that this came as a directive from the Lord, but not knowing the place mentioned, they visited the Chicago Public Library. An atlas showed the location as the northeastern coastal state of Pará in Brazil. In 1910 they departed for the capital city of Belém, where they began their ministry—on faith, without pledged support. While Vingren engaged in pastoral work, Berg worked as a foundry man in a steel mill and with his earnings paid for their living expenses and lessons in the Portuguese language. From the labors of Berg and Vingren, as well as the work of the Italian-American Luigi Francescon in the south, Pentecostalism, with its emphasis on the supernatural dimension of Christian living and evangelism, grew to encompass millions of believers (Stewart-Gambino and Wilson 1997, 229–30).

Because of its attention to spiritual gifts, Pentecostalism has been contextualized easily in Latin America, Africa, and Asia. Adapting Pentecostal spirituality to indigenous church principles led to spectacular church growth, particularly after mid-century as missionaries handed leadership responsibilities over to indigenous Christians. The Spirit's direct conferral of leadership gifts also generated independent leaders and movements that have seen rapid expansion (Satyavrata 1999, 206–7). All that a believer required was the calling and infilling of the Spirit before launching out and starting her or his own congregation. This also opened the door for women because Joel's prophecy included them. Missiologist Melvin Hodges perhaps described the phenomenon best: "The faith which Pentecostal people have in the ability of the Holy Spirit to give spiritual gifts and supernatural abilities to the common people . . . has raised up a host of lay preachers and leaders of unusual spiritual ability—not unlike the rugged fishermen who first followed the Lord" (Hodges 1953, 132–33).

Charismatic Renewal

Beginning in the 1950s and 1960s "Pentecostal" movements arose among mainline Protestants, Roman Catholics, and, to a lesser extent, Eastern Orthodox Christians (Hocken 2002, 479–85). The "charismatic renewal" quickly attained global dimensions, and features of its spirituality could be found in large sectors of Christianity. Today, an unprecedented number of evangelicals, from Lutherans in Ethiopia to Presbyterians in Korea, pray for the sick, engage in charismatic worship (singing of praise choruses, lifting of hands, clapping), and seek for the spiritual gifts (Christenson 1987, 369–70; Shim 1998, 120–23). Although many charismatic Christians have not embraced all the teachings of the Pentecostal movement, the breadth of the renewal indicates that twentieth-century Pentecostalism challenged virtually every branch of Christianity to review its understanding of the role of the Holy Spirit in the life and mission of the church.

In the Roman Catholic Church the renewal has strongly supported the "New Evangelization" called for by Pope John Paul II. According to theologian Avery Dulles, "The evangelical shift brought about by Vatican II, Paul VI, and the present pope

149

is one of the most dramatic developments in modern Catholicism" (Dulles 1995, 32). Catholic evangelization in some areas has been marked by signs and wonders and resulted in improved relationships with evangelicals (Ganaka 1995, 108). In southern India, tens of thousands of Indians have visited the Divine Retreat Centre north of Cochin for the gospel and healing services of the Catholic evangelist Mathew Naickomparambil—called by some the "Billy Graham of India" (Duin 1994, 88).

The Third Wave

By the 1980s, interest in charismatic spirituality had grown in conservative evangelical ranks, notably in the spiritual gifts, prayer for the sick, and the usefulness of exorcisms. As the movement grew, insiders called it the "Third Wave" of the Holy Spirit (Wagner 1988, 15–19) (leaders shied away from identification with the Pentecostal and charismatic movements, believed to be the first two waves). C. Peter Wagner traces the roots back to the early 1980s when John Wimber, pastor of the Vineyard Christian Fellowship in Anaheim, California, began lecturing with him at Fuller Theological Seminary's School of World Mission. Wimber's lecture, "Signs, Wonders and Church Growth," eventually developed into the popular course "The Miraculous and Church Growth." Though provoking dissent at Fuller (Smedes 1987, 62–70) and beyond, it generated widespread interest among evangelicals previously resistant to Pentecostal spirituality.

Wimber's books *Power Evangelism* (1986) and *Power Healing* (1987) were particularly influential, as were others by Charles Kraft (*Christianity with Power* [1989]), Timothy Warner (*Spiritual Warfare* [1991]), Jack Deere (*Surprised by the Power of the Spirit* [1993]), and C. Peter Wagner (*Confronting the Powers* [1996]). They variously highlighted "power encounters," "strategic-level spiritual warfare," and "spiritual mapping" in evangelism and mission. The views of these proponents on "spiritual warfare" have exceeded those held by nineteenth-century radical evangelicals (McGee 1997, 90–95). By the 1990s, the spotlight turned to a new form of restorationism: the "New Apostolic Restoration" of Christianity. Complete with apostles and prophets, this represents, advocates believe, "the most radical change in the way of doing church since the Protestant Reformation" (Wagner 2000a, 21–22).

Not since the first-century church has so much importance been placed upon the role of the Holy Spirit in mission. While the lines between North American Pentecostals and evangelicals blurred over the course of the twentieth century, others ministering within the Pentecostal/charismatic tradition have continued to press for an ever more radical restoration of New Testament practices.

VATICAN COUNCIL II AND CATHOLIC MISSION

In 1925 Rome witnessed the greatest display of missionary curios ever assembled in the history of Christian mission. The "Vatican Mission Exposition" promised to be a "window on the world" for visitors. Over twenty exhibition halls sported items such as elephant tusks from Africa, a Chinese altar to the Goddess of Mercy, a hut from Ecuador, a hall devoted to the contributions of medical science in treating tropical diseases, pictures of famous persons and events, and statues of heroes such as Jean Théophane Vénard and Cardinal Lavigerie. "The day of a mass movement by Catholics of the world, for the winning of the thousand million souls still unconverted, is only now dawning," lauded one promoter of the event, "and the . . . Exposition is the aurora in the sky" (Considine 1925, 28).

Despite the triumphant prospect, Catholic missions struggled with many of the same problems that faced Protestant missions. European clergy dominated the mission churches, little progress had been made in indigenizing the faith and worship, and Catholic authorities invariably aligned themselves with conservative forces in society that resisted social change and land reform. Finally, because of the minimal progress in preparing an indigenous clergy by 1919, Pope Benedict XV lamented, "There are still countries where the Catholic faith has been preached for several centuries, but where you will find no indigenous clergy, except of an inferior kind" (Barry 1985, 1236).

Fifty-five years after the Vatican exposition, on March 24, 1980, in a church in El Salvador, a bullet fatally wounded Archbishop Oscar Romero as he celebrated Mass (Brockman 1989, 245). In a nation torn by civil war Romero had become a champion of the poor and an advocate of justice, much to the displeasure of fellow clerics, government officials, and right-wing "death squads." Romero's martyrdom dramatically showed how much the understanding of mission had changed.

Conversation with the World

The Second Vatican Council (1962–65) profoundly affected the outlook of the Catholic Church on the modern world, the contextualization of the faith, other Christians, and the non-Christian religions. The rise of religious skepticism in the Enlight-

enment, followed by the French Revolution and other revolutions in its wake, had pushed the church into a defensive posture (McSweeney 1980, 28–42). Confiscation of church property, anticlerical regimes in traditionally Roman Catholic countries, and increasing secularism undermined the church's role as the guardian of Christian culture. Little wonder that Pope Pius IX, in his famous *Syllabus of Errors* published in 1864, censured critics who said that "the Roman pontiff can and ought to harmonize himself with progress, with liberalism, and with modern civilization" (Barry 1985, 996). One hundred years later the issues of the modern world no longer could be ignored. Rather than attacking the world, the church would now engage it in conversation.

Vatican II impacted mission in several ways, two of which will be examined here. First, the council broadened the scope of those who will be redeemed. In an extraordinary action it referred to Protestant and Eastern Orthodox Christians as "separated brethren" in whom the Holy Spirit is at work (Abbott 1966, 346–49). Furthermore, the council recognized that those who have not yet heard the gospel have a relationship to the "people of God" in some fashion: "Those also can attain to everlasting salvation who through no fault of their own do not know the gospel of Christ or His Church, yet sincerely seek God and, moved by grace, strive by their deeds to do His will as it is known to them through the dictates of conscience" (Abbott 1966, 35). Hence, sincere seekers after God (Heb. 11:6) who have never heard the gospel in this life ultimately will be saved in the mystery of Christ.

To some extent, the aggressive conversionary evangelism championed at the exhibition gave way to interreligious dialogue because varying measures of truth could be found in all the non-Christian religions. This created a dilemma for Catholic mission and resulted in a lessened emphasis on traditional evangelism, but it did not eliminate the importance of working toward conversions (Sullivan 1992, 167–68). "Christ knew that we live in a world of religious pluralism; that other religious leaders have promoted different ways to go to God," maintains missiologist Edward Le Joly, "and that people of good faith can obtain grace whilst following other paths than the one he indicated"; notwithstanding, "he commanded us to go to the whole world to preach the Word of God, to baptize, to consecrate to the Blessed Trinity all who would receive his message with open hearts and obedient wills" (Le Joly 1986, 26–27). For Catholics and many Protestants alike, the eternal state of those who never heard the gospel "through no fault of their own" remains a vexing theological and missiological issue (Erickson 1991, 33). We will return to this issue in chapter 18.

Liberating the Oppressed

Equally controversial, but with stronger political and social overtones, the council affirmed, "Whoever in obedience to Christ seeks first the kingdom of God will as a consequence receive a stronger and purer love for helping all his brothers and for perfecting the work of justice under the inspiration of charity" (Abbott 1966, 282). That the mission of the church included working toward social justice, land reform, and helping the poor represented a seismic shift away from the defensive posture of the nineteenth century. Indeed, "those who are oppressed by poverty, infirmity, sickness, or various other hardships, as well as those who suffer persecution for justice' sake—may they all know that in a special way they are united

with the suffering Christ for the salvation of the world" (Abbott 1966, 70).

Catholic missions have a long record of ministering to the suffering, with none more famous in recent years than the Albanian missionary Mother Teresa. Called to work amongst the "poorest of the poor" in Calcutta, she founded the Missionaries of Charity to assist in her endeavors. Missionaries such as Frédéric-Vincent Lebbe in China ardently worked to indigenize the Catholic faith into local cultures despite intense criticism. However, "liberation theology" represented the most successful attempt at contextualizing the faith after the council, combining compassion for the suffering with social and political activism. Beginning in

> Let the poor, seeing you, be drawn to Christ. Poverty makes people very bitter, and they speak and act without realizing what they do. But do they remember Christ when they see you—even if they get angry—because you remind them of Christ?
>
> Draw them to God but never, never to yourself. If you are not drawing them to God, then you are seeking yourself, and people love you for yourself and not because you remind them of Christ.
>
> Mother Teresa
> (Thomas 1995, 167–68)

Latin America, its influence spread around the world. To put the ideals of the council into practice, Latin American bishops met in 1968 at Medellín in Colombia, where they shifted the focus of the church from the hierarchy to the laity, condemned political oppression, grieved over the harsh poverty of most Latin Americans, and highlighted physical and spiritual liberation (Dussell 1976, 113–16). Along with the conference, a book by Peruvian theologian Gustavo Gutiérrez, *A Theology of Liberation* (1973), set the movement in motion.

Unlike the traditional method of formulating theology, liberation theology started with where the people lived. Catholic laity met in small groups known as "base Christian communities" to study Scripture, re-

> *The Christian life is a Passover, a transition from sin to grace, from death to life, from injustice to justice, from the subhuman to the human. Christ introduces us by the gift of his Spirit into communion with God and all men. More precisely, it is because he introduces us into this communion, into a continuous search for its fullness, that he conquers sin—which is the negation of love—and all its consequences.*
>
> Gustavo Gutiérrez (1973, 176)

flect on their circumstances, and consider what action might be taken to change their world. Liberation theology's call to alleviate the suffering of the masses triggered the hostility of elements in society with vested interests in maintaining the existing social order. In effect, it challenged the form of Christendom that had survived in Latin America—the marriage of ecclesiastical and political elites—which through economic and political policies dehumanized millions of people and repressed all their hopes for a better life. "The evangelical witness which the world finds most appealing is that of concern for people, and of charity towards the poor, the weak and those who suffer," wrote John Paul II in his encyclical *The Mission of the Redeemer;* "the complete generosity underlying this attitude and these actions stands in marked contrast to human selfishness" (John Paul II 1990, 73). Illustrating the evil that human selfishness can produce, the assassin who had intended to silence Romero once and for all in fact created the best-known martyr of liberation theology.

Evangelicals, too, began to look more favorably on the relationship of the gospel to social action. Opinions have varied, from those who remain suspicious that social action will replace the value set on gospel proclamation, to those who have called for even more involvement in society. Leading proponents have included Orlando Costas, author of *Christ Outside the Gate: Mission Beyond Christendom* (1982), and Ronald Sider, author of *Rich Christians in an Age of Hunger* (1990). From within the furnace of conflict in South Africa, Anglican Archbishop Desmond Tutu received the Nobel Peace Prize in 1984 for his efforts to end apartheid. A fellow countryman, Pentecostal pastor Frank Chikane, was arrested by civil authorities for his political activities. During his imprisonment he underwent torture, ironically at the hands of a white deacon in his denomination—a sad commentary on how Christianity can become captive to a culture (Chikane 1988, 126–28).

GLOBAL MISSION ADVANCE

Never before in the history of Christianity had so much attention been placed on mission and missions than in the latter half of the twentieth century. Missiologists such as Donald McGavran (*The Bridges of*

153

God [1955]) explored the many aspects of presenting the Christian message in cross-cultural contexts and what factors produced church growth. The vastness and many shapes of Christianity became evident in David Barrett's *World Christian Encyclopedia* (1982). Moreover, world conferences, schools, academic societies, journals, and books wielded considerable influence on the mission enterprise.

Strategy figured strongly in the work of world conferences. At the Lausanne Congress on World Evangelization in 1974, Ralph Winter challenged delegates to evangelize the vast number of "unreached peoples" and make the global church aware of the existence of people groups still untouched by established churches and mission agencies. To his disappointment, many Christian organizations, "ranging widely from the World Council of Churches to many U.S. denominations, even some evangelical groups," have concluded that traditional missionary work has become obsolete. Instead, "local Christians everywhere" should continue the witness for Christ (Winter 1975, 213). "Far from being a task that is now out-of-date," declared Winter, "the shattering truth is that at least four out of five non-Christians in the world today are beyond the reach of *any* Christian's . . . evangelism" (Winter 1975, 221). This surprised many evangelicals and sometime later led to the forming of the "A.D. 2000 Movement" with its emphasis on evangelizing the 10/40 Window, which comprises the least evangelized part of the world (Coote 2000, 160–66).

Far from the auditoriums of world conferences and the boardrooms of mission agencies, grassroots North American and European evangelicals have displayed an unflagging commitment to mission.

Whether through funding missionaries or going themselves on short-term mission assignments, the scope of their involvement has been impressive: street evangelism, church construction, food distribution, and medical assistance. With the world becoming a global village and thousands of foreign students enrolled in American colleges and universities, visionary campus ministries have looked at their potential for ministry. For example, Chi Alpha Campus Ministries not only works to convert and disciple students, but also prepares them to evangelize when they return home.

Despite this vitality, the Western nations of the now defunct Christendom have continued to slide into secularism. However, missiologist Lesslie Newbigin rejects this notion. The West has not simply become secular, but pagan. Furthermore, "its paganism, having been born out of the rejection of Christianity, is far more resistant to the gospel than the pre-Christian paganism with which cross-cultural missions have been familiar. Here, surely, is the most challenging missionary frontier of our time" (Newbigin 1986, 20). Indeed, the North Atlantic countries had become mission fields themselves.

SHIFTING GRAVITY

The great surprise at the end of the twentieth century came with the realization that the gravity of Christianity had shifted to the southern hemisphere, signaling the end of Euramerican domination. Birthed in the Jewish world, raised in Greco-Roman culture, and then exported to Europe, Christianity now has experienced a third massive cultural change: southward and eastward. Alongside historic beliefs and practices stand new forms of the Christian faith at the beginning of the third millennium.

Today, the world's largest congregations can be found in countries such as Brazil, Nigeria, and Korea, where their memberships number in the tens and sometimes even hundreds of thousands. But, whether large or small, denominational or independent, non-Western mission boards and individual churches send thousands of their own missionaries: Brazilians to North America and Angola; Koreans to East Africa; Singaporeans to China and Africa; Africans to Europe; Indians to the Middle East; Pacific Islanders to Central America; and Latin Americans to Africa and Asia. With this robust vigor has come theological reflection. If missionaries championed the "three self's," these Christians have explored the fourth: "self-theologizing." They have also taken keen interest in the ministry of the Holy Spirit, resulting in millions of Christians worldwide sharing features of Pentecostal spirituality (Barrett 2001, 385). The significance of indigenous Christians contextualizing the faith and its implications for doctrine, spirituality, ecclesiastical authority, and traditional rites within their cultures cannot be underestimated for the future development of Christianity.

Missionary J. Herbert Kane remembered that Chinese believers in Anhwei province grew weary of the China Inland Mission hymnal, even though singing from it only on Sunday mornings. The imagery of songs such as "Down in the Valley," "Rock of Ages," and "Jesus, Savior, Pilot Me" made little sense to Kane's audience; they lived on a vast plain, had never seen stones larger than a human fist, and had no conception of what an ocean was like. The coming of an indigenous movement known as the "Jesus Family" brought hundreds of short new songs set to native tunes that became immensely popular. Easily sung without a piano or organ and thoroughly Chinese in expression, they could be understood by the illiterate and the educated alike and were sung at home, on the roads, and in the fields (Kane 1947, 22–23). The story of mission in the twentieth century ends with the sound of Christians around the world singing the "great Redeemer's praise" in a myriad of songs, languages, and cultural expressions.

CONCLUSION

Christian expansion over the centuries resulted from the dedicated labors of uncounted missionaries and laypersons determined to carry the gospel into all the world for the redemption of humankind. The foundation set out here in chapters 6, 7, and 8 gives us solid footing for encountering the practical life of missionaries—the focus of the remaining parts in the book.

Encountering Missions as a Candidate

C alling, preparing, and going—all are important steps for the missionary candidate. In this section we explore each of these three in turn.

In chapter 9 we consider several important questions about the missionary call: What is it? Does it even exist? If not, then why do missionaries talk about it so much, and how does God guide Christians into service? If you have been called into full-time Christian ministry, what further guidance do you need to determine where God would have you serve? Is there more than one call? In this chapter we explore these and other important questions related to your calling into God's service.

Chapter 10 focuses on what happens after you sense that God would have you serve him cross-culturally: How do you get ready? Is training really necessary? What types of training are best? Where can you get training? These and other issues about preparing to become a missionary receive our attention in this chapter.

In chapter 11, the final one in this part, we explore what it takes to get from where you are now to where you will serve: What are the important things for you to look for if you go with a mission agency? What other options are available for getting to a cross-cultural setting? What are the possibilities and potential hazards of the various options? How can you make a good choice? This chapter offers insights into the many options that are available for missionary service today.

9

First Steps:
Have You Been Called?

INTRODUCTION

One of the more mysterious areas of mission is that of "the call." What is a call? What does it involve? What are the theological principles behind the idea of a call to missionary service? In fact, some people question whether the idea of a missionary call is even defensible. J. Herbert Kane, missionary educator, expressed his frustration with the mystery surrounding the idea:

> The term *missionary call* should never have been coined. It is not Scriptural and therefore can be harmful. Thousands of youth desiring to serve the Lord have waited and waited for some mysterious "missionary call" that never came. After a time they became weary in waiting and gave up the idea of going to the mission field. (Kane 1978b, 41)

Kane was not ready to throw away the term, but he was tired of the misunderstandings tied to it. In light of his comments, then, how can the questions that we pose above be answered? In this chapter we start with a personal story. Then we will explore some of the misunderstandings surrounding the

idea of call and look at what the Scriptures have to say about it. We conclude the chapter with several helpful guidelines related to the missionary call.

A PERSONAL STORY

Scott Moreau received his call to full-time Christian service quite unexpectedly. While in college, he regularly attended a noon prayer meeting sponsored by a Christian student ministry. One day during a prayer meeting he suddenly felt that he wasn't at the meeting. Instead, he was standing directly before God, who asked him, "What are you going to do with your electrical engineering degree?" The tone of the question led Scott to answer, "Nothing, I guess!" God's response? "It's time to get moving."

The next thing Scott knew, he was back in the group and they were closing the meeting in prayer. He had never physically left the room, and he wasn't sure whether he had had a vision or simply fell asleep and dreamed. Whatever the answer, he realized that it was time to move to a college that offered more solid theological training than did the state university he attended at the time.

Was Scott's experience a vision or a dream? Having had plenty of sleep the night before, and generally not being a nap-taker, Scott wondered what had happened. Eventually, he realized that the answer to that question was not very important. What was important was that he was convinced that God had called him into ministry.

He told his friends what had happened, and he began the process of transferring to another school where he could get some foundational ministry training. The next semester, he enrolled at Wheaton College as a junior.

Over the next two years God slowly began to make Scott aware of mission as an option for fulfilling the call he had received. Scott's initial dramatic experience was not repeated. Instead, he felt a quiet, persistent drawing that took place through a growing interest in missionary service, an excitement about an opportunity to connect his undergraduate training in a meaningful way in another part of the world, and enthusiasm generated through people who were experienced and who could offer meaningful advice. The general issue of "career focus" or vocation was dealt with in a dramatic experience; the specific issues of location, "career path," and organization were resolved more in gradual growth and development.

Is Scott's experience a normal one? Should every Christian expect some type of dramatic vision as a call to ministry? To answer those questions, we first need to explore some common misunderstandings about the missionary call.

MISUNDERSTANDINGS ABOUT THE MISSIONARY CALL

Many wrong ideas about the missionary call are found among Christians today. It will help to identify them and respond to each briefly before seeing what the Scriptures have to say. To spur your own thinking, sidebar 9.1 provides quotations from several mission leaders through history. They offer a wide spectrum of perspectives on the missionary call.

Misunderstanding 1: The Call Is a Definite Event

Scott's story, told at the beginning of this chapter, is an example of what some believe to be a typical missionary call. His call, however, was to full-time service rather than to missionary work. In fact, it was another two years before Scott realized that the place of service that God apparently had for him was outside of North American borders. The term *call* is perhaps not the best one to describe the leading that he received to go to Africa; the word *guidance* might be a better fit. Sometimes guidance comes in a flash of light, a dramatic insight, or a miracle such as a vision or dream. At other times it comes simply through a gentle but undeniable tug on the heart to be involved in a certain part of the world or with a certain people or in a certain type of role. It might start with a growing interest in a current event. It might come through prayer as guidance is sought from God. It sometimes happens that a friend mentions something in a way that strikes you, and you can't forget it or let go of it as it grows in importance in your thinking. To limit it to a dramatic event, however, is to limit God and how he actually deals with Christians.

Misunderstanding 2: Paul's Macedonian Call (Acts 16:9–10) Is a Model of the Missionary Call

On his second journey Paul had a vision in which a man from Macedonia appeared

SIDEBAR 9.1
THINKING ABOUT THE MISSIONARY CALL

Read the following quotations about the missionary call to see the variety of positions that people have taken on it. As you read them, and as you read this chapter, develop your own thesis statement about the missionary call—what it is and how it works.

Ion Keith-Falconer: "While vast continents are shrouded in darkness . . . the burden of proof lies upon you to show that the circumstances in which God has placed you were meant by God to keep you out of the foreign mission field" (Speer 1909, 190).

Isobel Kuhn: "I believe that [in] each generation God has 'called' enough men and women to evangelize all the yet unreached tribes of the earth. . . . Everywhere I go, I constantly meet with men and women who say to me, 'When I was young I wanted to be a missionary, but I got married instead.' Or, 'My parents dissuaded me,' or some such thing. No, it is not God who does not call. It is man who will not respond!" (Kuhn 1947, 224).

Thomas Hale: "Being a missionary begins with being called. You don't choose to be a missionary; you're called to be one. The only choice is whether to obey" (Hale 1995, 16).

Gordon Olson: "If we have a choice and unless there are compelling reasons to the contrary, the Christian worker should choose the place of greatest need! Failure to give adequate consideration to this factor has caused the incredible inequity in the distribution of workers" (Olson 1998, 86).

Alistair Brown: "No-one escapes the general call to mission. No-one can say, 'Witness is not for me.' The critical question is not whether we're called, for we are. The critical question is 'Where am I called to?' The answer may be to serve Jesus right where we are already, among those we live with and work beside. That is a wholly legitimate calling" (Brown 1997, 104).

Alistair Brown: "But a call isn't valid unless shared—like one person's guidance before marriage isn't to be accepted unless the intended partner gets the same guidance. In the case of mission there are lots of partners whose leading must all be the same. As well as the potential missionary, usually that's also his or her church, a mission agency, and a local church or union of churches in another country. All must believe the same. If they do that harmony of thought is persuasive evidence of God's will. Without it plans must be rethought" (Brown 1997, 110).

James Gilmour: "Even on the low ground of common sense I seemed to be called to be a missionary. Is the kingdom a harvest field? Then I thought it reasonable that I should seek to work where the work was most abundant and the workers fewest. . . . In place of seeking to assign a reason, for going abroad, I would prefer to say that I have failed to discover any reason why I should stay at home" (Gilmour 1895, 42–43).

Thomas Hale: "This distinction between God's 'general call' and his 'specific call' is very similar to the distinction between God's 'general will' as revealed in Scripture and his 'specific will' for the individual. God's general will (call) is that I be a witness. His specific will (call) is that I be a witness in Nepal, or Chicago, or wherever" (Hale 1995, 17).

to him and asked him to come. This event certainly was an important step in God's guidance of Paul on the journey. It showed Paul the next step to take in his full-time service of bringing the gospel to the Gentiles. However, it most definitely was not a call to missionary service—Paul already was a missionary. Those who teach that this call is a model for missionary service must go back to Luke's account, place the event in its actual context, see it for what it is, and stop spreading this unfortunate misunderstanding.

Misunderstanding 3: Calls to Missionary Service Always Come through Mystical Experiences

This misunderstanding frames the call in a mystical or emotional border. The border is seen as the main determiner that an experience is a valid call. In some Christian circles the teaching of a need for this type of call puts pressure on people who may very well (consciously or unconsciously) build themselves up and even manufacture an experience that they then mislabel a "call." Perhaps they see others around them being called and they don't want to be left behind. Maybe they feel that they are not special in God's eyes, and only this type of experience can help them connect to the desire they have for significance. Whatever the reason, believing that a mystical experience is a requirement of a call, they may embark on a journey to have or even generate the experience themselves.

Misunderstanding 4: You Cannot Become a Successful Missionary without a "Call"

Many factors determine the success of a missionary. It is just as easy to imagine the failure of a person who feels called, moves to a new culture, and proceeds to live a miserable life simply on the basis of this feeling as it is to imagine the failure of a person who goes to a new culture to minister without a clue as to what God actually intended. On the one hand, it is true that the memory of a dramatic experience can indeed give a person an anchor to cling to during times of trial. But on the other hand, that memory also can weigh that same person down in guilt or unrealistic expectations if he or she has an inappropriate view of what that "call"

really meant and who may have actually generated that "call."

In response to the belief in the necessity of a call, we point to the many believers who have served successfully in new cultural settings on the basis of deeply held biblical convictions rather than a well-defined experience of a call. Such convictions include the need of the lost to hear the gospel, the need to enable all peoples of the world to hear the message of Christ in a way that makes sense to them, and the privilege of serving as Christ's ambassadors. These convictions have impelled many into fruitful mission service. They can serve as an even greater anchor than an emotional experience because there is less need to doubt their interpretation when the going gets tough.

Misunderstanding 5: A Call Is the Best Test of Fitness for Missionary Service

In fact, a *misguided* sense of call may be the worst test of fitness for missionary service. Alistair Brown tells the following story to illustrate the point:

> Joe's an enthusiast. Reads his Bible, says his prayers, attends church meetings, talks to others about Jesus. He turns up on his minister's doorstep one day, saying he feels he should be a missionary. Minister is overjoyed. Church is overjoyed. They've never had one of their members become a missionary before. At last someone has offered to go. They recommend him warmly to a mission agency. The agency is impressed with Joe and the church's backing of Joe, and within a year he's off to win the world.
>
> Is that how the world's missionary force should be formed? It's often how it is. It has all sorts of dangers, not the least of which is that the church may be so enamoured of

the idea of Joe becoming a missionary, or so impressed with his sense of calling that they don't choose to tell the mission agency that Joe has started ten different projects in the last two years and never finished any of them. Nor do they mention that Joe is a smooth-talking charmer who has played havoc with the emotions of every young lady in the church, and that his sensitivity to people's feelings scores about minus 5 on a scale of 1 to 10. If they knew these things most mission agencies would instantly be hesitant. But, because Joe is so good with words and so confident of his calling, and because he comes with impeccable references from his church, they enrol him gladly and only find out the problems later. Those problems will come out, and usually worse than before. Place someone out of his own culture, alongside colleagues with whom he may have no natural affinity, and give him work to do which is stressful and often unfruitful, and personality flaws increase rather than reduce. Joe may well have a miserable time as a missionary, and cause big problems for others too. (Brown 1997, 105)

Although Joe is not a real person, his story accurately illustrates one of the complex factors that mission boards face: it is exceedingly difficult to discern motivations for missionary service. A putative call that is based on guilt or manipulation, the desire for significance or adventure, or simply a wish to escape a bad home situation probably will not stand the test of time. Motivations such as these, although strong enough to get a person to a cross-cultural setting, are insufficient to sustain him or her for fruitful service. Such motivations must be transformed by God or they will fall apart.

Although it is helpful to ensure that missionary candidates have a deeply embedded sense of God's work in their lives and that they sense his leading into full-time Christian service, better tests of fitness also will include an assessment of the candidate's understanding of God's heart for the nations, his or her dependence on God, the ability to adapt to new settings, flexibility, and a sense of what can be accomplished in ministry.

Misunderstanding 6: A Call to Full-Time Christian Service Is Given Only to Especially Gifted People

This misunderstanding parallels the misunderstanding of the missionary as a supersaint as described in chapter 1. The response to it is that God is the one in charge of who is called to full-time Christian service and who is not. With God's calling comes the equipping to accomplish what he has called a person to do. God does not limit his call to so-called supersaints, as is clearly seen in the apostles Peter and John, who are described by the Jewish leaders as "unschooled, ordinary men" (Acts 4:13).

Misunderstanding 7: A Call Is Completely Irrelevant to Becoming a Missionary

As we will see in the upcoming discussion of calling in the Bible, God calls *all* Christians into witnessing service for his kingdom. No one who claims allegiance to Christ escapes the Great Commission. However, God also leads some of those who have come to Christ into full-time service for the sake of the kingdom. A call is not irrelevant, but neither is it the final test of fitness. Rather, it is one piece in the larger picture of God's leading of his children into fruitful service.

163

Misunderstanding 8: A Call Involves Only God and the One Who Is Called

God has given to every Christian a community of believers who have mutual responsibilities toward each other. The community confirms God's leading, as it did with Paul and Barnabas. Some might argue that at times Paul went against the directions of the church, such as when he ignored the community's exhortations not to go to Jerusalem at the end of his third journey (Acts 21:7–14). It is true that in this case Paul overrode the will of the community, and there still are times today when God's leading is so clear that a person may have to do likewise. At the same time, however, over and over again in Paul's life Acts portrays the involvement of the church community in confirming God's leading. Barnabas introduced him to the church in Jerusalem, easing their fears (9:26–28). Barnabas later came to Tarsus and brought Paul to Antioch to help with the church there (11:19–26). The church at Antioch confirmed God's call on Paul prior to the first missionary journey (13:1–3). Paul reported to the Jerusalem church after the second and third missionary journeys (18:22; 21:17–19), and he followed the recommendations of the Jerusalem council between his second and third journeys (15:22–35). After his third journey he followed the advice of the Jerusalem elders to participate in a Jewish ritual (21:20–26). In these instances Paul's going against the church was an exception rather than the rule. The misunderstanding says, "God and I make a majority." The truth is that God gives every Christian the body of Christ as a resource to confirm his or her calling and leading. Whoever ignores this tremendous resource does so at their own risk!

CALLING IN THE BIBLE

Perhaps you sense that you have been called. Maybe you have had a visionary experience, or maybe you grew up simply knowing that you were to become a missionary. Or perhaps you have been feeling a growing conviction that you ought to be involved in God's work but aren't quite sure how that will be worked out. What are the ways God calls people into service? The best place to look for an answer is the Bible.

The Bible, however, does not provide an exposition of what should constitute a "call." Though there are several examples of calling, and various types of calling, there seems to be no single pattern or experience that fits them all. Some are miraculous. For example, Moses was called from a burning bush (Exod. 3); God told Joshua what his responsibilities were to be (Josh. 1:1–9); and Isaiah received his call in a vision (Isa. 6). By way of contrast, some calls come from divinely inspired but humanly made choices. Among the many examples we could mention, Nehemiah was distressed on hearing of the plight of Jews in Jerusalem, pouring out his heart to God (Neh. 1); Barnabas was sent by the Jerusalem church to Antioch (Acts 11:22); and Timothy accompanied Paul as a traveling companion because Paul wanted him to do so (Acts 16:3).

Although no single method is found, there are at least four types of calls seen in the Scriptures (the first three are mentioned in Peters 1972, 270–72), ranging from the broadest to the narrowest: (1) the call to salvation, (2) the call to discipleship or holiness, (3) the call to full-time ministry, and (4) the call to a specific assignment or task.

The Call to Salvation

Through Jesus, God calls people to enter into a relationship with him through salvation. Jesus came to call sinners to salvation (Matt. 9:13; Mark 2:17; Luke 5:32), and the writers of the New Testament use the same language to speak of our salvation experience (Acts 2:39; Rom. 1:5–6; 8:28–30; 1 Cor. 1:9, 24–26; 7:15–24; Gal. 1:6; 5:13; Eph. 1:18; 4:1–5; 1 Thess. 2:11–12; 1 Tim. 6:12; Heb. 3:1; 9:15; 1 Pet. 2:9; 5:10; 2 Pet. 1:10; Jude 1:1).

Admittedly, a point of controversy over the extent of this calling arises between those who follow the teaching of John Calvin and those who follow the teaching of Jakob Arminius. Though there are spectra of ap-

> *Would that God would make hell so real to us that we cannot rest; heaven so real that we must have men there; Christ so real that our supreme motive and aim shall be to make the Man of Sorrows the Man of Joy by the conversion to Him of many.*
>
> J. Hudson Taylor
> (Mueller 1947, 112)

proaches in both camps, Calvinists typically maintain that God's call is always effective, and therefore he calls only those who will respond to Christ (and those are the only ones for whom Christ died). Arminians, on the other hand, typically believe that God calls all people (and Christ died for all) but only some choose to respond. The question is far too complex to address fully here, but for our purposes we may say that whatever the actual extent of the call to salvation, it is the broadest of the four types of calls given by God.

The Call to Discipleship or Holiness

Those who have responded to God's call to salvation have a deeper call given by God: they are called to discipleship or holiness. Originating with the call to the apostles and culminating in Jesus' life with the Great Commission (especially Matt. 28:18–20), the call to a Christlike life is emphasized most clearly in the letters of Paul and Peter (e.g., 1 Cor. 1:2; 1 Thess. 4:7; 2 Thess. 2:13–15; 2 Tim. 1:9; 1 Pet. 2:21; 3:8–9; 2 Pet. 1:3).

In being called to become more like Christ, Christians have the responsibility to teach others to obey all that Jesus taught (Matt. 28:20). Consequently, a commitment to follow Christ involves at the heart a commitment to mission. If nothing else, this means at the very least that Christ's followers must be contagious agents carrying the "Jesus plague" (see sidebar 9.2).

This call is issued to all Christians. This is not to say that all Christians are "missionaries" in the narrow sense of the word or engaged in full-time service for the kingdom per se, but that all are to be involved in the process of growing to be like Jesus and helping others to do the same. To put it the way John Piper would, Christians better reflect God's glory and most effectively worship him when they fix their sights on enjoying God and find their deepest satisfaction in relating to and serving him (see Piper 1986).

The Call to Full-Time Ministry

God calls some Christians to serve him as their full-time vocation. Again, examples of various types of "full-time" lifelong calls can be found throughout the Scriptures. Abraham was called to leave his home, go to a new land that God would show him, and to be a blessing to the nations (Gen. 12:1–3;

SIDEBAR 9.2
PLAGUE-SPREADING CHRISTIANS

Jim Reapsome
(Reapsome 1999, 42–44 [used with permission])

Remember some of those old clichés we used to hear at missionary conferences: "You're either a mission field or a missionary!" "If you aren't called to stay, you're called to go!" I've often wondered how many people heard God's call despite the faulty theology of those well-meaning slogans. Anyway, I've come up with a new one that I think has some biblical validity: "Every Christian should be a plague-spreading Christian!"

Now that the plague has revisited the planet, we have a perfect model of how the gospel originally infected the world, and how it should continue to do so. The plague suddenly struck Surat, India, and despite frantic efforts it soon spread to other parts of the country. Now health officials at airports around the world are checking arrivals for the plague. Wouldn't it be something if Christians of all nations were so infectious with the gospel?

My point is that it's bunk to suggest Christians ought to go to the mission field if they're not called to stay home, or that anyone who is a Christian (i.e., not a mission field) is automatically a missionary. But it is gospel truth that all those who have been infected by the Jesus plague ought to pass it on to others. That doesn't make them missionaries, just obedient disciples of Jesus.

Somewhere along the line our thinking got badly fuzzed by the notion that anything we do for Jesus qualifies as "missionary" work. Your neighbor breaks his leg and you take him to the clinic. Does that make you a missionary? Of course not. It makes you a kind person, not a missionary.

Furthermore, our thinking also got scrambled by the heresy that only missionaries, pastors, and evangelists are carriers of the Jesus plague. That was a winner, because it conveniently excused hordes of Christians from their responsibility to spread the Jesus

---

cf. Acts 7:4; Heb. 11:8). Moses was called to join with God in setting the Israelites free from bondage in Egypt (Exod. 3). Jeremiah was called as a prophet to the nations before he was formed in his mother's womb (Jer. 1:4–10). Ezekiel was called through an awesome vision that drove him prostrate before God (Ezek. 1). The apostles were called by Jesus to leave their jobs and join him (e.g., Matt. 4:19; 9:9; Mark 1:17). Other examples of full-time service to God include Paul's calling as an apostle (Rom. 1:1; 1 Cor. 1:1; Gal. 1:15) and the high priest's calling to that office (Heb. 5:4).

Remembering that missionaries are "sent ones," we find that an examination of the term *send* sheds light on the concept of call. Jesus, of course, was himself sent by God

(Luke 4:18), and likewise he sends his followers (John 20:21). Similarly, he implores the disciples to pray that God send laborers into the harvest field (Matt. 9:35–38). Mark comments that the apostles were appointed so that they could be with Jesus *and* be sent to preach (Mark 3:14), and Paul notes that people will not hear the gospel unless preachers are sent (Rom. 10:14–15).

Two parables in particular also express the idea of God sending someone in service. In the parable of the vineyard, the owner (God) sends his servants (the prophets and, eventually, Jesus) to collect the fruit harvested by the tenants (Matt. 21:33–44; Mark 12:1–11). The king in the parable of the wedding banquet likewise sends servants to

plague, too. God does not call every believer to be a missionary, but he does call all of Christ's disciples to spread the Jesus plague.

One of the reasons Christians find it uncomfortable even to ask God if they should be missionaries is that they've never been good at spreading the Jesus plague. They like to cheer the plague spreaders to foreign shores, but please don't ask them to spread it to the folks next door. They get excited about an outbreak of the Jesus plague in Mauritania, but get mad when the Muslims take over their local Dunkin' Donuts shop.

Hard as we may try, we cannot sever the lifeline between local and foreign plague carriers. You cannot send plague carriers overseas unless the church is full of plague carriers here. Eventually the Jesus plague will die out, unless all Christians spread it next door and everywhere. Nobody will want to carry it overseas because nobody cares enough to carry it next door. Oh, the overseas carriers will go on for a little while longer, but when they expire no one will take their places, because the churches—even the so-called "missions-minded" churches— didn't spread the Jesus plague in their own backyards.

In the Philippines, where hundreds of thousands hire out for work, in other countries, the churches train the Christians among them how to be Jesus plague carriers wherever they go. There are more house servants among them than businessmen and scientists, but they are very good at spreading the Jesus plague. On any given day scores of American Christians arrive in virtually every airport in the world. They are not missionaries, but they should carry the Jesus plague. Wouldn't it be something if they somehow radiated Jesus so brilliantly that they set off alarms at the baggage X-ray checkpoints? Before they go, we have to identify them as plague carriers and tell them how to infect others. They, too, are part of God's commitment and strategy to save the world.

REFLECTION AND DISCUSSION

1. What are some of the ways you have carried the "Jesus plague" to others?
2. If it was hard for you to answer question 1, what steps can you take to change that?

---

call the people to come to his son's wedding banquet (Matt. 22:1–14).

Finally, to clarify, a call to full-time service for Christ does not preclude the possibility that at times the one called may need to pursue vocational opportunities that generate income. Paul's work as a tentmaker while in Athens (Acts 18:1–3) is a case in point. And Clarence Jones points out that the call to full-time ministry can unfold slowly:

> If God had suddenly shown us everything he was going to do in the years to come, I would have said, "Wait a minute, you've got the wrong man! . . ." But God inched up the curtain just a little bit at a time and said, "Take a look, and take a step." (Neely 1980, 82)

The Call to a Specific Assignment or Task

In addition to the call to full-time service for God, Scripture contains cases in which God provides more specific calls to people who are assigned limited duties or tasks. For example, Jesus sent the disciples out on a specific preaching mission *after* telling them to pray for laborers to enter the harvest field (Matt. 9:35–10:42). Peter and John were sent by the Jerusalem church to investigate what was happening in Samaria under Philip's ministry (Acts 8:14). Barnabas was sent from Jerusalem to Antioch to follow up on the church that had been planted there (Acts 11:22). Barnabas and Paul were sent to Jerusalem with an offering from Antioch (Acts 11:27–30; 12:25). God set apart Barna-

---

CASE STUDY:
THE CALL OF GOD

Lillian Lau

"What can I do? It seems that every answer leaves someone disappointed—I feel caught between a rock and a hard place," Nathan whispered to his friend Lim. Lim knew Nathan was desperate for an answer that would satisfy everyone, but he had no idea what that could be.

Lim had known Nathan from childhood. Nathan grew up in Lim's neighborhood in the United States as the eldest son of Chinese immigrants. He deeply loved his Buddhist parents, and had many fond memories of learning about the Chinese traditions and ancestral worship rituals while growing up. In the best sense of the word, Nathan had been a good Chinese son. In everything he did, he worked hard to bring honor to his family and please his parents. This included diligent study and living an upright moral life.

Nathan's success became a source of great pride to the family. He was an excellent student and after graduation at the top of his class from a prestigious university he accepted a job as an engineer with a starting salary of $75,000 per year. His parents could not have been more pleased with the way things turned out, and often reminded him of his heritage and responsibilities towards the family.

He would never forget the first invitation he received to go to church. A decade after he graduated from college and started work, a good friend of his asked him to go to a church service. He had never gone to one before and was mildly curious about why his friend went to church every Wednesday evening and Sunday morning. He decided to go.

During the service, the pastor talked about the story of the rich young ruler. He challenged the congregation to consider following Jesus in spite of their "need" for material wealth. Nathan went home and pondered this challenge. After a month of asking a lot of questions and quiet deliberation, he decided to give his life to Jesus.

He was so excited about sharing his faith—even though his parents disapproved. For the first time in his life, however, he sensed he was not a source of honor for his family, and they applied regular and subtle pressure for him to return to his old ways.

---

bas and Paul from the church in Antioch as full-time workers to the Gentiles (Acts 13:2). As Gordon Olson points out, however, God had already called Paul to be an apostle to the Gentiles. As with the Macedonian vision, this was a confirmation of that call and further leading in how that call was to be worked out in Paul's life, not an initial "missionary call" (Olson 1998, 82).

Additional examples from the Book of Acts include Paul being sent with Barnabas to be part of the Jerusalem council's wrestling over the question of circumcising Gentiles prior to inclusion in the church (15:2). After the meeting, the Jerusalem church sent a delegation to carry the letter they wrote to the Gentile believers in Antioch, Syria, and Cilicia (15:22–33). Once Barnabas and Paul split up over John Mark, Paul chose Silas to join him on his second missionary journey (15:40). Early in the journey Paul added Timothy to the team simply because he wanted him to join him (16:3). As we mentioned previously, the Macedonian vision (16:10) was not a call to missionary service, but a specific guidance or calling from God leading Paul away from Asia and into Europe as the next step of his ministry to the Gentiles.

FIRST STEPS: HAVE YOU BEEN CALLED?

A year later, however, Nathan's pastor asked him to consider a short-term mission trip to China to teach English to high school students. He prayed about it, got permission to take a month's leave from work, and went off into one of the poorer, undeveloped areas of central China. Over the month he was there, he developed several deep friendships with his students and was able to share the Gospel numerous times. God used this to change his life.

He came home excited and enthusiastic about the work that he did and tried to share this excitement with his family and friends. He informed them that he was considering giving up his engineering job to go teach English in China full-time.

While his church friends were excited and shared his joy, his parents couldn't understand his euphoria. They reminded him

that they had many unpleasant memories of their lives in China. Why would he want to return to a place of such hardship? Couldn't he use his job to send money for others to go, if it meant that much to him? They tried to convince Nathan to concentrate on his work and to settle down and get married. His father reminded Nathan that he was getting older and needed to quit playing around. When Nathan persisted with his ideas, subtle threats began to surface. His parents constantly reminded him of his obligations to them and to the family as a whole. Leaving everything would shame them all, and this was the greatest fear Nathan had.

Nathan tried to take his parents' advice but felt more and more unsettled. He knew that his heart and thoughts were elsewhere but he didn't know what to do. He yearned to do what God wanted him to but he also wanted to

honor and respect his parents' wishes.

Lim and Nathan wrestled with the questions together. Should Nathan give up his good-paying job to live and teach in the countryside of China, earning a pittance? Should he hope that these pullings and tuggings would go away with time? Maybe he could earn enough that he could send ten instead of being the one to go! At the same time, Nathan knew that the Bible taught that God was to be his first priority. But was this really God's call on his life, or was he just imagining things? How could he live with himself if he disappointed his parents? Together Nathan and Lim struggled before God, but no clear answer seemed to come to them. Eventually, Lim realized what he needed to say to Nathan. Breathing a prayer for wise words, he said …

GUIDELINES ON THE CALL

In light of this discussion, what guidelines will help Christians understand the call to missionary service? We propose the following four.

God's Call Comes in Many Ways

Among the various examples of calling and being sent in the previous two sections, we do not find any single method used by God to enact his call on an individual. Calling and sending can come through a specific experience such as a dream or vision, but it can also come through a settled conviction

that God places on the heart(s) of the one(s) being sent or through a local body of believers assigning a task to a person or team.

All Are Called, Some Are Assigned

All Christians are called to engage in discipleship as a way of life. They are all to call unbelievers to repent, believe the gospel, and worship God, and to delight in serving God by becoming more like Christ in all they do, following the examples of people such as Priscilla and Aquila by serving Christ wherever circumstances may lead them (Acts 18).

169

At the same time, God does set apart some Christians for full-time lifelong service to the kingdom. He also gives people specific assignments or tasks of a temporary nature to be carried out, often perceived and assigned through a local body of Christians.

Assignments Are Not Permanent, Even When Calling Is

As seen in the examples of temporary assignments found in the Bible, missionaries are not required to sign up for life. This is an important issue to people today, especially when the idea of a permanent assignment seems overwhelming. Those who sense a full-time call to the vocation of ministry should be willing to accept short-term assignments as part of the means God uses to fulfill his call in their lives.

For most of us, God does not lay out the entire life plan in a single call. Rather, he leads step-by-step along the way. Many missionaries accept their assignments from God one term at a time, whether that term is a few weeks or several years. The recent stagnation in long-term North American missionary appointments (of four years or longer [Moreau 2000c]) does not prove that the missionary movement itself is stagnating. The explosion of short-term missionaries shows that interest in mission is still strong, but the focus on a so-called career orientation has shifted dramatically in the past few decades. All three authors of this book are counted as former missionaries who are no longer on the field. At the same time, however, all three continue to serve God's call in their lives through the teaching and promotion of mission in their respective contexts. They illustrate that the means of working out the call can vary widely from person to person.

The Body of Christ Plays an Important Role in the Call

Although the one who ultimately calls or sends is God, often in the immediate context it is a local body of believers who sense or confirm a call and delegate the associated assignment or responsibility to an individual or team. The body of Christ, then, has a significant role to play in the calling of people into ministry. As did the church at Antioch, they confirm and enact on behalf of God what the calling entails. The local body of believers, who usually best know the individual or team, should be able to affirm the call or leading and play a key role in helping the call to be fulfilled.

CONCLUSION

Do you feel that you have been called? Or do you have a growing burden for a people, a country, or a culture that you cannot shake and wonder whether this might be part of God's call? If so, you should seek to have that call examined in the context of a local church or community of believers, recognizing the function of the body of Christ in the lives of every member of that body. You should also bear in mind that God is more flexible in how call is worked out than many Christians are. Additionally, opportunities or assignments that come our way in the future may be further means that God is using to confirm or extend the work he has chosen to accomplish through his children (Eph. 2:10). The case study for this chapter exemplifies these issues by focusing on a young man's response to what seems to be God's gentle call when pressures around him pull him in many directions.

If you sense that moving into missionary service for Christ is for you, or if someone you know is coming to you for advice on following his or her calling, the next issue to consider is how to prepare for walking in this commitment. In the next chapter we will turn our attention to the means of preparation for missionary work.

10

Missionary Preparation

INTRODUCTION

Linda was ready. She felt called to go and minister, and God had confirmed her call in numerous ways. She even knew the people that God wanted her to reach: the eight hundred thousand Algerian Arabs living in France. She had studied French in high school and college, and she even spent a year in France as an exchange student, so her French skills were good.

Deeply burdened with a desire to reach people for Christ, she wondered about getting some specialized training but also was disturbed that every day Algerian Arabs in France who had not had an opportunity to respond to Christ were dying. That thought left her in agony, especially when she considered that it might take a few more years before she could go. "Why waste my time with unnecessary training? After all, Algerian Arabs speak French, and I spent time as an exchange student in France and feel comfortable with French culture," she reasoned. There was also this nagging thought: what would she feel if Jesus returned while she was being trained?

The Linda of our story is not a real person, though her thoughts and turmoil typify a number of the questions that people raise about training in preparation for mission. Today, more training opportunities are available than ever before. Local churches sponsor Perspectives on the World Christian Movement courses; short-term mission trip opportunities are easy to find; and intensive training conferences are affordable and geared specifically to prepare people for the field. More traditional training methods at schools and seminaries give better academic foundations, but they take longer and cost more.

Biblically, there are several "models" of missionary preparation. Timothy learned "on the job" as Paul simply chose and circumcised him prior to bringing him along on his second missionary journey (Acts 16:1–4). Paul himself spent three years in Arabia, briefly visited Jerusalem, and then returned to Arabia for fourteen years before Barnabas brought him up to Antioch (Gal. 1:13–2:1; Acts 11:22–26). Perhaps the most extreme example is Moses, who was trained in the ways of Egyptian culture for forty years and then spent forty years in the wilderness before receiving God's call into ministry (Acts 7:20–32).

In this chapter we will focus on how you go from where you are now to where you sense God is leading or how you might advise someone who asks you about getting prepared to cross cultures. As we look at training options, we will point out several steps, but we do so with the warning that God does not typically lead people on any particular path. God loves every person so deeply that he carves out a unique path for each one, with various elements coming at different times. With that in mind, we will look at a number of ways people have used to prepare as missionaries.

WHY GET TRAINING?

So missionaries, *real* missionaries, are people just like you. They face circumstances that many who remain in their own culture never face, they have to deal with questions that they may have never had to answer at home, and typically they have to learn how to adjust to a new environment. How can they get ready to do those things well?

Anytime a person gets ready to do a specialized task, training can help make the task easier and enable the person who is trained to do a better job than one who is not. Missionary preparation is no different. Crossing into a new culture and bringing a message that may not make sense to a group of people whose language and ways of life the missionary neither knows nor understands is a complex task.

Don't get confused, however. Training doesn't happen only in the classroom (see table 10.1). Some training is informal; it happens in the daily events of life. Some is nonformal; it comes through experiences

TABLE 10.1
TYPES OF EDUCATION

Type	Basic Description (Steffen 2000)
Informal	Happens anytime, anyplace, without cost, as people dialogue about a host of personal or ministry topics
Nonformal	Tends to be held in locations of convenience, be participatory in nature; addresses specific topics in depth, focuses on individual or group improvement, and tends to be short in duration, making it more affordable
Formal	Tends to take place in designated locations, be expert-centered and sequenced; focuses on individual achievement, covers topics broadly and in depth, and takes extended amounts of time, making it costly

that are geared for learning but that don't take place in traditional schools or training institutes. Finally, some types of training are formal; they take place in institutions established for the purpose of providing education in the traditional sense. All three have strengths and weaknesses in preparing for missionary service. In each of the areas we will explain options for training experiences. For additional help, see sidebar 10.1, where we mention several other areas in which training takes place and provide reflection questions that help you think through important issues.

WHAT IS THE GOAL OF TRAINING?

The overall goal of missionary training is to equip the prospective missionary to be a godly person who is both competent and effective in his or her missionary service. This involves a blend of the following (adapted partly from Dodd 1991, 273):

1. *Genuine growth toward spiritual maturity.* The missionary does not have to be

---

SIDEBAR 10.1
TRAINING GROUNDS FOR MISSIONARIES

REFLECTION
AND DISCUSSION

Steve Hoke and Bill Taylor (1999) note the following as areas that shape people into who they are. Each has been a "training ground" for you and is part of the process that God already has been using for you to become a missionary.

1. The home shapes you.
2. The job/marketplace teaches and hones skills.
3. The church stimulates development of character, ministry skills, and a degree of important knowledge.
4. Formal schools focus on knowledge and some skills.
5. Mission agencies take a careful look at character, skills, and knowledge and may offer their own specific equipping.
6. The future national church with which you may serve will shape you in all areas of your life.

7. Other kinds of interpersonal relationships mold you.

The following may be added to the areas that Hoke and Taylor provide:

8. The genetic fabric of who you are, molded by God at the moment of conception, provides parameters that shape your personality and character.
9. The reality that you have a sinful nature that has been transformed by grace provides you with an approach to the world that is, at the same time, both holy and tainted. This plays an important role in both the brokenness you experience and the fact that God works in and through you in redeeming ways and shapes who you are today.

1. Think through each of these nine areas and ask yourself what impact it has had on shaping who you are and what type of missionary you have the potential to be.
2. Are there other areas you can identify that have had or could have an impact on preparing you for missionary service?
3. Which of the nine areas have had the most positive impact on your character and ministry development? What are the implications for you as a future missionary?
4. Which of the nine areas have had the most negative impact on your character and ministry development? What are the implications for you as a future missionary?

---

mature in order to cross cultural boundaries, but should be growing throughout his or her life. This includes things such as trusting God in strange and new circumstances, knowing how to go to the Scriptures for sustenance and nurture, and maintaining a healthy prayer life.

2. *The ability to carry out one's assigned task.* The focus here is on having the appropriate ministry or professional competency and skills to do the job for which the missionary goes, whether that job is church planting, hospital construction, or something else. Whatever one's professional skills may be, evidence of spiritual fruit as seen by others is an important consideration of readiness for missionary service.

3. *The ability to interact well with people in the new cultural setting.* This ability will include, in addition to language-learning capabilities, things such as skills in appropriateness, friendliness, and clarity when discipling or training in ministry skills or teaching. These will be discussed in greater detail below.

4. *The ability to adjust well by coping effectively with culture stress and dealing with the adaptation process.* The shock of being in

a new culture in which the mental "maps" that people normally use to navigate life no longer work can deeply wound them and render them ineffective or, in extreme cases, even counterproductive for the cause of Christ.

5. *The ability to facilitate adjustment and manage stress for family and significant others.* Family and team relationships, especially with recent trends of increase in intercultural marriages and teams, also are significant areas for the missionary.

6. *The ability to develop genuine partnerships with national Christians in which both parties have something to offer to each other.* The days of colonialism are over, but many of its attitudes remain. A feeling of cultural superiority all too readily pervades missionaries going from cultures with technological, educational, or financial advantages over

> *And people who do not know the Lord ask why in the world we waste our lives as missionaries. They forget that they too are expending their lives . . . and when the bubble has burst they will have nothing of eternal significance to show for the years they have wasted.*
>
> Nate Saint (Hitt 1959, 158)

the host culture. Engaging in two-way relationships with national Christians finally is being increasingly emphasized. Risks come with this ability, but they must be taken if Christians really want to see local churches living in a relationship of dependence on God rather than on the missionary.

This list is not exhaustive. We could add many more things to it. The temptation is to add too many, which would mean that no

one could hope to ever meet all the demands. The items mentioned are indicative of the types of things that missionary training—formal, informal, or nonformal—should seek to foster in those who have responded to Christ's call to minister in his name in a new context.

Recent research in intercultural communication has indicated that for successful cross-cultural adaptation a person needs skills or development in four important areas: character traits, ministry or professional skills, specialized knowledge, and social skills. With adaptations, these same areas apply to the missionary as well.

TRAINING IN CHARACTER TRAITS

What character traits should characterize a missionary? Here we blend ideas from two different worldviews: Scripture and contemporary intercultural communication research. Scripture provides the foundational spiritual focus for the missionary, and intercultural communication research adds elements that typify people who successfully cross cultural boundaries and are effective in their work.

What Character Traits?

By "character traits" we mean those qualities that characterize how a person sees the world, responds to varying circumstances, and is oriented to life. In our discussion we will place less emphasis on the spiritual character traits only because there is a wealth of Christian literature available dealing with these areas (see sidebar 10.2). In contrast with the wealth of literature on Christian maturity, very little Christian literature focuses on the other character traits that exemplify a person who is more likely to cross success-

175

fully to another culture. Furthermore, many of the character traits listed are also marks of spiritual maturity; the dividing line between these two areas is somewhat arbitrary and at times quite blurred.

SPIRITUAL CHARACTER TRAITS

1. *Genuine dependence on God.* This does not mean developing an "overspiritualizing" attitude, but having a genuine attitude of submission to God's sovereign oversight and a willingness to obey as he leads. This includes a life characterized by regular communion with God in prayer.

2. *Humility and teachability.* These attitudes are built on proper self-appraisal. Jesus taught that Christians are to deny themselves. His intention was not that they demean themselves or engage in self-destructive thinking and mistake that for humility. Rather, it refers to a Christian having the attitude that other people really are important (Phil. 2:1–4) and understanding accurately how truly small he or she is in the totality of God's scheme. Humble people do this without playing a game of "worm

> *I used to think that prayer should have the first place and teaching the second. I now feel it would be truer to give prayer the first, second and third places and teaching the fourth.*
>
> James O. Fraser (Dick 1987, 34)

theology" in which their true worth in God's eyes is denied.

Included with this spiritual quality is the teachability of the candidate. This is more crucial than ever before in a day when partnership is valued across the world church, as a missionary who is not teachable and who comes across as the one who only can give and never receive from others (especially from indigenous Christians) is one who will find it difficult to work alongside national churches in fruitful partnership. A teachable person is one who recognizes the inherent worth and wisdom of others. In fact, a person who never receives from others is not allowing them to grow and develop. Their own spiritual growth will be stunted, and they will be more likely themselves to pass on this unbiblical model for the next generation of Christians.

3. *The fruit of the Spirit.* The success of our striving together with the Holy Spirit to be conformed to the image of Christ is the major emphasis of this set of character traits. It is exemplified by love, joy, peace, patience, kindness, goodness, faithfulness,

> *Prepare for the worst, expect the best, and take what comes.*
>
> Robert E. Speer (Wheeler 1956, 69)

gentleness, and self-control (Gal. 5:22–23). Space limitations prevent us from exploring each of these, but we note that only to the extent that they are evidenced can a Christian say that he or she is displaying the fruit of the Spirit. For the missionary, of course, the ability to understand how the fruit is perceived in cross-cultural perspective is also important. First Timothy 3:1–13 and Titus 1:6–9 provide additional characteristics of Christian leaders that should also exemplify missionaries.

OTHER CHARACTER TRAITS

In addition to the spiritual qualities discussed above, what other traits and attitudes are important for the missionary?

The following eight traits to emulate were developed from a variety of intercultural communication resources (including Dodd 1991, 279; Ruben 1982; Barna 1982; Dinges 1983; Kealey and Ruben 1983; Lustig and Koester 1996). In listing these traits separately from the spiritual qualities named above, we are not implying that they are somehow not spiritual. Certainly they embody strong spiritual values and should be descriptive of Christians in general. We separate them here simply to identify them as traits that have been found in secular studies to be important for effective intercultural communication.

1. *More emphasis on people, less on task.* A person with this trait is approachable and is able to establish contact with others easily. A person with this trait does not need to be extraverted, but should feel comfortable meeting people in new settings. Perhaps most important, this person can let go of tasks when people are at stake. This does not mean that tasks are unimportant; rather, they are viewed in the perspective of kingdom priorities, which emphasize that people submit to God and learn from each other.

2. *Ability to withhold unproductive criticism.* People with this trait are able to avoid unnecessary and unproductive criticism of local customs, beliefs, and ideas. Instead, they show respect by treating others in ways that make the others feel valued. They also have the capacity to communicate that they respect others. This does not mean that no criticism can ever be given or that these people hide what they really feel, but that the emphasis is on withholding criticism that would be unproductive (coupled with the ability to see things from more than one perspective). A constant barrage of criticism of the host culture by missionaries is not

only unbecoming, but also damaging to the cause of Christ and growth of the local church.

3. *Tolerance of ambiguity and flexibility.* This trait is perhaps hardest to learn, especially for those who depend on predictability in life for security. New cultural settings are rife with ambiguous situations for those who do not know how to read the signs, and many cultures even value that ambiguity because of the way it keeps options open and life flexible. Tolerating ambiguity can be developed through growing trust in God coupled with willingness to let go of control. For many, this can be very difficult, especially when culture and family upbringing have taught them to avoid ambiguity.

4. *Empathy.* It is especially important that empathy be shown in culturally appropriate ways of listening and accurate perceiving of the other's point of view. It includes the ability to "walk in the other person's shoes" (or sandals) so that the other feels understood. This requires more than just an understanding of another culture; it includes the skill of seeing the world as another person does and making allowances for that person's perspective.

5. *Openness in communication style.* This may be threatening to some potential missionaries, especially if they have a particular doctrine or theological system on which their Christian life is based. The idea of being nondogmatic is important, but it does not mean that Christians cannot have deeply held convictions. The issue at stake here is more how they communicate those convictions, and whether they are perceived by others as tolerant and able to genuinely interact with people regardless of their differences.

People who are constantly defensive or argumentative are not winsome, and this

177

is especially true of missionaries who feel that they can give no ground to people who do not hold the same beliefs and convictions that they hold. It is not our job to defend God, though it is our job to call people to faith in Christ. Distinguishing these two tasks can help missionaries be more open and less threatened (and threatening) in their communication.

6. *High cognitive complexity.* This character trait refers to the ability to avoid quick black-and-white judgments and reject simplistic stereotypes. This is critical in cross-cultural settings, where quick evaluations by people who do not know the culture well are likely to be wrong. This is most important when it involves motivations. Those who consistently come to snap judgments—for example, as to why someone was late for a scheduled appointment ("He does not respect me") or why someone says yes when no is really meant ("She is a liar")—will be less able to see the nuances of culture and will develop a reputation of being insensitive or even hypocritical.

7. *Good personal relational skills in the home culture.* This can be seen both in the ability to trust others and in the capacity for turn-taking and partnering with others to accomplish objectives. Typically, missionaries who want to minister in a new culture but cannot relate well in their own culture will find that their relational problems will be more, not less, difficult in the new culture.

8. *Perseverance.* This refers to the tendency to remain in a situation and feel positive about it even in the face of difficulties. It does not mean an attitude of stubbornness or refusal to change as God leads.

Spiritual Disciplines to Develop These Traits

Typically, the spiritual and character traits listed above are not emphasized in the school curricula. More often they are developed in informal or nonformal settings. To grow in them requires spiritual discipline. Naturally, then, we feel that a prospective missionary should be a person who is making progress in those disciplines as a way of life. In the limited space we have here we will overview only five of the disciplines; we invite you to consult some of the key resources listed in sidebar 10.2 for further discussion.

Three foundational spiritual disciplines for any missionary are study, memorization, and meditation on God's word (adapted partly from Moreau 1997a, 110–13). *Study* is not an end in itself. Paul instructed Timothy, "Do your best to present yourself to God as one approved, a workman who does not need to be ashamed and who correctly handles the word of truth" (2 Tim. 2:15). Christians do not handle the word of God accurately through some mystical process. It takes disciplined study to know and understand God's word, followed by practical and thoughtful reflection to apply it to life. Although original language skills are helpful, they are not necessary for the type of study that builds missionary character and spirituality.

Christians also should immerse themselves in God's word through the discipline of *memorization.* In his responses to Satan during the temptation (Matt. 4:1–11), Jesus demonstrated that he had memorized God's word and was able to apply it correctly. He did not carry around a pocket Bible to refute the enemy! Instead, he had hidden God's word in his heart. He also knew the context

---

SIDEBAR 10.2
RESOURCES FOR GROWTH IN SPIRITUAL DISCIPLINES

Below are listed several books to help you develop spiritual disciplines and grow in the characteristics that are important for a missionary. They are chosen because in addition to providing a variety of perspectives on spiritual growth, they are practical, encouraging, and deeply insightful in challenging you with solid thinking about critical spiritual growth issues.

Of course, engaging in the spiritual disciplines requires more than simply reading—after all, they are disciplines! One way to help develop and maintain them is to join or start a small group of like-minded Christians who will read these books (or others like them), practice what is learned, and keep each other accountable for the issues discussed.

Dan B. Allender and Tremper Longman III, *Bold Love* (1992)

Brent Curtis and John Elderidge, *The Sacred Romance: Drawing Closer to the Heart of God* (1997)

Brennan Manning, *Ruthless Trust: The Ragamuffin's Path to God* (2000)

Andrew Murray, *With Christ in the School of Prayer* (1953)

Eugene H. Peterson, *A Long Obedience in the Same Direction: Discipleship in an Instant Society* (1980)

Jeff VanVonderen, *Tired of Trying to Measure Up* (1989)

John White, *Changing on the Inside* (1992)

---

of the teachings that Satan used to tempt him and had the ability to respond instantly because he knew them so well.

Missionaries from the West, coming from cultures that emphasize writing rather than oral tradition, often neglect memorization. Even when they do memorize, they may focus more on passages from the New Testament Epistles than other sections of Scripture. Memory is like a muscle: it only grows through exercise. We encourage you to strengthen this area of spiritual discipline so that you will be better equipped to face the temptations of the enemy and the trials of the field.

Followers of Jesus also are to immerse themselves in God's word through the process of *meditation*. According to John White, meditation is

the deliberate, disciplined practice of focusing our attention on a truth or an aspect of reality—ideally, on the truth of the loving presence of Christ in and with us. Meditation consists of dwelling on reality,

and God in me is reality. . . . Meditation means reflecting on truth, letting it sink in. Meditation involves silent musing . . . taking time daily to sit and ponder what is real. (White 1992, 137–38)

In meditation, one reflects, repeats, and continuously turns over a passage or idea. The basic image comes from a cow chewing its cud: the cow chews it, swallows it, and brings it back up for more chewing. Meditation for the Christian, therefore, is not a meaningless emptying of the mind; rather, it is a filling of the mind with God's truths, allowing them to percolate within so that they become part of our "mental programming." Societies provide their members with a type of mental "software" (Hofstede 1991). Software is a set of instructions that computers use to function. Although the freedom to make choices of their own volition sets humans apart from computers, people still operate on a set of basic software instructions that guide how they respond to the events in life (social scientists refer to these as "scripts" [see Nuckolls 1991]). That "software" is developed as people grow, and it is shaped by family experiences, cultural surroundings, and the choices made in responding to their influences in their lives. Meditation on biblical truths gives Christians the opportunity to modify their "software" so that they respond in a godly way to the events in life.

Another foundational discipline is that of *prayer*. The goal is to cultivate an atmosphere of prayer in your life. This is the only way you can obey Paul's command to pray without ceasing (1 Thess. 5:17). When he told the Ephesians to put on the armor of God in order to stand against Satan, he explained that they were to do it in a manner that was permeated by prayer in the Spirit (Eph. 6:18). The idea is not focused on spending lengthy devotional times every day (those should be an outcome of a life of prayer); rather, it is to cultivate a continuous two-way communication with God over all of the events and details of life.

The last discipline we will mention is *praising and thanking God in all circumstances*. In spite of years of life filled with physical pain resulting from a climbing accident, Tim Hansel maintains,

> Pain is inevitable, but misery is optional. We cannot avoid pain, but we can avoid joy. God has given us such immense freedom that he will allow us to be as miserable as we want to be.
>
> I know some people who spend their entire lives practicing being unhappy, diligently pursuing joylessness. They get more mileage from having people feel sorry for them than from choosing to live out their lives in the context of joy.
>
> Joy is simple (not to be confused with easy). At any moment in life we have at least two options, and one of them is to choose

an attitude of gratitude, a posture of grace, a commitment to joy. (Hansel 1985, 55.)

Luke records a surprising account of the disciples' response after being whipped for preaching Christ in Jerusalem (Acts 5:17–42). This ragtag band of deserters who had hidden in fear just weeks ago now went on their way "rejoicing because they had been counted worthy of suffering disgrace for the Name" (Acts 5:41). They had learned the secret of being content apart from their circumstances. They took the punishment and turned it upside down. They didn't just see it happen; they were the ones who were abused. Even so, they simply continued obeying what God had told them to do, thankful and joyful that God considered them worthy to suffer because they were associated with Jesus.

This dramatic statement of the disciples' reaction to their whipping provides a challenge for us. Like those disciples, Christians are to cultivate a personal "atmosphere" of trusting and thanking God in all of life's circumstances. The author of Hebrews reminds readers that Jesus endured the cross because of the joy that was set before him (Heb. 12:2), and also commends them for sympathizing with those in prison and joyfully accepting the confiscation of their property (Heb. 10:34). James tells his audience to consider it pure joy when they face trials (James 1:2). Peter urges his persecuted readers to rejoice that they participate in the sufferings of Christ (1 Pet. 4:13). Christians are to learn how to turn bad things upside down in their perspectives. They can see them through the lens of God's continuing sovereignty. The critical question here is of focus: Are you focused on the world around you as the means by which your needs are provided, or are you focused on God?

Many other spiritual disciplines could be explored. The focus of these disciplines is growth in loving God and loving others. Christians grow to love God by enjoying and pursuing him; submitting to him in obedience; repenting before him; communing with him through prayer and worship; and fearing, trusting, and thanking him in all of life's circumstances. They pursue him as people empowered by the Holy Spirit whose hunger for him comes from the Spirit's work within them.

Followers of Christ also grow in loving others as they love themselves. This they do by being filled by the Spirit, stripping off the old self and putting on the new, walking in the light, fellowshiping with one another, taming their tongues, forgiving and reconciling with those who have hurt them, and resisting Satan. They resist Satan by standing humble yet firm, denying themselves, taking every thought captive to Christ, putting on spiritual armor, refusing to let fear dominate them, choosing truth rather than deception, and proclaiming truth.

Being part of a small community that goes to the Scriptures on a regular basis together, or being discipled in a one-on-one or small-group setting, offers opportunities to develop the spiritual traits listed. Finding someone who can mentor you in the character traits is more difficult. Ask God to give you a mentor as you look for someone around you who emulates the traits needed to be a missionary. People who are good candidates for this type of mentoring role include retired missionaries or ministers, people with extensive successful cross-cultural experience, and people who have successfully crossed cultural boundaries in your home setting.

TRAINING IN MINISTRY AND PROFESSIONAL SKILLS

In many schools and seminaries today young people are forming teams prior to even looking for a mission agency. Often they assign roles within the team that respect the gifting of each individual and yet provide the overall skill mix that is necessary for mission in a pioneer setting. Some provide ministry skills, while others bring business or professional skills, with the latter perhaps earning the money necessary to keep the whole team on the field. In these cases each team member may need a different type of training, depending on the role that he or she will play.

Whatever your role, in addition to developing character traits, to enjoy a successful missionary experience it is important that you have good foundations in appropriate ministry and professional skills. We will look at each separately.

What Ministry Skills?

Missionaries moving into different ministry assignments may need differing sets of skills. Those engaged in pioneer church planting need ministry skills different from those moving into leadership development or educational ministries.

However, there are some skills that are important for every missionary no matter how he or she serves. These include the skills involved in discipleship, which are essential for all Christians. Skills such as the ability to build good relationships (with the addition of cultural sensitivity for the missionary [see chapters 14 and 15]), leadership development and delegating skills, and mentoring skills are included. These skills do not need to be public ones—ones used in front of large groups. Some of the best ministry is done one-on-one or in small groups or among families, and the basic skills listed here do not have to be the same as those for large-group settings. For example, the skills for leading a good Bible study discussion are not the same as for teaching a class or preaching a sermon. The former are necessary for all missionaries, while the latter are necessary only for those in ministries that require missionaries to teach or preach in front of large groups.

Missionaries often must face the reality that the skills they thought they would need on the field are significantly different from what they actually need once they arrive. The attitude that new skills can be developed as needs arise is just as important as having skills in place prior to departure. Primarily this involves teachability and flexibility on the part of the missionary.

Often, the more training the missionary has had prior to field experience, the less flexible he or she may be, since greater time was invested in getting ready and expectations are proportional to the level of professional training. This does not mean that missionaries should not get the best training possible, but that throughout their preparation for the field they should be realistic about how the skills they are learning may or may not be applicable once they are engaged in ministry in a new culture.

What Professional Skills?

If your missionary focus is church planting, then the ministry skills you need to develop *are* your professional skills. If, however, you sense God's leading to serve in a different way, you will need development as a professional to meet the challenges you will face. Here we offer some introductory thoughts; we will return to tentmaking in greater depth in chapter 11.

One axiom to remember is that tentmaking missionaries do their jobs best when they have high-quality training and they are linked with people in the field who have the necessary ministry skills to follow up on contacts that the tentmaker provides. Those links may be with indigenous believers or missionaries or both. In any event, the important consideration is that the tentmaker sees himself or herself as a team member rather than a "Lone Ranger" who does all the work without help.

Professional skills that are helpful in a variety of cross-cultural settings may be found in a wide variety of areas. Training is available on all levels. The amount of skill development you will need will be a balance between your own abilities and the needs of the organization or field. A partial list includes agriculture (all areas), aviation (pilot, mechanic, administrator), business (management, administration, entrepreneurship), communications (television, radio, photography, other mass media), computer science (hardware, software, training), construction (all areas), engineering (all types), education (teaching, administration, specializations [such as TESOL]), health (doctor, nurse, dietician, community health worker), maritime work (shipping, ship repair and maintenance, navigation), performing arts (music, dance, drama), social work (advocacy, counseling, support for underprivileged populations), sports (coaching, performing), veterinary services (farm, household), and writing (journalism, promotional literature). There are numerous Internet resources that offer more complete lists and can help you catch a vision for the types of skills that are useful. Four with which to start your search are: (1) Mission

Finder (www.mfinder.org/level2.htm), with hundreds of opportunities in dozens of areas; (2) MisLinks (www.mislinks.org/practical/rdorgs.htm), listing relief and development organizations; (3) the World Evangelical Alliance Mission Commission (www.globalmission.org), which lists hundreds of long- and short-term opportunities in a searchable database; and (4) the Interdenominational Foreign Mission Association (IFMA) (www.ifmamissions.org), which lists hundreds of opportunities utilizing professional skills.

How Can You Develop These Skills?

What better way to develop ministry skills than to engage in ministry? Many denominational missions recognize that schooling alone usually does not prepare people for actual ministry, and that prospective missionaries require a number of years of work in a local church setting prior to field assignments. Do not begrudge the added years of waiting. They will prove to be invaluable when you finally arrive on site.

Likewise, professional apprenticeships may also be important to hone skills learned in the classroom. The risk, however, is that the apprenticeship may extend into a career without the prospective missionary ever crossing into a new cultural setting.

The foundation for these skills typically is established through appropriate education. This may range from college to a specialized program, whether at a trade school or in a postbaccalaureate setting such as medical or law school. You need to consider how God has "wired" you and what professional activities energize you. Maybe full-time church planting is not your calling, but you have the necessary gift mix to make a great engineer and you

enjoy cultivating relationships in the work setting with people who do not know Christ. If this describes you, it will be worth your time to find a school or institute that offers the type of training you need to become a top-quality professional. Those who are true professionals with solid training will be more valuable both to the local culture and, ultimately, to the cause of Christ than those with shoddy training who can barely function professionally.

TRAINING IN SPECIALIZED KNOWLEDGE

What Knowledge?

Experts in cross-culturalism recognize two types of knowledge that are helpful in preparing a person to adjust successfully to a new culture. The first is *general* knowledge that enables a person to understand how and why cultures differ. This serves as a foundation for understanding the specific differences encountered in a new cultural setting. It includes basic awareness of insights from the social sciences (anthropology, sociology, psychology, and so on).

If you have access to courses that give you broad perspectives on humans and the cultures and societies that they create, we strongly encourage you to take them. They will help lay the type of foundation of general cultural knowledge that you need.

The second type of knowledge builds on the first. You may know that cultures do indeed differ, but be without a clue as to how that applies to your specific setting. This second type of knowledge is *culture specific*, and it relates to the idiosyncrasies of the culture that is your new home. In contrast to general knowledge, this is the knowledge of the specific social skills necessary to develop good relationships within a particular culture. For example, general knowledge includes the awareness that each culture has ideals of time, while culture-specific knowledge is to be aware that when a Swazi arrives an hour late for an appointment, it may communicate that this person feels comfortable with you as a friend and not that he or she is irresponsible, and thus to interpret the timing of the arrival correctly. It also means knowing that in Uganda you should not shout out to someone older than you whom you see across the street because it is disrespectful to your elders. Or it means understanding that in Korea, avoiding direct confrontation is highly valued. We will offer more examples of this in chapter 16.

How Can You Develop This Knowledge?

To obtain general cross-cultural knowledge, one option is to attend a traditional degree-granting institution, such as a college. They typically have programs available in anthropology, communication, sociology, mission, and so on.

A second option is to find a well-designed cross-cultural institute, which also can provide the general knowledge necessary for successful adjustment in another culture. Although lacking in the depth that the longer degree programs offer, these shorter institutes still can provide a good foundation of helpful knowledge compressed into a short time. Since they have an exclusive focus on cross-cultural issues, the prospective missionary can come away from them with more helpful knowledge than from the general degree programs.

A third source for general cross-cultural training is the popular Perspectives on the World Christian Movement course that is available in many settings across North America (for a list of available locations, see www.perspectives.org).

Typically, training for knowledge of a specific culture is available in several ways. First, you can take advantage of the fact that the world has come to our door: there are many pockets of people scattered across North America that might be the same as, or very close to, the culture of those among whom you will live. Use this to start your ministry here before you go there.

Second, good local language programs in your host culture will incorporate cultural elements as well. If you go with a mission agency, its personnel usually will know the better programs that are available. If you are not going with an agency, you may need to investigate through local contacts the reputations of various language-learning programs before you choose one that is right for you.

Third, mentoring from a missionary who has significant cross-cultural experience in your target culture can provide invaluable help, as can a cultural informant who understands how to communicate information about the culture in a way that makes sense to outsiders. Although missionaries and indigenous cultural informants almost always are helpful, keep in mind that each one provides only one person's perspective. It is advisable to find more than one informant so that you can gain a broader perspective and be less likely to misread actions or events because you have received biased information.

TRAINING IN SOCIAL SKILLS

What Social Skills?

In the first week of his term in Swaziland, Scott Moreau walked to a small kiosk to purchase some food items. Seeing the well-stocked shelves, he asked the man behind the counter, "You don't have peanut butter, do you?" "Yes," the man answered. Scott said, "Great! I'd like some, please." The man said, "But we don't have any." Scott objected, "But you just said you did." To which the man replied, "No. I said, 'Yes, we don't have any,' which is what you asked me." This simple exchange sent a shock through Scott's system. It was a small but vivid reminder that even in a country in which people spoke English quite well, the wording he used in his question and how he interpreted the answer were dead wrong.

Over the course of your life, you have learned literally thousands of "scripts" for events in daily life. Going to the store, asking for help, dealing with a problem, proper eating habits—all of these and uncounted others you learned as you grew up. One of the ways culture shock hits is when you realize that your scripts no longer work, as Scott found out at the kiosk.

People who successfully navigate culture shock are those who best learn the critical social skills that are required in the new culture (see Bochner and Furnham 1986). It is not so much that they adjust to a new culture as that they learn the important techniques of social behavior (or scripts) of the new culture:

> These include expressing attitudes, feelings and emotions, adopting the appropriate proxemic posture; understanding the gaze patterns of the people they are interacting with; carrying out ritualized routines such as greetings, leave-taking, self-disclosure, making or refusing requests; and asserting themselves. (Bochner and Furnham 1986, 14–15)

Social skills are one of the crucial areas of specific knowledge that the missionary needs. They are specific; that is, they apply in a particular setting and may or may not apply in any other setting in the world. Knowing what type of eye contact is appropriate, how to greet and take leave, what communication patterns are between the sexes, how to deal with an older person, and so on are important skills that the newly

> *There are many phases to a missionary's life. The least of these is to preach, so you don't have to look for those who are especially gifted or learned to become missionaries. Kindness is the big thing.*
> Malla Moe (Nilsen 1956, 146)

arrived missionary must learn as part of the adaptation process.

Day-to-day social interactions may seem mundane in your home culture, but the feelings associated with the discovery that your tried-and-true methods do not work can be quite strong. You may feel that you have been cast adrift in uncharted, and sometimes dangerous, waters. The process of learning new ways to do familiar tasks, such as doing the laundry, will take extra time and energy and will drain you more quickly than you realize, especially when you have to find out how to do them while speaking in a new language.

In fact, until these new skills have become second nature in the new setting, the missionary will feel like an outsider. It may help you to note that often those cross-cultural workers who learn these skills the best may have the hardest time readjusting to life back in their home culture. They go through culture shock all over again (called reentry shock), having grown used to the ways of their new culture and needing to readjust to the old.

How Can You Develop These Social Skills?

You learned your social skills when you were growing up. As already mentioned, you memorized, through the course of your life, literally thousands of scripts that you employ without even having to think. Something as simple as going to the store to buy food might require dozens of those scripts. Driving a car or catching a bus in a place where traffic etiquette differs from that of your home country; finding a parking space or knowing when and how to get off a bus; choosing food (which in many cultures might still be alive at the time you choose it), negotiating a fair price for it in a new language, knowing the proper method of payment, and getting it from the shop(s) to the car or bus and from there to your house—all the things you take for granted at home when you decide to go out and get some ice cream late at night—may be difficult or even outright dangerous in your new setting.

Social skills in general typically are taught in cross-cultural or intercultural communication courses. Learning general rules about how people communicate provides a foundation for understanding the particular ways they communicate in any given culture. Rules of nonverbal communication; how time is valued and understood; roles for relating to all types of people based on age, gender, and status—all these, in addition to many other culturally based social skills, do have patterns that often apply to more than one culture (we will return to these issues in chapter 14). Basic cross-cultural training is readily available through courses in schools and institutes. We strongly advise you to get some training in intercultural communication as a foundation for understanding the particular behaviors that you will encounter in a new culture.

Social skills specific to a setting may be learned at cultural institutes in the home country. However, the more remote the setting, and the smaller the number of people going there, the less likely it will be that an appropriate training program exists outside of the target culture. As with the culture-specific knowledge skills discussed above, resources that are helpful for the development of social skills include local language courses, a missionary mentor, and local informants. Typically, some combination of all three of these is the best way to learn the social skills needed to navigate the new culture successfully.

One important step in the process, however, is simply to recognize that as a newcomer you lack the basic social skills that everyone else in the culture takes for granted, and so adopting a learner's posture will go a long way in easing your transition into the new culture. Your mental map of how to simply get along needs to be significantly changed. The sooner you come to grips with this and what it means, the sooner you can make the necessary adjustments.

TYPES OF TRAINING AVAILABLE

In each of the sections above we have mentioned types of training that are helpful in preparing for missionary service. In this section we will summarize the types of training available and offer helpful information on each.

Training at Home or Church

Training at home or church runs the gamut from personal reading and study to the semester-long Perspectives on the World Christian Movement class (www.perspectives.org). It can include one-on-one discipleship with missionary mentors and distance learning through a Christian college or university. In more recent years, excellent Internet resources have become available that offer quick access to high-quality information (www.strategicnetwork.org) and multiple links to mission-related resources (www.mislinks.org).

As mentioned earlier in this chapter, a

> *Education for missions belongs to churches. They nurture believers and develop spiritual gifts. They recognize vocations and send out missionaries. They care for missionaries at home or on the field. Mission agencies and training programmes are servants of the churches and partners with them in training endeavours.*
>
> Lois McKinney (1991, 247)

prospective missionary should not neglect the fact that immigration in North America has brought the world to our door. Field experience among numerous people groups might involve only some investigative work and a short drive. Are you going to minister in a Muslim setting? Look around in your local community to see if there are Muslims with whom you can begin your preparation where you live—some perhaps even from the same country or people group you are interested in. If you start your ministry here, where those you reach are more likely to understand Americans, they can help you learn cultural and communication issues before you leave. The same is true for almost any group you choose, and more so if you live near just about any major city in North America. Joshua Massey, an experienced missionary, relates how his U.S. contacts significantly helped set up his transition into the country where he served because he had taken the time to get to know them on this side of the ocean. In fact, he recommends that agencies not even let prospective missionaries go to a new culture until they have significant ministry time among populations similar to those they eventually will serve (Massey 2002).

Training in Short-Term Institutes

There are numerous short-term institutes that offer specialized training for missionaries. These programs typically are brief (two weeks to a few months), intensive, focused exclusively on issues of cross-cultural preparation, and practical in readying people for effective service. For an updated list of mission training programs from around the world, browse to www.mislinks.org/research/progs.htm.

Some of these programs were developed as in-house training for mission agencies. For example, Campus Crusade for Christ's Agape International Training (www.aitusa.org) was developed for Campus Crusade but accepts people from other agencies.

Other programs are offered through organizations that specialize in pre-field training, such as the Center for Intercultural Training (www.cit-online.org) and Mission Training International (www.mti.org).

Still others are affiliated with educational institutions and offer academic

187

CASE STUDY:
WIFE BEATING

William A. Benner
(Hiebert and Hiebert 1987, 57–58 [used with permission])

The Reverend Solomon Begari, chairman of the Pastor's Disciplinary Committee, looked at the other two members of the committee and said, "We must decide whether Pastor Trombo should be disciplined for beating his wife, and, if so, what that discipline should be. There is no doubt that he beat her, but she disobeys him and embarrasses him in public. The question is, is this something for which we should discipline a husband, particularly a pastor?"

The missionaries who lived by the church had brought the problem before the committee. One afternoon Pastor James Trombo returned home and found his young daughter playing with rat poison, which was scattered on the floor around her. His wife, Paeyam, was nowhere to be seen. He rushed his child to the hospital to have her stomach pumped, just in case she had eaten some of it. When he returned home, he beat his wife after he found out that she had gone to town to buy a dress. She had left their daughter asleep on the floor, expecting to be gone only a short while. Pastor Trombo had scolded his wife several times before this for leaving the child when she was asleep, but

Paeyam had taken to ignoring his rebukes and sometimes publicly embarrassed him out of spite.

Immediately after her beating, Paeyam went across the street to the home of Carl and Lynne Hansen, the missionaries in the area. Paeyam had worked for them for several months, ever since their arrival in the South Sea Islands. Carl and Lynne both liked Paeyam and were shocked to see her weeping and bruised. Although Carl had found it hard to work with Pastor Trombo, who seemed to him to be arrogant and authoritarian, he and Lynne had to admit that the pastor's church was flourishing. Beside the many highlanders who attended the church, Pastor Trombo had a real ministry among the coastal people working in the town.

Carl went immediately to talk to Pastor Trombo, but he would not

---

credit through them. Examples include the Institute for Cross-Cultural Studies, offered through the Billy Graham Center and Wheaton College in Wheaton, Illinois (www.wheaton.edu/bgc/icct/); and Mission-Prep (www.timcentre.com/missionprep), affiliated with MI Canada and Tyndale College and Seminary in Toronto.

Training in Residential Educational Institutions

Over 270 institutions offer residential programs in mission and evangelism studies across North America (Welliver and Smith 2002). They range from associate degrees to the Ph.D., and from general missiological training to specializations such as Islam-ics, church growth, leadership development, theology, and so on. Academic programs range from the very practical to the highly theoretical. If you are interested in finding out what programs are available, EMIS, in the most recent edition of the *Handbook of Schools and Professors of Mission and Evangelism,* offers a complete listing (Welliver and Smith 2002).

CONCLUSION

Prior to the twentieth century missionaries typically went to new countries of service with little or no training in cross-cultural adjustment skills. A quick look at the criticisms of the cultural attitudes and

listen to Carl's remonstrance. "This is the custom of our people," he said. The missionaries felt that they could not drop the case, so they reported it to the Pastor's Disciplinary Committee of the Zion Churches of the South Pacific Islands.

Rumors of the beating circulated among the church members, causing various reactions. Some of the older people felt that Paeyam had finally gotten what she deserved and now would probably straighten up if the committee affirmed her husband. After all, wife beating was common in the highlands cultures. Many others who had been raised in the church were concerned. They felt that Pastor Trombo had done wrong and might even have committed a sin, although they were not exactly sure what kind of a sin. The new converts from the coastal people were generally confused. They liked Pastor Trombo and found him to be a good pastor, but they were used to treating their wives with more equality than the highlanders. Their wives were not beaten, except by an occasional drunk husband.

The members of the committee considered all these facts and the possible consequences of various decisions. They realized that if they affirmed Pastor Trombo, many people, including the missionaries and coastal people, would not understand. It would seem to them that the committee was condoning the practice of wife beating. Moreover, it would cause friction between the church leaders and the missionaries.

On the other hand, if the committee decided to discipline Pastor Trombo, it would cause problems with the older highlanders in the congregation and detract from his ministry. The committee's decision would affect the future of the church, Pastor Trombo's ministry, and his relationships in his family. No matter what they did, it seemed as if someone in the church would not understand.

Pastor Solomon Begari looked at the other committee members and said, "As the disciplinary committee of the Zion churches, we must make a final decision in this case. We have talked to Pastor Trombo, to the missionaries, and to our other pastors, and no agreement seems possible. And we cannot put off the decision without seriously hurting the church and the people involved. What should we do?"

blunders of missionaries of the past serves as a warning that missionaries should not continue that same practice today.

While theological training has been available for centuries, formal mission training did not start until the second half of the nineteenth century. Though relatively new, many training opportunities offer high-quality preparation that will pave the way for a smoother cross-cultural adjustment and enable a more effective and enjoyable ministry experience. Today's missionary cannot afford to move to a new culture without some type of pre-field training. The case study for this chapter shows how difficult it can be to apply those insights in light of biblical standards, illustrating why training can help prepare you to face situations you might never face in your home culture.

11

Charting a Path from Here to There

INTRODUCTION

In chapter 9 we told the story of Scott Moreau's call to ministry. Though the call to ministry was unexpected and dramatic, the tug toward mission as the place where God would have him serve came much more slowly.

Having no memory of being exposed to missionaries while growing up, Scott had no idea of what is involved in becoming one. During his last year in college, announcements in chapel about opportunities to teach in Nigeria came on a regular basis. God provided the money for Scott to attend the 1976 Urbana Conference in which over seventeen thousand college students joined together to learn about mission. There he met with representatives of several missionary organizations to find out where he might fit. Eventually he joined Campus Crusade for Christ for a two-year term of teaching science in a national high school in Swaziland, a small country in southern Africa.

If you sense that God would have you in full-time ministry in a cross-cultural setting, one important issue to consider is how you will get from where you are now to where

God will have you serve. In Scott's case that took a year of exploring, interviewing, support raising, and final training. In your case the time may be shorter or longer.

Today there are more choices than ever. In chapter 9 we saw that there is no single way God calls people into service. In chapter 10 we saw that there are many ways to prepare to become a missionary. In this chapter we will see that, especially today, there is no longer a single path by which a person can be involved in missionary service.

In addition to the traditional path of

> *I know enough about Satan to realize that he will have all his weapons ready for determined opposition. He would be a missionary simpleton who expected plain sailing in any work of God.*
>
> James Fraser (1958, 10)

going with an agency, a multitude of other options are open. Many people have technical skills that enable them to find international jobs. Professional organizations are available to help by networking to send people with appropriate skills overseas. Relief and development agencies enable those who can sensitively serve needy communities find meaningful places to help around the world. Some of the larger churches have been acting like mini-agencies, funding and overseeing their own missionary forces. Before looking at those, however, we must detour long enough to explore an exploding phenomenon that many see as a contemporary bridge from here to there: short-term mission trips.

SHORT-TERM MISSION TRIPS

Short-term trips are one of the hottest trends in contemporary missions. A world made increasingly smaller by the speed and relatively low cost of modern transportation, coupled with the ease of making and

> *Short-term work, whether two weeks or two years, can indeed be effective and pleasing to God. Yes, it can cost a lot of money, disrupt nationals and missionaries, encourage short-term thinking, and inoculate some against career missions involvement. But done well, it can open participants' eyes to the sometimes gritty realities of the world, make them aware of their own ethno-centrism and the gifts and courage of non-Western believers, and spark a lifelong commitment to missions. In the best cases, some real kingdom work gets done, too.*
>
> Stan Guthrie (2000, 89)

maintaining contact with people serving all over the globe, have fueled this movement. There is so much going on in this area that it merits special consideration in its own right, and we provide an analysis of this important phenomenon in chapter 17. At this point, we explore important issues of short-term mission trips and how they might fit into training for long-term missionary service.

The 2001–3 edition of the *Missions Handbook* reported an increase of over 50 percent in the number of people embarking on short-term projects through mission agencies from 1996 to 1999, with over ninety-seven thousand people going (Moreau 2000c, 34). This does not include the large numbers of others who go through local churches, schools, or on their own. A wealth of material has been developed and posted on the Internet to prepare you for short-term missions and to help you navigate the paths available. For example, MisLinks Short Term Missions (www.mislinks.org/practical/shterm.htm) offers dozens of links to Web sites dedicated to short-term missions, and is a good place to start your search.

For North Americans, short-term mission projects are comparatively inexpensive ways to "test the waters" of mission service. They provide an opportunity to live in another culture, experience the ways people live in other parts of the world, and be used of God to reach others for Christ. Short-term mission projects range from sports camps to construction to teaching (often English) to evangelism.

If your intention in a short-term mission trip is to discover whether long-term mission is the direction you should be going, you should consider several important factors both in the trip you choose and in what you look for during the trip.

If you sense the desire to go with an agency for the long haul, it makes sense to "try out" the agency through a short-term trip. The

SIDEBAR 11.1
SEVEN QUESTIONS TO ASK WHEN CHOOSING A MISSIONS
AGENCY

John McVay (McVay, www.askamissionary.com [used with permission])

John McVay, an experienced missions pastor and developer of the Ask-A-Missionary Web site, poses the following questions to ask of a missions agency.

The following seven issues present discussion points as you talk with various agencies. This list should not replace divine guidance, and there will be other questions that you will ask.

1. What is God's calling on the agency? In some cases that will be broad. For example, Youth With A Mission (YWAM) has a calling to evangelism, to training, and to mercy ministries. Within this broad calling much of their activity is in training and short-term missions. But with over 7,000 full-time workers, they have many missionaries involved in almost every missions activity! Other groups, though large, may have a specialized mission. Wycliffe Bible Translators seek to translate the Bible into every language. One-half of their 6,000 full-time workers are translators. The other half are support personnel: some in North America, others overseas. Many serve as teachers, administrators, bookkeepers, secretaries, etc.

2. What doctrinal areas are important to you? Important questions include worship style and speaking in tongues. For example, charismatics should look into agencies that fit them and be aware that a few agencies only accept those who do not speak in tongues. The Frontiers agency allows both persuasions, but usually each overseas team is one or the other. WEC International and Operation Mobilization typically have mixed teams, though a missionary must agree not to push his or her understanding.

What roles can women have in the mission? Some groups allow and encourage women to rise to leadership. Others believe that only men should be leaders. Some agencies hope for the married woman to serve the mission; others prefer her to be a full-time homemaker.

3. What is the financial policy of the agency? Some agencies, like WEC International, major on faith and prayer. Their missionaries may answer any question, but just as George Mueller expressed his needs to God and God alone, they will not ask anyone to make a financial gift.

In contrast, other organizations encourage their missionaries to take some initiative. Wycliffe practices full information, no solicitation. Other groups encourage missionaries to ask a potential supporter for a specific monthly commitment. Some agencies allow their missionaries to use any of these approaches.

What are the monthly support requirements? Some agencies may have a higher support level that includes medical, retirement, and other support services. It may take more effort and time to get to that level. Other agencies may give you a target, but if you sense God's leading, you may still go and live at a sacrificial level.

After you're on the field, what happens if your finances fall short or if you have an emergency? Some agencies have funds for such purposes. Others are not structured to facilitate such situations.

What contacts are available for raising support? Does the agency provide some leads or does the missionary develop all these alone? The mission board affiliated with your denomination can often provide numerous contacts. Also, some denominations have developed relationships with certain agencies.

4. What support services does the agency handle? What contacts are available for support raising? Some agencies take care of many needs: a car for furlough, processing contributions, newsletters, etc. Others are not able to do any of these. Perhaps your local church or a missionary service organization can help with such needs.

5. What structure does the agency have and how flexible are they? Some older agencies have learned from mistakes and have policies and structures to prevent repeating the past. In contrast, some younger agencies are more flexible and open to new ideas. One isn't better than the other, just different.

Learn where decisions are made. Is the authority centralized in an international office? How much authority is delegated to the field? Is the international director or the field director a strong personality? Does an effective board control the organization? What is the leadership style of those at the top?

Talk to the agency about how missionaries are placed. Who chooses where the missionary goes? Do you pray and then talk to your leaders or do they pray and then ask you?

Read a biography of the founder. WEC International was founded by C. T. Studd. Cameron Townsend began Wycliffe Bible Translators. If you are interested in YWAM, read the story of Loren Cunningham, *Is That Really You, God?* With a smaller agency, try to meet the director when he or she travels near your area.

6. Which countries and people groups is the agency working among? One missionary leader has said, "The team you're playing with is more important than the stadium in which you're playing." Let the Lord decide where He wants to place you in His world. Perhaps you have a specific geographic call that's clear and will focus your selection of an agency. But for most, God has given gifts and a desire to respond.

For example, half of those who join one worldwide agency don't begin with a geographical call. They know they are called to missions and to that agency.

Some agencies have global opportunities. Other groups have a focused geographical calling, such as Greater Europe Mission. The agency name may or may not indicate that focus. For example, Christian Associates International also works mainly in Europe.

Study the articles, advertisements and the career missions opportunities in the Great Commission Opportunities Handbook (www.aboutmissions.com). Look at which agencies are working in various countries as you pray through the book Operation World (www.opera tionworld.org). Look at online

listings in www.mfinder.org and www.peopleteams.org.

If you are called to a specific country, read the Mission Handbook, available from billygrahamcenter.org. This lists 800 North American–based agencies in alphabetical order with cross references for countries of activity, types of mission work and church tradition. I know a man who heard God speak to him to go to Zaire (now Democratic Republic of Congo). He found Zaire on the map (it's in central Africa) and then used the Mission Handbook to find an agency that was active in Zaire in Bible teaching and open to his church background. Then he and his wife spent ten years serving there!

7. Is God bonding you with the agency? Do you sense a connection with the agency? Are you ready to join their family? The other issues should serve as confirmation to what you sense in prayer.

Selecting a mission agency is like selecting the right family. Missions organizations are as eager to find the right match as you are. As you take time to prayerfully search out God's choice, you can look forward to long-lasting and fruitful service to our Lord.

short-term project can be something like a "date" between you and the organization. Both of you use the time to explore the possibility of a long-term relationship without either of you making a final commitment.

You also might consider a trip to a country or people group that has drawn your attention. There are many resources that will help you find an agency and a country that match your needs, especially on the

Internet. For example, ShortTermMissions (www.shorttermmissions.com) provides a searchable database of short-term mission opportunities. They offer detailed descriptions and requirements on short-term opportunities from many organizations. The site also has information on agencies, articles on short-term missions, and discussion forums. Globalmission (www.globalmission.org/st.htm) also offers a large database through which you can search for a short-term project.

CHOOSING A MISSION AGENCY

The process of choosing a mission agency has been compared to the process of dating. Without detailing the analogy, we can say that the reality of a "good fit" being found is important in choosing an agency, just as it is in marriage. People who are considering lifelong careers in mission will do well to take their time getting to know the agencies with which they sense a good fit. In earlier times doctrine took center stage. Today's generation of potential missionaries, however, tends to worry less about explicit doctrinal standards than they do about philosophy of ministry.

It would be wise to be asking yourself before you begin the investigative processes what you consider important in choosing an agency. Are there doctrinal boundaries (e.g., authority of Scripture, Pentecostal issues, eschatological beliefs, etc.) that you find crucial? Do you feel that the agency you enter should have a more aggressive or less aggressive approach to evangelism? Would you rather raise funds for a central pool or more directly for yourself? Do you feel comfortable telling people about your financial needs or do you sense a need to be quiet and let God lead them to give without

your raising the subject? If you are single, what are the agency's marriage policies? How does the agency handle school debt? How much choice do you have in your final assignment? How does the agency deal with care of missionaries who have or develop special needs? All of these questions, and more, are important in finding an agency that will provide you an opportunity to be fruitful in God's work. In sidebar 11.1 John McVay, an experienced missionary, presents a list of seven of the most important questions to ask when considering an agency.

There are several means by which people go into missionary work through an agency. Some find an organization and decide to join. Scott Moreau, as a student, was involved with Campus Crusade for Christ on two campuses before joining staff with that organization after graduation.

Others sense God's guidance to a particular country and find an agency that serves in that country. The most recent edition of the EMIS *Mission Handbook: U.S. and Canadian Christian Ministries Overseas,* for example, lists under each country all of the agencies that reported having missionaries serving there.

Still others already have a set of professional skills that they want to use in God's service. They focus on finding an agency or organization that enables them to use those skills most effectively.

A fourth option, mentioned in chapter 10, is for people to form a team before they do anything else. They may come together as a result of attending the same church or school or may even be friends from childhood. Scott has seen teams form among students at Wheaton and also seen teams send some of their members to Wheaton for training. The team then makes group decisions such as emphasis in ministry, placement of service, and mission agency for affiliation. Agencies are more open than ever to people joining as a team, but they still rightly require that each member of the team be fully qualified to join the organization.

CONNECTING WITH A LOCAL CHURCH

For most missionaries, raising support is among the least favorite aspects of their lives. It is not fun to rely on others to meet your financial needs, even though it is biblical for God's people to partner in this way. The issue is made more difficult, however, when there is an inadequate understanding of how things actually work.

The consensus view through much of the twentieth century was that the way to raise support was to travel as widely as possible, presenting your vision to individuals and churches. Connection to the church through a friend, relative, or previous involvement was always considered helpful, but not essential as long as people would give you a hearing. This approach favored those who were effective speakers or who had the most spine-tingling stories to tell. The downside was missionaries spending most of their home-assignment periods (what used to be called "furloughs") in a car.

Today the picture has changed considerably. If the older methodology described above was ever a good one, it is much less so now. This is largely because the church landscape has changed so dramatically. In much of North America megachurches have largely replaced churches of one hundred to four hundred members as the places where

many evangelicals worship (see sidebar 11.2 for an example of how one such church is successfully financing missionary work).

The implications of this for raising missionary support are not inconsequential. Whereas at one time it may have been opportune for a missionary to fill the church's pulpit and share a vision during a worship service, that is seldom true today. In fact, the most common opportunities that were available, a Sunday evening worship service or a Wednesday evening prayer meeting, no longer exist in most churches.

It is important, therefore, that missionary candidates understand the need to focus on their connections with subgroups within the churches (Bible classes, fellowship groups, children's classes, etc.) and with individuals. In either case, relationship is more than advisable. It is essential.

When Gary and Dotsie Corwin came to the conclusion that God was leading them toward long-term missionary service in Africa, they felt led to put something of a fleece before the Lord. They prayed that the Lord might confirm their sense of his leading by providing the bulk of their support through churches and individuals who knew them well, and with whom they had been involved in ministry in some fashion.

One of their biggest fears was a lack of prayer support, and they didn't want to be one of fifty faceless names on the back of church bulletins scattered across the breadth of the continent. They wanted supporters who knew them, cared about them, and would pray for them and their ministry. They also realized that they might be misreading God's direction, and they wanted to provide opportunity for God to show them otherwise. Or perhaps they just needed to be involved in more people's lives before they went. As it turned out, their support was

Missionary Financial Support at Park Street Church (Boston, Massachusetts)

This church's wide-ranging mission vision has it doing a lot of things. These include a comprehensive ten-day mission conference, Barnabas teams (to get behind individual missionaries), partnerships with international leaders and ministries, short-term mission trips, ministry to internationals in the Boston area, and encouraging 100 percent involvement in various city works. What has revolutionized its mission program more recently, however, is its approach to mission sending and support (Telford 2001, 79–80).

A mission pacesetter since its founding in 1809, this church made a difficult but defining transition in its approach to mission support in 1997. The purpose was to build stronger relationships between the church's missionaries and its members. In a letter to the church's missionaries, Senior Pastor Gordon Hugenberger wrote,

> On November 4 the Missions Committee of Park Street Church voted unanimously to adopt a new policy that is intended to radically strengthen the relationship between our church and our active missionaries. Within a mutually agreeable time frame, we will work to redefine our relationship with our active missionaries so that they will be considered as *members of our church's ministerial staff*, except that they will be seconded to various missionary organizations, other than during furloughs.

This new approach required adjustments in finances as well as furloughs, as the letter explains:

> In view of this, our policy will be to provide *full financial support* . . . just as we would for any other member of our ministerial staff. In turn, as with any other member of our staff it will be expected that our missionaries will consider Park Street Church to be their home church. . . . Further, without diminishing the indispensable role of missions agencies, it is expected that our missionaries would seek to involve Park Street Church in any and all major decisions that affect their ministries. Finally, when they are not away on the field, missionaries should normally spend their furloughs at Park Street Church (Telford 2001, 76).

Although some bumps were encountered along the way, the results have been dramatic. By the end of 2000 some sixty-five missionaries were supported by Park Street Church, fourteen of them for 100 percent (Telford 2001, 78). Before this new 100-percent-support venture began, missions giving at Park Street had been in decline over a number of years. However, since the new program has begun, giving has increased, and in 1999 the missions budget ended with a surplus. The belief of the leadership was that giving would increase when there was a significant investment in fewer missionaries. As far as Park Street goes, they were right. The year 1999 saw the decrease in giving ending and the goal of $1.25 million exceeded (Telford 2001, 78).

raised in seven months, and the great bulk of their supporters have stayed with them more than two decades in spite of several changes in their ministry and location. They commend the method to those needing to raise support.

PROFESSIONAL SKILLS OPTIONS: TENTMAKING MISSION

David English of Global Opportunities, an organization dedicated to enabling tentmakers to fulfill God's calling on their lives,

196

estimates that there are some five million jobs filled by Westerners working overseas (English 2002). Thus, many who want to bring the gospel to new cultures do not need to go through traditional missions agencies. Instead, they choose an educational path that provides them with professional skills in the anticipation that they will work in cross-cultural settings as contemporary tentmakers, following the model of Paul and Apollos in Corinth. In sidebar 11.3 Patrick Lai offers a helpful categorization of tentmakers. Terminology aside, the distinctions that Lai makes are important to know when thinking of the full range of tentmaking options.

Done well, tentmaking is not easy. The demands of the job and the need to perform well enough to satisfy your employer can make it more difficult to learn the language and culture. It also takes more time to cultivate and keep formal ties to sending churches or agencies, since none may be required. Christian fellowship and support on the field for you and your family may be more difficult to find. Some organizations may require you to sign a "no evangelism" clause in a contract. Latin America Mission director David Befus concisely summarizes the difficulties:

> The big problem with overseas jobs is that the job takes up all of one's time, and little time is left for ministry activity. There is often limited freedom to learn the language and the culture, or even to decide where to live, or for how long. The connection with the North American supporting church may not exist, as financial support is not necessary so prayer support is not available either. But the basic problem of tentmaking has been the focus on making the tents—it just takes so much of one's time. (Befus 2001, 62)

Even so, tentmakers have some advantages over the regular missionary. For example, they have regular contact with people who do not know Christ and thus more natural opportunities to share Christ.

Tentmakers who are connected with a local mission community can provide a bridge for those who choose to follow Christ into a local church or ministry. Tentmaking is a viable option for cross-cultural service, but those who want to pursue this option should go into it with their eyes open to both the benefits and the problems. In sidebar 11.4 we offer a list of questions that tentmakers should ask about the opportunities they have.

In prior decades people who wanted employment in a new country and were not already employed with a multinational organization typically focused on skills in short supply around the world. The most frequently chosen paths included engineering (civil, industrial, mechanical, and so on), agriculture, education, and health.

However, since the 1980s no professional skill has grown more quickly in use than that of teaching English. Referred to by various terms (TEFL [Teaching English as a Foreign Language] and TESL [Teaching English as a Second Language]), the practice's currently preferred acronym is TESOL (Teaching English to Speakers of Other Languages).

How big is the demand? The fact that there are more people learning English (at all levels) in China than there are English speakers in North America puts it in perspective. The demand for English language skills has swelled tremendously over the past fifty years as English has evolved into a world language. North Americans, most of whom speak English as their first tongue, have a built-in advantage in teaching English to speakers of other languages.

SIDEBAR 11.3
A SPECTRUM OF TENTMAKING OPTIONS

Patrick Lai (Adapted from Lai 2001 [used with permission])

T–1: Hired by a company in their home country to do a job they are uniquely qualified for in another country, T–1s are sincere Christians who are active witnesses for the Lord at home as well as abroad but are overseas not out of any special calling or desire to minister, but because they have been sent there by their company.

T–2: The T–2 is fully supported through his or her job. However, T–2s differ from T–1s in that they do have a calling from the Lord to reach out to a specific people group. A person may choose to work and minister as a T–2 because the country of the people group of call restricts traditional missionary activity or because of a desire to minister among a group of people that is less reached than others. T–2s may be associated with a traditional mission for emotional support and guidance.

T–3: The T–3 . . . is partially or fully supported by the church at home. Thus, back home a T–3 is considered by at least some people to be a missionary, while overseas the T–3 has a nonreligious identity. Most T–3s serve under or have a relationship with a mission or a team of like-minded people. The primary differences between a T–2 and a T–3 concern time and money. T–3s work part-time or operate their own businesses. T–3s supplement their salary by raising partial or full support, as would a traditional missionary. The T–3 sees his or her job first as a vehicle to enter the country, second as a way for reaching out to people, and last a means of financial support.

T–4: The T–4 is not a tentmaker in the sense of working a regular nine-to-five job for a company, but is not a traditional missionary either. A T–4 is someone such as a missionary dentist, doctor, or a social worker. T–4s have actual jobs and do real work, but it is usually in the line of charity and often among the poor. T–4s may even be students studying in a local university. T–4s are fully missionary at home and are supported as missionaries, but due to their jobs, they are recognized as something other than a religious professional on their field of service. T–4s normally are connected to a mission organization through which they raise financial support, receive guidance, and are held accountable for accomplishing their ministry goals. T–4s seek to minister full-time through their predetermined strategies and methodologies.

T–5: The T–5 actually is a regular missionary, not a tentmaker. However, since the place or people they are ministering to is in a country that does not grant "missionary" visas, T–5s have created an identity for themselves that is something other than being a missionary or religious professional. T–5s may have a job with a business, but by prior agreement they really do not work for the company. Some T–5s create "shell companies" to enable them to reside in the country. The company, whether functioning or not, simply provides a "cover" visa by which the T–5 may enter and reside in the target country. T–5s fulfill all the criteria for categories 1 and 2, and, like a T–4, they raise their salary support as a regular missionary does. T–5s are always connected to a mission-sending organization, and they have clear ministry objectives.

A native accent is a valuable tool in teaching English, but many have mistaken the fact that they speak English as their first language for the idea that they can easily teach it without specialized training. This generally is not true—as many, to their chagrin, have found out.

English-language programs (whether TESL or TEFL) have proliferated around the world, especially in Asian contexts. At the same time, training programs in TESOL also have increased significantly in North America in both Christian and secular contexts. There is no longer any reason to go

---

SIDEBAR 11.4
QUESTIONS TO ASK ABOUT TENTMAKING OPPORTUNITIES

Global Opportunities, an organization dedicated to helping tentmakers, provides extensive advice on their Web site (www.globalopps.org). For those who want to become tentmakers but aren't sure how to get started, consider the following questions (Siemens 2002):

1. What are my best aptitudes, gifts, and interests?
2. What do I like to do?
3. What do I do well?
4. What vocations are helpful in a needy world?
5. What skills are marketable in my target country?
6. What career will enable me to support a family and make me marketable at home and abroad?

If you are interested in becoming a tentmaker, or if you anticipate providing guidance for those who want to pursue tentmaking options, we highly recommend *Working Your Way to the Nations: A Guide to Effective Tentmaking* (Lewis 1996) as an excellent resource.

---

to a new culture to teach English without the proper training (and credentials) that will enable you to do your job to the best of professional standards and thereby develop a more effective witness for Christ. In fact, countries are increasingly becoming selective in the types of credentials they will accept for people coming to teach English, with an accredited M.A. in TESOL (or equivalent) becoming the normal minimum requirement.

Although it is true that TESOL skills are currently the most in demand, skills in areas such as engineering, health, education, and agriculture continue to be valuable for gaining legitimate professional entry into another culture. This does not eliminate other creative options (such as opening a Web café, starting a travel agency, launching an import-export business, and so on) that entrepreneurial missionaries have used. In fact, these types of income-generating

activities may be the future mainstay for missionaries from the majority world (Befus 2002).

Finally, with an economy now globalized to an unprecedented degree, the availability of multinational corporations with offices scattered throughout the world has made it easier than ever to find a job in one's home country with the intention of serving the same company in a new setting in the future.

RELIEF AND DEVELOPMENT OPPORTUNITIES

Another entry path to cross-cultural ministry is that of relief and development. The reality of ongoing pain and suffering stemming from natural and human-made disasters as well as the overwhelming need for development in many countries in the world make this path to ministry one that is strategic for human development and

CASE STUDY:
WHEN A WOMAN
SHOULD BE A MAN

Frances F. Hiebert
(Hiebert and Hiebert 1987, 205–8 [used with permission])

Karen White stared out the window of the bedroom-cum-office in her home. Snow had fallen softly during the night and settled on the pine branches that framed the window. Now the sun was shining brightly, and the day glistened with all the promise of a winter reprieve. But Karen was only half aware of the winter wonderland outside. She was, in fact, quite deeply troubled about the future of her mission organization.

It was her organization. She had begun it and for several years had been its director. The purpose of the organization was to provide interim medical personnel for mission hospitals and clinics. Doctors and nurses from the United States took their vacation time, sometimes extended, to serve in place of missionaries who had gone on furlough. Karen's organization recruited the temporary workers and put them in touch with mission agencies that needed them.

Karen worked with a volunteer committee of Christian doctors in the Boston area. At their last meeting, one of them, Dr. Brown, threw a bombshell into the discussion—at least from Karen's perspective. He raised the issue of having men under the authority of women, citing a radio preacher he had heard that day. He asked whether, now that the mission was well established, they should not consider recruiting a man to be in charge. Karen, he said, could certainly remain as assistant director and would be invaluable in training the new male director. But, with a man in charge, the mission would be in line with their evangelical constituency and with Scripture.

The rationale given for this proposed change of administration had caused turmoil in Karen's mind all week. Her background, training, and present commitment were to the full authority of the Bible. It had never occurred to her that she was doing anything "wrong" when she answered God's call to mission and administered the agency that she was sure God had called into being. The discussion in the meeting had left her thoroughly confused. She was a single woman. Did the instructions to wives in the New Testament mean that all women were subject to all men? Were they universal, for all time and every place? Or were the injunctions about women addressed to a particular situation for a particular reason?

Dr. Fleming, another member of the committee, at the same meeting had voiced concern about changing to a male administrator. With things going so well, he asked, why should they risk the slippage that is an inevitable part of change? He admitted that he didn't know quite what to think about the biblical issues and the church interpretations, but he did know about a real situation that was very much like this one.

A number of years ago, Dr. Fleming told the committee, a young woman named Julie Smith, who had been his wife's close friend while he was in medical school in Canada, had worked on various university campuses for a well-known campus-ministry organization. She was also very interested in foreign mission and did her best to interest the students with whom she worked. She participated with great enthusiasm in the Urbana Conferences.

During the time she worked for the campus ministry, the Lord gave Julie a vision for a need that she felt was not being met. Many young people committed themselves to mission but had little guidance as to how they should go about getting involved. Julie felt called to set up an organization that would help match the gifts and abilities of young people with mission organizations and agencies overseas that could use them.

Then one of the board members whose opinions she respected told Julie that it was time to turn leadership of the organization over to a man. He recommended a certain man for the job. Julie was reluctant about choosing that particular man only because he had no overseas experience. She was no "feminist." If a man would be more acceptable to the evangelical public, she was ready to go along with the change. Besides, it would free her to concentrate on improving the service.

It was not long after this man took charge, however, before the organization was in deep trouble. Julie had built up a large file of well-prepared applicants, and many others had already been placed in ministry positions overseas. But, soon after she turned over the leadership, the placement counseling was eliminated and the service dwindled to almost nothing. Financially, the organization was now always broke, although Julie was still out doing the fund raising.

Friction arose because Julie was still the *de facto* head as far as the evangelical community that supported them was concerned. Because of her long overseas experience, invitations to speak in churches about their mission came to her rather than to the man in charge. He had no mission expertise.

The small board was too far away and too busy to know what was really going on. Tired of the financial problems, the board finally decided to dissolve the organization.

Julie—on the recommendation of local mission leaders and her pastor and feeling a strong sense of call from the Lord—in the same week that the old organization was dissolved, incorporated a new one with the same goals. This time the board was composed of local people with whom she could stay in close contact. They rejoiced with her over how promptly God provided all their needs and how quickly the new organization became even more fruitful than the earlier one.

"This difficult experience has made Julie more sympathetic to women in leadership," said Dr. Fleming to Karen and the other committee members. "And I think there are some valuable lessons for us in her story. We should be careful not to repeat past mistakes."

The mention of women in leadership had made Dr. Brown bristle, and Karen herself flinched, because she always tried to avoid that discussion. She wanted to get on with the work of evangelism and avoid being embroiled in hassles over who should be in charge.

"And yet," Karen thought, as she reached for her coat and scarf, "I am in the middle of it just because I am a woman—whether I like it or not." When she opened the door, a fluff of snow landed on her head. She thought of 1 Corinthians 11:10 and smiled in spite of herself. Was the snow a sign that her authority was on her own head? No, she would need more concrete guidance than that.

Her heart lifted as she took in the grandeur of the day. But the weight of the decision she must make was still on her. Should she resign and be submissive in the way that she, like many other evangelical women, had been conditioned? Or should she follow the new urging that she had been convinced was a call from God, and continue the work that God had begun in her?

As she walked away from the house, leaving a trail of footsteps in the soft snow, Karen realized that her decision, like Julie's in the story told by Dr. Fleming, would be a precedent for many other women who were struggling to live out their calls to mission and ministry, in spite of misunderstandings and traditions in some sectors of the contemporary evangelical church. As she looked at the brilliant sky and the snow-crowned earth around her, Karen suddenly remembered the words of the psalmist: "I will trust and not be afraid."

for sharing Christ. Many Christian organizations either are exclusively focused on relief/development ministry or have subministries whose focus is on this area. An active list of such organizations, with links to them, can be found on the MisLinks site (www.mislinks.org/practical/rdorgs.htm) (Moreau and O'Rear 2002). Skills in areas such as community health, microeconomic development, large-scale emergency response needs, administrative tasks, education, agriculture, and the like are useful.

As a final note, the warning offered by Befus (above) for those working as tentmakers applies also to those working in relief and development. In the midst of facing desperate needs it can be easy to lose the focus of mission as calling others to repent, turn to Christ, and come worship the King of kings. As we outlined in chapter 5, mission that engages in relief and development but omits evangelism, discipleship, and church planting is not truly holistic mission; it has simply replaced one focus for another (Myers 1995).

MEGACHURCH MISSIONARIES

A more recent option available to people following God's leading to serve as missionaries is to simply go through their own local church. This option generally is limited to a few megachuches. Some of them have decided that traditional models of missionary agencies are not the best means of sending people overseas and have, in effect, established their own agencies. In the process, however, they are learning that the work of supporting people far away from home requires a great deal of time and resources.

CONCLUSION

Whatever path one chooses to go to the nations, multiple opportunities and a wide variety of options are available. We encourage you to chart a path that both honors God's call and leading in your life and reflects the fact that he has created all Christians as a community of believers who are to encourage each other (1 Thess. 5:11), equip each other (Eph. 4:11–13), and help each other fulfill the works that God has established in advance for them to do (Eph. 2:10). The case study for this chapter focuses on a situation in which a woman, following God's call, started a ministry and is now being challenged about an ongoing role with the ministry because she is a woman. Her situation illustrates how complex and difficult it can be to move "from here to there" in our contemporary world.

PART 4

Encountering Missions
as a Sent One and as a Sender

Y ou have been called out, prayed over, trained, underwritten, packed up, and sent off. So what happens now? In a word: adjustment—to a new role, on a new team, in a new place, among a new people with a new culture. And that's just for starters. Even after you've been there for a while, you still will have ongoing personal, family, strategic, cultural, and relational issues to deal with. "You mean this is not going to be easy?" That's right, this is not going to be easy—but it can be done. God's grace is sufficient for you, just as you have already experienced, and, just as it has always been for the thousands upon thousands who preceded you.

Mission never has been the province solely of those who go; it also belongs to those who send—by their prayers and by their gifts. Though the dividing line between the sent and the senders is less pronounced today because of the many senders who also go (often for multiple short-term ministry trips), the distinction still is important. It

is important not because it creates a hierarchy of relative value, but because each role encompasses a particular spectrum of responsibilities and challenges.

In this part we explore issues of importance to the missionary once he or she arrives on location. In chapter 12 we discuss issues of importance to family and mission team; in chapter 13 we cover issues of strategy and ministry; and in chapter 14 we overview the missionary work of developing relationships with people who are culturally different. We also turn to those who are senders, especially those commissioning churches that form the backbone of any missionary endeavor. We briefly examine the agencies, training institutions, and mobilizers who play crucial roles alongside the churches in getting the sent ones from here to there. Thus, in our final chapter of the part, chapter 15, we turn the focus around to explore challenges that face local churches, agencies, and training institutions—the senders of missionaries.

12

Personal
and Family Issues

INTRODUCTION

At the center of any worthy endeavor is the issue of personal preparedness. For the believer, an additional issue is that of conformity to the will of God. And what is true for the individual is true also for his or her family. Personal and family issues are not secondary matters when it comes to success or failure in the mission enterprise. They are foundational.

At least four subject areas require our attention under the broad category of personal and family issues: (1) assimilation (life as a new team member); (2) enculturation (life as a language and culture learner); (3) lifestyle (life as a rich person among the poor); and (4) special challenges (life as a displaced person or family).

ASSIMILATION: LIFE AS A NEW TEAM MEMBER

Although the term *pioneer* is still a familiar one to describe a good deal of contemporary missionary work, the adjective *lonely* is much more rarely applied than it used to be. This is because most missionary work today is done in teams. For the sent one, this brings both good news and bad news.

The good news is that loneliness is less of a problem, strategizing is more effective, and spiritual gifts and natural abilities are more broadly represented. In addition, a more holistic representation of the body of Christ is made visible in the host culture, whether churches of any kind currently exist there or not. The bad news—or better, perhaps, hard news—is that the new missionary family needs to learn not only the culture and cues of the host culture, but also about their new teammates. Sometimes the resulting tensions can be enormous, and with the internationalization of teams becoming more and more common, both the blessings and tensions are multiplied.

In many ways, Scott Moreau's first two years of missionary service were the most difficult years of his life. Separated from family by a distance of twelve thousand miles, and having left behind an important dating relationship, he wrestled with loneliness and culture shock bound inextricably together.

His first assignment was to lead his team of four in the northern part of the country. He and his roommate taught at a rural high school, and the other two teammates, both women, taught at another school in a nearby town. They enjoyed each other and generally got along well, but the stress of living and working in a new culture at new jobs (none had ever taught high school before) and ministry responsibilities weighed heavily on all.

Loneliness, compounded by isolation and differences in personality styles, eventually took its toll. Eighteen months into his first two-year term, Scott felt as though he had been through an emotional divorce from his teammates. Although they were all on speaking terms and friendly with each other, Scott felt isolated and distant, without support or interest in pursuing change.

One saving grace was the team of missionaries with his organization. At the time, there were numerous other single missionaries scattered around the country who had been through pre-field training together. They provided emotional support at critical

> *Infighting among personnel is more devilish, desperate, and devastating than anything from the outside.*
> Clarence Jones (Neely 1980, 37)

times and helped Scott keep his focus on Christ rather than on his circumstances.

Scott's experience is far more common than many realize. Culture shock is bad enough. Add to that the reality of living with people who are different from you, and having wrong expectations that they would not be as different as they really are, and you have a recipe for frustration, disappointment, and hurt.

Choosing to lean on God at this time is perhaps the most foundational decision in

avoiding burnout and early attrition. It is important to enter the field knowing that ordinary stresses in your home culture will be magnified because life in general is a stress when culture shock hits. If you know from the outset that your teammates will be different from you, it can make it easier to handle things when the differences seem larger than you ever imagined.

Developing a Team, Finding an Agency

One recent trend seen among North Americans is that of people forming teams and then focusing on an area of the world and finding an agency to join. Teams formed in the home culture prior to departure typically will have worked through many of the relational issues that come up on the field. However, they too need to be prepared for the intensity of feelings that surface when differences continue to be unresolved after arrival at their destination.

Agencies so far have relatively mixed reactions to teams formed in this way. On the positive side, a ready-made team is always welcomed in God's work. However, these teams are not immune to the problems faced by teams formed on the field. If they end up dissolving (and this happens), the emotional turmoil and resulting casualties can be higher than in the case of a team that was formed on the field of service.

International or Multicultural Teams

Another facet of globalization in mission has been the development of teams comprised of individuals from many cultures and languages. More often than not, these teams have to use English as the only medium of communication. Though the team members have at least that much in common, those members whose first language is not English find themselves at a distinct disadvantage when it comes to communicating the nuances necessary for healthy team dynamics.

These teams do have the advantage of displaying in very practical ways the diversity of the body of Christ (Cho and Greenlee 1995, 179). They also have an intrinsic system of checks that help them distinguish cultural from biblical values, since different cultures are represented within the team itself. As they work through their differences, they display to the local church the ability to cross cultural, economic, and linguistic hindrances in relationships. They are less likely to be seen as politically motivated, since they come from many nations. Finally, their home churches benefit from seeing the diverse nature of the body of Christ and developing connections with parts of the world they may have not known previously.

Multicultural teams also have significant difficulties to overcome. Missions must address this issue in the years to come because international teams will become increasingly common, as will the fallout of the team breakups that inevitably will occur. International teams especially have to find ways to adjust to the cultural differences that can make the team setting just as stressful as the field setting. Devising ways to blend teams of internationals together remains a perplexing issue for agencies.

General Guidelines for Teams

What, then, are the keys to coping? We offer three. First, be certain before connecting with a team that you and your teammates are on the same page regarding the purpose and priorities of the team. Your agency or sponsoring church should have done most of the legwork on this before you came aboard, but it is important that you confirm compatibility for yourself. Second, beyond the issue of purpose and priorities, be willing to give up your rights. As C. S. Lewis wrote many years ago, "The man preoccupied with his own rights is not only a disastrous, but a very unlovely object" (Martindale and Root 1989, 520). Third, view diversity on the team as an asset and an enriching factor, not a bother. To have the varied gifts of other team members at your disposal and to enjoy the variety of their cultural and personal backgrounds is something to be treasured, not trashed.

It is almost as predictable as the sun rising tomorrow that the time will come when you as a new team member will be asked to do something for the good of the team for which you consider yourself neither well trained nor well suited. This is the test of your commitment to teamwork and of your faith in the God whose grace is sufficient for you. Respond positively if at all possible. You need not take on the job as an open-ended assignment, but your willingness to fill in until a suitable substitute can be found is an important part of what teams are all about.

It should be remembered about teams that they do come in various shapes and sizes, depending largely on their purpose and origins. Among many things, they can be long term or short term, monocultural or multicultural, ministry specific or multiministry, theologically uniform or theologically diverse. The point is that although all teams have many things in common, they also differ widely with regard to policy, practice, and ethos. Do all you can to know the team you are joining, and be honest with yourself and others concerning the things about which you can be flexible and the things that for you are nonnegotiable.

ENCULTURATION: LIFE AS A LANGUAGE AND CULTURE LEARNER

Crossing cultural barriers for the work of the gospel, or for any purpose for that matter, raises significant issues of role. This is true even for roles that transfer relatively easily (male, female, spouse, parent, etc.), because such roles undoubtedly will have some different expectations attached to them in the new culture. Often more tricky

> *Learning a language and culture through relationships in a community requires a tremendous commitment to the people of the new language. . . . If your goal is to live with people, to love and serve them, and to become a belonger in your new community, then learning the language will prove to be a great means to that goal. And learning the language will probably become quite manageable!*
>
> Tom Brewster
> (Brewster and Brewster 1986, 4)

still is the role that describes why you have come to this new culture, and how you will carry yourself as a guest within it.

Although ultimately you will want to communicate that it was the love of Christ that constrained you to come, there is a more basic place to start: the role of the learner. It is a role that is universally received and appreciated, and it communicates that you think highly enough of your hosts, their

culture, and their language that you want to learn more about all three. Rather than rushing ahead to drop "gospel bombs" on all with whom you come into contact, you listen and you learn from them, thus nurturing a relationship of trust and mutual respect.

"But," some will ask, "what about my home church and supporters, who are waiting eagerly to hear of souls saved, churches planted, and ministries established?" The short answer is that they will need to learn, as you will learn, that before anyone can reap a harvest, ground must be tilled, seeds planted, and seedlings watered and weeded.

What is a reasonable amount of time to devote to prerequisites of language before one can enter into formal ministry? If you want to become truly conversant in the language, be prepared to put in at least one year of intensive language learning prior to engaging in formal ministry. Experts in language learning recognize that even with a language of average difficulty, it generally will take a full four-year term before you will feel comfortable speaking the language in most settings (Dickerson n.d.[a], 2). Though you may feel stifled during your initial language-learning experience, keep in mind that the method you choose to learn a language can open doors to future ministry. Thinking of language learning as a foundation may ease the burden and provide motivation, even though it will not make the task any easier.

Preparation for Language Learning

Lonna Dickerson, director of the Institute for Cross-Cultural Training, offers the following five steps that you can take at home to help you prepare for language learning on the field (Dickerson n.d.[b]).

First, take a course in Second Language Acquisition (SLA). Those who take these courses consistently report that the time and money saved more than compensate for the cost of the course.

Second, find a native speaker to begin practicing with for at least two hours a week. Developing an ear to hear the sounds as well as make them correctly requires time and effort on your part, and doing this before leaving for the field will ease your transition when on the field. Dickerson recommends that you "work on learning 'survival language'—the kind of language you'll need right away in your new country—and some basic 'building blocks' such as the alphabet, numbers, and a few of the most basic sentence patterns" (Dickerson n.d.[b])

Third, gather as many language resources as you can before going to your assignment. Language textbooks, dictionaries, articles, and the like will be valuable tools for your language-learning process. Having them in hand prior to your arrival can ease your work, and they may even be more readily available at home than on the field.

Fourth, look for CDs that teach your target language. They can be especially helpful in developing your listening comprehension, since any quality program on CD should include native speech for you to practice comprehension on.

Fifth, take a course in the language. Many community colleges offer language courses at reasonable rates. In addition to helping lay foundations for you, such a course might also provide you the opportunity to contact more native speakers of your target language who live nearby. As mentioned in chapter 10, practicing language and ministry skills at home among native speakers of the language can greatly ease your transition. It may even provide valu-

able field contacts, in the relatives of those who helped you at home, before you ever arrive on the field.

Always bear in mind, however, that as important as language learning is, it alone does not provide you all you need to know to successfully communicate across cultural barriers. Working in the Philippines, experienced missionary and church planter Tom Steffen discovered that it was far easier to track how well he was learning the language than how well he was learning the culture. The resulting integrated approach that he developed to learn culture and language at the same time (Steffen 1993, 103–12) is a reminder that intercultural communication involves more than just the language. The culture-learning component will be developed in chapter 16.

Short-Term Missions and Language Learning

The emergence of short-term missions as a widely used model has raised questions concerning some of the earlier assumptions about language learning. Some, focusing on speed and efficiency, have gone so far as to assert that language learning isn't really that important and that working through interpreters is quite sufficient. Whether this is the result of predetermined commitments to types of ministry, or the primary determining factor for them, is open to question.

A carefully reasoned suggestion more faithful to earlier assumptions, however, is that up to 50 percent of one's time given to learning language and culture is not too much to expect even for short-term missions. The reason is that learning language and culture is much more than a prerequisite to ministry; it is the first step and a solid foundation for almost any ministry one can envision. Such learning establishes rapport, builds relationships, and communicates the respect that opens up multiple doors of opportunity.

LIFESTYLE: LIFE AS A RICH PERSON AMONG THE POOR

Few things are as heart-wrenching as coming to terms with one's own relative wealth in a context of overwhelming poverty. If it were simply a matter of a poor person or family in your midst, they could be cheerfully assisted and their woes ameliorated to the greatest extent possible. But

> *What are we here for, to have a good time with the Christians or to save sinners?*
>
> Malla Moe (Nilsen 1956, 132)

when the vast majority of people in a culture are in some type of significant need, one's inability to respond meaningfully can be most disheartening.

The problem is complicated further by the conflicting priorities that so often come into play. The missionary who has a spouse and children bears the responsibility of caring for and protecting them in a culture that is not their own, often thousands of miles away from the supportive care of friends and extended family. With much that is new and sometimes dangerous, this responsibility can stand in acute tension with the need to incarnate and identify with the host culture in which the missionary now resides. In such a context the potential for wallowing in feelings of guilt is substantial.

One of the areas in which the tension most often is seen is the employment of domestic help. For most middle-class Americans, the thought of having paid helpers in the home to do things that the family always has done for itself is repulsive at best. This assessment has a tendency to change, however, when the realities are carefully assessed:

"Everything seems to take twice as long, or even longer, to do here."

"Foreigners sure have a hard time getting things at a reasonable price in the market."

"Visiting with people certainly is an enjoyable and necessary form of ministry, but it sure can eat up the time."

These and similar concerns prove decisive for many in coming to the conclusion that they do need and want to employ household help. Another factor that weighs heavily for many is the realization that they can provide gainful employment for someone who otherwise might be unemployed and unable to support his or her dependents.

As reasonable as the foregoing considerations are, they seldom totally eliminate the feelings of angst that accompany the practice—all the more so when and if employer-employee issues emerge over time.

More difficult still is the perennial issue of how to respond to beggars, particularly in contexts where the number of beggars is overwhelming. This is an area where missionaries walk more by faith than by sight. As one of Gary Corwin's colleagues said, "Sometimes I give, and sometimes I don't. As much as anything, I look for the Holy Spirit's promptings, and I recognize from the outset that sometimes I will be right and sometimes I will be wrong. Sometimes I will give to charlatans, and sometimes I won't give to the worthy. The Lord knows, so I don't need to stress out about it."

Dealing with beggars is more art than science, more waiting upon God than doing extensive investigation (frequently there is simply no time for the latter). Most important is to recognize that there is no perfect, ultimate solution to the challenge, but only the daily walk of dependence on the Lord.

Unfortunately for those in the camp of the already perplexed—"Can missionary life get any more complicated?"—larger and more systemic issues arise that relate to this problem as well. These include the relational, communication, and strategic consequences of missionary affluence, as well as the more basic theological, ethical, and biblical considerations that should guide every Christian in assessing personal behavior and lifestyle.

No one has attempted to respond to these issues in a more comprehensive way than Jonathan Bonk in *Missions and Money: Affluence as a Western Missionary Problem* (1991), and we commend that book for your consideration. Bonk doesn't claim to have all the answers, but his diagnosis is insightful, his questions are probing, his tone is sympathetic, and his transparency in the struggle is refreshing. In the concluding section he writes,

> As long as we North American Christians and leaders demonstrate that we have learned only to abound, it will be hypocritical to insist that missionaries from among us should learn how to be in want. The Laodicean Church cannot inspire its members to great sacrifices for the sake of Christ. Only a community of believers who themselves have chosen to reject the materialist spirit of the age can stir its members to pursue genuine self-sacrifice abroad. A wealthy church is bound by the rules of propriety to support its missionaries according to its own ever-inflating notions of adequacy. On the other hand, missionaries so supported are not morally obligated to conform to Western

standards of consumption and privilege. They are free—indeed morally obligated as Christ's followers—to practice stewardship of these resources according to the dictates of the consciences. . . .

> In the final analysis, Christian stewardship is not something we do, but something we become. Not a technique but a way of living. (Bonk 1991, 129, 131)

In this area, as in so many others, the challenge of being is the ultimate one, and this comes only by spending lots of time with Jesus and in God's word.

SPECIAL CHALLENGES: LIFE AS A DISPLACED PERSON OR FAMILY

Growing out of life in a new cultural context are several issues concerning the sense

> *If Jesus Christ be God and died for me, then no sacrifice can be too great for me to make for Him.*
> C. T. Studd (Grubb 1945, 13–14)

of disruption that is part and parcel of such a change. Five that bear most significantly on new missionaries are issues of security and significance, singleness and mission, loneliness and romance, educating kids, and home assignment and reentry.

Security and Significance

At the upper end of Maslow's hierarchy of human need are the twin issues of belongingness and significance (Maslow 1970). Maslow posits that once the more basic needs for food, shelter, and security are met, people still need to belong and to feel significant. Though both of these latter needs are important for males and females

211

alike, and how they are expressed will vary widely across cultures, we have observed that North American male and female missionaries do not give them equal priority. In fact, it is remarkable to note the difference in response that commonly occurs during the first year of ministry in a new culture.

The first two months seem to be particularly difficult for the women, and the primary issue seems to be one of belongingness. They have, after all, left their homes, friends, and extended family—in short, most of the relationships and familiar things that heretofore provided stability, comfort, and predictability to their lives. They now find themselves having to reestablish a home and make new friends in a new place, in the context of a culture and a language that also are new to them. No wonder the first two months are so stressful.

Once those new relationships and a new place called home begin to be established, however, they quite often take on a new spirit of optimism and peace. This certainly was the case for Gary Corwin and his wife, Dotsie. Toward the end of their first two months in Ghana, Gary was beginning to wonder if Dotsie would ever get past breaking down in tears over the smallest things. To his delight, she did so at about the two-month mark, and it was clear that it coincided with new friendships developing both for them and their two boys, and the achievement of a certain level of order and routine in the home.

Gary, on the other hand, had entered their new context brimming with optimism and with a clear focus on the job to be done: to establish an evening Bible school so that urban churches could have well-trained leaders, and wider outreach could be facilitated. He was greatly relieved when Dotsie's crisis passed, and was somewhat surprised

when his own surfaced about four months later. For him, as for many men, the crisis centered more on significance. All the things that he had hoped to achieve had not been accomplished, and everything seemed to take far more time than he had thought possible. This raised questions in his mind about the wisdom of the course he was on. Fortunately, his wife's newly found sense of belonging provided an anchor of stability through which the Lord could remind him of the significance of what he was doing.

Though for some time Gary and Dotsie considered this experience to be nothing more than personal history, subsequent years of ministry with new missionaries on several continents convinced them that this pattern is much more the rule than the exception.

We are convinced, therefore, that it is crucial for husbands and administrators to be especially vigilant and sensitive in their ministry to wives and other women during those highly vulnerable first couple of months. Likewise, wives and administrators need to be vigilant and sensitive to the vulnerability of men as they come to terms with new realities. When they come to realize that their "Eight-Point Plan to Complete World Evangelization," or whatever their particular vision is, may not be achievable in the way they had projected, it can come as quite a blow. And they will especially need encouragement when it really hits home that life in this new culture is going to require some new coping skills, including large doses of patience, flexibility, and perseverance.

Singleness and Mission

Any discussion on singleness and missionary work must emphasize that singleness is not somehow a less-than-ideal state for a missionary. Jesus was single, and single men and women carrying the gospel message to other cultures have been part of the history of the church since the days of Paul (1 Cor. 7:7).

Among evangelicals, "single" traditionally meant being celibate and never having married. Today, however, it also includes the bereaved and the divorced (Foyle 1985, 134).

Although singleness applies to both genders, in Protestant circles, especially from the 1800s on, far more single women than single men have populated the missionary ranks (Tucker and Liefeld 1987; see also Douglas 1988). Historically, Protestant missionaries who went to the field as singles generally did not consider themselves singles for life. Exceptions included, for example, those women's agencies in the nineteenth century that required their candidates to sign a pledge to remain single (Beaver 1980, 181).

What, then, are the advantages and challenges of being a single missionary (see also Hale 1995, 350–52; Lum 1984, 105–11)?

ADVANTAGES FOR SINGLE MISSIONARIES

The first advantage to being a single missionary is noted by Paul. Married people have to devote time and energy to each other, while those who are not married may focus exclusively on God's work (1 Cor. 7:32–35). The single missionary can be more productive simply because her or his entire life focus can be ministry, including language learning, preparation for teaching, spontaneous evangelism, and so on.

Second, singles tend to be more flexible in location and ministry assignment. Uprooting families is usually more traumatic than uprooting singles. Singles can adjust to harsh conditions more quickly than whole families can. This advantage must not become an agency policy, however, because singles also need stability and should not be subjected to administrative whims or fads.

A third advantage is that singles have significantly less financial support to raise than married couples do, and especially those with families. Although we never should let finances become the bottom line for missionary "efficiency," the fact remains that singles are a more efficient use of financial resources than missionary families. Related to this is that singles can live a less cluttered lifestyle, as Ada Lum notes:

> Singles can get along with temporary furnishings that are impractical for a family. They can live out of a suitcase but a family cannot. A bicycle often suffices for a single person, but a family usually has to have a car. So not only do singles spend less money on personal and household furnishings; they spend less time maintaining them. In short, singles can keep their lives uncluttered materially and mentally. This should make it easier to keep their lives emotionally uncluttered too. (Lum 1984, 108)

Finally, singles are able to spend more time developing close relationships with nationals in the community they serve. Not having a spouse or children, who need time and attention, singles are freer to intermingle with those they serve.

CHALLENGES FOR SINGLE MISSIONARIES

Single missionaries often receive less consideration in regard to housing and ministry assignments. Agencies, assuming that singles are more flexible, may reassign them more quickly than they do married missionaries and unnecessarily disrupt ministry. In addition, singles rarely get to choose their roommates, and being placed in a housing situation with a person whom one does not know can add to the stress of living cross-culturally.

Single missionaries must deal with loneliness. Singleness is still not thought of in many cultures as a "natural" state. The local culture may wonder what role the single person serves. Fellow missionaries may unconsciously communicate this feeling as well, even trying to make matches between single missionaries. When done inappropriately, this communicates to singles that they are in some way incomplete without a spouse, even though that may not be the intention of the matchmakers.

Single missionaries need special care to ensure that their relational needs are being met. It may become routine to find "fillers" that take the place of relational intimacy. Work, ministry, hobbies—any or all of these may be used as substitutes for the relationships that every human needs, and singles should be wary lest those good things crowd out the better things.

Finally, singles must deal with unfulfilled sexuality. This is potentially a dangerous area. The fact is that every normal, healthy single missionary will face sexual tension. Finding appropriate, creative, and helpful ways to recognize and relieve the tension will be a long-term issue for the single missionary. Marjory Foyle explains two areas of sexuality that must be faced and offers helpful advice:

> *Biological sexuality.* This is the urge, the instinct, the innate drive to mate and to reproduce. Many Christians believe the sex drive has a deeper significance than other drives—such as hunger—and this may be true. Nevertheless, it is a basic bodily drive that we can never expect to lose.
>
> Here single missionaries make a mistake. Because they remain sexual beings they think their dedication is inadequate. Some ask God to remove sexual feelings if they are not going to marry. This, of course, God will not do, for it would make them less than human.
>
> It is also futile to attempt to feel totally fulfilled. Single people [*who have never mated nor had children*] can never be fulfilled biologically. . . . In dealing with biological urges, it is important simply to accept them as indications of normality. Continued trust in God's overall plan for their life, together with a wise life pattern, helps the single missionary maintain celibacy for as long as God wishes. But it is important to use common sense. Single missionaries need to be wise in avoiding situations that may make chastity difficult to maintain.
>
> *Creative sexuality.* This aspect of the sex drive is utilized in many different ways: care of children, service, maintenance of good personal relationships, work, and many other things; all are powered by creative sexuality.
>
> Creative energy is reduced when single persons use a lot of energy in resenting their singleness. In reality, this energy holds abundant possibilities for personal fulfillment. A profitable habit single persons might adopt is to thank God at the end of each day for the volume of creative sexuality expended during the day's ministry. (Foyle 1987, 139–40)

Loneliness and Romance

Matters of the heart are tricky in every culture but can become doubly so when multiple cultures are involved. Besides the usual complexities associated with love and loneliness, additional considerations arise when ministering cross-culturally.

SIDEBAR 12.1
THINKING OF MARRYING SOMEONE FROM ANOTHER
CULTURE?

Bill and Carol O'Hara
(O'Hara and O'Hara 2002 [used with permission])

Cross-cultural marriages offer significant advantages and disadvantages. But before you cross cultural boundaries in marriage, you should carefully consider the following set of questions written by Bill and Carol O'Hara, missionaries in Latin America.

Are you willing for your children to not really know your parents?	Marrying someone from another culture means that one of you will be living outside of your home nation permanently . . . which means that . . . your children will see very little of one set of grandparents.
Are you willing for your family members to not be able to communicate well with your children?	Not only will your children not have the opportunity to know one set of grandparents very well, if there is a language barrier, one set of grandparents will not be able to really communicate well with your children.
Are you willing to take the time to explain why something is funny to you? . . . Are you ready to just accept the fact that you won't be able to share each other's humor?	Marrying someone from another culture means that you will have a hard time understanding each other's humor.
Are you willing for your children to grow up with a different set of family traditions than your own?	Marrying someone from another culture means that one of you must be willing to not give your children the cultural traditions and national heritage that you have.
Are you willing to live in your spouse's home country indefinitely?	You need to be aware that the day may come when you may need to move to your spouse's home country.
Are you willing to lose your place in society?	You may need to consider that the socioeconomic class one holds in one culture may not cross over in another culture.
Are you willing for your children to grow up with gender role models you don't approve of?	Growing up in another culture means that the gender role models for your children may not be what you would consider to be good role models.
Have you considered how the "home court advantage" may affect your marriage relationship?	You may need to consider the effect of the "home court advantage" on your marriage. If a foreign man marries an American woman and they live in the United States, she would be cast in the leadership role in some aspects of their relationship. . . . Whereas if they lived in his nation, he would be able to lead out more effectively in their marriage.

For those who are single but interested in the possibility of marriage, it will be obvious that there are fewer members present from the home culture when one is residing in another cultural context. To the extent that this is important to an individual, it needs to be faced squarely. If, on the other hand, one is open to the possibility of cross-cultural courtship, then a different set of issues needs to be considered: What would marriage to an individual from another culture mean? Would your expectations of marriage and life be compatible? Would you need to make more compromises than you are willing to make? Romano (1997) and others have documented general characteristics of cross-cultural romances. More significant, perhaps, is that such romances tend to be more intense in two ways in comparison with intracultural ones: first, the flame of romance certainly can burn brighter, but, second, cross-cultural romances tend to fall apart faster and with more negative energy.

Adjustments are part of every marriage, but there are particular adjustments that cross-cultural couples need to be aware of prior to committing themselves to marriage. In sidebar 12.1 Bill and Carol O'Hara provide a helpful set of questions and comments to help you see some of the issues involved.

For those who are single and not necessarily interested in marriage at all, there are still issues to be faced. With whom are you going to relate as "family" in your new context? How will you maintain adequate links to your real family without becoming e-mail dependent or otherwise disabled to the extent that you cannot relate well in your new culture? These issues should be faced squarely, early, and with the benefit of counsel from a number of fair-minded sources.

Educating Kids

No subject is more sensitive than this one. People generally, and Christians even more so, often can be quite tolerant of unfavorable circumstances where only their own preferences and desires are thwarted. Let their children be impacted negatively, however, and very quickly they can begin to act more like a mother bear whose cub is threatened than a dove of peace.

The missions enterprise has passed through a difficult time over this subject in the last few decades. The context has shifted from a time when "ministry adultery" was a dominant model, and almost any sacrifice of one's family for the cause was considered noble, to a time when "family idolatry" is too common, and no family sacrifice for the sake of ministry is permissible. Fortunately, in the midst of this changing context some very good things have happened with regard to the education of missionaries' children.

First, mission policies have moved away from a one-size-fits-all approach that usually meant that boarding school away from parents was the only option. In its place, multiple-option and highly flexible approaches suited to individual family needs have become the new norm.

Second, homeschooling, which in recent years has swept over the landscape in North America, is now accommodated in mission circles not just as an acceptable choice for missionary families, but even as a preferable one during early years of education. This has made it possible for many families to envision themselves ministering in the remotest pioneer situations when previously they might have dismissed out of hand the possibility of such service.

Third, an increasingly important question is the effect that missionary choices may have on nationals. In many countries homeschooling resources are not available to national missionaries, and the choices that expatriate missionaries make may have an impact on the ways nationals want to educate their children. There are no simple guidelines in this matter, but it is a factor that should be taken into account in establishing mission policies for the education of children.

Finally, many traditional mission boarding schools have reengineered themselves to become highly desirable options for private education in their local context. They minister more effectively now not only to the children of missionaries, but also to the children of national and international church, business, and government leaders. They have become in many cases not just support ministries, but true outreach ones.

Home Assignment and Reentry

A challenge of a very different sort looms large for those who return after several years from another country, particularly those coming from one of the poorer nations of the world to their own, more wealthy, home country. To the extent that they have adapted well to their new environment, learned the language, and identified with its people and culture, the reentry challenge is that much more severe. Suddenly, people and contexts whom a missionary has known for decades seem out of touch and quite foreign to the person he or she has become.

Likewise, missionaries often seem disturbingly different to many of the people with whom they have had deep relationships for years. Reentry is, in many ways, a difficult time. Often, the reunion with family and friends that has been fondly anticipated for a long time is a disappointment because

it has become so idealized in their minds. The things and activities that meant a great deal to the missionaries in earlier days, including the pursuit of personal peace and affluence, may suddenly seem trivial and mundane.

For those missionaries with families, an accompanying challenge that often surfaces is the sense of confusion among children as to where home is. Home for most of them is where they have just come from, the culture that hosts their parents' ministry. Yet they incessantly hear words of "welcome home" from a myriad of family, friends, acquaintances, and supporters. Though their parents perhaps still have important roots that they cherish back in the sending country, it may be a very different story for the children. They are not called "third-culture kids" for nothing. Not fully at home in either their parents' birth country or their ministry country, they truly are of a third culture.

Issues of money are never far from the missionary's consciousness on home assignment either. The very essence of home assignment is to report back to those who have prayed and given to sustain you in your missionary labors over the last several years. This can be a great joy, but it also can be a bit threatening, particularly

> *Wants are things we think we need; necessities are things God knows we need. God will supply our needs, not our wants.*
>
> Thomas J. Bach (1951, 41)

if you sense that the labors in which you have been engaged may not be fully appreciated by those churches or individuals

217

Case Study:
Trouble with Servants

Matt Howell
(Hiebert and Hiebert 1987, 240–42 [used with permission])

"Mark, what are we going to do with Nadine?" Linda was at her wit's end. Her husband gave a sigh. Nadine, their maid in Haiti for over two years, had refused to do her full job the last few weeks. Mark knew they could hardly let her go. She seemed like family now and she would have no place to go and no means of support if she were fired.

When Mark and Linda first came to Haiti, they both planned to work full-time. Mark was a hospital administrator, and Linda taught high-school English at the local missionary school. They found out when they arrived that just keeping house in that subtropical country was a full-time job in itself. Occupied fully with their jobs, neither one had time to go to the market and bargain for the food that had to be bought daily to ensure its freshness. Nor had they the time to soak the fruits and vegetables in permanganate solution to kill bacteria, to boil all the water needed for drinking and cooking, or to kill and clean the chickens, which were still running around when they got them in the market. Around the house, the garbage had to be burned, food protected from insects, floors mopped, laundry hung and rehung to dry, and a daily ritual performed of wiping the dust that came in freely off the unpaved roads. They soon found themselves overwhelmed with domestic duties that kept them from fulfilling the tasks of their mission. Their colleagues encouraged them to hire a Haitian maid.

The idea of having a maid did not sit well with Mark and Linda at first. The last thing they wanted to do was help perpetuate white supremacy in an already oppressed society. But they began to realize that besides freeing themselves from household chores so that they could use their abilities in ministry, they could also provide adequate housing, a balanced diet, and a Christian witness to a Haitian that had known none of these before.

Through the recommendation of a friend, they hired Nadine to help them around the house. They knew at once they had made the right decision. Nadine worked hard and did everything she was instructed to do, even though she had to be reminded at times. Between her broken English and Mark's and Linda's limited Creole, they were able to communicate adequately enough to get the job done. Nadine was also able to get better bargains at the market than her employers, because she knew the barter-trade system inside out. Mark and Linda and Nadine soon became good friends.

From a Haitian perspective, Nadine now had a high-paying job with room and board in a "blanc's big house," and she was therefore looked on with envy by her Haitian friends. At first she enjoyed the prestige, but then it began to go to her head. Her old friends saw less of her, as Nadine began to associate with other Haitians who were better off.

After a while Mark and Linda began to notice that Nadine had become a bit more lax in her responsibilities, but they brushed it aside as nothing important. Nadine had become like family

---

who have been your supporters. This may be true because of perceived shortcomings in your performance, or it may simply be the result of altered priorities on the part of the supporters, most commonly a local church missions team.

But this is not the only place where monetary issues arise. Salaries that were quite adequate to sustain the family back in the ministry culture may be quite insufficient to deal with the inflated prices and expectations for behavior that they now

to them, and they were enjoying the little community that had formed. Soon after Nadine was hired, her husband, an older man who could not work because he lacked skills, had moved in with her in the basement apartment. Not long after that, she became pregnant, and Linda was given the opportunity to become a midwife. With the birth of her baby girl, Nadine's young niece moved in from the country to help around the house until Nadine could get back on her feet. Mark and Linda were glad they could help these Haitian people and were especially pleased when the family started attending a local Haitian church.

Then Linda realized that again the house was not being kept very well. She had to remind Nadine to do her regular chores more often. She spoke to Mark about this, and he in turn talked to Nadine, who simply smiled and explained that as a new mother she had many responsibilities, but she would see that the chores got done.

Mark and Linda began to see less and less of Nadine. Her niece was sent in to help, but she did not do a good job. It was finally obvious that Nadine did only the essentials of her duties and made her family members cover the rest of her work load, which was poorly done.

Mark could no longer stand the way things were going. Now Linda was pregnant and had to do more and more around the house with the result that her strength and patience were decreasing daily. Finally Mark confronted Nadine. Lovingly, yet firmly, he demanded to know why she had ceased doing some of her chores. She replied that she had been freed from lower Haitian work. She was now beyond those duties because she had been "raised up" by the good treatment of her missionary friends. Mark and Linda were now her friends; and she would help share the chores but could never again work like a lower Haitian for them as before.

Mark now realized their innocent mistake. In befriending Nadine, they had raised her social status to a point where she no longer considered herself to be of the lower working class. In her mind, Nadine had been liberated from mopping floors by the friendship of her white saviors and the money she had collected and saved for her family from her generous wages.

Mark and Linda discussed what they should do. Nadine could not be shaken from her attitude, even though they threatened to fire her. They could barely afford Nadine, much less hire additional help. If they fired her, she could not get another job without a good recommendation. Moreover, Nadine said that now she would only work for "good white people" like Linda and Mark, but such jobs were almost nonexistent. Unemployed and homeless, Nadine would face a cruel world with a baby and two other dependents to feed. When they asked their Haitian friends for advice, they told the missionaries to beat her at once and put her in her place.

When Mark and Linda's baby was due, and good help around the house became even more a necessity, they knew they would have to do something about Nadine. It was a tough decision for Mark and Linda to make, because they felt responsible for creating the dilemma in the first place. Finally, after much discussion and prayer, they decided what they had to do and called Nadine into the house....

face back in the sending country. Things such as higher housing costs, dining out, various kinds of lessons for children, youth retreats, and keeping up with clothing styles can very quickly make a family budget look minuscule. And overhanging this challenge is what generally is considered to be the least favorite missionary task: receiving and, even harder, asking for money from others.

A final hurdle that tends to further complicate the already complex set of circumstances known as home assignment is the challenge of effective communication. How do you tell the story of four years in ten minutes—or even less (see Bruce 2000)?

As churches have tended to become larger and more diverse in their functions, fewer opportunities seem available for missionaries to address congregations as a whole. The task then becomes one of determining which subgroups within congregations to target and finding appropriate opportunities for communicating with them.

CONCLUSION

Rarely in today's world is the missionary task in a local setting the responsibility of the isolated individual. Knowing how to be a team member is a necessary skill for any prospective missionary. Additionally, the challenges posed by missionary life are such that one must see them up front and prepare for them prior to encountering them on the field. The case study for this chapter shows how complex relationships can be. Not all missionaries have domestic help, but in many parts of the world the tasks of daily living require far more time and energy than in North America, and the income of many missionaries often allows them to hire domestic help so that they can focus on the tasks that God has given. Most new missionaries are not accustomed to being employers, and they tend to bring their own cultural values to the work setting, especially when that setting is their home. Complications can arise, as the case study clearly shows.

13

Strategic and Ministry Issues

INTRODUCTION

In addition to personal and family issues, individual missionaries also will face important strategic and ministry ones in the course of their career. These are in addition to, or overlap with, strategic and ministry issues that arise from a missionary being part of a team or overall field endeavor. Though some of these issues may also have been faced during the candidating stage, almost all of them normally will require at least some further attention.

What follows here, though by no means exhaustive, represents some of the most important strategic and ministry issues that a "sent one" is likely to face. First, there is the question of peoples and places. Is your calling to a particular people or people group, or is it to a particular place? Though it may seem that this question would be resolved before one leaves home, that often is not entirely the case. Second, a focus of attention flows from the important point that the church to be established is not the missionary's church. It is Christ's church first, and the local believers' church second. Third, we need to discuss money as

a burden. Certainly, money is a blessing in many ways, but it has that unique capacity to be as damaging when used badly as it is helpful when used properly. Fourth, we will look at leadership as a bad word. It is described this way because of the reluctance that many exhibit when challenged to assume the mantle of leadership. Fifth, we offer some thoughts on issues related to the role of women in mission.

PEOPLES OR PLACES?

Since the Lausanne Congress on World Evangelization in 1974, the priority of reaching unreached peoples (as opposed to unreached people; see map 13.1) has been established in global mission strategy to the position of primacy, as discussed in chapter 5. And although many in the mission enterprise have adjusted their own strategies accordingly, ambiguities remain concerning the practical ways this commitment is to be worked out. These ambiguities reach all the way down to the lives of individual missionaries.

Even in contexts dominated by a particular people group, there is often a question of which subgroup to address. Likewise, in major cities in all parts of the world new identifications of various sorts (e.g., work related, neighborhood, religious, student groups, and associations of different kinds) often are in the process of displacing the relative significance of one's ethnolinguistic identity. What all this means is that decisions or commitments already made to focus on a particular people or people group sometimes can be challenged by the circumstances one faces on site in a particular location.

It takes a highly resolute commitment to stay the course in putting all one's energy into reaching a particular people group when, for example, knocking on your door every day for much-needed attention are representatives of a much more receptive group. Or, as is often the case in an urban situation, a new multiethnic ministry is desperate for the particular spiritual gifts (e.g., teaching or mercy) that are your forte.

It is not our role in this book to tell you what to do when faced with such a situation. The decision is highly personal, and the Lord's leading should be the final arbiter. It remains an indisputable fact, however, that many of the least-reached peoples remain that way because when choices need to be made, other avenues of service appear much more fruitful and attractive. Reaching the least reached requires so much energy and focus that it rarely fares well when more immediate and receptive competitors have a stake in the missionary's time.

IT'S NOT YOUR CHURCH

One of the most important and strategic ministry issues that missionaries face is their understanding of the church: What

is it? Who should lead it? How should it function?

In addition to the theological discussion on the church in chapter 5, a key point to remember is that the church (or churches) with which you are working, even as the primary church planter, is not yours to possess in any fashion. It is, first of all, Christ's church, both locally and as part of his universal body. He has promised to build it, and he is its leader.

Learning to appreciate the local church is another area that missionaries at times have to deal with. All of us, including missionaries, are naturally drawn to churches in which we understand the language, agree with the doctrine and philosophy of ministry, feel com-

> *A recent WEF survey on mission attrition showed that one of the main causes of missionaries returning prematurely from the field was because they were not rooted and grounded in a local church.*
> Patrick Johnstone (1998, 205–6)

fortable in the worship service, and, if we are parents, find space for our children to grow in their love of Christ. In the urban and suburban settings, finding such a church might be relatively easy. In rural areas, however, the choice may be limited to one church, and it may not fit the missionary's ideal of what a local church should be (see sidebar 13.2).

One of the dangers, however, of finding a church in which you feel comfortable is that new Christians in the culture likely will not feel comfortable in that church. Since it offers familiarity to you, it probably will not offer familiarity to them.

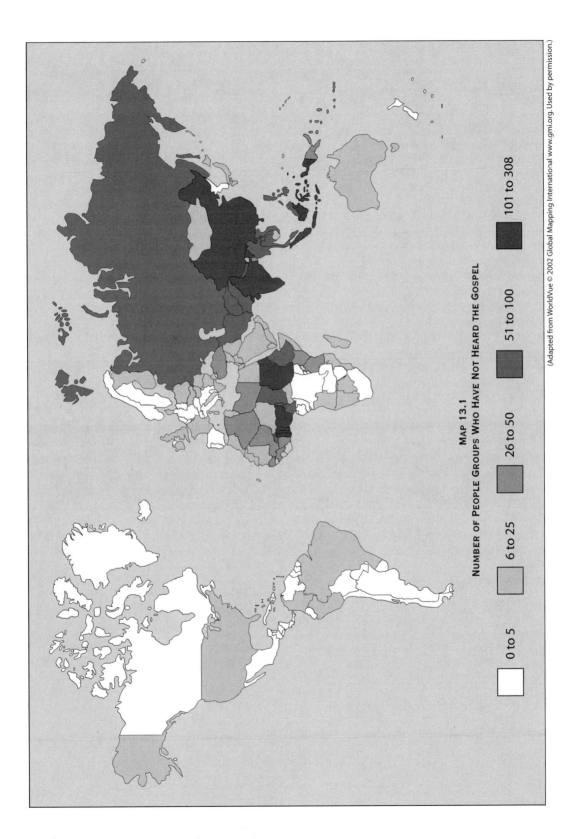

MAP 13.1
NUMBER OF PEOPLE GROUPS WHO HAVE NOT HEARD THE GOSPEL

0 to 5   6 to 25   26 to 50   51 to 100   101 to 308

(Adapted from WorldVue © 2002 Global Mapping International www.gmi.org. Used by permission.)

SIDEBAR 13.1
REACHED AND UNREACHED MISSION FIELDS

Robertson McQuilkin
(McQuilkin 2000 [used with permission])

Since the mid-1970s intense debate has raged over what a mission field is and what it means for a field to be reached. In general, since the Lausanne Congress on World Evangelism of 1974, the concept of a people group, defined by common language and culture, has displaced the older idea of a nation-state. There continues to be a discussion of whether the people groups to be evangelized should be defined more in terms of language or dialect (with over 12,000 in the world) or of culture (over 20,000). But leaving some latitude for those definitions, the chief ethnolinguistic groups have been identified.

But how do we determine when a group has been "reached"? In the mid-1980s there were said to be 12,000 unevangelized groups, but by 1990 that estimate was reduced to 6,000. With the advent of the A.D. 2000 and Beyond Movement, this was reduced to 2,000, then by 1995, to 1,600. Did the missionary enterprise advance that rapidly? No, the definition of "evangelized" or "reached" changed. Does "evangelized" mean that every person would hear with understanding the way to life in Christ as Mark 16:15 and Acts 1:8 seem to indicate? Or, as the objective set by some in recent years, does "evangelized" mean that every person would have access to the gospel? That is, when a church is near enough or there are radio broadcasts or book shops, the Bible has been translated into their language—everyone could hear the gospel if they wanted to. This greatly reduces the number of unevangelized people groups. Others opt to focus on Matthew 28:18–20 and Luke 24:47–48 and the goal of evangelism is said to be discipling the "nations" or people groups. But what is it to "disciple"? Some have said that when there is a witnessing church movement, the missionary task is complete. Others point out that a witnessing church movement in a tribe of 1,000 may mean the group is evangelized or "reached," but what if the group is 40 million in size? So others add the phrase, "capable of reaching its own people." If there is such a church movement, no more outside help would be needed to complete the task of evangelism, however defined. Still others define a reached people as those which are majority Christian. If "Christian" is used in an evangelical sense, however, no

---

Beyond that, as a local manifestation of Christ's body, the church is under the stewardship of those in that culture who comprise its membership. That stewardship may produce various structural forms, depending upon the ecclesiastical and cultural traditions that are its chief influences. The ultimate decisions about what those forms will look like, however, should be made locally, in accordance with culturally and biblically appropriate decision-making patterns. Such decisions should not be made by the missionary, and the church never should be referred to by the missionary as "my church." Though the intentions of such language may be innocent enough, its

> *God grant us faith and courage to keep "hands off" and allow the new garden of the Lord's planting to ripen.*
> Lottie Moon (Allen 1980, 185)

imperialistic and paternalistic overtones are counterproductive at best.

The implications of this understanding should be visible in the leadership structure and functioning of the church. With rare

more than a handful of very small ethnic groups could be considered "reached" on that definition.

This debate is not academic nit-picking; it is very pragmatic, defining the task that remains and targeting those areas in which a church or mission should invest precious, limited resources. The consensus that seems to be emerging at the end of the twentieth century is to have a scale from "least reached" to "most reached." On this basis it can be said that there are at least 1,600 people groups larger than 10,000 in size in which there is no witnessing church movement capable of reaching its own people. If smaller groups are included, the number of unreached escalates to at least 6,000, including many with no gospel witness at all.

The majority of the least reached groups fall within the 10/40 Window, a band of ethnic groups stretching east between the 10th and 40th degree latitudes (north) from the Atlantic Ocean to Indonesia in the Pacific. This embraces nations in northern Africa, the Middle East, and the Far East in which the least reached religious groups are concentrated: Islam, Hinduism, and Buddhism. These are not only the least reached, they are the least reachable, the most resistant. In fact, because of religious, political, and cultural barriers, they are also the least accessible.

If "Christian" is defined as one who has a personal relationship with God through faith in Jesus Christ, and "mission field" is defined as any ethnolinguistic group in which there is no witnessing church movement capable of evangelizing that group, perhaps half the people groups of the world have been "reached." The other half need outside assistance, commonly called missionaries. If those groups with fewer than 10,000 were excluded from the tally, then the majority of the remaining people groups have been reached. If, on the other hand "reached" focuses on individuals rather than ethnic groups, and "access to the gospel" is the criterion, perhaps more than half the individuals of the world have been reached. If, however, "reached" means they have actually heard the gospel with understanding, far less than half could be considered reached.

REFLECTION AND DISCUSSION

1. What would be the impact on missionary strategy of each of the approaches to defining "reached" and "unreached"?
2. Why are those who are least reached at the same time the hardest to reach? What are the implications for missionary work over the twenty-first century?

exceptions, the missionary should not be the pastor, but rather the coach of the pastor and/or elders. From the very beginning local leaders should take the lead publicly, with the missionary functioning at most as part of a leadership team. This is a crucial element to the church becoming truly indigenous in its worship and ministry life.

In addition, every effort should be made to promote freedom and creativity, so that biblically acceptable but culturally natural styles of worship and governance can be incorporated from day one. Culturally relevant church life will flourish best where it is incorporated early.

MONEY AS A BURDEN

Money is to mission what fire is to the human condition: God's gracious provision for our survival, empowerment, and even our enjoyment. Like fire, however, it is also capable of wreaking havoc. The challenge of handling it well is often what makes it a burden.

The ways that money impacts world mission, both good and bad, are almost

---

SIDEBAR 13.2
BUILDING UP RESISTANCE

Scott Wisely
(Wisely, personal correspondence [adapted; used with permission])

In the movie *The Princess Bride,* Wesley drinks poison but doesn't die and answers simply, "I have spent my life building up a resistance to Iocaine powder." I think this is what is needed in order to attend local church here—a lifetime of building up resistance.

After being in the United States for four months, we got spoiled with great church in our home culture. Screaming children are in children's church, the sermons are structured in points that one can follow, there are worship teams,

the Scripture can be understood in modern language, and so on.

Since we got back, almost two months ago, I've been gearing up to go to our national-language church, but until this morning I haven't been brave enough. I dressed and got there forty-five minutes late, which meant I was one of the first ones in the door. The ten people inside had just sung their first song, "How Great Thou Art," which is slow, but they slowed it down to a funeral dirge tempo and sang so far off key that even I could tell. I sat while we

went through Scripture reading and more dirges that seem to have no meaning whatsoever to 99 percent of the congregation, since very few of them understand the official language.

I sat in the back and watched as all the people filed in. Men went to the right, women and children to the left. The women all seemed to have at least one baby in a net bag hanging on their back and another two-year-old in tow. Each mother walks in stooped over, sits down, hauls out a breast over the already stretched-out neck of a T-shirt for the kids, and then starts a murmured conversation with the ladies next to her.

Meanwhile, the two-year-olds who aren't nursing gather in the center aisle and start wrestling,

---

too numerous to count. It is the sustenance that sends missionaries cross-culturally to places where the gospel has not yet taken root. It is the fuel that keeps the organizational machinery of mission running, which sustains those who are working cross-culturally. It is the bricks and mortar for new urban church facilities or leadership training centers. It is the seed that enables an expatriate or national church planter to begin a new work or a Bible translation to go forward. Unfortunately, it is also sometimes the addictive foreign drug that keeps indigenous church members from learning the joys of Christian stewardship. It may also be the conscience-disturbing sand in the gears of effective ministry decisions, just as it is in personal ones.

Given its great potential, then, for both positive and negative impact, how should money be thought of and used appropriately in mission? Here are some observations and suggestions:

1. *Money is no substitute for passion, but it can be an effective expression of it.* God's glory and the desire to see him universally worshiped and enjoyed should be a primary passion for all believers. For many, pouring financial resources into that cause can be a wonderful expression of that passion. Missionaries need to develop appropriate pathways for it.

2. *Money ought to be used only where clear and justifiable ends and means are plainly in view, and when even in a worst-case scenario the money will not hinder the ultimate ends of developing healthy indig-*

laughing, screaming, and doing less mentionable things, like all good two-year-olds will do. Everyone but the pasty white guy in the back is oblivious to all this.

The men for the most part are sound asleep by the time the sermon comes around, since the pastoral prayer lasts between ten and fifteen minutes. About half the sleepers are dozing with the head-jerk approach, but the others are deep in REM cycles with wide-open mouths and heavy breathing, looking more dead than angelic.

Those who aren't sleeping are all intent on reading anything they can find while the pastor stands up and speaks, but I can never follow beyond the first five minutes because he starts going in circles and my mind has been trained to think in points. As his circles get wider, I get lost and start to look around at all the three- to seven-year-olds, who are staring wide-eyed at me. I gain five minutes of time making them smile with funny faces, but then I catch the pastor's eye. He seems to be distracted by my smiling at the kids but not by the two-year-olds screaming and pulling hair right in front of the pulpit.

I make it fifteen to twenty minutes into the sermon, and then I think of something really urgent that needs to be done, such as write an update e-mail to you all, and I sneak out rationalizing that I blend in with the constant stream of traffic going in and out. What an ordeal. I justify my behavior by telling myself, "I am building up a resistance, and one can't be expected to take the whole dose right in the beginning—this will take me a lifetime!"

I hope this paints a realistic picture of national-language church here. The local-language churches are much better, but since I don't speak the local dialect, I am limited to one option here. My wife doesn't even pretend to try.

REFLECTION AND DISCUSSION

1. What would you say to this missionary couple to encourage them?
2. What would you do if you found yourself in a position similar to the one described here?

---

enous churches and ministries. The law of unintended consequences needs to be kept in mind constantly, as money has as much potential for evil as it has for good.

3. *Money ought never to be used as a power wedge for one part of God's family to enforce its will on other members of the family.* This pattern has existed for too long with much of the mission activity from the West.

4. *Stewardship of financial resources is for everybody.* Those who have much should assist those who have little. Those who have little should do what they can. All should live modestly and humbly as unto the Lord.

5. *Those who will not work should not eat.* This is a very biblical idea (2 Thess. 3:10). At the same time, though, those whose work is insufficient to provide self-sustenance (however industrious they may be) should be assisted in every way possible to make their work productive enough that they can feed themselves. This may involve dealing with oppressive overlords or finding ways around climatic or other conditions that are beyond control, and it ought to be a first line of assistance.

The number of places where an individual missionary will need to make substantial financial decisions in isolation is, hopefully, much smaller today than it used to be. Good teams and partnership arrangements have gone a long way toward improving that situation. Having good principles in mind to guide one's own participation, however, is as important as ever.

227

Leadership as a Bad Word

Evangelical books and seminars on leadership make much of the concept of "servant leadership." And well they should. It's a solidly biblical concept. After all, our supreme leader himself said, "I come not to be served, but to serve, and to give myself as a ransom for many" (see Mark 10:45). It's that last clause, however, that Christians don't always fully appreciate in the context of discussions about leadership. It was not only for Jesus to give himself; it is for all who want to bear the name "servant leader."

There is a thesis about leadership that goes something like this: *You can exercise and sustain personal leadership only to the extent of your capacity to bear pain.* If you can bear only your own pain, then you can't really lead. If you can respond to and bear

> *The sense of being led by an unseen hand which takes mine, while another hand reaches ahead and prepares the way, grows upon me daily.*
> Frank Laubach (Medary 1954, 124)

only the pain of your family, then your family represents the full scope of your leadership potential. If, however, by God's grace you can recognize and bear the pain of those around you, then the breadth of your leadership potential is limited only by the scope of your burden and capacity.

All this talk about bearing pain may seem off-putting to some. You may be thinking, "Isn't leadership more about vision and the ability to inspire than about pain?" Not really. To be sure, there is a kind of leadership that can rouse people to action for a short

time, but enduring leadership invariably will be built upon a confidence that those whom you call "leader" would sacrifice themselves not only for the cause they share with you, but even for you yourself.

Leadership development has begun to catch on in mission circles in a big way in recent years, and with good reason: nobody seems to have enough good leaders. Several mission agencies and associations have undertaken leadership development programs, and some top seminaries, such as Fuller School of World Mission, have had outstanding leadership programs going on as part of their mission curriculum for a decade or more.

What remains to be seen is how effective any or all of these efforts ultimately will be in overcoming "leadership lethargy," an apathetic response to the challenge of taking on leadership responsibilities. At its base there is no especially good reason for taking on leadership responsibilities in mission, unless one is doing so out of a passionate love for Jesus. In most cases no additional pay comes with the job, and the "pleasures of power" (whatever they may be) usually are more than counterbalanced by the headaches and other assorted pains that come with the position.

What are the types of pain that particu-

> *If we are going to wait until every possible hindrance has been removed before we do a work for the Lord, we will never attempt to do anything.*
> T. J. Bach (Watson 1965, 121)

larly shadow those involved in positions of leadership in mission? There are scores of them, no doubt, but perhaps these half dozen represent some of the most common or most grievous:

1. *Being fatigued.* When, as is often the case, there is no one else to do a task, it falls to the leader.

2. *Being overwhelmed by an avalanche of conflicting duties.* Different constituencies often are looking for different things. When it comes to sorting out the conflicts and setting a course for the future, it falls to the leader.

3. *Being the bad guy.* When there's bad news to convey or someone has to be dismissed, it falls to the leader.

4. *Babysitting the self-centered.* Whether they come in the form of new missionaries, old missionaries, short-termers, or visiting experts, demanding types will always be around. When either they or their problem must be dealt with, it falls to the leader.

5. *Bearing the burden of decision-making in times of crisis.* When revolution or anarchy emerges and lives are at stake, there's one sure place where tough decisions must be made: it falls to the leader.

6. *Bearing the pain of others.* When others are hurting and tears must be wiped, it falls to the leader.

Given all this pain or potential pain, why would any sensible person voluntarily stand on its receiving end? The only reason that makes any sense is the call to emulate the Savior, who offered himself as a ransom for many.

Our age does not put a high premium on sacrificial service. The word *duty* is almost lost to our vocabulary, even among Christians. As Francis Schaeffer liked to point out, "personal peace and affluence" is our controlling passion.

Though many important things must be learned about effective leadership, the most important thing comes only by spending sig-nificant time at the feet of Jesus, becoming mesmerized by his heartbeat and captured by his love. If the present crisis in leadership is to be solved, if adequate numbers of quality leaders are to step forward, then many significant efforts will have to be made. But it will all be for nought unless the battle of the heart is won first. Only a heart like that of Jesus can bear the pain.

WOMEN IN MISSION

"Fools rush in where angels fear to tread!" That pretty well summarizes the audacity required for three males to address the topic of women in mission. The history of the issues is not new to us. We are acquainted with the huge and typically unheralded contributions of women to global mission over the last two millennia (see, e.g., Athyal 2000; M. Kraft 2000; Robert 1996; Tucker 1988). They are the "Two-Thirds Force" in ministry to the "Two-Thirds World." We have personally seen the results of their diligent and sacrificial efforts up close in Africa, Asia, and South America.

In wrestling with the issues involved (see, e.g., the case study for chapter 11), all of us must acknowledge forthrightly the important biblical, interpretation, cultural, and historical questions that will not go away and that must be addressed and resolved if any kind of permanent peace is ever to exist over these matters. But—and this is an important *but*—first there must be repentance and forgiveness between the sexes before the underlying issues can be fruitfully addressed. So much hurt and moral disquiet festers just below the surface that dispassionate and honest theological reflection is nearly impossible right now.

CASE STUDY: THE REVEREND CHU'S DECISION

James Chuang
(Hiebert and Hiebert 1987, 188–90 [used with permission])

"What am I going to do? No matter what I do, one of them is going to be hurt very seriously." Reverend Chu, capable chairman of the Taiwanese National Church Union, was at a loss for words for the first time. The air was unusually tense. On the faces of the weary committee were signs of frustration and despair. It was already the fourth meeting, yet they were exactly where they started four meetings ago.

The Gospel Church, one of their local congregations, was desperately in need of a pastor. The former pastor had left some time ago, and the church was experiencing a serious decline in attendance. It brought a great hope and excitement when one of the missionaries, Reverend Johnson, located Mr. Wang, a willing and able worker. The

case was quickly presented to the executive committee and it voted eight-to-one to approve the proposal. The missionary had exclaimed, "Great, let us install the man as pastor immediately." But Chairman Chu said, "No, we cannot." The only negative vote came from Reverend Mah, the former chairman. What would he do if they installed Mr. Wang as pastor?

By far the greatest difficulty for the growth of the church in this particular field was the serious lack of qualified workers. Out of 2,300 Protestant churches in the country, there were more than 300 without full-time pastors. It took at least four years to train a new worker. Therefore it was a special discovery when the missionary located Mr. Wang, who at the time was working in

an orphanage as a chaplain. He was a very sensitive, friendly, and experienced Christian worker. He felt the call of God to be a pastor of a local church and was looking for an opening. Reverend Johnson felt that it was God's guidance for him to become acquainted with Mr. Wang just at the time when he was open to a new appointment and when the Gospel Church was in need of a pastor.

Chairman Chu was a highly respected leader who always took into consideration every aspect of the matter in question. He was particularly sensitive to this case, because a few months before he had been elected chairman of the National Church Union over Reverend Mah, who had served as chairman for more than two decades. The latter had ended up being the vice-chairman, and this made things more complicated.

Mah was also a very respected leader. He had been with the denomination from its

Steps toward Healing

What might some preliminary steps toward healing and clarity look like? We believe that they would include at least the following five elements.

First, a repentant spirit would permeate the overwhelmingly male institutional leadership of the mission enterprise. Men would confess both to God and to their female colleagues the abuses of power that have characterized too much of our interaction together. At the same time, repentance

would characterize both men and women for all their subtle and blatant manifestations of selfishness.

Second, people would recognize that the real issue is the fulfillment of each one's calling as God, in mercy and grace, has established it. They would not wrongly characterize the debate as a fight between those who support second-class status for women and those who don't, or between those who support obedience to the authority of Scripture and those who don't.

beginnings. Although he sometimes tended to be more subjective than objective, he had proved himself a faithful servant of the church. He had led the churches in their early years, and brought them to their present state as a body of autonomous, self-supporting congregations.

The committee took Mah's opposition to the selection of Mr. Wang as pastor very seriously. It chose two representatives to conduct further investigations into Wang's background. They returned with positive reports, finding nothing that would disqualify him for joining the National Church Union. However, they heard from another source that Wang's wife once worked for Reverend Mah and, on an important occasion, had failed to fulfill her responsibilities, causing a serious problem for him. Ever since that incident, her former employer had labeled her as "unfit" for God's service. Although many years had passed, Mah had not forgotten the experience.

The missionaries, who had had no part in the decision-making processes, were impatient with the delay. They remarked at times that they had turned the responsibilities over to the national leaders prematurely. Privately they told Chu to ignore Mah and to install Wang on the basis of a majority vote. But the chairman knew that this would not work. In the Chinese culture, interpersonal relationships were very sensitive and most important. Although each member of a committee was given one vote, not every vote carried an equal weight. In this case Reverend Mah's vote was of great significance.

Chairman Chu knew that he could say to the committee, "Dear committee members, Reverend Mah has been chairman of this committee for the past twenty years. He knows what is best for our entire church organization. Let us support his decision and make our vote unanimous." Most of the members would go along

with such a recommendation. After all, maintaining unity was one of the highest values in Chinese culture. Moreover, if the committee members were forced to choose between Reverend Mah and Mr. Wang, they would be obliged to side with Mah who was an older insider. But if Chairman Chu allowed such a showdown to occur in the committee, and the committee supported Mah out of respect, it would become Mah's committee! Moreover, such a decision would be fair to neither Mr. Wang nor the Gospel Church.

On the other hand, if Chu ignored Mah's opposition, he knew that there would no longer be unity and harmony within the executive committee. Moreover, since the church organization was small, Mr. Wang would soon feel the tension, and would not be able to work at peace within the church.

Looking around the table at the weary committee members, Chairman Chu said …

Third, given both the biblical and the historical records of women's ministry, people would forthrightly acknowledge that women have been effective and fruitful in spiritual endeavors traditionally reserved for men. At the same time, they would honestly acknowledge that this has been more the exception than the rule. Why this is so requires deeper exploration on both sides.

Fourth, we would better understand the importance and parameters of lay ministry in juxtaposition to ordained office. Although many agree that certain functions in the Bible are reserved for those set apart for ordained office, too broad an understanding of those functions may, in addition to other problems, be a root cause of tension between men and women.

Fifth, commitment to the integrity of the biblical text as given must be maintained as both starting and ending point. Rewriting or mistranslating the Bible to fit a particular view is not an option.

The Look of Resolution

Resolution may come in one of two ways. It may come in the all too common American way: increased division and hardening of positions. Signs are strong today that this is the likely outcome, as genuine dialogue laced with intellectual honesty and winsomeness of spirit is increasingly hard to find. The alternative way, the establishment of a new consensus, requires more grace and generosity than has been evident heretofore.

If, however, a new consensus is found, it will be characterized by (1) faithfulness to the teaching of Scripture without recourse to translation tampering or "escape hatch" cultural hermeneutics; (2) a recognition and celebration of the essential and varied ministry gifts of women, as seen both in the Scriptures and in history; and (3) a renewed sense of the dignity, uniqueness, and irreplaceability of all God-ordained roles.

The Importance of the Culture of the Target Audience

Finally, however missionaries may answer the vital questions being asked, they should not forget the importance of the context of their ministry and the cultural values seen there (for discussion on culture and gender role, see Adeney 1987; Hofstede 1998). They may violate the local culture's values whatever position they take, and when they feel that biblical principles require such a violation, they must be ready to face the cultural backlash that may very well occur. Subordination of women in Sweden may have as negative an impact as gender egalitarianism does in Saudi Arabia. Missionaries will do well to be aware that societies may not be ready for their understanding of gender role distinctions, especially if they are rigid in their answers. "Gender role colonialism" should be avoided. Missionaries rather should live lives faithful to the message of the gospel and walk humbly in the knowledge that God extends salvation to and values equally all categories of humanity (Gal. 3:28).

CONCLUSION

Although the particular strategic and ministry issues that each generation faces may change, the fact that each generation of missionaries and mission shareholders faces them does not. One hundred years ago, thinking about reaching peoples was not on the mission map the way it is today. Fifty years ago, male-dominated missiology all too readily ignored the essential contributions of women in mission. Change varies, but the challenge to change remains the same. The case study for this chapter illustrates one of the ministry issues faced by missionaries and national churches. How might you advise Reverend Chu as he helps guide his church members through the important decision of choosing their next pastor?

14

Relating to People of Other Cultures

INTRODUCTION

One of the distinct pleasures of being a cross-cultural missionary is meeting numerous people of backgrounds radically different from one's own. It is also one of the frustrations. Developing relationships with people of other cultures takes a long time, and negotiating relational waters that are filled with eddies and undertows can be tricky. At the same time, developing close relationships with others can bring a

> *The most important factor in your effectiveness and happiness overseas is the way you relate to other people. All of your concern for culture, your knowledge of the country and its people, and your skills in coping are less important than your manner of dealing with fellow workers and people of the host country.*
>
> Ted Ward (1984, 130)

foretaste of heaven. In this chapter we will look at the process of developing friendships across cultures, discuss ways that Ameri-

cans form relationships, and explore some of the types of relationships that a missionary typically has.

DEVELOPING RELATIONSHIPS: A PROCESS

Every culture has its ebb and flow in developing relationships. Although each relationship may be seen as unique and following its own path, in general three phases may be seen in relationships across cultures: (1) initial acquaintance, (2) developing friendship, and (3) growth in intimacy. The separation between the phases may be fuzzy, and relationships can proceed both backwards and forwards, but those three phases nonetheless typify progress in a relationship. Furthermore, people may wander back and forth through all three simultaneously as a relationship develops. Certainly, progression toward deep friendship is one of a missionary's goals, especially since relationships are central in discipling people. Sidebar 14.1 carries the discussion further by helping you think through five types of changes that take place in growing friendships.

Stage One: Who Are You?

The first stage of relationships is characterized by the simple fact that the two potential friends do not know each other. American culture is strongly individualistic, and for the individualist it is normal to develop friendships with new people. Those from collective cultures, in contrast, often are born or initiated into a group of people who are their friends for life (Bell and Coleman 1999, 3), and strangers are not always people with whom friendships are developed. We will come back to these two orientations in chapter 16.

During this early exploration two barriers can stop the growth of the relationship. The first comes from the human tendency to stereotype. Before intimacy can have a chance to grow in a cross-cultural relationship, each person must be able to stop seeing the other as "one of them" and instead see that person as an individual. Reducing the uncertainty about the other person is a skill that is developed within the culture, and each culture has its own

> It takes energy. Making friends across cultures requires time and work and frustration. Understanding does not turn on like a light. But at the end is unparalleled satisfaction. You are bringing into being, in a partial way, the climax of history.
>
> Tim Stafford (1984, 38)

rules as to how this uncertainty is reduced (Lustig and Koester 1996, 260–63). In Asia an American might be asked how much money he or she earns, which is offensive to Americans. An American might ask how many children an African has, which might be considered personal information rather than public information. Americans tend to try to reduce uncertainty by being friendly (upbeat, smiling, "chipper") and relatively shallow in meeting strangers, which is not always interpreted the way they intend it to be. Among Middle Easterners, for example, the friendliness of American women can be interpreted as sexual aggressiveness, leading to serious misunderstandings on both sides. In the Japanese corporate world people meeting for the first time may exchange business cards with enough detailed information for each to gauge the other in terms of status and hierarchy. The cards are a means of reducing uncertainty that seems entirely foreign to Americans.

It may be apparent to the reader that our discussion is built on the presupposition that relationships, and especially friendships, are voluntary associations. That is, at any time either party in a relationship can choose to pull out or deepen the ties. This view fits well with an individualistic orientation to life, but, as we noted, not as well in collective cultures, where people are born into extensive in-group relationships that they must maintain throughout life. Missionaries, however, as outsiders who have crossed cultural boundaries, are never born into the collectives of the people whom they seek to reach, and thus missionary relationships with members of the local culture are, by definition, voluntary relationships.

This fact plays a key role in the potential for a relationship to develop. For example, Americans may look for common interests, hobbies, skills, and the like before they "volunteer" friendship. Chinese, on the other hand, want to know the extent of *yuan* in a relationship before they will proceed further. *Yuan* is what accompanies all relation-

---

SIDEBAR 14.1
CHANGES IN DEVELOPING FRIENDSHIPS

Intercultural communication specialists Myron W. Lustig and Jolene Koester (1996, 246) note five changes that take place in friendships crossing cultural boundaries.

1. Friends interact more frequently; they talk to each other more often, for longer periods of time, and in more varied settings than acquaintances do.

2. The increased frequency of interactions means that friends will have more knowledge about and shared experiences with each other than will acquaintances, and this unique common ground probably will develop into a private communication code to refer to ideas, objects, and experiences that are exclusive to the relationship.

3. The increased knowledge of the other person's motives and typical behaviors means that there is an increased ability to predict a friend's reactions to common situations. The powerful need to reduce uncertainty in the initial stages of relationships . . . suggests that acquaintanceships are unlikely to progress to friendships without the ability to predict the other's intentions and expectations.

4. The sense of "we-ness" increases among friends. Friends often feel that their increased investment of time and emotional commitment to the relationship creates a sense of interdependence, so that individual goals and interests are affected by and linked to each person's satisfaction with the relationship.

5. Close friendships are characterized by a heightened sense of caring, commitment, trust, and emotional attachment to the other person, so that the people in a friendship view it as something special and unique.

REFLECTION AND DISCUSSION

1. What are the risks in each of the changes in a cross-cultural setting?

2. How might awareness of these areas of change impact the way you disciple someone in a cross-cultural setting?

---

ships, determining the extent that any can go. *Yuan* is not the cause, but it attends the relationship, mediating its progress (or lack of progress). To the American missionary this may sound fatalistic, but to the Chinese it traditionally is significant in determining the extent of a relationship with a stranger (Chang and Holt 1991).

The second barrier to a deeper relationship can be expressed in a simple question: "Are you enough like me to commit to a deeper relationship?" Of course, you are unlikely to actually pose this question to another person, but it is implicit in your desire to get to know the other person. At least initially, you may be attracted *because* of the differences. Even so, too many differences eventually will make it difficult to develop genuine intimacy. If mutual satisfaction, acceptance, and trust for each other develop during this stage, then the relationship can move on to the next level.

Stage Two: Let's Be Friends

The second stage of relationships requires both parties to consider the risks of changing enough to accommodate each other. Both must make some compromises if the friendship is to be mutually valued. Since you are a stranger in a new culture, nationals who form relationships with you are taking certain risks. They may see advantages in those risks, which can include status and access to the relative wealth you represent, or simply an opportunity to connect to someone who represents new opportunities. However, they may consider that the advantages do not outweigh the disadvantages and decide that pursuit of a deeper relationship is too risky.

During this stage important elements will include a growing emotional openness and finding ways to deal with conflicts. Missionaries of the past often had the attitude that they should not show any weaknesses to the nationals. They were afraid that the message of the gospel would be diluted or weakened if they were weak themselves. The resulting glittering image they presented was of people who needed no help.

Nationals, however, could see through this disguise, and recognized that an un-

> *Do not be sensitive. Perhaps you are by nature, but you can get over it with the exercise of common sense and the help of God. Let things hurt until the tender spot gets callous. Believe that people do not intend to be unkind; some are too busy to think of the feelings of their fellow-workers, and others have not the nice discernment that ought to guide even the busy brain and tongue. Sensitiveness is only another kind of self-consciousness, and as such we should seek deliverance from its irritating power.*
>
> Isabella Thoburn
> (Thoburn 1903, 258)

fathomable distance stood between themselves and the missionaries. Intimacy was difficult to develop in this relational climate. Contemporary missionaries from the West

are less likely to deny their own weaknesses. However, learning how to be emotionally open with people who you think do not understand you is still a risk that is difficult for many people to take.

A basic truth that all missionaries must learn if they want to disciple effectively in another culture is this: when missionaries don't allow others to help them, they deny those others dignity. In refusing to admit that they hurt and need help and support, missionaries effectively deny those of the host culture the chance to see themselves as people who have something to offer the missionaries. Relationships developed with this weighing them down will be one-dimensional because the missionary only gives and the indigenous people only receive. That is not healthy for discipleship or local church development.

Handling conflict is an important part of this stage. All relationships face conflict sooner or later, and the coping strategies that people use to resolve conflict were ingrained deeply in them as they grew up. Cultures value differing ways of handling, or even admitting to, conflict. Learning the ways people do this in your new culture is a key step not only in your culture-learning process, but also in helping you to develop deeper relationships with those you have come to serve.

Stage Three: Intimate Friendship

This last stage is reached in a relationship only when one party or the other chooses to focus on developing the friendship. As Harriet Hill, long-term missionary in West Africa, notes, "Without a clear-cut decision to pursue friendship, missionaries could find themselves filling their time with an assortment of other relationships

Kindness. It seems to "come naturally" for some; it requires continuous self-reminding for others—no matter, it pays large dividends in one's own sense of worth and in a healthy respect for others. "Be kind to one another" is still sound advice.

Patience. The "get-ahead" person is especially apt to be impatient. Being able to accept the time it takes others to think and act is basic. Learning to be more patient with oneself helps too.

Valuing People. Sometimes things are allowed to become more important than people. Even getting one's job done "well" and promptly tends to get in the way of a proper focus on people. People, not things, are what life is about.

Politeness. The proper mixture of respect for customs, respect for other people, and willingness to be a person among persons goes a long way toward offsetting the dissonances that naturally arise from the differences between oneself and others. Irritability, harshness, and the need to be noticed can work against good relationships.

Thinking the Best of Others. Showing respect demands investing trust in others. Suspicion, aloofness, coldness, and "distance" come between people. Holding a grudge or keeping a list of one's hurts, real or imagined, is a sure way to turn a relationship sour. Even when it seems that someone has let you down, try to find some way to look at the situation that gives the other person the benefit of the doubt.

Persistence. Some might call it faith—faith in another person, or faith in others, in general. Fidelity and stubborn commitment to make things work will pay off. Building and maintaining good interpersonal relationships require a commitment that is strong enough to persist in the face of all sorts of setbacks.

REFLECTION AND DISCUSSION

1. The need for these qualities seems obvious. However, societies define the ways kindness, politeness, valuing people, and so on are demonstrated quite differently. In what ways might culture impact how people interpret what we do as being kind, polite, patient, or persistent?
2. How might these different interpretations help or hinder you in developing friendships in a new culture?

and activities" (Hill 1993, 266). Hill's seven points on the realities of cross-cultural friendships are accurate and well stated (sidebar 14.3).

Ideals of intimacy vary from culture to culture, especially when two friends are on opposite sides of the individualism-collectivism spectrum. The collectivist tends to identify intimacy in terms of the amount of time spent together, the relative lack of privacy, mutual dependence, and issues of face (the "social impression that a person wants others to have of him or her" [Lustig and Koester 1996, 253]). The individualist tends to prefer to maintain a level of privacy and independence that seems distancing to the collectivist. Note the feelings of an Asian American toward American friendships:

I grew up for a good portion of my life in the United States. In the course of living here, I've made many American friends. My relationships with them are very close, in

---

SIDEBAR 14.3
SEVEN REALITIES OF CROSS-CULTURAL FRIENDSHIPS

Harriet Hill
(Excerpted from Hill 1993, 266–68)

---

1. Cross-cultural friendship must be intentional. In monocultural situations, we often gravitate effortlessly toward those who become our friends. But establishing cross-cultural friendships requires more intent.

2. Cross-cultural friendship requires proximity. Reflecting on his cross-cultural experiences, Daryl Whiteman speaks of one experience as successful and another as less successful. In the first, he lived in a village and developed good relationships. In the second, he taught in a school, lived on the school compound, and came away with very few relationships with nationals. His values or model hadn't changed, but his proximity to the people had. Those who can live in the middle of the community have a great advantage. Those who cannot must regularly get close to the people.

3. Cross-cultural friendship must appreciate differences and similarities. Anthropology greatly helps us understand people of different cultures, but it can also hinder us. . . . If differences are our primary focus, we will not be able to have real relationships. We must balance the understanding of our differences with a realization of our common humanness.

4. Cross-cultural friendship will cross economic classes. This barrier seems at times more difficult than crossing cultures. We can understand another's etiquette, values, and social structure, but the contrast of our income and theirs spews out a host of problems. We feel guilty about having so much, both materially and in terms of opportunity. We are accustomed to a certain lifestyle and function very poorly when all of our props are removed.

5. Cross-cultural friendship involves vulnerability. . . . When cross-cultural workers experience the death of a child, they often report suddenly being taken into a new level of intimacy with the people. In the depths of their grief, all modeling and role playing set aside, bonding with the people occurs to an extent never thought possible.

6. Cross-cultural friendship must be selective. On any continent, you can only relate meaningfully to a handful of people. The same holds true in most cross-cultural situations. Without selecting a few people as close friends, your attention will be too diffused to be significant. But with a few friends, you will gain a window on the culture.

7. Cross-cultural friendship must be flexible. The goal is friendship, but the strategies must remain flexible. Each situation is different, and each missionary is different. Your lifestyle might look significantly different than someone else's, but if you both have good relationships with the people, you've both succeeded.

REFLECTION AND DISCUSSION

1. Identify which of the seven you consider to be areas of strength for you. Do you think that they would be strengths in a cross-cultural setting also? Why or why not?

2. Choose one of the seven that you find most difficult and explain what it might take for you to grow in that area.

---

that I even confide in them, but somehow I feel something is missing. There seems to exist a barrier against how close we can really be. I guess this is especially notice-able to me because of the fact that my early childhood was spent in a culture that put a great deal of value on friendship. (Her 1990, 185–86)

SIDEBAR 14.4
"GOOD NEIGHBOR" SKILLS: A STORY FROM INDONESIA

Duane Elmer
(Elmer 1993, 65–67 [used with permission])

Culture shock blasted the ears of Pat and Steve the very first night they moved into their house in Jakarta, Indonesia. As they were getting their children ready for bed, talking and praying, there was a sudden siren blast. It was the Muslim call to prayer.

Steve and Pat soon learned that the siren's source was very near their house, with the speaker pointed in their direction. The siren went off several times each day, and for them these blasts were not a major problem. But the nightly disruption of their family time proved unbearably frustrating. If the children were put to bed early, they would be awakened by the noise of the siren screeching through their house. Sometimes it frightened them.

With her patience wearing thin, Pat resolved to change the situation. Back home in the United States a person with this sort of problem would just go to the proper authorities, explain the problem and hope a solution could be worked out. If not, one would appeal to higher authorities and to noise-abatement laws, if necessary.

As Pat prepared her speech to the authorities at the local mosque, a thought crossed her mind. Shortly before departing for Indonesia, she and her husband had attended a seminar on conflict resolution in the Two-Thirds World. The content started coming back to her, and quickly she realized that the approach she had envisioned would not work. In fact, it could do great damage. There was an alternative, and she began to think about how to make it happen. She would have to take an indirect approach.

Using a mediator was one of the seminar suggestions. But who? And how? Would it work? The whole idea seemed very awkward and unnatural. Yet it was worth a try. What was there to lose?

That evening, the guard Pat and Steve had hired to watch the house each night appeared for his usual 6:00 shift, and Pat realized that this person might be the answer she was seeking. He didn't have much status, and since she was new in Jakarta she had no idea of his network of relationships. Nevertheless, it was worth a try.

She explained the situation to the guard, and he in turn began to talk with other household guards in the area about Pat's dilemma. Eventually an area supervisor of these guards heard the story. The supervisor, as it happened, had a friend who worked at the mosque. The friend in the mosque talked with someone in authority.

This process of communication took a number of days. In the busyness of settling into her new home, Pat left behind her concern about the siren and almost forgot her conversation with the guard. But one night she realized that it had been some time since the mosque siren had disrupted the evening talks and prayers with her children. Had she simply become used to the sound and failed to notice it? Or had something changed?

The next night she listened carefully. The siren went off at the appointed time, but it was definitely quieter, and it seemed as though the loudspeaker was no longer pointed directly at their house.

"It works! Mediators really work" was Pat's gleeful conclusion as she reported the story to me.

REFLECTION AND DISCUSSION

1. What are the qualities of a good neighbor that Pat used?
2. Why was her method effective?
3. How might you choose a mediator when you face a conflict situation in a new culture?

CASE STUDY: TO DRINK OR NOT TO DRINK?

Dennis Teague
(Hiebert and Hiebert 1987, 97–99 [used with permission])

It had been a long evening. What had started out as a real privilege had turned into a real disaster. John had already insulted and upset the Professor by refusing the aperitif, the wine, and the beer. Now, as they sat in the living room after the meal, Professor Piaget set a glass in front of John and began to pour the prized Brittany cider. Was it right for John to continue to anger, insult, and alienate his host—or would it be all right just this once to forget all that teaching in Bible College, forget his alcoholic father, forget what the Smiths would think and say, and drink a little cider, which did not contain much alcohol anyway?

John had spent the past two summers in France and now was enrolled at the University of Nantes. It was not an easy decision, but in obedience to what he felt to be the will of God, he returned in October and entered the beginning course in French. John had never studied French before. He found a room in the dormitory, hoping to make contacts with French students. He worked with the Smiths, who were starting a new church in Nantes. John had just graduated from a Bible College, a conservative school that took a strong stand against drinking alcoholic beverages. Besides, the Smiths had warned him about a few missionaries who had started

drinking wine with the French and had later become alcoholics. John knew the suffering that alcoholism brought, because his father was an alcoholic.

One day John received an invitation to have dinner with his professor, along with three other foreign students. Professor Piaget had very graciously opened his home to them. John realized that it was a real privilege in France for French students to be invited to a professor's home, and an even greater honor for foreign students. When the night arrived for the dinner, the Smiths loaned John their car so that he could pick up his Japanese friend, Isao. The two students were excited as they arrived at the house. Little did John suspect that this would turn out to be such a problematic experience.

Dr. and Mrs. Piaget were very friendly and cordial. John spoke less French than any of the other

Furthermore, for the individualist, face is more the responsibility of the individual, while collectivists see it more as a group responsibility. The polarity in defining responsibilities may make it difficult for the friends to know how (or whether) to help each other when face is threatened. For individualist missionaries moving to a collective culture, understanding issues of face within that culture will be essential in developing intimate relationships.

Finally, any intimate friendship sooner or later will have to face the need for forgiveness. The fact that we all not only make mistakes but also at times act in sinful ways toward even those who mean the most to us underscores the need for missionaries to know both how to forgive and how to repent (see Allender and Longman 1992; White 1992). Relationships without these spiritual disciplines rarely will pass from friendship to the deeper intimacy that Christ wants all Christians to experience as part of his body. Those who are working in a new culture must take the time to see how forgiveness and repentance are expressed within that culture, so that they know how to read cues that are key to the survival, let alone the growth, of relationships.

students, but they had been very patient with him. After all the students arrived, Professor Piaget offered everyone an aperitif. Everyone accepted except John. He wanted to be a good witness for his Lord, so he refused. John thought the professor seemed ill at ease, because for a moment he appeared not to know what to do. After an uneasy silence he offered John some lemon drink and it was accepted. The awkwardness of the moment passed and John breathed a sigh of relief.

When dinner was served, John partook heartily of the beans and roast beef. But when Dr. Piaget began filling the guests' glasses with the customary wine, John politely refused his share. It was clear that this time the professor felt not only awkward but somewhat angry at this foreigner in his house who refused his hospitality. Though he offered John a Coke instead, the atmosphere had changed. Due to the length of French meals and the thirst of the people there, the host soon got more wine. Again it was only refused by John.

Dinner being finished, everyone sat around the table and discussed various subjects. Mrs. Piaget cleared the table of the last remains of dessert and coffee. It had been a great time for everyone except John and perhaps his host. John wondered, "Was it right to offend Professor Piaget the way I did? Was the Lord really pleased with what had taken place? Will I ever be able to share my faith in Christ with Dr. Piaget? Is it really so bad to drink just a little wine, and is it not worse to build a barrier between oneself and someone who does not know the Lord?" All these questions and more had run through John's mind throughout the meal and particularly now, when everyone was enjoying the conversation and relaxing.

It was then that Professor Piaget excused himself. He was gone for a few minutes but reappeared carrying a tray. On it was a large flask surrounded by neat-looking glasses. He began to tell his guests how good the Brittany cider was and, especially for John's benefit, that it contained only a little alcohol. The host set glasses in front of everyone and began to pour.

John became anxious as the professor moved closer. Should he refuse once again, even though the professor had pointed out for his sake that it contained little alcohol? Was he going to build an even higher barrier between his teacher and himself? Or should he ignore the teachings of the Bible College and the warnings of the Smiths? When Professor Piaget paused before John and put a glass before him with a smile, John …

AMERICAN FRIENDSHIPS

What do people from other cultures think of Americans (adapted from Kohls 1976, 6)? Americans are thought of as outgoing, friendly, hardworking, generous, and wealthy. Additionally, they are seen as typically being informal, always in a hurry, and confident of having all the answers. Each of these may be viewed positively or negatively, depending on the context. Characteristics that typify Americans that are more negative include being loud, rude, boastful, immature, extravagant, wasteful, and disrespectful of authority. In many cultures, influenced by exported American television shows such as *Baywatch*, people view American women as promiscuous. It is helpful to be aware of these stereotypes as you encounter people of other cultures because they may comprise the grid through which your actions and attitudes are analyzed.

How do you develop friendships? The following characteristics of a typical American approach are a reminder that strategies for finding and developing friendships are culturally determined to a high degree (adapted from Stewart and Bennett 1991, 100–103).

First, Americans tend to choose their

241

friends based on spontaneity, mutual attraction, and warm personal feelings. These choices are made quite quickly. Many American parents will have vivid memories of a child coming home from the first day of the new school year proudly announcing that he or she met a new "best" friend. The

---

We will see the importance of forgiveness as a central category in relating to others to the extent that we see every relationship enmeshed in a war that leads to a taste of heaven or hell.

Dan Allender
and Tremper Longman (1992, 88)

---

quickness characterizing American friendships can be unnerving to those who are used to letting friendships develop more slowly. For example, Japanese friendship patterns involve obligation, duty, and ritualized interaction. This combination of factors makes it virtually impossible to imagine meeting a "best" friend on the first day of school.

Second, American friendships, though starting fast, tend to be relatively shallow in comparison with friendships in other cultures (Althen 1988, 78–79; Smith 2002, 484). Valuing their independence and individualism, Americans keep people at arm's length longer than people in other cultures do, and they value independence in their relationships rather than dependence.

Third, Americans' relations with their friends are kept separate from work or social obligations. Many other cultures do not separate these two spheres, seeing life more holistically than most Americans do.

Fourth, American friendships are formed in shared activities. They like to do things

together. They have church friends, school friends, bowling friends, hobby friends, and the like (Lustig and Koester 1996, 275). Generally, they keep these friendships compartmentalized, which allows for a large number of friendships. Additionally, as they become interested in new activities or lose interest in old ones, they add or drop friendships related to those activities. American Christians form neighborhood Bible studies but limit the obligations that people have to join the group. They may study a Gospel or an Epistle from the New Testament (or, rarely, a short book from the Old Testament). Once that study is finished, however, there is no cultural obligation to continue with the study. Members may lose contact with those who lose interest and drop out. This pattern allows for a larger number of friendships but results in a diminished ability to develop the type of intimacy seen in longer-lasting friendships found in other cultures.

NEW NEIGHBORS, FRIENDS, AND ACQUAINTANCES

Today's missionaries are less likely to live on a missionary compound than were missionaries of previous years. This is an important and positive development. Though they may have less contact with other missionaries, they have more opportunity for contact with people in the community, and thus more opportunities for witness in the context of real life. At the same time, this can bring added strain, as the "strangeness" of everyday life can be pressing. This looms large especially in cultures with gender roles that limit the freedom of females to travel unchaperoned in public, or when the very strangeness of the missionary invites staring or perhaps even aggression.

Learning to live as a good neighbor, then, is an essential missionary skill. Qualities of neighborliness will vary from culture to culture, just as they vary from rural to urban environments in North America. One of the early adaptations that missionaries must make is learning what the new "neighborology" is—what makes for good neighbors, what bothers people in the neighborhood, and what roles there are for the stranger who comes to a new neighborhood. In sidebar 14.4 Duane Elmer tells a wonderful story of one couple's struggle to adjust to life in their new neighborhood and to learn how to live as good neighbors while at the same time wisely dealing with an issue that could have been a source of tremendous frustration for them.

CONCLUSION

Discipleship is built on relationships. Relational values and skills are culturally learned, and the wise cross-cultural worker will invest significant time in learning how friendships are developed in that culture so that he or she can disciple well. Indeed, developing deep relationships in the host culture is not optional for missionaries who want to faithfully call others to worship Christ. The question is not *whether* missionaries develop significant relationships; the question is *how well* they do it. The case study for this chapter offers an example of one set of cultural values directly clashing with another, and the distress of finding ways to deal with conflicting values in the process of developing a relationship.

15

Relating to Churches and Other Shareholders

INTRODUCTION

What are shareholders? And who are they? Good questions both, and important prerequisites to the more crucial question in mission: How are they doing and what could they be doing better?

When we speak of shareholders in the missionary enterprise, we note a primary division between the sending and receiving functions, though any particular geographic entity can and should be participating simultaneously in both. That's the message behind the rallying cry "Mission from all continents, to all continents."

The shareholders that we have in mind here are those entities with a serious share in the mission enterprise: taking the gospel of Jesus Christ to all peoples and making disciples of them. Shareholders may come from the supply side, the recipient side, or both. Those from the recipient side include, among the more obvious examples, indigenous churches, Christian leaders, unreached peoples, and agencies working in the area.

To the extent that any city, nation, region, or continent is participating in the sending function (the focus of this chapter), share-

holders are likely to include churches, agencies, trainers, and mobilizers (i.e., assemblies, agencies, academics, and admonishers). These are the typical shareholders of missions sending.

THE CHURCHES

Churches, of course, are the primary senders. This wasn't determined by chance or by a vote. God made the church—the "bride of Christ" (see Rev. 19:7; 21:2, 9)—his primary instrument for accomplishing his purposes on earth (Matt. 16:17–19). Foremost among the roles that churches play as local manifestations of the universal church is to prepare members for Great Commission work (Matt. 28:19–20). Churches do this by teaching the full counsel of God regarding the global task, by preparing all members to find and perform their particular part in it, and by sending out those called to go (see Acts 13:1–3; 3 John 5–8).

As Gary Corwin points out, "Well-grounded disciples of Christ are the building blocks of any mission outreach, and only the churches can provide them. The work of academics, agencies and admonishers only builds on the most basic work that churches do of training disciples" (Corwin 1994a, 46). As the fountainhead of missionary training, churches are the chief guardians of the process of character formation, as well as the chief venue for ministry experience. They also are, or ought to be, the chief broker and quality-control mechanism for all other aspects of training provided by other shareholders (Corwin 1994b, 170).

Although churches have a somewhat exclusive role in actually sending those who go, at least in the sense of commissioning and providing necessary resources, they usually share the selection and training roles with others. This is because churches generally are unable to provide all the specialized services and training necessary to send and sustain well-prepared missionaries in difficult places. There are exceptions to this, of course, particularly among some of the largest churches, but most still welcome the unique contributions of other shareholders who are willing to work under and alongside the churches. Failure to pay more than lip service to the latter has been a significant factor where friction has existed between churches and the other shareholders (Engel and Dyrness 2000).

THE OTHERS

The other primary sending shareholders—agencies, trainers, and mobilizers—can be sorted according to the nature of the relationship they usually have with churches. Agencies generally have the longest and most interconnected relationships with the churches because they share common members over a long period. This has declined somewhat in recent years with the surging of short-term missions and the simultaneous decline of long-term recruits, but it still distinguishes the relationship between these two groups. The joint commitment to the welfare and effectiveness of common members acts as a glue that requires them to stick together. This does not, however, mean that churches are inclined any longer to defer to the strategies of the agencies. More and more churches are developing quite explicit strategies of their own, and this has created a certain level of uncertainty in terms of how the two entities ought now to relate (Pierson 1998; Engel and Dyrness 2000). We will return to this issue in chapter 17.

What is true for the agencies is true also for the trainers, especially for those who operate on a more traditional academic and institutional model, such as Bible colleges and seminaries. However, a lower priority usually is given to this relationship by the churches, at least as far as the sending function is concerned. This is so for two reasons: first, the period in which they have "members" in common with the churches is not as long (usually four years or less); second, the stakes of failure are not understood to be as high (either financially or for the individuals involved). Where churches are sending their own members, however, and making use of the less formal forms of mission training that are available today, the relationship may be quite intense, though often short-lived.

The mobilizers, on the other hand, generally have a very different kind of relationship with the churches altogether. Depending on their particular mission and purpose, they may provide awareness seminars for whole congregations, consultancy for church missions committees, or resources and services that address particular felt needs in the local church context. They tend to be viewed by the churches much more like a consumer outlet, where distinct services may be procured for a price. Their credibility, however, often is assessed on the basis of multiple years of consistent quality service.

Each of these "other" shareholders, then, has a unique role to play in the sending function, which is the primary responsibility and purview of the churches. Increasingly, their effectiveness in playing that role depends not only on the quality of their services, but also on their ability to work amicably and in genuine partnership with and under churches. In some cases they will act as a junior partner needing to follow the churches' lead; in other cases the churches will look to them to be more proactive. Clearly, it is a challenging time for these "others," and the need for them to be flexible and adaptive is enormous. The plus side for them, though, is that they are given much clearer opportunity to do what they have always declared as their goal: to serve the churches.

THE CHALLENGES

As they are faithful to their God-given responsibility of taking the lead in the sending function of mission, churches invariably face many challenges. In this section we will look at two main sets of challenges that confront local churches most directly.

Rallying the Troops

No task related to the sending function is more important or foundational in the local church setting than keeping the vision of outreach and mission before the congregation. Unless there is zeal fed by knowledge in the hearts of the people, you can say good-bye to the vision of being an effective sending church.

But what is the biblical vision for outreach and mission that must be kept in view? Is it a heart for the lost? The Lord's command? A love for the world's peoples? A desire to see Christ return? Simply a love for Christ? A passion for God's glory? Some combination of these and other motivations? Proposing balanced answers to the question of vision has consumed hundreds of pages in the literature of mission. John Piper, whose thinking was presented in chapter 5, has captured the imagination of many mission-minded people with his thesis that "missions exists because wor-

> *A church not involved in mission will forever be a mission field.*
> Yemi Ladipo (1989, 20)

ship doesn't" (Piper 1993, 11). That is to say, God deserves and requires the worship of all peoples, and mission exists to bring that about. Mission one day will end, as time becomes eternity. Worship, however, the stuff of eternity and the fountainhead of all human joy, will go on forever. But what does it take for this message to capture the hearts of God's people, and for it to propel them into effective participation in mission? Four things may be mentioned.

1. *It takes a right balance of information with inspiration.* Neither is sufficient alone. The heart must be stirred, but also the mind must be informed. William Carey, the simple cobbler from Northampton, England, grew in his passion through study of both God's word and the world. He became convinced that foreign mission is the chief responsibility of the church as he developed a biblical perspective as a lay preacher, while also reading vision-expanding sources such as *Captain Cook's Voyages* (Tucker 1983, 115). The multitude of sources available today,

both in written and other media forms, would seem to him a miracle.

Evangelical churches and educational institutions in the era in which this book's authors were growing up seemed to err most often on the side of too much inspiration and too little information. In more recent decades, in an era of "scientific" mission, that tendency seems to have been reversed. That may be a result of better information and delivery systems being available today. But it may also be because there is less to inspire—fewer lives that set remarkable standards of commitment and service to God—or it may be simply that Christians are more cynical and harder to inspire. Undoubtedly also in play is the widespread lack of clarity in understanding biblical teaching concerning the supremacy of God in the process. Whatever the reasons, churches that want to fulfill their responsibility as senders must inspire as well as inform.

2. *It takes good pathways for gaining experience in service to the task.* This is where short-term missions done well have made such a powerful contribution. There simply is no substitute for hands-on ministry when the goal is creating hearts burdened for the task. Done poorly, however, short-term missions can produce results detrimental to the task and dispiriting to the participants (see chapter 17 for the marks of good short-term mission endeavors).

Regular and faithful ministry in the local church and community context is an even more fundamental avenue for gaining experience. The biblical model of the older people mentoring the younger in ministry is really hard to beat. And rarely is a young person permanently damaged from being overchallenged. Young people thrive on challenge. Unfortunately, many of them seem to have suffered the effects of being underchallenged.

3. *It takes the reinforcement of targeted and effective teaching and training.* This is true at the congregational level. It is true at the missions committee and pastoral staff level. And certainly it is true at the level of those who are being sent. Though the training needs of this last group are widely recognized and have been discussed at some length in chapter 10, often the needs of the first two groups receive scant attention. It is here that shareholders taking the role of admonishers can be effective.

In the years since the first Lausanne Congress (1974) put the mission spotlight on least-reached peoples, it is the admonishers who have been most effective in mobilizing global evangelicals to see churches planted among these peoples. Initiatives and groups such as the Perspectives on World Mission courses, the U.S. Center for World Mission, Operation World, Adopt-A-People, Global Mapping, Caleb Project, ACMC, and Joshua Project 2000—to mention just a few—have made a huge difference. Yet, in spite of their best efforts, the mobilization task remains enormous.

Multitudes of churches remain asleep to the task. Though the statistics are debated, Patrick Johnstone has estimated that there are approximately seven Protestant churches in America for every missionary that is sent (Johnstone 1998, 181).

The teaching and training, therefore, must continue and accelerate. Pastors, especially, must be energized with the message so that they can energize others with their preaching and teaching. Though a minority of the pastors do eventually become energized, this is seldom caught in seminary, so the challenge to the mobilizers remains large.

SIDEBAR 15.1
CHURCH MODELS THAT WORK

Mobilizing Children for Mission at Mechanicsville Christian Center (Mechanicsville, Virginia)

Getting kids excited about mission is the focus that makes this church unique, and its people have proven that it is a successful method for mobilizing the whole church. It's also highly effective for recruiting missionaries. Some of the top ideas that they have developed for mobilizing kids for mission include (Telford 2001, 52–55):

1. Start a mission library for kids.
2. Use the mission "P words" (see below).
3. Launch mission prayer for kids.
4. Start a monthly mission emphasis in Sunday school, children's church, or midweek kids' program.
5. Teach kids the biblical basis of mission using material designed for kids.
6. Develop a mission resource area for teachers.
7. Provide opportunities for kids to give to missions.
8. Conduct a kids' mission retreat.
9. Hold a mission conference for kids during the regular mission convention.
10. Encourage a Sunday school class to adopt a missionary, especially a family with children their own age.
11. Start kids' ministry clubs at church.
12. Start an outreach team composed of children.
13. Develop MED (missions education) teams.
14. Never stop looking for resources.

Mission "P Words" for Kids (Telford 2001, 53–54)

Purpose: God's purpose is to make his name known in all the world. This is the point of the Bible. Genesis 12:1–3 tells us that God's purpose through the whole Bible is actually twofold: to bless us and to make us a blessing to all tongues, tribes, peoples, and nations.

Power: God makes his name known by demonstrating his power to people. As we pray, God's power is shown to people. Exodus 9:16 says that God shows his power so that his name might be proclaimed throughout all the earth.

People: God wants all people to know him. People have been created with needs. We can help people know God when we meet these needs by being bridge builders between people and God. The name of the children's mission teams at Mechanicsville Christian Center is Bridge Builders.

People-Moving: People are moving all over the world, and this creates needs in their lives. At this point in history it is believed that half the world has moved to and live in large cities. God uses migration of people to make himself known to them.

Passport to the World: God always has told his people to go into all the world, but we need to know what the world looks like. We need to have a global perspective.

Preparation: Before we go into the world, we need preparation. There are many careers or jobs that God can use to help others know him. God is preparing you now for his purpose and mission.

Possessions: Possessions are time, talent, money, and material things. We need to use our possessions for God's mission, not just for ourselves. We need to learn the difference between what we need and what we want.

Projects: We need to mobilize for action now. Sometimes this means giving our money for projects that meet the needs of people. Projects give us hands-on opportunities to make a difference right now.

Partnership: We are in partnership with God in the task of making his name known in all the earth. We can make a difference in God's mission when we join with other people. We all need each other to make God known to all peoples. No one group can do it alone.

Proclamation: Half the world still does not know about Jesus. We need to learn how to tell people the good news.

And those who spearhead mission in local churches through committees or teams need to be given the assistance they need to do it well. Too often, it seems, they fall into one of two unhealthy categories: no policies or rigid policies. Thoughtful and flexible policies will be produced only by knowledgeable and passionate people. And because they need the resources to make wise decisions, they also need more and better training. But how do they get it? That's where the final item comes in on our list of what it takes for the message of mission to capture the hearts and minds of God's people.

4. *It takes resources that make a difference.* Fortunately, myriad resources are available today, and they come in just about every variety imaginable. Among the most active and helpful is ACMC (Advancing Churches in Missions Commitment), which for years has engaged effectively in direct ministries of consulting, providing resources, and working with local churches to improve their mission impact. One of their number, David Mays, has developed and made available on the Internet multiple lists of books and other resources that can benefit any sending church (www.davidmays.org/booknotes.html). In sidebar 15.2 we provide an organized sample of the types of books that Mays summarizes and recommends on his Web site.

Balancing the Portfolio

One of the most significant challenges that any church faces concerning global mission is how to balance the "portfolio" of its involvements. Besides the inherent complexity of the task and the enormous number of things to consider, particular pressures and precedents seem to come in from every side to influence the decisions that are made. Complicating things further is the fact that mission leadership in local churches tends to change either too often or not often enough. This frequently results in pressures and precedents that are the product not of well-reasoned policies and conviction, but of the personal preferences and/or relationships of a few. Over time the portfolio begins to look less and less coherent and rational.

In trying to combat these seemingly intractable tendencies toward incoherence and reduced overall effectiveness, churches must understand and articulate their own vision and periodically review their commitments based on it. That is not to argue for wholesale reversals of commitments every few years, but to suggest that regular and thoughtful reflection on where things are and where they are going can make such reversals far less likely.

The twin realities of the church's particular vision and giftedness, together with the global strategic needs of the gospel task, need to be regularly overlaid and reflected upon. Where major change is needed, it should be accomplished in a way that still values continuity. This is both for the overall sake of the work and for the welfare of those who have faithfully given of themselves in the task. Abrupt and careless change does a great disservice to both.

Whether significant overall change ultimately is the result or not, certainly categories of decisions will need to be made along the way. Four major areas include decisions about (1) geography and peoples, (2) frontline and support personnel, (3) ministry areas, and (4) short-term versus long-term endeavors. Let's look now at some of the issues related to each.

SIDEBAR 15.2

A STARTER LIST OF INVALUABLE BOOKS ON MISSION

Books for Thinking and Practice

Paul Borthwick, *How to Be a World Class Christian* (1991) and *Six Dangerous Questions to Transform Your View of the World* (1996)

David Bryant, *Stand in the Gap: How to Get Ready for the Coming World Revival.* Rev. ed. (1997)

Michael Griffiths, *Get Your Church Involved in Missions: Some Suggestions for Ministers and Congregations Disenchanted with the Traditional Muddle* (1981)

Patrick Johnstone, *The Church Is Bigger Than You Think: Structures and Strategies for the Church in the 21st Century* (1998) and *Operation World* (2001)

Robertson McQuilkin Jr., *The Great Omission: A Biblical Basis for World Evangelism* (1984)

A. Scott Moreau, gen. ed., *Evangelical Dictionary of World Missions* (2000)

Bryant L. Myers, *The New Context of World Mission* (1993)

John Piper, *Let the Nations Be Glad! The Supremacy of God in Missions.* 2d ed. (2003)

Tom Telford, *Missions in the 21st Century* (1998)

Ruth A. Tucker, *From Jerusalem to Irian Jaya: A Biographical History of Christian Missions* (1983)

Books for Pleasure Reading and Inspiration

Elisabeth Elliot, *Through Gates of Splendor* (1957)

Thomas Hale, *Don't Let the Goats Eat the Loquat Trees: Adventures of an American Surgeon in Nepal* (1986); *On the Far Side of Liglig Mountain: Adventures of an American Family in Nepal* (1989); and *Living Stones of the Himalayas: Adventures of an American Couple in Nepal* (1993)

Bruce Olson, *Bruchko* (1978)

Jim Reapsome, *Final Analysis: A Decade of Commentary on the Church and World Missions* (1999)

Don Richardson, *Peace Child* (1974) and *Eternity in Their Hearts* (1981)

Martin St. Kilda, *Near the Far Bamboo: An Insightful Look at Cross-Cultural Clashes through the Eyes of a Tentmaking Missionary* (1993)

Bill and Amy Stearns, *Catch the Vision 2000* (1991)

Books for Ministry to Missionaries

Marjory Foyle, *Honourably Wounded: Stress among Christian Workers.* 2d ed. (2002)

Kelly O'Donnell, ed., *Missionary Care: Counting the Cost of World Evangelization* (1992)

Neal Pirolo, *The Re-Entry Team: Caring for Your Returning Missionaries* (2000)

William Taylor, ed., *Too Valuable to Lose: Exploring the Causes and Cures of Missionary Attrition* (1997)

GEOGRAPHY AND PEOPLES

The focus and assumptions of modern mission have altered significantly since Ralph Winter made his famous address "The Highest Priority: Cross-Cultural Evangelism" (Winter 1975) to the Lausanne Congress on World Evangelization in 1974. Because of the flurry of activity that rippled out from that event, scarcely an agency or a church today is unaware of the need to target ethnic peoples. This has resulted in the need to rethink priorities not only on mission fields, but also in local church missions committees.

The reality, however, is that most of these committees and the churches they serve find themselves resourcing a potpourri of causes and individuals without much reference to the needs of least-reached ethnic peoples. This is partially the result of inertia and "the way things always have been done," but it is also impacted by a lack of knowledgeable and thoughtful dialogue about priorities.

The real need is for churches to ask, "Without limiting ourselves to whatever commitments we have currently, among which of the least-reached people groups of the world can we make a significant difference by investing our prayer, personnel, and financial resources over the long haul?" The same question can be asked appropriately about prime geographic categories, such as world-class cities or Islamic centers. These are also home to many of the least-reached peoples, although their specific ethnic identity may be a less important social characteristic to them in these contexts than in more rural settings.

The key point for the local church committees, however, is to factor in the "peoples" issue in their allocation of resources. It is crucial to keep in mind the Lord's promise to surround his throne with some from "every nation, tribe, people, and language" (Rev. 7:9–10), as well as his command to his people to "make disciples of all nations [peoples]" (Matt. 28:19). When this consideration is kept on the front burner, perhaps many different and more fruitful decisions will be made.

People-group thinking also helps to put in perspective and provide guidance to the issues of potential conflict that arise concerning the expenditure of resources on international or domestic outreach. Either one can be strategically more important at any given time, depending on the people-group focus. In a world in which the migration of people is so common, particularly to North America, huge opportunities, once unthinkable, now exist to impact particular peoples in new ways and places. And peoples impacted, not geography, is the determining factor.

FRONTLINE AND SUPPORT PERSONNEL

The issue in view here has to do with the role that particular individuals play in a larger organizational or project strategy and, very often, where they will be located to accomplish it. More than many areas, this is one that has been dominated too often by some very shallow thinking. It is not unheard of, for example, for an individual who is promoted into a leadership role in an agency to be dropped from local church support because he or she no longer will be located in a frontline (often translated "overseas") location. The fact that this person's influence and impact for the cause will be expanded seems at times not to enter into the equation. Sadly, the same is also too often true for those who may be working in the same "frontline" evangelism or church-planting role among the same ethnic people, but their location has changed to one of the great cities of North America. This ought not to be.

In the military realm it has long been recognized that a significant number of support personnel are needed to keep a soldier functioning effectively at the front. It has been said that the ratio reached ten-to-one for the five hundred thousand American soldiers who participated in Desert Storm in 1990–91 (Pelletier 1999, 174). That is a huge percentage of support personnel needed to get the job done. Though the ratios may not be exactly equivalent, the same principle holds true in mission. It is essential, therefore, that resource providers, especially local churches, which are chief among them, not lose sight of this crucial fact and that they get behind them. Balance is not possible, just as the task is not possible, without support personnel. Their roles may not be as exciting, but they are every bit as essential.

MINISTRY AREAS

In seeking to maintain a balanced mission program, deciding which types of ministries to resource and what degree to resource each are important considerations.

251

Maintaining balance requires knowledge, reflection, and prayer.

Generally, at least four broad types of ministry come into view: (1) church planting, (2) church nurture and leadership training, (3) translation and media, and (4) mercy. The fourth type can be divided further into relief, development, and justice categories, with components in areas such as medicine, education, and economic assistance. Each has a particular and unique role to play.

Church Planting

This generally is considered to be the heart of the missionary enterprise, and rightly so, as it is the fulfillment of Christ's declaration "I will build my church," as well as the clear objective of mission as it plays out in the New Testament (see chapters 3, 4, 5). As a result, it is also the area that senders tend to get most excited about.

Nothing could be clearer, then, than the central place that church planting ought to occupy in any church's mission planning. More nuances, however, that should be considered often go unrecognized. Some key questions that any church should ask include the following three.

First, do our church-planting plans have a strategic focus emphasizing the needs of those peoples with least access to the gospel, or is creating more churches "like us" the most important consideration? If it is the latter, then resistant peoples (the least reached) will almost always get the leftovers of mission energy and attention. Workers and plans invariably will gravitate toward more receptive peoples and situations.

Second, do our church-planting plans take into account the church as it already exists in an area, even if the tradition or theology of that church is very different from ours? We are not suggesting here that the existence of other churches ought to rule out new work automatically, but it certainly ought to be looked at very carefully. Even if engagement clearly is needed, it may be possible to accomplish the goal by coming alongside what is already there rather than starting something completely new. The same would be true for the work of other mission groups working in that context.

Third, is the church-planting methodology to be employed one that holds promise for the establishment of a self-sustaining indigenous movement, or is it the imported kind that is totally dependent on the foreigners? If it is the latter, it may not be worth the effort.

Yes, church planting ought to be the anchor and epicenter of mission involvement, but all church planting is not equal. Nor is church planting all there is. In fact, without many of the ministries that follow, its impact may be hollow.

Church Nurture and Leadership Training

Wherever there are churches, whether newly planted or long-rooted, there is need for godly, effective leaders. Helping to provide and multiply them through training and mentoring has been, and undoubtedly will always be, a major focus of mission work. Church nurture, likewise, is the work of training at a larger congregational level, often in specialized areas such as children's or youth work, developing indigenous worship music, or evangelistic methods appropriate to particular groups.

Sometimes church nurture and leadership training flow outward from formal educational institutions such as seminaries or Bible schools. Other times it is accomplished primarily through itinerant Theological Education by Extension (TEE) ministries. More recently, distance-learning programs over the Internet or by means of other electronic distribution are gaining in usage. Sometimes, however, it is simply a key missionary facilitator coaching local leaders through one-on-one training and encouragement. Whatever the means, though, the need is ever present and must be a significant part of healthy sending-church mission endeavors.

Translation and Media

A bit farther out on the spectrum from church ministries per se are ministries of translation and media, which to about an equal degree have both an inward and an outward focus. Translating the Scriptures, for example, clearly is on the inward side in terms of its importance to the functioning of healthy churches and effective believers. But the word of God is also the chief bridge to those who are coming to faith. Clearly, both roles are essential and verifiable historically.

Though in a less dramatic way, the same is true of media ministry. Whether literature, radio, cable and satellite TV, audiotapes and videotapes, or CDs and DVDs, there is almost always an application to strengthen and build up believers, as well as one of outreach evangelism.

It is hard for Westerners to imagine a world in which the advantages brought into their own lives by both these areas of ministry, translation and media, are not readily apparent. It ought, therefore, to be easy to see the need for each of them to be a ready part of any church's mission endeavor.

Mercy

This is almost certainly the most complex and multifaceted of any of these ministry areas. It is distinguished first of all by its twin foci of relief and development—the former aimed more at short-term and emergency work, and the latter more at long-term and structural work.

It is further distinguished by the many ways in which acting mercifully and promoting justice are fleshed out. It may be educational, medical, well-drilling, fish-farming, famine relief, microloans, agricultural development, desert reclamation, advocacy on behalf of oppressed peoples, ministering among political leaders for legislative reform, and other things too numerous to mention. And perhaps never are God's people more Christlike than when they engage in these ministries, loving others as they love themselves (Matt. 22:39), and doing good unto others as if they were doing it unto Christ himself (Matt. 25:40). No well-balanced local church mission strategy worth the name can be without such ministry, as long as these critical activities do not become replacements for the focus on calling people to worship Christ.

SHORT-TERM AND LONG-TERM EFFORTS

This fourth major area in which significant decisions will need to be made is one that has grown exponentially in its importance over the last couple decades.

When Gary Corwin and his wife, Dotsie, went overseas for the first time in 1975, short-term missions of the type they were doing (a two-month teaching assignment in Ghana) were fairly new. Prior to this time, most "short-term" ministry was for a year or two, and it was carried on almost exclusively under the direct auspices of mission agencies. Things have changed considerably since then.

Today, short-term mission trips are as common as high school proms, and each year hundreds of thousands of youth and adults travel considerable distances overseas and domestically to "do missions."

These short-term trips also have changed rather dramatically in some of their most basic characteristics: (1) the majority of them are conducted directly by churches rather than under the auspices of a mission agency; (2) their typical length is one to two weeks; (3) the median age of the participants probably is under twenty; (4) their primary purpose is much more clearly focused on what they will do for the spiritual growth and worldview of the participants rather than on the strategic contribution they will make to the Lord's work where they are going; (5) because congregational experience tends to trump strategic impact as the reason for short-term mission trips, a lot of sound missiological principles are being violated, and vast sums of money for mission are being spent without a lot of positive results to show for it.

Fortunately, the last two of these five characteristics are not the whole story. Some churches indeed are making a great contribution to the health and expansion of the Lord's work in various places. The things that distinguish them from the majority include: (1) a commitment to relate effectively to what is already happening in an area (Palmatier 2002); (2) a commitment to go back to the same places year after year so that strong relationships can be developed and contributions can be targeted to real felt needs (Tucker 2001); and (3) a commitment to doing the hard work of learning sound missiology so that unnecessary errors can be avoided.

Besides the obvious applications of all this for evaluation of short-term endeavors by any local church, another key question is raised. That is the question of what balance actually looks like in the relationship between resource investments in long- and short-term missions. Clearly, the pendulum has swung in emphasis to the short-term side, and the jury is still out on what effect this ultimately will have on the North American contribution to global evangelization. But the early evidence is not particularly good. Churches interested in real effectiveness, therefore, should be ready to examine and monitor this balance closely. Two good places to begin looking for helpful tools are on the Internet at www.acmc.org and www.mislinks.org/practical/shterm.htm.

MISSIONARY CARE

Inescapable among the many responsibilities that all senders have to deal with is the care of the missionaries they send. It is part and parcel of the unwritten contract between the senders and the sent. It is also the clear instruction of Scripture (3 John 5–8)—senders are to perform this duty with diligence, but also with joy. This is not to say that churches have the only, or even the primary, role in this particular task. In fact, a strong case can be made that the agency involved has a larger responsibility in this because of the more direct contact and the closer involvement it has in missionary supervision.

Missionaries themselves, furthermore, also need to play a significant role in their own care. The difficulty with that, however, comes most clearly into view at the point where the missionary is already wounded, burned out, or ready to call it quits. Such circumstances clearly call for the intervention of others, but so do the causes that lead to them.

We now look at some of the chief considerations related to missionary care, and, in particular, how they relate to senders: (1) the challenge of maintaining wholeness; (2) the particular roles of senders; (3) avoid-

ing attrition and assisting the broken; and (4) resources for missionary care.

The Challenge of Maintaining Wholeness

It may seem to some that the very title of this section is overly dramatic or exaggerated. "Surely," some may contend, "missionaries are not so delicate or unusual that they need special preemptive attention in order to keep their bodies, souls, minds, and families on an even keel." No, it is not because they are delicate or unusual that such attention is called for. The reason is simply that they are ordinary human beings, while the pressures on them are out of the ordinary.

The two sidebars that accompany this section, "Burnout" (15.4) and "Focus on the Missionary Family" (15.5), provide insight into those pressures and the impact they can have.

An additional pressure, too often overlooked, is the stress of spiritual warfare and the fact that it actually is warfare. Wars produce casualties. Good armies take care of their wounded. The fact is that there is a real enemy who desperately wants to foil the ministry success of the Lord's servants and to do them harm to the extent he is permitted. Senders need to be ready to respond and come to their aid.

The Particular Roles of Senders

As we mentioned previously, the task of providing member care belongs to at least three entities: (1) the missionaries themselves, (2) the agencies with which they serve, and (3) the churches that have sent them forth. Because of their unique contexts and circumstances, none of the three is capable of doing the job alone, yet each has a role to play that only it can do well.

First, for the missionaries themselves, that role involves both self-care and one-another care. This is the first line of defense. It involves all those things that believers do to sustain their own spiritual, mental, and physical health (too many to mention here), as well as all those encouragement and admonishing roles that believers are to exhibit toward "one another." The Bible is full of such references, which for their own benefit every reader is encouraged to review regularly with a concordance. For missionaries, such reviews and the practice

of what they say is more than an option; it often is a matter of survival.

Second, for the agencies corporately, the challenge is a very different one, though obviously, individual mission leaders face the very same challenges mentioned above. The agency challenge corporately is to create an atmosphere in which missionary care can flourish and to ensure that it is actually happening at a healthy and sustainable level. This will include both elements of missionary self-care described above, as well as the employment of programs, training, and professional personnel that carry missionary care to the next level. The reader is referred to Kelly O'Donnell's "Touring the Terrain:

SIDEBAR 15.4
BURNOUT

Gary R. Corwin
(Corwin 2000a [used with permission])

Burnout is the state of emotional, physical, and/or spiritual exhaustion that makes the missionary unable to carry out his or her work. While it is not normally terminal in life-and-death terms, it is often fatal to missionary effectiveness.

Potential causes of burnout are many, but overwork, undersupport, and prolonged exposure to the pressures of living and working cross-culturally are three of the most important. Learning the language and becoming bicultural can be particularly stressful to newcomers; living in the public view, facing unfulfilled expectations, and issues of self-esteem may be more important

burnout issues for longer-term veterans.

Unfortunately, all these challenges are often compounded by a lack of pastoral care or by mission administrators insensitive to the psychological pressures their missionaries face. Reliable figures are hard to come by, but some estimate that between 20 percent and 50 percent of new missionaries fail to return for a second term. This attrition is seldom the result of theological difficulties or problems in communicating the gospel. It is almost always attributable, at least in part, to an inability to adapt to the kinds of issues that lead to burnout.

Increasingly, mission agencies are seeking ways to address the causes of burnout before they occur. Training seminars, mentoring programs, team-building efforts, pastoral care ministries, and more flexible schedules have all proven helpful. But the rigors of missionary life, particularly among some of the least-reached peoples of the world, are still significant. And the limitations of human and material resources available to the worldwide missionary enterprise would seem to suggest that the issue of burnout will not soon pass from the scene.

REFLECTION
AND DISCUSSION

1. Why does God allow missionaries to burn out?
2. What steps can you take to prevent your own burnout?

An International Sampler of Member Care Literature" (2001), which provides multiple resources relevant to this issue.

Third, for the sending churches, the challenge is to stay fully engaged with the missionaries they have sent and to make sure that effective missionary care is actually taking place. The latter may require them to give a series of nudges—asking tough questions until what needs to be done is actually done. Among more regular duties, they should focus on the kinds of communication and home-assignment encouragement that convey the sense of love and concern that all missionaries need.

Avoiding Attrition and Assisting the Broken

One could wish that it were not even necessary to include a section such as this, but it is. In *Too Valuable to Lose*, the best book available on missionary attrition, William Taylor describes the heart-wrenching scope of the problem from a study done on a global scale:

> Let's take a look at one of the prime findings of the ReMAP research: In terms of the global missions force, it is estimated that 1 career missionary in 20 (5.1% of the mission force) leaves the mission field to return home *every year.* Of those who leave, 71% leave for *preventable* reasons. (Taylor 1997b, 13)

That is a staggering finding when one calculates the loss to the cause financially alone, not to mention the more tragic loss in human terms. But it does happen, and the need must be addressed.

Fortunately, the need is being addressed, and on a global scale. *Too Valuable to Lose* and the international conference and research project of which it is an outcome bear eloquent testimony to that. Unfortunately, the fine recommendations that the book contains are still a long way from anything like full implementation. This is true of a myriad of helpful preventative measures, as well as of efforts to "assist the broken."

So who are the broken, and what can be done to help them? Put simply, the broken are those who leave ministry prematurely for preventable reasons. It may be their body, mind, or spirit that is broken, but they share a common need for healing.

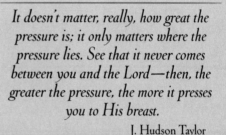

> *It doesn't matter, really, how great the pressure is; it only matters where the pressure lies. See that it never comes between you and the Lord—then, the greater the pressure, the more it presses you to His breast.*
>
> J. Hudson Taylor
> (Taylor and Taylor [1932?], 152)

The conditions needing healing cover the same gamut of afflictions, addictions, and maladies that inflict the population generally. The missionary population simply has more pressures and occasions for wounds because of living cross-culturally and as missionaries.

Resources for healing are much more plentiful than they were just a decade or two ago (the next section will discuss some of these), but the understanding and support necessary to enable hurting missionaries to take advantage of these resources has not always kept up. That's where well-informed and compassionate churches can play such a strategic role, ensuring that neither a lack of funds nor a lack of moral support and encouragement will keep wounded mis-

SIDEBAR 15.5
FOCUS ON THE MISSIONARY FAMILY

Gary R. Corwin
(Corwin 2001, 418–19 [used with permission])

It's difficult to imagine a class of people less understood than missionary families, unless maybe it's missionaries in general. To their advocates they are heroes and creators of family faith legacies. To their detractors they are fools and irresponsible toward their children. The truth is that they cannot be summed up neatly in a descriptive phrase.

Having said that, however, there are some characteristics and needs that tend to be common among them, and there are some resources and responses that many have found helpful. Please keep in mind that the observations offered here are based on anecdotal evidence and personal intuition.

First, what are some of the characteristics of missionary families that set them apart from other families?

1. They tend to be more closely knit and unified in their focus. Being a missionary family involves everybody in the unique challenges and blessings associated with the calling. Living cross-culturally is, obviously, the biggest part of that, particularly when it's among the disenfranchised. One should not forget, however, challenges such as raising support, relative wealth overseas, and relative poverty at home, to name just a few other areas. Nor should one forget the quantity or quality of time together, or the exhilarating feeling of striving together for a goal so worthy of the energy and sacrifice, to name just a couple of key blessings.

2. They tend to be more out of touch than most with the cultural cues, fads, and fashions of their home culture. Indeed, the better adjusted they are to their ministry culture, the more out of touch they are likely to be.

3. They seem to produce a higher percentage of exceptional and gifted children than their own numbers would justify. And this was true even before homeschooling became the rage, though many of the same factors that have tended to push up the achievement statistics for homeschoolers (e.g., parental involvement, focused and flexible learning, personal attention) are no doubt in play here as well.

Second, what are some of the needs unique to missionary families?

1. They tend to face the challenge of transitions much more frequently and to a greater degree than do most families. Changing cultures requires a much larger adjustment than changing cities, and going back and forth between cultures every two to four years is a much greater challenge to maintaining healthy psyches, especially for children.

2. Home tends to be an elusive concept, and while a sense of loss may be the

sionaries from the healing resources they need.

Resources for Missionary Care

The variety of resources for missionary care and healing available today is large and growing. It ranges from books, to collections of articles, to centers with trained psychologists that cater specifically to those in cross-cultural ministry. Although decisions to employ these resources generally are made by the missionaries themselves or their agencies, it is important that churches, as the chief source of funding, be aware of them and the conditions that require their use. Less than a decade ago the process of becoming

dominant feeling that this may engender for oneself and one's spouse, a sense of guilt may accompany it with regard to children. For some close families, distance from grandparents, aunts, uncles, and cousins can seem an overwhelming sacrifice.

3. Financial issues tend to be a bigger deal for missionary families than for others. It's simply not a lot of fun to ask people to support you. And shortfalls cannot be responded to by moonlighting or working harder. On the contrary, they usually require communication of the need to others so that they can "bail you out." Yes, it may be biblical and it may be right, but it still doesn't feel very good from the missionary family side of the equation.

Finally, what steps can missionaries, their agencies, and their supporting churches take to strengthen missionary families?

1. Take full advantage of books, seminars, and other resources available in the Christian community to strengthen families. Where needed, agencies also should be developing new resources to address issues peculiar to missionary families (culture adjustment issues, customized financial planning, etc.).

2. Agencies can create an atmosphere that communicates not only that it is okay, but also that it is essential and expected, that couples and whole families spend periodic time apart from their assignments—time to recharge their batteries, enjoy some privacy, and pursue hobbies or other recreation. Churches can reinforce this idea by occasionally giving a small gift designated for this kind of use only.

3. Successful marriages always require hard work, patience, and commitment. Successful missionary marriages are no exception, but they do require something more: recognition that there are additional stresses that will have to be faced. Issues of culture, distance, transitions, privacy, support raising, and so on can compound the challenges that exist in any marriage and family. It's important to acknowledge this fact going in, to prepare oneself mentally and spiritually for all that will be required, and to plan for the practical steps that will provide periodic respite.

Missionary families aren't from Venus, Mars, or anywhere else outside of our atmosphere. But they do have some special characteristics and needs, and those concerned for their welfare (including themselves) ought to be proactive in meeting them.

REFLECTION AND DISCUSSION

1. Choose one of the unique needs of missionary families and brainstorm in small groups about how a local church supporting a missionary family might help meet that need.

2. Generate a list of at least three additional ways agencies and supporting churches can strengthen missionary families.

aware was time-consuming and difficult. How difficult usually depended on one's proximity to agency headquarters or training institutions where such resources, or at least guides to them, could be found. That is all changed now with the ubiquitous Internet. All this material can be found there, and access to it is just a few clicks away. MisLinks provides a page full of links to helpful resources that we encourage you to check out (www.mislinks.org/practical/membcare.htm; Moreau and O'Rear 2001). Additionally, we encourage you to check out recent print resources such as the January and October 2001 issues of *Evangelical Missions Quarterly* and Kelly O'Donnell's *Doing Member Care Well: Perspectives and Practices from around the World* (2002).

SIDEBAR 15.6
CHURCH MODELS THAT WORK

Member Care at Hershey Evangelical Free Church (Hershey, Pennsylvania)

This church does many things well, but the place where it really shines is missionary care. Telford describes it as "the benchmark by which other churches should evaluate their missionary care. If there's a way to make missionaries feel loved and cared for, Hershey Free has thought of it" (Telford 2001, 28).

The people of Hershey Evangelical Free don't just rise to the occasion when missionaries need special care; they have a full-orbed strategy that cares for missionaries when they are at home as well as abroad, and it is designed to help the whole church become part of that caregiving. This in turn makes for a congregation that really knows its missionaries and feels like a part of their ministry (Telford 2001, 28).

New ideas and creative services are standard features of the ways this church seeks to change the lives of its missionaries and its members through caring. The church employs unique communication methods, extravagant hospitality, persistent prayer, small-group support teams, short-term teams, special field visits by leaders and the senior pastor, accountability that requires quarterly reports, retreats for missionaries, and various kinds of individualized care, particularly in making anniversaries and birthdays special. And this list doesn't begin to do their efforts justice (Telford 2001, 31–36).

CONCLUSION

Challenges faced by local churches in mission are not new, though certainly they have contemporary twists that are particular to our day and age. Although such new twists can make the challenges seem daunting (as outlined in this chapter), new resources also are available to help those concerned tackle the challenges effectively. The case study that follows shows the ways in which different groups (in this case, two different national churches, a ministry setting, and the mission agency itself) with competing interests can place the missionary at the center of a storm full of conflicting challenges. Wisdom to navigate such times is hard-won but well worth the pursuit.

CASE STUDY: THE AUTHORITY DILEMMA

Mark Danielson
(Hiebert and Hiebert 1987, 199–201 [used with permission])

Eileen Thompson, a North American missionary in the San Isabel Valley of Mexico, was committed to working within the structures of local church authority. It was important to her that the church be an indigenous expression of God's kingdom, so she was glad to submit to national leadership. The problem was that there were competing indigenous authorities who laid claim to her ministry. Eileen had just completed her furlough and was getting ready to return to Mexico. First, however, she and her mission board would have to decide where she would next be assigned to work.

Several different local groups had great plans for Eileen's life. She could not choose any of the options without offending people who wanted her to serve elsewhere, and her decision carried the potential for long-term consequences. Eileen had been put in the position of either defying the authority of the local Mexican church, to the possible detriment of its future growth, or dropping a fruitful ministry among some 15,000 migrant farm workers. To complicate things further, the hospital where she had worked during her first term as nurse-anesthetist and evangelist also had designs on Eileen. According to the doctor in charge, the zeal for evangelistic outreach at the hospital had diminished considerably while she was away on furlough.

During her first years of ministry, Eileen had been assigned to the hospital, but she also began to evangelize the valley's migrant farm workers, whose ethnic identity was Indian rather than Mexican. Just before her furlough, after ten years of work among the Indians, she had begun to reap the fruit of her ministry. Several small congregations sprang up in a number of the Indian villages.

Eileen had carried out this ministry to the farm workers under the authority of the local national Baptist church. At the time she left, the infant Indian congregations still depended entirely on the Mexican church for leadership, support and nurture. Eileen trusted that the relationship would continue in the same way without her.

Soon after Eileen went on furlough, something else happened that seriously affected the Indian work. The pastor of the Baptist church left, and his successor gave very low priority to the Indian work. Pastor Gonzalez believed that attention should be focused instead on the Mexicans.

A group of national nurses from the mission hospital had tried to preserve the ministry to the Indians by teaching classes at the various camps throughout the week and arranging transportation to the Mexican church on Sundays. Because of the hospital's isolated location, however, it was difficult to keep their staff. So, within four months of Eileen's departure, two of the three nurses working with the Indians left the valley. The third nurse complained that her zeal for the Indian ministry had waned considerably for lack of support. She had tried to get incoming hospital staff interested in helping her, but it became harder and harder. The ministry to the Indians gradually slipped downhill.

When the Indian ministry went into decline, the leaders of the Indian villages took unprecedented action. They met together and drafted a letter to the mission board that sponsored Eileen, asking them to send her back to the valley to renew the ministry she had begun among them. Eileen was certainly willing to do that, because she had come to love the migrant Indian workers. Her mission board was also sympathetic to their appeal.

The problem was with the pastor of the local Baptist church. Pastor Gonzalez insisted that if a woman

(continued)

261

missionary were to be in the area, she would have to be under his authority. He would assign Eileen to playing the piano for church services and teaching a women's Sunday school class in the Mexican church. He gave two reasons for not allowing her to work with the migrant Indians. First, he believed it was wrong for a woman to teach men; and second, he emphasized the fact that his own ministry was to the Mexicans and not to the Indians of the valley.

Members of the Mexican church expressed a desire for a missionary to come and work with them because they felt the church was dying and in need of rejuvenation.

The pastor, on the other hand, was cold to the idea of *any* missionary coming to work with the church, citing some bad experiences with North American missionaries in the border town from where he had come. He complained that the missionaries "always came in and did things their way" without heeding his authority.

Some church members who were close to the pastor expressed the fear that if Eileen came to the valley and carried on her own ministry outside the authority of the pastor, it would reinforce his negative feelings about missionaries in general. This would further diminish their chances of ever getting a missionary to work with their church again.

Eileen now faced one final meeting with her mission board, during which they would have to make a decision regarding her assignment. She still could not see a way to resolve the conflict of other people's agendas for her ministry. It was still her deep desire to work within the national church structure. But now the Indian work also represented the "national church." Which national church had priority—Mexican or Indian? She hoped and prayed that her mission board would be able to help her make the right decision.

PART 5

Missions Encountering
the Contemporary World

As we noted in chapter 1, the contemporary world presents numerous and formidable challenges to the church. Even so, God calls all Christians to faithful service for his kingdom no matter what the world brings against the church. In this part we provide four chapters that lay out the encounter of mission in the contemporary world.

Chapter 16 starts this part with an overview of cross-cultural communication, a critical foundation for encountering the many cultures of the world. Chapter 17 surveys contemporary issues in mission in general, especially issues not already covered in the rest of the book. Chapter 18 looks at what promises to be the largest challenge that the church will face in the next century: the religions of the world. In chapter 19 we close the book by presenting our perspectives on some of the challenges that the future will bring to mission.

16

Communicating with People of Other Cultures

INTRODUCTION

On Paul's first missionary journey he and Barnabas encountered the reality of communicating across cultural boundaries (Acts 14:8–20). In Lystra they healed a man crippled from birth. The people immediately were aroused by the miracle and began to shout in their own language that these two strangers in their midst were the gods in human form. Paul, not knowing the language, was unaware of their misinterpretation until he received a translation.

In the meantime, the residents of Lystra already had started to organize a sacrifice in honor of Paul and Barnabas, mistaking them for Zeus and Hermes. When Paul finally discovered what the Lycaonians were thinking, he and Barnabas tore their clothes in anguish and barely managed to persuade them that they were not gods and that the sacrifice being planned was unacceptable. Shortly thereafter, however, the crowds were turned against Paul and Barnabas. They stoned Paul and left him for dead.

The perils of intercultural communication are vividly captured in Luke's account. In a very short time, Paul went from being

declared a god to being stoned and left for dead! Although Paul's treatment was extreme, the reality is that misunderstandings in communication due to culture are a regular part of the life of a missionary. Luke's story illustrates a fact that every missionary must face: people "read" you in ways that make sense to them. Furthermore, their understanding of you and the message you bring can be radically different from what you intended.

Paul penned the following verses, which have become widely used in support of intercultural communication:

Though I am free and belong to no man, I make myself a slave to everyone, to win as many as possible. To the Jews I became like a Jew, to win the Jews. To those under the law I became like one under the law (though I myself am not under the law), so as to win those under the law. To those not having the law I became like one not having the law (though I am not free from God's law but am under Christ's law), so as to win those not having the law. To the weak I became weak, to win the weak. I have become all things to all men so that by all possible means I might save some. I do all this for the sake of the gospel, that I may share in its blessings. (1 Cor. 9:19–23)

Paul exhibited a "willingness to accommodate himself to whatever social setting he found himself in, so as 'to win as many as possible' [i.e., evangelism]. . . . Thus Paul's first concern in such matters is not whether he offends or does not offend—although that too is a concern (10:32)—but whether the gospel itself will get its proper hearing (cf. 10:33)" (Fee 1987, 426–27).

Paul made the choice to live within his context freely, and he did so in light of the gospel. Though on the behavioral level his actions were inconsistent, they followed a higher priority (and integrity) than slavish behavioral observance. In this context, he specifically dealt with food bought in the open marketplace. He drew the line on the fact that he remained under Christ's law even when living like a Gentile. For example, Paul would hardly murder someone,

> *Added to the difficulty of learning to speak the language was the greater difficulty of finding terms to express the ideas which the missionary had come halfway round the world to convey. . . . In many languages the most precious truths of Christianity had to force their way by bending stubborn words to new ideas, and filling old terms with a new content.*
>
> Helen Barrett Montgomery
> (1910, 90)

no matter how favorably the culture might look upon it.

Paul was not saying that he changed the *content* of the gospel message from group to group, but that he changed *how he lived or behaved* while in different groups as he communicated the changeless gospel message (Fee 1987, 432–33). He was advocating that Christians pay attention to people's self-perception when communicating the gospel, and act in such a way that their audience can understand the message from within their own environment.

Why do you want to be effective in intercultural communication? Your ultimate desire should be to communicate Christ. To do that in a cross-cultural setting, you must be effective in intercultural communication. Not only will you be a better communicator, but also, in the long run, you will be better able to enjoy your cross-cultural experience.

IMPORTANT COMMUNICATION FACTS

We discussed language learning in chapter 12, and that certainly is crucial for successful intercultural communication. However, that is only one of the key components of the process. To set the stage, it will help you to understand five foundational truths about communication.

1. *Everything that people do communicates.* It is impossible for any person to stop communicating (Kraft 1983, 75). From a sigh to a wink, from a laugh to a yawn, every word, every gesture, and every action of yours can be seen to have meaning by another person, whether you intend it or not.

2. *The goal of communication is always more than just to impart information.* Persuasion, or at least influence, is behind everything that people do (Hesselgrave 1978, 58). Even a simple "hello" is a communication act that needs a response—you want

the other person to acknowledge you, and you may feel insulted if your friendly word is ignored.

3. *The communication process is more complex than most people realize.* People always communicate messages through more than one channel (e.g., words, tone of voice, and body language are separate channels) and always communicate more than one message. These "multiple" messages may contradict each other (see Kraft 1983, 76; Hesselgrave and Rommen 1989, 180; Filbeck 1985, 2–3). You learned how to read these channels when you were growing up, and you take your interpretations for granted. All this changes when you go to a new cultural setting. There, the rules you normally use to interpret communication no longer work, and it doesn't take you long to notice this fact.

4. *The communication process is dynamic, not static.* To understand what is happening in any given instance of communication, the interpreter must "get into" the context, understand the worldview, and examine the give and take (and much more) of the communication event in question (Hesselgrave and Rommen 1989, 188).

5. *The ability to develop communication patterns that build trust is an invaluable missionary skill.* If a missionary wants to communicate effectively across cultural barriers, the foundational consideration for his or her communication should be, "What can I do to build trust on the part of the audience?" (see Mayers 1974, 30–79).

CULTURE AND COMMUNICATION

Every human being is to a large extent a product of cultural values. God has designed people as learning beings, and the rules of culture that people learn while growing up provide maps that they use to interpret the world around them. No human being escapes culture, and none escapes the way culture impacts communication.

Like individuals, cultures are not static. They are dynamic and always changing. Rules of what it means to be a proper human being are part of the cultural fabric that affects every person. Among many others that could be mentioned are rules and ideas about fairness and justice and how (or whether) people deal with injustice, ways that good leaders act, how the younger relate to the older, power and how it operates, how male and female are to interact, the meaning of friendship and family, values about making decisions and conflict resolution,

> *The Gospel has not yet been preached to them in their own tongue in which they were born. They have heard it only through interpreters . . . who have themselves no just understanding, no real love of the truth. We must not expect the blessing till you are able, from your own lips and in their language, to bring it through their ears into their hearts.*
>
> Mary Moffatt, to her husband
> (Deane n.d., 67–68)

how to be a good host and a good guest, and so on. Intercultural communication is the formal study of these things and how people deal with them when they come from different cultures.

One foundational rule that people who are communicating across cultural divides must keep in mind was illustrated in the story about Paul and Barnabas that opened this chapter: *people interpret your words and*

267

actions in ways that make sense to them. Often, therefore, what you think you are communicating is not what they are receiving. If nothing else, knowing this may help you be humbler in attempting to convey the greatest message of all.

WORLDVIEW

Worldview essentially describes the way people understand and interpret the world around them. It is something like a referee at a ball game. As long as the game proceeds without a violation of the rules, you might never know that a referee is present. But as soon as a violation occurs, the referee stops play, perhaps assesses a penalty, and then allows play to resume. How that happens in life depends on worldview. If the violation is severe enough, the "game" might be ended violently. More often, however, it is ended quietly, and one side might not even be aware that it has ended, as the following story illustrates.

Li (not his real name), a Chinese student at a U.S. Christian college, was with a group of fellow students on a short-term mission trip in Hong Kong. On the first morning after their arrival they visited a local marketplace. The Americans, amazed at seeing live animals rather than packages of prepared meat, whipped out their cameras and started taking pictures. Li backed away from the group, watching the faces of the shopkeepers in the marketplace as they looked at the Americans. Simply by looking at the shopkeepers' faces Li could tell who among them would or would not be responsive to any message that the Americans might bring in the future.

The Americans, in their wonder and curiosity at the novelty, unfortunately engaged in a behavior that violated the local

"rules of life." The local marketers judged the American actions in light of the local rules, not in light of the Americans' values or rules.

Li obeyed the local rules. By backing away from the group of Americans he was communicating that although he was physically with them, he did not agree with their actions. Without knowing it, the Americans had shut doors to their message among many of the shopkeepers. On the other hand, Li knew the local rulebook well enough to see what had happened. He tried to keep the doors open for his own ministry among the shopkeepers, and also to make it possible to serve as a mediator later by distancing himself from the rest of the group.

This story illustrates ways that worldview lies at the core of all communication. The shopkeepers' worldviews were a set of belief systems (Dodd 1991, 75; Olthius 1985, 155) that defined the ways they "leaned into life"; it gave them a mental map (Walsh 1992, 18) or a lens (Kraft 1983, 222) through which they interpreted the behavior of the American students.

The Americans also had mental maps, and their maps did not include live meat at the market! The curiosity that was aroused was handled in part by their desire (arising from worldview) to document what they saw so that people back home would understand how "strange" the marketplace was. The relatively innocent act (according to their worldview) of taking the pictures was also a way to deal with the shock of what they saw.

In sum, there was one scene with two widely differing sets of worldviews to interpret the scene. Both focused on "strangeness" (the Americans' behavior was just as strange to the Chinese as the Chinese market was to the Americans). Each worldview judged the other, and both judgments had a long-term impact on future communication. Fortunately, the study of intercultural communication offers helpful tools for understanding what happened and preventing similar mishaps in the future.

CULTURAL VALUES THAT AFFECT HOW WE COMMUNICATE

From 1960 on, anthropologist Edward Hall wrote a series of popular books showing how culture and communication intertwined (e.g., 1960; 1973; 1981; 1991a). Hall's ideas had a profound and lasting impact on intercultural communication theory and practice. His two main ways to explain culture and communication focused on (1) how societies value the role of direct communication versus indirect communication, which he called "low" and "high" context respectively, and (2) how societies understand and value time, which he called "polychronic" and "monochronic." We will explain these below.

In the late 1960s social psychologist Geert Hofstede performed a massive study of people from around the world (1980; 1991; 1998). He found that four sets of cultural values played an important role in the major differences seen from one culture to another. They were how societies idealize (1) the self (individualism and collectivism), (2) the separation of gender roles, (3) the distribution of social power, and (4) dealing with uncertainty. Later studies supported the first three of Hofstede's dimensions (e.g., Chinese Culture Connection 1987), and these have become standard topics in intercultural communication textbooks and courses (e.g., Gudykunst and Kim 1992; Dodd 1991; Lustig and Koester 1996; Storti 1999).

To explore all six of the values identified by Hall and Hofstede would go far beyond the scope of this chapter. Thus, we will focus on the three that are the most helpful for cross-cultural workers: (1) high and low context, (2) polychronic and monochronic time, and (3) individualism and collectivism. We encourage you to explore the cultural values not discussed in this chapter through other resources such as Craig Storti's *Figuring Foreigners Out* (1999).

High and Low Context: Indirect and Direct Communication

Children in North America learn early in life why they have three names: parents use all three to let their kids know that they are angry—"Arthur Scott Moreau, come here!" By adding extra, unnecessary information (the middle and last names) and changing the tone of voice, parents communicate that they are unhappy, and children feel their displeasure. For those who grew up with this, it is taken for granted and done without thinking. It is an example of "contexting," the act of putting information in a context.

All people learn how to context information as they grow up. Their skills at contexting information and the value they place on contexting it are built by the experiences and values that shape them as individuals. Indeed, every communication act takes place in a context, but not every society assigns the same weight to that context in interpreting (or understanding) the message. Hall situates societies along a spectrum. At one end are those that more consciously value the context of communication and pay less attention to the actual words used, called "high-context cultures." Asian, African, Latin American, and southern European

269

DIAGRAM 16.1

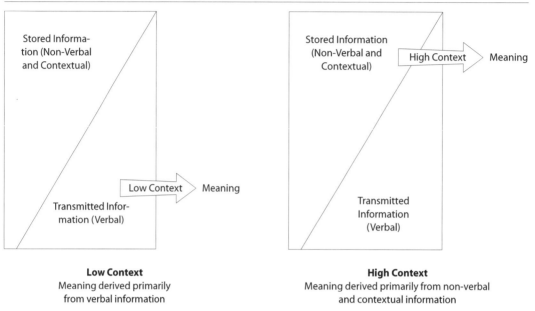

Low Context
Meaning derived primarily
from verbal information

High Context
Meaning derived primarily from non-verbal
and contextual information

(Adapted from Hall 1991a, 61)

societies tend to fit this profile. At the other end of the spectrum are those societies that pay more attention to the words themselves and less to the context in which they are spoken, referred to as "low-context cultures." This is more descriptive of North American and northern European societies (see, e.g., Ting-Toomey 1985; Gudykunst and Nishida 1986; Chua and Gudykunst 1987; Elgstrom 1994; Dsilva and Whyte 1998).

The differences between the two approaches to communication are illustrated in diagram 16.1. The main difference is in the extent to which it is expected that "stored," or contextual, information will be necessary to understand what is being communicated. Such stored information includes language and nonverbal cues, as well as the surroundings, the mood, the history of the participants, and numerous other contextual factors contributing to the atmosphere in which communication happens.

For example, a Japanese husband (high context) might come home and find that a picture in the hallway is slightly tilted or that flowers are not arranged neatly in a vase in the entryway. Looking for meaning in the context rather than in any words used, he might assume that something is out of sorts with his wife. He then would tune his communication "radar" more carefully toward her conversation. Rather than asking her directly what is wrong, which would be a low-context approach, he places value on being able to "read" how she talks, what she talks about, what she avoids talking about, and so on. During the course of the conversation, he notices that she mentions her mother-in-law several times. Nothing overtly negative is said, but neither is anything positive mentioned. He understands that she is communicating that she is having problems with her mother-in-law, his mother.

Without saying anything directly about the problem he senses, he also begins to talk about his mother. Perhaps he uses positive and negative ideas, and as he does so, he carefully watches to see how his wife responds. Eventually, without either of them stating directly to the other that there is a problem, both recognize that they have communicated about it. He mentions that he has not visited his mother lately and that it might be good to do so. She tells him that that would be nice and suggests that he take her a gift. He smiles, she smiles, and they both know that, at least for now, some of the tension is released.

This is a classic example of high-context communication. Neither person uses words to state the problem. Americans probably would say that both of them were "beating around the bush." This indirect method of addressing the problem, however, allows both to save face. No direct complaints about the mother-in-law were made, and the husband has no need to defend his mother to his wife. The wife is satisfied that the husband knows what the problem is, and that he is helping her by bringing a small gift to his mother as a gesture of reconciliation. The fact that they communicated without having to actually discuss the problem strengthens their bond by making both feel more deeply connected. A Japanese observer would understand what had happened; an American observer might not have a clue.

Orientation to Time: Polychronic and Monochronic Cultures

As a young missionary in Africa, Ben often was confused about how to handle appointments. Fresh from college experi-ence in the United States, where life was dominated by schedules and appointments, he saw the idea of not keeping close track of time as downright rude. When he made an appointment with someone, he "knew" without even thinking that it was important to arrive close to the stated time, even a few minutes early if possible. He also learned that a person who was more than twenty to thirty minutes late was unlikely to show up.

Jabulani, on the other hand, grew up in a totally different world and had a totally different orientation to time. When Ben invited him to dinner, Jabulani "knew" without even thinking that to arrive exactly at the stated time would communicate that it was all business. For a true friend, Jabu-lani knew that it would be better to arrive a little late, and for Jabulani "little" meant about an hour.

You can imagine how dinner went. Ben prepared the meal so that it would be ready to eat roughly thirty minutes after the time he expected Jabulani to show up. After all, he knew that Jabulani might not show up exactly when planned. When Jabulani did show up one full hour after Ben expected him, Ben's emotions were unsteady, to say the least. Thinking that he had communi-cated closeness by being relaxed about when he came, Jabulani was taken by surprise when Ben berated him for coming so late. The fact that Ben was quite upset commu-nicated to Jabulani that their relationship was only about business after all, and not a real friendship. Ben lost an opportunity to be a true friend that day, and Jabulani never really understood what had happened.

Ben's story illustrates the differences be-tween monochronic (Ben's) and polychronic (Jabulani's) cultures. Time is a reality for every culture. In teaching how to value time, families and societies give their members an invisible "rulebook" that tells them how they should understand time and the ways it is used in relationships. This is known as social time, and, as opposed to clock time, it has been called the "heartbeat of culture" (Levine and Wolff 1985).

More than simply regulating seasons and days, social time is an integral part of every interaction in life, from how people converse (rules for taking turns, interrupting, starting and ending and so on) to how educational institutions decide on the length of degree programs, politicians the length of terms in office, and judges the appropriate length of sentences to fit crimes committed.

In North America time is perceived as a tangible commodity that is available in limited amounts. It must be "spent wisely" and utilized in ways that value efficiency and avoid "wasting" or "losing" it. This is especially important in evangelical circles, where stewardship is highly valued, and evangelicals are taught very early in life to be good stewards of the time God has given to them. Think, for example, of the number of verbs that Christians attach to the word *time* in their churches: they spend, save, waste, kill, and lose time—they even multiply and redeem it! Hall refers to this approach to time as "monochronic" (1990, 13–16; 1991a, 44–58; 1991b). For people of monochronic cultures, time is thought to be like a ribbon or road that can be sliced only in one way. This influences their ideals in ideas such as respect (showing up "on time" for appointments), business (short- and long-term planning), and architecture (valuing private offices rather than open areas, where there is no sense of boundary), and it is deeply embedded in North American church life. In North America Christians value privacy ("*my* time") and dislike interruptions.

Promptness is defined by conformity to the clock, and people schedule their lives so as to make the "best" or "most efficient" use of the time they have allotted.

Not all cultures perceive time in this way, however. Hall calls the opposite approach to time "polychronic." People in polychronic cultures see time as a point rather than a ribbon or road. They value multilevel, simultaneous involvement. Business or even very personal decisions can be made in public places with multiple conversations going on simultaneously. For privacy, people move away from the public space rather than behind closed doors. They remain visible, but they are isolated by degree of proximity. Interruptions are not irritants; they are part of the rhythm of life. Rigid adherence to schedules is not valued, because it reduces people to little more than blocks of time. Such a demeaning communicates "official business" rather than intimacy. Furthermore, promptness is not defined by the clock, but by the relationship: the more intimate the relationship, the less value placed on clock time. In fact, one way of communicating personal distance or displeasure in a relationship in a polychronic setting is to show up exactly at the stated time!

Jabulani and Ben both valued time. However, each one's way of interpreting the messages embedded in the time-related behavior stood at opposite ends of the spectrum. Jabulani tried to communicate friendship by not coming at the stated time, but Ben read that as disrespect. Ben reacted by talking about issues of respect, and Jabulani did not know what Ben's problem was or why it was such a big deal to Ben.

Missionaries need to recognize that people in other cultures treat time differently. If missionaries want to communicate Christ well in their new homes, they must learn their hosts' perspectives on time and find ways to reset their own internal clocks to match those in the new culture. Too often, monochronic missionaries end up communicating that following Christ is a business venture rather than an intimate relationship simply because they do not understand the messages they communicate when they demand that services start on time, that prayer meetings follow a prearranged schedule, or that Bible studies end after exactly one hour.

Orientation to Self: Individualism and Collectivism

Scott Moreau found out that in Kenya one way to get help when dealing with official business with officials is to start conversations with a simple statement: "I have a problem and I don't know how to deal with it." Just the opposite happened when he barged in after a perceived injustice, insisting that his problem was the fault of the official and demanding that it be straightened out right away. The simple action seen in the first approach is referred to as "one-downing" (Elmer 1993, 80–98). It highlights another important value in intercultural communication: the way people define the self, more commonly referred to as individualism and collectivism. Among the fifty countries studied by Hofstede, the United States was the most individualistic. Generally speaking, Western countries (e.g., Australia, Netherlands, Great Britain, Germany) are more individualistic, while majority world countries and regions (e.g., Guatemala, Indonesia, Pakistan, Taiwan, West Africa) are more collectivistic. There is no dimension of cultural difference of more significance in affecting the way

people behave than that of individualism and collectivism (Triandis 1992, 71).

INDIVIDUALISTIC AND COLLECTIVE PROVERBS

Proverbs in various cultures often express their values. The Chinese say, "The tallest tree gets knocked down by the wind first." Likewise, a Japanese proverb states, "The nail that sticks up will be hammered down." Both express the idea that the willful individual, by standing out from the rest, needs to be put in his or her place. Contrast those proverbs with an American one: "The squeaky wheel gets the grease," which assigns value to standing up to get one's needs met. Westerners say, "I think, therefore I am," with the focus on individual identity apart from social context. Africans say, "We relate, therefore I am"—a sharp contrast to the American idea.

Scott's one-down statement typically worked in the Kenyan setting because with it he placed himself in a position of vulnerability that drew on the collective values present in the culture. When a person is vulnerable and is perceived to be either a member of one's group or behaving with social tact, an implicit obligation rests upon the one in power to help the helpless person so that he or she is not shamed. In collective societies parents teach children early in life not to cling to their own individual rights, but to ensure that group needs are given higher priority than individual needs.

INDIVIDUALISTIC AND COLLECTIVISTIC VALUES

Table 16.1 summarizes actions and attitudes valued by collectivistic and individualistic cultures (contents adapted from Markus and Kitayama 1991, 230). These are generalizations and the ways they are worked out will vary from society to society and be moderated by other types of values also found in the society. However, knowing these will provide you with a good foundation for understanding how the values of individualism and collectivism affect the ways people communicate.

TABLE 16.1
VALUES OF COLLECTIVISTS AND INDIVIDUALISTS

Collectivists Value	Individualists Value
Belonging, fitting in	Being unique
Occupying one's proper place	Expressing self
Engaging in appropriate action	Realizing internal attributes
Sustaining social obligations	Avoiding social obligations
Promoting others' goals	Promoting one's own goals
Being indirect: "read other's mind"	Being direct: "say what's on your mind"
Keeping conflict hidden; using indirect resolution methods	Facing and resolving conflicts openly

The collectivist (for these examples, a male) wants to fit in and belong to the group. The individualist (for these examples, a female), on the other hand, is taught that she should be unique and not simply follow the crowd. In order to fit in, the collectivist develops skills early in life that enable him to blend into the group by changing behavior and, to some extent, even personality so as not to stand out. The individualist sees that as hypocritical, and she values being herself no matter what pressures are brought to bear by the group.

The collectivist wants to occupy his proper place, which involves behaving in appropriate ways. That place is determined by age, status of birth family, gender, and a host of other factors, most of which are determined at birth and very few of which are under the control of the individual. These in turn determine what appropriate behavior is, and they change throughout life (appropriate behavior for a child is, of course, different from that for an adult). The individualist, however, is taught to express and be true to herself by realizing her own internal attributes. Rather than fitting in, the individualist is encouraged to carve out a niche for herself that uniquely fits her gifts, talents, and attainments. Ideally, she does not have to fit in as long as she is being true to herself.

The collectivist also learns early in life that social obligations or debts are the glue that holds the collective together. These debts may be passed on from generation to generation. For example, in rural Japan an extensive list of social debts is kept that spans multiple generations. If you are Japanese and following traditional customs, favors offered to your grandfather are debts that are still carried by you. When a friend whose grandfather helped yours has a need, you are obligated to respond and thereby pay off your social debt. However, you may very well respond in a way that places your friend in debt to you, and that debt may carry on to both sets of grandchildren, yours and your friend's. Carrying this debt from generation to generation thus keeps people connected—an important value in collectivist societies. By contrast, the individualist often does what she can to avoid social debt. If a friend invites her to dinner, she might offer to bring dessert. If that does not work, she will invite her friend to dinner the next time to ensure that the social debt is evened out. The individualist values standing on her own and not owing favors to others, while the collectivist sees those favors as glue holding people together.

SIDEBAR 16.1
INDIRECT WAYS TO SAY NO

REFLECTION
AND DISCUSSION

People in indirect cultures have several ways to say no without actually having to use the word "no." Missionaries from direct cultures often have great difficulty hearing the "no" that is being communicated, because it does not come directly. They may even think that a person lied. The reality is that they did not know how to hear the actual message being communicated and that the words being used were not as important to the indirect communicator as the translation of how the words were used in context. Don't be too quick to judge indirect communicators, as North Americans also use "white lies" ("I really like your new haircut") over what they think of as relatively small matters to help keep relationships working well. Some indirect ways to say no are:

1. Silence or avoiding a direct response
2. Hesitation, postponement
3. Blaming a third party or circumstances
4. Acceptance but no action (relational or power "yes")
5. Diverting to another proposal or idea
6. Tepid approval

1. Americans, preferring direct communication methods, often think that indirect communication methods are deceitful. What might you say to a fellow missionary who asks, "Why don't they just come out and tell the truth?"
2. Identify some circumstances in American culture where it is considered acceptable to be indirect (e.g., a noncommittal response to a friend's new outfit, or silence when your boss proposes a new idea that you have mixed feelings about).

Additionally, the collectivist is taught to promote the goals of others who are part of his group. He is responsible to ensure that they attain their goals, which in turn brings additional status to the group as a whole. Similarly, failure by an individual in his group can bring a loss of status to the group. Thus, all members of the group will work to ensure that none fail—especially important when failure will result in a loss of status to the group. The individualist, however, is responsible for attaining (or failing to attain) her own goals. She speaks of a "self-made" person, someone who does things his or her own way and who climbs the ladder of success based on abilities and perseverance.

The collectivist also learns, by watching others around him, that indirect or high-context methods are preferred in communicating with others. The ability to know the thinking of other members of the group by being aware of the situations they are in and by knowing their nonverbal cues is an important skill for the collectivist. In effect, each person lives in an "ocean of information" (Hall 1981), and collectivists value knowing not only the ocean, but also the currents within the ocean. The ability to discern someone else's unexpressed want is an important signal of intimacy for collectivists. Indirect communication is preferred for its subtlety, if for no other reason than it helps to ensure that no one loses face by having to offer or receive a direct denial (sidebar 16.1 illustrates this by showing some of the ways that "no" can be communicated in cultures that favor indirect methods).

In contrast, the individualist generally prefers more direct communication tech-

---

SIDEBAR 16.2
PROVERBS ABOUT INDIRECT CONFLICT

Many cultures idealize ways of avoiding rather than confronting conflict, as is illustrated in the following proverbs (from Augsburger 1992, 234–35).

Of the thirty-six ways of handling a conflict situation, running away is the best. (China)
Trumpet when in a herd of elephants, crow in the company of cocks, bleat in a flock of goats. (Malaya)
Love has no dispute. (Kenya)
Money softens a dispute like water softens clay. (Nigeria)

The second word [the answer] makes the quarrel. (Japan)
When one doesn't want, two don't quarrel. (Brazil)
A meager peace is better than a fat quarrel. (Latvia)
A good silence is better than a bad dispute. (Russia)
The squirrel does not talk back to the elephant, it just goes back into the hole. (Angola)
It is best to let an offense repeat itself three times. The first may be an accident, the second a mistake, only the third is likely to be intentional. (Kongo)

Silence produces peace, and peace produces safety. (Swahili)
All is never said. (Ibo)
In playing chess, there is no infallible way of winning, but there is an infallible way of not losing—that is not to play chess. (China)
If a quarrel gets too hot for you, pretend it is a game. (Hausa)

REFLECTION AND DISCUSSION

Discuss the value placed on avoiding conflict in each proverb. How would this value affect you if you were ministering in one of these cultures?

---

niques. This is not surprising, since the value of being unique results in each individual having his or her own orientation to life and set of cues and not expecting people to be able to read an indirect communication unless they know them. In one sense, the better you know someone, the more likely you are to use indirect communication methods and expect them to be understood. However, since individualists know relatively few people that intimately, they most often use direct communication methods.

Dealing with conflict is one of the areas in which the divide between individualism and collectivism is most readily seen, and often it is the area that missionaries are least prepared to handle.

Generally, collectivists value indirect methods of conflict resolution (see sidebar 16.2), while individualists value more direct means. Interestingly, an individualistic culture generally tends to have more conflict than a collectivist one (Ting-Toomey 1985; Chua and Gudykunst 1987). That makes sense, since conflicts typically arise over clashes in values, and individualists are expected to hold to their own values while collectivists are expected to share values. Though individualistic cultures tend to have more conflicts, those conflicts generally are confined to the individuals involved and have less impact on the group as a whole.

In contrast, when conflict does arise in collectivist cultures, it involves entire groups, and everyone has to take a side according to his or her collective obligations. The conflict involves more people and therefore is more serious. Missionaries from individualistic cultures, often used to small-scale conflicts between individuals, can be taken quite by surprise when an entire church is threatened by what they saw as a minor incident. It is no wonder that understanding the different approaches to

CASE STUDY:
WHOSE FACE TO SAVE?

Cai Yong Xian

The sound of the clock tower resonated throughout the campus as it struck six. Audrey left her apartment and walked to the soccer field where her Chinese colleague, Xiao Wang, was playing the game of football with Michael, Nathan, and Tasha. They were Audrey's North American teammates who came to Hua Mei School in Guangzhou, China, to teach and share.

As a form of outreach, Michael, Nathan, and Tasha had been getting together every Saturday afternoon for the past month to play football with anyone on the campus who was interested. Xiao Wang had joined them, looking forward to football every Saturday and enjoying learning how to play. He especially enjoyed getting to know Michael and Nathan, the male foreigners.

Xiao Wang highly regarded Michael and Nathan and was excited to bond with them, even though they were foreigners. He considered Audrey like a little sister. It seemed natural to him because, even though one of the foreign teachers, she was Chinese-American.

Earlier in the week, Xiao Wang talked to Audrey about his desire to take them out to dinner after their game of football and asked if she would join them. Xiao

Wang wanted Audrey to be there because she was his closest foreign companion and he didn't know Michael and Nathan very well yet.

Shortly after Audrey arrived at the soccer field, the game ended and Michael, Nathan, Tasha, Xiao Wang, and Audrey left the campus for dinner.

"Where would you like to eat?" Xiao Wang asked as they walked through the campus gates. Immediately, Nathan made a suggestion of a particular place down the street. Audrey felt uneasy. As a Chinese-American, she was aware of how cultural values play out in both the Chinese and the American settings. Among Americans, Nathan's suggestion was appropriate, but here it was different. Audrey struggled with being a Chinese-American in China, especially when she was caught in the middle of a cultural *faux pas* and she was unsure of what to do or whose face she should save. In this case, she knew that the proper Chinese way to select the place to eat was for her teammates to insist that Xiao Wang be the one who choose, since he was the host. Once Nathan made his suggestion, however, Audrey wondered what should she do or say. If she corrected Nathan

in front of Xiao Wang, the latter would be distressed over the loss of Nathan's face. But Nathan had already made Xiao Wang lose face by not letting him choose where they ate. Xiao Wang graciously agreed with Nathan's suggestion, and Audrey decided it better not to say anything.

When they got to the place Nathan had suggested, the waitress came to the table and gave a menu to Xiao Wang. This made sense as he was the only person who could read and order in Mandarin. As Xiao Wang flipped through the menu to pick entrees that he would like his foreign friends to try, Michael pulled out a generic Chinese-English menu from his wallet and started ordering a few dishes, reading off the ping yin that he learned.

Audrey was again frustrated. She knew that the proper way to handle the order was to let the host be in charge, which allowed him the honor of treating his guests well. Again, she faced a dilemma. What should she do? Should she speak against her teammates, by suggesting that Xiao Wang choose the dishes? If so, Xiao Wang may insist on what they ordered to save his foreign friend's face anyway.

While Xiao Wang was speaking with the waitress, Tasha asked who would like a cold drink. Seeing that Michael already had a bottle of water, Tasha went to the stand next door and bought two bottles of ice tea, one for her and

(continued)

one for Nathan. Audrey became aware that Tasha didn't buy enough drinks for everyone at the table. Should she motion to Tasha to buy a few extra to save her face or should she just go buy a couple extra bottles for herself and Xiao Wang?

After eating, the bill came. Instead of fighting for the check, each of Audrey's teammates pulled out their wallets to pay for their percentage of the meal. Audrey felt uncomfortable with the individualism of paying for

yourself being displayed. Should Audrey step in and fight for the check with her host?

Audrey had never had to talk with her teammates about their behavior when invited to eat with a Chinese host. But now she experienced an almost unbearable tension, and felt stuck in the middle. If she kept quiet and did not correct her teammates, they would continue to dishonor Xiao Wang, their host and Chinese friend. The friendship would not last long

with that type of behavior! Not only that, Audrey herself would be shamed, being associated with these well-intentioned but culturally rude guests. However, if she did speak up, her teammates might not understand what she was trying to say. In fact, they might even disagree openly in front of Xiao Wang—or, even worse, ask Xiao Wang to settle the disagreement. Audrey was trapped; what could she do?

conflict as they apply in collectivist cultures is such an important skill for a missionary to learn (see Augsburger 1992; Elmer 1993).

CONCLUSION

Crossing cultures and effectively communicating God's call to worship is tricky business. The annals of missionary history are littered with shipwrecks that happened simply because the lines of communication were crossed and misunderstandings esca-

lated to the point where relationships were broken. We encourage you to find appropriate training in intercultural communication even if you have no intention of becoming a missionary. In our increasingly globalized culture the ability to navigate cultural differences successfully is no longer an option. This chapter's case study wonderfully illustrates the ways that cultural values influence communication, and the ways that these values can put missionaries in difficult positions.

Mission Trends and Paradigm Shifts

17

INTRODUCTION

Many new realities exist for mission today. The primary one that missionaries and mission senders must face at the moment is rapid change. This is the information age, a time when travel around the world is relatively inexpensive, access to knowledge of places and peoples is easily obtainable, and communication with those far away is instantaneous. Important shifts have taken place in mission as a result. What follows here is a partial accounting of the new realities faced in the mission enterprise today. They make mission interesting, challenging, and exciting—sometimes all three simultaneously!

SHORT-TERM EMPHASIS

For many years it has been assumed (and even promoted) that people who go on short-term missions are more likely to come back as career missionaries. However, the tremendous upsurge in the number of short-term workers without any corresponding increase in the ranks of long-term missionaries indicates that the assumption

perhaps is wrong (see Moreau 2000c). As of this writing, we need more data before the validity of the assumption can be proven one way or the other.

The Ups and Downs of Short-Term Missions

Many pros and cons of short-term projects can be noted. On the extreme end of the negative side, career missionaries can be sidetracked by having to watch over a loud, brash group of young people who are insensitive to the host culture and unaware of the images they project. It literally can take years to undo damage done by more extreme groups who fail to take into account the realities of culture and the expectations they bring. On the positive side, however, short-term projects not only can be a healthy vehicle for people to consider long-term service, but also, in the best of cases, they can assist long-term missionaries or nationals in completing significant projects for God's kingdom that would not otherwise ever be done.

In sidebar 17.1 we offer two sets of "Ten Commandments" written by veteran mis-

---

SIDEBAR 17.1
"TEN COMMANDMENTS" FOR SHORT-TERM MISSION TRIP PARTICIPANTS

Here are two sets of "Ten Commandments" (nine, actually, in the case of Culbertson) written by seasoned long-term missionaries for short-term mission participants.

Set 1
Howard Culbertson, mission professor at Southern Nazarene University (Culbertson 2001)

---

1. Thou shalt not expect to find things as thou hast them at home, for thou hast left thy home to find things differently.

2. Thou shalt not take anything too seriously. A willingness to accept things as they are lays the foundation for a good trip to another country.

3. Thou shalt not let other group members get on thy nerves. Thou raised good money and set aside this time to enjoy thyself.

4. Thou shalt not forget that, at all times, thou dost represent thy own country and the Lord Jesus Christ.

5. Thou shalt not be overly worried. He who worrieth hath no pleasures. Few things people worry about are ever fatal.

6. Remember thy passport (or other identification document) so that thou knowest where it is at all times. A person without documents is a person without a country.

7. Blessed is the person who says, "When in _____, do as the _____ do." If in difficulty, use common sense and thy American friendliness.

8. Do not judge all _____ by the one person with whom thou hast had trouble.

9. Remember, thou art a guest in _____. He who treateth his host with respect shall be treated as an honored guest.

Set 2
Paul Cull, leader of Projeto Casa Esperanza (House of Hope Project) in Brazil (Cull n.d.)

---

1. Thou shalt always remember that the primary function of a short-term team is to learn, and not to help.

2. Thou shalt always defer to the long-term missionaries, even when thou dost not agree with them.

3. Thou shalt surely leave all thy agendas at home before thou arrivest on the mission field.

4. Thou shalt be prepared to spend large amounts of time doing nothing, for thus verily is the way of the mission field.

5. Thou shalt be careful to obey, in all details, the security rules and advice of the project which thou visitest.

6. Thou shalt be both attentive and accurate in the communication with the mission base before thy visit.

7. Thou shalt be careful to pay for all the expenses of thy visit.

8. Thou shalt take great care in thy giving and thy spending, lest thou appearest to be filthy rich.

9. Thou shalt be careful to respect the doctrinal and theological views of the project which thou visitest.

10. Thou shalt surely keep thy word in regards to follow-up activities.

REFLECTION AND DISCUSSION

---

1. Read each commandment carefully. What are the implications of each? Why, in your opinion, does the author consider each one important?

2. Choose the ten "best" commandments from the two sets to form your own set. Perhaps you'll need to add some of your own.

---

sionaries for those participating in short-term missions. They are provided to help short-term project coordinators consider how best to prepare a team to fit into the local setting and to be of the greatest benefit to the local work of God.

Whatever the data ultimately shows, however, the reality of short-term missions appears to be here to stay, at least for the near future. Some people in the agencies view this as a cause for concern because of the huge investment of financial and human resources that seems to be diverted into it. There are ways of looking at this phenomenon, however, that can increase the comfort level of those in the agencies and increase the effectiveness of the whole endeavor. We will explore those next.

The Message of Short-Term Missions

Critics have referred to short-term missions as the "amateurization of missions" or "drive-by missions." Some long-term missionaries despise it; many agency planners and recruiters tolerate it; and there are people in the pews who actually do love it. It has been around for decades, though its time frames clearly have been getting shorter. Not all that long ago its definition referred to those going out for a year or two, but today it is more likely to refer to someone going out for a week or two.

The meaning of this phenomenon is bound up with what it reflects about North American culture and time. Eras in mission, like eras in anything else, grow out of a context. The same spirit that launched the conquest mode of the high imperial period in European and world history also launched the inland mission movement. Both grew out of a context of broad optimism concerning the rightness of the cause and a spirit of sacrificial service and adventure. Both sought to bring the hard to reach into a new orbit of existence.

Likewise, the post-WWII missions boom was a reflection of the can-do spirit of GI optimism combined with a personal and deeply experienced sense of global need. Widely honored elements of military discipline and organizational style were brought to bear on the gospel task for which many had seen the need firsthand. The same spirit that provided energy for the great economic and entrepreneurial boom of the last half-century also spurred the mission enterprise to new feats. So what is the message of short-term missions for today? And what does it say about the future of the evangelical mission enterprise from North America?

Above all else, the enormous popularity of short-term missions is a reflection of local churches' desire to be involved more directly in global mission. Growing distrust of institutions and of centralized models of governance has impacted the status of mission agencies, just as they have other institutions in the society. Though this shift has occurred more slowly for mission agencies because of a higher trust level to begin with, and because of the higher proportional importance of support from institutionally oriented older church members, it has taken place nevertheless.

The tidal wave of short-term missions is also a reflection of the cultural reality that relationships and choice, rather than authority and institutional loyalty, now rule the day. Mission agencies, like the military services, have had to work much harder to secure and retain good recruits.

Short-term mission programs, on the other hand, like skydiving and bungee jumping, have attracted a lot more courageous souls to "give it a try," often at the encouragement of a close friend.

When the costs are so minor on the downside (e.g., separation from family and friends, long-term health risks, lower standard of living), and the reinforcements are so plentiful on the upside (e.g., feeling

281

good about helping others, doing one's part in God's mission to the world, traveling, camaraderie), why not?

Is the short-term-mission movement here to stay, or will it be a fading phenomenon? It seems that most likely it will be around for a long time. One possible spoiler is a huge economic downturn. Without affluence and affordable travel, short-term missions may survive, but they cannot thrive. Short-term missions are largely the product of a particularly wealthy and mobile historical context. Change the attendant conditions, and the methods will change. That's what made monastery transplants so important in the sixth century, and emigration so important to the Moravian missionary efforts in the seventeenth and eighteenth centuries. None of this is to deny that almost all methods retain some sort of following in all contexts and times, but popularity and effectiveness certainly are impacted by the larger societal and cultural scene.

CHURCHES AND AGENCIES IN TENSION

Perhaps no one in recent years has stimulated discussion in mission circles more than Jim Engel and William Dyrness with their *Changing the Mind of Missions* (2000), a book that portrays story after story of the tensions within contemporary missions. Churches, especially the larger ones, are pulling back from unquestioning support of the agendas and methodologies of established mission agencies. In fact, missionaries are being sent out directly by local churches, often bypassing the agencies altogether.

The flexibility in such an approach, however, often is offset by the lack of experienced on-field supervision. The real danger, ironi-

cally, is that the thing that churches so often are frustrated with will be the very thing that they perpetuate. Will they simply replace one type of hegemony (that of the agency) with another (that of the megachurch)?

The short answer often is yes, they will and they are, and frequently it is a less knowledgeable and less benign form of hegemony than the one they replace, or at least think they are replacing. The real "hegemony," at least in places where mission has been carried on well, lies with the indigenous church that has been established.

On the other hand, sometimes it is possible to see great things accomplished by older churches of the West (or elsewhere) relating directly to newer churches, thereby going around excessive agency bureaucracy in the cause of new outreach or church development. Predictably, the relative merits of each approach—church or agency—often are in the eyes of the beholder.

But is it necessary to choose one approach over the other? Not really. It is possible, given right attitudes and clear thinking, to see healthy synergism rule the day, wherein churches and agencies work together not only in implementation, but also in setting agendas in conjunction with believers in a region to accomplish things that none of them could achieve alone.

This is a goal worth fighting for and expending huge amounts of energy to achieve because it is so much more effective, it enables the world to see "how much these Christians love one another," and because God smiles upon it. Of course, not every church and not every agency will be willing or able to adjust long-standing attitudes and entrenched methods enough to do this effectively. But some will, and it behooves those who care about effectiveness and God's glory to do everything in their power to be numbered among those who can make it work.

As a byproduct of the tensions already discussed, money issues have become increasingly visible in missions thinking and action. On the one hand, the U.S. economy has changed so that running missions on the generosity of spare change is becoming less and less viable. At the same time, megachurches are developing their own mission programs tailored to their particular philosophy of ministry. They want to see the money given by their members used in ways that provide them with a greater sense of ownership. Clearly, the disconnect is serious. We examine some of the nuances next.

FINANCING MISSIONS

Reported income for overseas mission work among U.S. agencies was just under $3 billion in 1999, an increase of more than 21 percent from 1996 to 1999 even after adjusting for inflation, and this increase was a broad-based one (Moreau 2000c, 34, 45). This is good news, but it is put into perspective by the fact that in 1999 Americans spent $6.1 billion on computer games (Interactive Digital Software Association) and Burger King enjoyed over $10 billion in sales!

Tom Sine (1991) and others have long warned that financing for mission is tenuous. They have wondered what will happen when our economy bottoms out. Will missions giving follow suit and our ability to finance our part in the ongoing task be lost? In light of the recent downturn in the dot-com boom, corporate financial scandals, and the U.S. stock market fallout, the prognosis, from a human perspective, does not look particularly good.

This state of affairs has clear demographic overtones, including the aging and passing off the scene of the generations that have carried the funding of missions for so long, and the theological slippage of the generations that have followed them (particularly regarding the lostness of the lost). In effect, North American Christians are seeing the retirement (and expiration) of a generation that was more financially committed and the subsequent transfer of wealth to a generation known for its greed rather than its generosity. Some prophesy doomsday scenarios, while others admonish, "Who owns the cattle on a thousand hills?" (see Ps. 50:10).

Rather than generosity or its lack, however, the core problem appears to be a scandal of the evangelical heart in North America, where it seems that God's people increasingly love the world and seek its approval more than they love and seek the approval of the Savior. In the words of Francis Schaeffer, they are seeking "personal peace and affluence" above God's glory. Furthermore, fewer and fewer know the Scriptures, thereby cutting themselves off from a chief motivation for repentance. This also means that fewer and fewer know why they are here. In short, things are deteriorating to a point that without a genuine revival it is hard, humanly speaking, to envision North America making a significant contribution to world mission much longer. Fortunately, God operates beyond human limitations to accomplish his purposes.

Further compounding the complexity of the financial issue is that the relative cost of financing missionaries from the West versus missionaries from the rest of the world has caught the attention of many agencies and church missions committees in the United States. It is noted that for the

283

SIDEBAR 17.2
CHURCH MODELS THAT WORK

Megachurch Missions Program at University Presbyterian Church (Seattle, Washington)

The most unique feature of this church's mission efforts is the absolute commitment of the leadership not to start anything, but to mobilize the resources of people who have their own dreams, and then to support those efforts to the hilt (Telford 2001, 112). Far from slowing inertia, this has resulted in a very large church that is incredibly innovative and purposeful in its mission endeavors. Some of their most challenging guiding principles include (excerpted from Telford 2001, 113–16):

Bottom-up Mobilization! There is no manual for what a task force should be or do. That makes some people frustrated, but the leadership believes that the day you organize what a task force is will be the day you take the fire away.

Give Missions Away! The purpose of the staff in the missions department is to pastor and mentor the laity who are doing the work of missions. They are not there to try to mobilize the laity to do something the leadership wants; they are there to empower and minister to the laity.

Open the Floodgates of Generosity! The leadership believes that if you allow the laity to create ministry, the money will flow.

Small Groups Relate! If you attend UPC, you're in a small group.

That's all there is to it! Small groups often become missions or ministry task forces. Bottom-up, relational, and generous small groups and task forces are what make the missions expansion at UPC a reality. It takes a certain kind of leadership to make it possible.

How does this flesh out? The model initiatives listed below demonstrate the range and depth of mission involvement in University Presbyterian Church (excerpted from Telford 2001, 117–20):

World Deputation: This is a scholarship opportunity UPC provides for university students to go on short-term missions trips. Many have ... gone into full-time ministry as a result of their missions experience.

Intentional Communities: With a focus on lifestyle ministry, the Intentional Community (IC)

---

cost of financing a family of four Americans to serve abroad, several (anywhere from six to twenty) indigenous missionaries can be sent. Additionally, they can be sent more quickly, as it takes well over a year for many American missionaries to raise enough support to depart. Many missions committees of local churches have been pulling back from financing U.S. missionaries because their dollars go further when they support indigenous missionaries.

Although an efficiency orientation is an integral part of American culture, that does not absolve Americans from sending their own people as missionaries. Nor does

sending money to fund local missionaries working in the missionaries' own country ensure that the least reached will have the chance to hear the gospel. It is often most

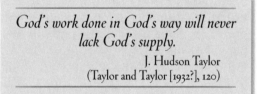

God's work done in God's way will never lack God's supply.

J. Hudson Taylor
(Taylor and Taylor [1932?], 120)

difficult for those closest to a cultural or religious boundary to cross over it.

Resolving the issues involved will continue to be a complex challenge, but reso-

program is committed to learning about life in community and in the city. Through its members, the IC program provides at least nine thousand hours each year to urban ministries in the city of Seattle.

TWAD: Travel With a Difference is designed to awaken and deepen a traveler's understanding of what ministries are going on as an extension of UPC.

Journey: Journey is usually a two-week short ministry experience to give members an opportunity for cross-cultural service. The leadership has a long-term goal that every member of UPC will eventually have an opportunity to go on a journey overseas to experience the spiritual growth and renewal that can result.

Ethnic Church Partners: UPC has had an opportunity to do missions right in their own city. They have planted a number of ethnic churches and have seen them become self-supporting, calling their own pastors. These churches first met at UPC but then were able, often through the help of UPC task forces, to acquire their own facilities.

Missionary Care: As the number of missionaries grew it became too difficult for the missions staff alone to adequately care for them. The Barnabas Ministry was created about ten years ago to mobilize the laity to participate in missionary care. A global care coordinator was hired to oversee and expand this ministry.

UPC Scholars: This is a scholarship program designed to help international students studying in the United States or abroad who intend to go into full-time ministry. UPC wants to come alongside these future leaders and work toward helping them reach their ministry goals.

Global Task Forces: Members who have a particular burden for or interest in a certain area of the world or ministry are encouraged and helped to be active, praying task forces. They encourage missionaries and make visible to the rest of the church the needs and initiatives in that area of the world. These groups have three goals: build relationships, mobilize resources, and support projects.

A New Model for Missions: As a result of UPC's intense involvement in Albania . . . they have developed a set of [still evolving] principles for strategic missions:

1. Begin with a lay vision.
2. See what God has been doing before we arrived.
3. Start with what we can do best.
4. Respect preexisting Christian ministries.
5. Empower local leadership.
6. Expect the unexpected.

lution will come in some fashion over the next few years. Decisions will have to be made, even if the theological justification and practical planning is found wanting.

MAJORITY WORLD MISSIONS

Thankfully, the heyday of colonialism is behind us. No longer should Western Christians be thinking that they carry the "White Man's Burden" or that the missionary task is theirs alone. A new day has dawned—a day in which all Christians must adequately recognize the gifts and strengths of those who hail from majority world countries.

In 1999 U.S. mission agencies reported over seventy-one thousand nationals working in their own countries for U.S. mission agencies, compared to just under forty thousand Americans. This may or may not be good news for those countries. It may only mean that the U.S. agencies are abandoning long-standing indigenous church-planting principles in favor of skimming off the leadership cream from the indigenous churches. Still, it does indicate a shift in the primary source of personnel doing mission even in U.S. based agencies.

The ratio only three years earlier was slightly more than thirty thousand nationals to just under forty thousand Americans (Moreau 2000c, 33–34). In three years the ratio of nationals to Americans more than doubled—an amazing number, given the relatively recent trend. Additionally, this accounts only for U.S. mission agencies. When the number of agencies from the majority world is added, the ratio goes even higher. Some may lament the lack of American involvement, but the explosion of missionaries from around the world is a cause for rejoicing rather than lamenting.

The past twenty-five years have witnessed significant developments in majority world missionary involvement in the task. This in turn has enabled the development of globalized strategies. It seems that the evangelical movement has finally caught up with the ecumenical movement in understanding the realities of mission as a phenomenon to and from every continent.

PARTNERSHIPS

The word *partnership* has reached the status of a buzzword in mission circles today. Creating and carrying out partnerships in which each member is valued and has something to offer to the partnership is difficult under the best of circumstances. This is especially true when the partnering organizations are from different cultures and have widely differing management and organizational structures and styles.

The difficulties are magnified when one of the partners brings the bulk of the necessary financial resources, as is most often the case when Western churches or missions partner with churches or missions from the southern hemisphere. It requires strong relationships and wise, godly interaction for the partnership to be genuine and

for all partners to feel that they are on an equal footing.

One group that has been most helpful as a midwife to effective partnerships is Interdev. Their name, under Phil Butler's leadership, became almost synonymous with the subject of partnerships. Another organization whose name has literally become synonymous with partnership is Partners International, formerly known as Christian Nationals, Inc.

Daniel Rickett, the long-time director of partner development for Partners International, describes seven mistakes that partners most often make (Rickett 2001, 308–17).

Mistake 1: Assuming you think alike. "One of the quickest ways to get into trouble in a partnership is to assume that others share your perceptions and expectations. I know. I made this mistake and it almost cost me a dear friend."

Mistake 2: Promising more than you can deliver. "You've probably heard stories of Christian tourists who promise the first one thousand dollars on the spot, and then leave the problem of raising the balance of a thirty-thousand-dollar project to their church back home. But making a promise you can't keep doesn't happen only to the novice. Experienced missionaries can also overestimate their abilities."

Mistake 3: Taking to the road without a map. "It is normal for partnerships to start with ambiguity, misunderstandings, and disagreement. A partnership is necessarily untidy as people negotiate values and interests. It is abnormal when major misconceptions emerge late in the relationship. This happens generally for two reasons. Either the partners did not clarify goals for the partnership at the outset, or they neglected to review and recalibrate their goals along the way. The net effect is like going on a journey without a destination."

Mistake 4: Underestimating cultural differences. "Succeeding at intercultural partnership requires at a minimum some understanding of the worldview, ways of being, and interacting, used by members of the partner ministry."

Mistake 5: Taking shortcuts. "I like to think I'm too smart for someone to play me for a fool. But it can happen, especially when I'm willing to take shortcuts. . . . Con artists who prey on Christians take advantage of trust and benevolence. You can usually spot them, though, when you start checking references. The chances of being scammed by a certified con artist are slim. Even the most modest investigation sends them scurrying. Where you're more likely to get hoodwinked is by someone you know."

Mistake 6: Forgetting to develop self-reliance. "It is a mistake to underestimate the destructive potential of foreign aid. Relief self-reliance has three interwoven qualities: organizational self-determination, relational interdependence, and financial independence. A self-reliant ministry is capable of making its own decisions, collaborating with the larger Christian community, and surviving on indigenous resources."

Mistake 7: Running a race with no end. "The easiest mistake to make in a successful partnership is to keep going with no end in sight. Long-term partnerships tend to make this mistake more than short-term, functional partnerships. Short-term partnerships are by definition goal-driven. When the goal is achieved the partnership is dissolved."

We are fortunate today to have a well-developed body of literature to assist those wishing to enter into cross-cultural partnerships. Like the material from Rickett

presented here, it is based on experience and is a highly valuable resource for any who will avail themselves of it.

At the same time, it should be noted that other changes have helped to encourage this process. For example, never before in modern history has there been such a high level of interagency cooperation, both within and across cultures. This has been facilitated in part by the shift in emphasis, especially in the West, from denominational/theological loyalties to ministry/philosophy loyalties.

SPIRITUAL WARFARE

Perhaps no area of missions is more controversial than that of spiritual warfare. Western missionaries often have the reputation of going to new contexts largely unaware of spiritual realities and belief systems linked to spirits in their new culture. The recent movement in magical directions in the United States (Moreau 1995b; 2002b), however, has resulted in a new type of American missionary. He or she is now more thoroughly trained in spiritual warfare and anticipates that it is the key to evangelism in any given area. "Spiritual mapping" and "strategic-level spiritual warfare" prayer are advocated as the means to reaching the unreached people groups (Moreau 2002a). Forays into enemy territory, prayer journeys, praise rallies, Jesus marches, identificational repentance, deliverance, and healing are all part of the package of missiological spiritual warfare training.

At times this leaves many in the national church confused. Weren't they taught by previous generations of missionaries that the demonic powers are nothing? Now they are told to look for objects that may have been cursed, to trace their ancestral lineage to see if any familial spirits are attached, and to see setbacks in ministry as satanic attacks that must be withstood through spiritual warfare techniques.

Clearly, the questions that arise are complex and difficult. Theological, cultural, practical, and historic issues all come into play. So what should those who seek to be responsible senders do? Minimally, they need to acquaint themselves with a fair and balanced overview of the issues involved; and then they need to make their plans and decisions based upon a careful assessment of them. With that in mind, we offer the following overview of the issues.

Definition

At the most basic level, spiritual warfare is the struggle that Christians have to live faithful Christian lives in the face of onslaughts of spiritual powers of darkness. By and large, Christians around the world have little trouble believing in these powers of darkness—except in the West,

> The only person who does not believe that the Devil is a person is someone who has never attempted to combat him or his ways. . . . The simple tribesman going through his animistic incantations is wiser than such a drugged intellectual. He, at least, knows there is a Devil; and he has ways to appease him temporarily.
>
> Isobel Kuhn (1956, 197–98)

where a tradition of mechanistic science opened doors of doubt in regard to the existence of such beings. The biblical evidence is clear, however, that Satan exists and harbors malice and hatred toward all people, especially those who, like Job,

most clearly reflect the image of God (see Moreau 1997a, 65–80).

Personal Spiritual Warfare

Missionary training in evangelical circles in the West largely ignored issues of spiritual warfare until the early 1980s, when a spate of courses and books appeared across North America (Kraft 2002a). The most popular author was not a theologian, but Frank Peretti, whose novels *This Present Darkness* (1986) and *Piercing the Darkness* (1989) sold well in both Christian and secular markets. His stories portrayed a heavy demonic influence over the lives of people and institutions and captured the imagination of many (Moreau 1995b).

Perhaps the most influential non-Charismatic evangelical has been Neil Anderson (*The Bondage Breaker* [1990a]; *Victory over the Darkness* [1990b]), who employs a counseling methodology based on Christians knowing, understanding, and declaring truth rather than outright demonic confrontation. Growing in influence is Ed Smith's theophostic approach. The word *theophostic* means "God's light," and the focus of this method is to expose the lies that people have believed to the light of God and invite Christ to respond to those lies (see Kraft 2002a, 190–91; also, see the Web site www.theophostic.com).

The focus with many who teach spiritual warfare is on the need for the missionary or evangelist to be equipped to face Satan's attacks. Missionaries often are engaged in frontline evangelism, and the reality of the attacks they face demands some type of preparation prior to field deployment. This typically includes, at the very least, the need to explore issues of personal sin and issues of our past as part of missionary pre-field training (Warner 1991; Murphy 1992; Dickason 1987).

Over the past several decades considerable discussion has taken place about the extent to which a Christian can be influenced (demonized or possessed) by demons. Many people experienced in ministering to the oppressed, based both on biblical studies and personal experience in cross-cultural settings, have concluded that demons can control even Christians (Arnold 1997; Dickason 1987; Kraft 1995; Moreau 1997a; Unger 1963). Others, more typically based on theological orientations, disagree (Ice and Dean 1990; MacArthur 1992; Powlison 1995). Worldview considerations are perhaps the most important element in the debate (Dickason 1987; Kraft 1989; 2002a; Wagner 1996). In a 1999 Lausanne Consultation on spiritual warfare, over the course of one week of discussion, participants could not agree on this issue (Moreau et al. 2002, xxv–xxvi). It appears that this debate will continue for the foreseeable future.

However Christians answer the question of Satan's ability to affect believers, the New Testament warnings to humble ourselves before God and be on guard so that we can resist Satan (1 Pet. 5:8–9) and stand our ground in the face of his attacks (Eph. 6:10–18) make it clear that Christians are not immune to his assaults. Missionaries, as frontline workers for the kingdom, must be prepared to face spiritual conflict as they minister in Christ's name.

Personal Ministry in Spiritual Warfare

In many parts of the world a belief in the ongoing activity of spirits is prevalent. Missionaries from North America may encounter phenomena that they have never seen at home (Moreau 1997a, 13–14; Kraft 1995; Blaschke, 2001). Thus, in addition to being prepared to face spiritual warfare in their own lives, they need preparation in ways to minister to the "harassed and helpless" (Matt. 9:35–38) whom they encounter.

Several approaches to spiritual warfare have been developed, ranging from outright confrontation of the demons (Dickason 1987), to engaging truth in the life of the victim (Anderson 1990a; Moreau 1997a; Smith 2000), to bringing God's power to bear through visualization techniques (Kraft 1992; 1994). All have strengths and weaknesses. The confrontational approach can move into abuse, especially when people try to get a demon to speak when no demon is present. The engaging of truth can deal with cognitive issues but leave emotions unhealed. Visualization methods open the door to imaginative speculations and spiritual counterfeits. The Scriptures do not present a clear picture of the best way to minister to the demonized (Moreau 1997a), and we encourage the readers to evaluate every method in light of scriptural principles (see also the brief discussions in chapters 4 and 5).

Strategic Spiritual Warfare

As we mentioned in chapter 8, some people more recently have advocated that a key element in missionary ministry is the confrontation and binding of spirits that are responsible for territories rather than individuals. This is referred to as "strategic-level spiritual warfare" (Wagner's preference [1996]) or "cosmic-level spiritual warfare" (Kraft's preference [2002a, 192–94]). Peter Wagner, one of the chief proponents of this method, feels that this is the most important spiritual power boost for missions that the church has had since the days of William Carey (Wagner 1996, 46). Associated with this is the practice of "spiritual mapping," in which Christians seek to discover, through a combination of research and prayer, the spirits that are controlling a geographic domain (such as a city or region) so that they may more effectively combat these territorial spirits in prayer. George Otis is perhaps the best-known advocate of spiritual mapping (see Otis 1993; 1997).

Although some people today maintain that no biblical case can be made for such spirits (Priest, Campbell, and Mullen 1995), the scriptural evidence does seem to indicate territory-oriented responsibilities assigned to demons (see Page 1995, 63–65; Arnold 1997, 150–57). Even so, this does not automatically mean that Christians are called to engage such spirits in prayer warfare over territories. Indeed, exaggerated claims of spiritual breakthrough, unsubstantiated

> There is the constant invisible warfare that has to be waged against the powers of darkness. . . . It is fashionable in the Western world to relegate belief in demons and devils to the realm of mythology, and when mentioned at all it is a matter of jest. But it is no jest in West Africa or any other mission field for that matter.
>
> Rowland Bingham
> (Tucker 1983, 297)

testimonies of territorial deliverance, and shaky use of the biblical texts weigh heavily against missionary engagement of territorial spirits (Arnold 1997, 185–90; Lowe 1998;

Moreau 2002a). Missionaries, like all Christians, are to stand their ground against the enemy. At times this will involve encounters with the demonic, but, more typically, it involves walking in light of God's truth and prayerfully standing firm when the enemy does attack.

TECHNOLOGY AND AN OCEAN OF INFORMATION

Technological advancements, together with shifts in conceptualizing the task of mission, have combined to yield a more accurate picture of the task remaining as well as the possibility of updating that picture in "real time." Technology can be harnessed for good or for ill in the task of reaching the world for Christ. On the one hand, e-mail communication makes it possible for the missionary to stay in touch with the home culture. On the other hand, that very fact may make it more difficult for the missionary to adjust to the new culture. Christian television shows designed for one culture are beamed across the world, usually without regard to their impact on another culture but simply in search of greater market share.

Development projects, while offering opportunities for new life choices and better lifestyles, bring with them a host of technological issues. Technology is never completely neutral; it always comes with its own culture and changes the cultures in which it is implemented. As one example, women who used to gather at the well traditionally connected with each other and built community while waiting their turn. Though initially they enjoy the easing of hard physical labor effected when the water is pumped faster through solar power, they discover in the long run that their com-

CASE STUDY:
PARTNERSHIP OR SEPARATION?

Richard C. Pease
(Hiebert and Hiebert 1987, 191–94 [used with permission])

"Are you really saying that if the mission sends the Parks to Japan, there may be no more official cooperation from the church?" the Reverend Robert Adams asked.

"Yes, we are sorry, but that is what we mean," replied Reverend Tanaka.

"Then we as missionaries must make a decision, and I must call the mission headquarters in California immediately and notify them," said Adams.

The four missionaries drove down the winding road to the village, past rice paddies where farmers were finishing the laborious task of planting rice seedlings by hand. In the town at the foot of the mountain, they stopped at a Japanese restaurant. The heat and humidity seemed even worse in the valley. As they ordered

lunch, each was deeply disturbed by this turn of events. The Parks were due to arrive in Japan in six weeks. Should the missionaries order the home office to delay their coming?

Adams's mind raced over the events of the past six months since the Parks were officially appointed. He remembered the long hours of private conversation he had had with the church leaders and the two joint meetings of the church and mission. How could something that seemed to be the leading of the Lord bring the church and mission to this crisis? He thought back over the key factors in the case.

The Faith Union Mission had worked in Japan since the turn of the century. The thirty-five churches and thirteen preaching points that made up the Faith

Union Church were the fruit of the missionaries' work. The mission had helped build a Bible College and a Christian camp, but the church was now autonomous and self-supporting.

In the early 1970s, the mission developed a policy for working in partnership with its overseas churches. In order to respect the equality and autonomous nature of the national church organizations, plans for cooperative evangelism were drawn up. These were called Joint Working Agreements. The committees that drew up these agreements were composed of the governing committee of the national church, the field governing committee of the missionaries, and representatives from the mission headquarters in America.

In 1979, the Second Five Year Working Agreement was signed between the Faith Union Churches of Japan and the Faith Union Mission. The church and mission agreed to cooperate in areas such as church planting, the

(continued)

munity ties are weakened when the new pumps dispense water so fast that they don't have sufficient time to connect with each other at the well. Additionally, because what used to take hours now takes minutes, an unprecedented surplus of time arises, and even adjusting to that surplus can be stressful. Certainly, we are not advocating banning technology that eases women's burdens. Nevertheless, missionaries will do well to pay attention to the attendant

circumstances that technology brings, because of the potentially huge impact on the local culture.

Information technology also is exploding. As the April 2002 issue of *Evangelical Missions Quarterly* noted, contemporary Christians truly are living in an ocean of information. New books, new CDs, new databases on the Internet—a whole new range of tools to approach the missionary task has appeared since the early 1990s.

Bible College, literature work, and the camp program. There would be two joint-committee meetings scheduled each year to discuss these areas of cooperation, as well as any other areas of mutual concern. All missionary assignments were discussed at the joint meetings. So far, these arrangements had worked out well.

The problem arose with the appointment of Reverend and Mrs. Park. Both were American citizens of Korean ancestry. Both had lived in Japan. In fact, Mrs. Park was born there. Both were fluent in Japanese as well as Korean. During his theological studies in America, God gave Reverend Park a deep burden for reaching Korean people living in Japan. The local Korean church affiliated with the Faith Union Mission was also concerned about the Koreans in Japan and pledged itself to support the Parks' ministry there. When the Parks applied to the Faith Union Mission, the board was impressed with their qualifications and high recommendations.

Shortly before receiving the Parks' application, the Faith Union Mission had made a major shift in its policy. It decided to begin evangelistic work among ethnic and social groups in which there was no significant Christian witness. The six hundred thousand Koreans living in Japan were just such a group, and the Parks seemed the ideal couple to head up this new venture of faith.

When the possibility of the mission's launching of a new ministry to reach Koreans in Japan was first presented to the Faith Union Church, Reverend Kashiwagi, its chairman, was not enthusiastic about the idea. Nevertheless, he promised missionary Adams that the church would discuss it. A month later, in a private conversation, Kashiwagi said that he thought the appointment of the Parks to Japan would cause problems within the church and consequently between the church and mission. Some of the church's main objections were that historically there were problems between Japan and Korea, and that the Koreans in Japan felt that the Japanese discriminated against them. The church felt it would be like mixing oil and water to have Koreans and Japanese in the same national church organization.

After hearing the church's objections, the mission came up with what it felt was a compromise solution. The Parks would work in Japan among Koreans, but their work would have no organizational link with the Japanese Faith Union Churches. When, however, Reverend Tanaka became chairman of the Faith Union Church of Japan, he opposed the new work more strongly.

Hearing of this opposition, the missionaries and home office reconsidered their plans. They were concerned about working harmoniously with the Japanese

On the traditional publishing side, the journal *Missiology* devoted one issue (January 2000) to the stories of several major reference works that either had been published or were in process of publication around that time.

One of the potentially significant developments to watch for in the future is interconnectivity through the Internet and the development of significant and relatively inexpensive missiological tools for use on computers (such as the *20:21 Library*).

Global Mapping has led the way on one frontier with the development of several significant CD tools, ranging from *Operation World* to *Operation China* to *The World of Islam* to the *African Proverbs Project*. Each CD includes books (fifty on *The World of Islam*), photos, outlines, maps, and so on. The text on every CD is searchable, letting the user search for important ideas through multiple resources at the same time.

The Internet is home to an explosion of mission-related resources (for numer-

church, which was the philosophy behind the Joint Working Agreements. At the same time, the mission was deeply burdened about the Koreans in the country who had little Christian witness among them. While the mission had the right under the terms of the agreement to launch a new ministry, they hesitated to do so over the objections of the national church. The Japanese leaders said that they had no plans for a work among the Koreans in Japan, but that when such a work was begun, they wanted to initiate it and be involved in selecting the personnel. After all, they were Japanese, and this was Japan! Moreover, although they had given a special status to American missionaries—for it was through the missionaries that they had come to know the Lord—they could not give the same special status to someone of Korean ancestry.

The home office felt deeply that the mission should begin a new work among the Koreans and that God had called the Parks for that ministry. The Parks, too, believed that God was leading them to Japan. They had sold their home and furniture and were preparing to leave for Japan.

The missionaries were strongly supportive of the idea of launching a new ministry, but they were saddened to see a breach developing in their own working relationships with these Japanese brothers and sisters. What would it do to their own ministries?

When the home office and missionary council agreed to launch the new ministry despite the objections of the church, the Japanese felt the mission was not treating them as equals. At the next joint committee, Robert Adams explained the decision of the mission. He pointed out that the mission felt a responsibility for the Koreans in Japan, but that it did not want to offend the Japanese church. Consequently, the Parks would be assigned to another area of Japan and would be completely separate from the Japanese church. Reverend Tanaka said that having the Parks work separately was "an American way of thinking." He added, "If the mission sends Reverend and Mrs. Park as new missionaries to Japan, it will be difficult for the church to continue working cooperatively with the mission." It was then that Adams had asked, "Are you really saying that if the mission sends the Parks to Japan, there may be no more official cooperation between us?"

"What shall we do?" Reverend Adams asked the other three missionaries seated around the restaurant table. "The Parks are due to arrive in Japan in six weeks. In this matter the home office will go along with our decision because we know the situation best. So what shall I say when I call headquarters tonight?"

---

ous resources and helpful thinking, see the January 2003 issue of *Evangelical Missions Quarterly*). Mission directories, databases of articles, profiles on unreached peoples, biblical exposition, and tools for churches are available. One place to start searching is MisLinks (www.mislinks.org). Designed as a "directory of directories," it provides several thousand links to resources of importance to missionaries, ranging from member care to financial helps to contextualization and world religions. Another resource to browse is the Network for Strategic Missions site, which includes a "KnowledgeBase" of over ten thousand articles—all with a mission heartbeat (www.strategicnetwork.org/index.asp?loc=kb).

CONCLUSION

Certainly, many more topics could be covered. For example, the challenge of the religions of the world is so great that we offer an entire chapter just to introducing it. If space permitted, we also would explore the impact on mission of AIDS, global economics, and issues of poverty and injustice. We invite you to choose one or more of these trends and pursue it yourself. Our case study is an example of one of the hotter topics: partnership. As the story shows, it is an area of great importance as well as great challenge.

18

Encountering the Religions
of the World

INTRODUCTION

On one crystal clear September morning of 2001 the dividing lines between Islam and Christianity became clearer than ever before, and the events that transpired irrevocably changed the religious landscape of the United States. The first impression of many Christians when they heard the news of the attacks on the World Trade Center and the Pentagon was that the world was at a watershed moment in history. Instinctively they knew that life could not simply go on as before. The attacks on U.S. soil ripped to shreds the idea that Americans are safe, and it was painfully clear that the missionary enterprise could not go on unaffected by those events. It is highly likely that missionary work among Muslim populations, and perhaps even among adherents of other religions, will never be the same.

A quick look at the 10/40 Window (see map 18.1) shows that the vast bulk of people who have yet to hear a clearly communicated invitation to repent, turn to Christ, and worship God are those who are deeply embedded in cultures that largely, if not exclusively, follow a religion other than Christianity. Those

who live in non-Christian contexts and come to Christ will inevitably come face-to-face with competing truth claims. These claims focus on issues that impact daily life rather than simply theoretical ones.

Should the Chinese Buddhist who comes to Christ stop all participation in ancestor veneration? Should the new African believer

> *The impact of agnostic science will turn out to be child's play compared to the challenge to Christian theology of the faiths of other men.*
> Max Warren (Clendenin 1995, 11)

stop going to the diviner when illness strikes his family? Should the Christian Pacific Islander not let her sons and daughters go through initiation ceremonies? Should the Christ-follower from Islam stop praying five times each day or fasting during Ramadan? These are questions that most North American missionaries have never faced in their own culture, but they are questions constantly faced by people coming to Christ from non-Christian religions.

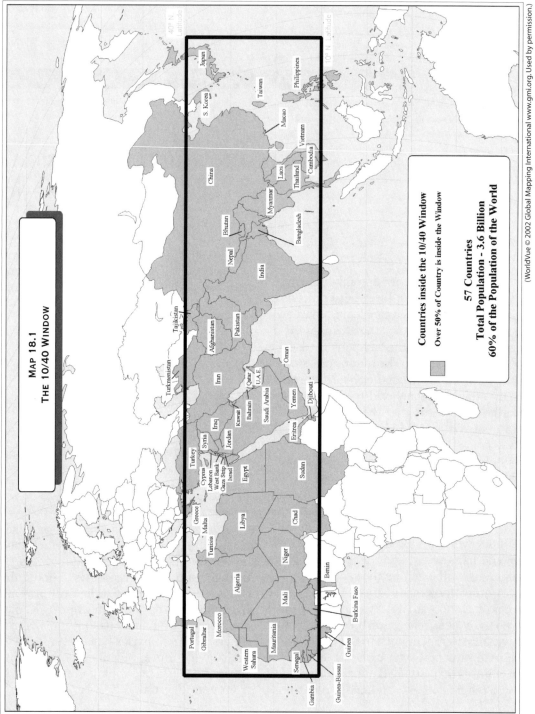

MAP 18.1
THE 10/40 WINDOW

Countries inside the 10/40 Window
Over 50% of Country is inside the Window

57 Countries
Total Population - 3.6 Billion
60% of the Population of the World

(WorldVue © 2002 Global Mapping International www.gmi.org. Used by permission.)

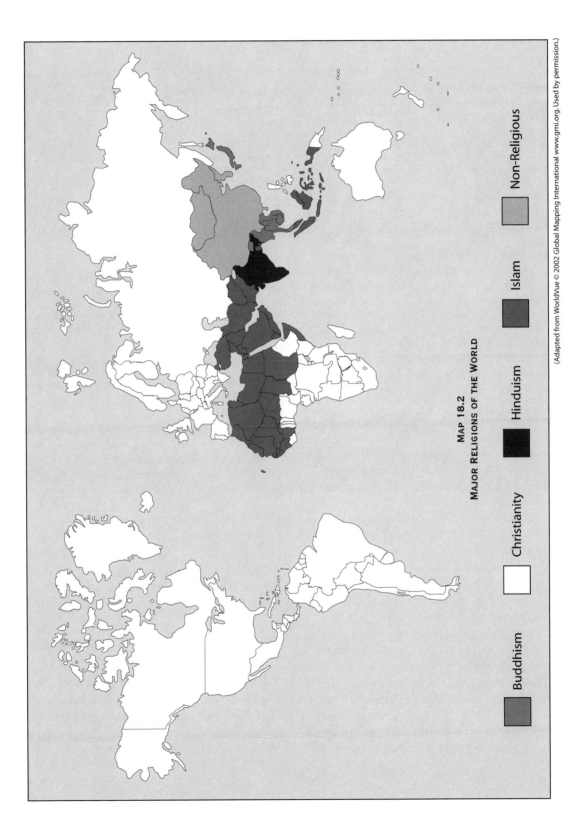

MAP 18.2
MAJOR RELIGIONS OF THE WORLD

Buddhism   Christianity   Hinduism   Islam   Non-Religious

(Adapted from WorldVue © 2002 Global Mapping International www.gmi.org. Used by permission.)

SIDEBAR 18.1
SPECTRUM OF MUSLIM CONTEXTUALIZATION

John Travis
(Adapted from Travis 1998 [used with permission])

The following chart shows the spectrum of practices in use today for contextualizing the Christian faith in Muslim settings.

*C1: Traditional Church Using Outsider** Language.* May be Orthodox, Catholic, or Protestant. Some predate Islam. Thousands of C1 churches are found in Muslim lands today. Many reflect Western culture. A huge cultural chasm often exists between the church and the surrounding Muslim community. Some Muslim background believers may be found in C1 churches. C1 believers call themselves "Christians."

*C2: Traditional Church Using Insider** Language.* Essentially the same as

C1 except for language. Though insider language is used, religious vocabulary is probably non-Islamic (distinctively "Christian"). The cultural gap between Muslims and C2 is still large. Often more Muslim background believers are found in C2 than in C1. The majority of churches located in the Muslim world today are C1 or C2. C2 believers call themselves "Christians."

C3: Contextualized Christ-Centered Communities Using Insider Language and Religiously Neutral Insider Cultural Forms. Religiously neutral forms may include folk music, ethnic dress, artwork, etc. Islamic elements (where present) are "filtered out" so as to use purely

"cultural" forms. The aim is to reduce foreignness of the gospel and the church by contextualizing to biblically permissible cultural forms. May meet in a church building or more religiously neutral location. C3 congregations are comprised of a majority of Muslim background believers. C3 believers call themselves "Christians."

C4: Contextualized Christ-Centered Communities Using Insider Language and Biblically Permissible Cultural and Islamic Forms. Similar to C3, however, biblically permissible Islamic forms and practices are also utilized (e.g., praying with raised hands, keeping the fast, avoiding pork, alcohol, and dogs as pets, using Islamic terms, dress, etc.). C1 and C2 forms avoided. Meetings not held in church buildings. C4 communities comprised almost entirely of Muslim background believers. C4 believers, though highly

---

In addition to these difficult issues, contemporary North American culture (as well as many religions of the world) preaches that all religions chart a path to the same God through different routes. Anyone who dares to declare otherwise is "intolerant" and simply "not up with the times."

Certainly, the missionary approach to the religions of the world cannot be founded on the attitudes of contemporary culture. The very fact that it is "contemporary" is a reminder that these attitudes are not set in stone. This does not mean, however, that Christians should completely ignore contemporary culture around them. They

should be sensitive to it, but not enslaved to it (see John 17:13–19). What attitudes and approaches should Christians, and missionaries in particular, have toward the multitude of non-Christian religions in the world?

LEARNING ABOUT AND STUDYING OTHER RELIGIONS

One important step that Christian missionaries should take is to become students of the religions that are so important to those among whom they work. This involves study and observation. Two related ques-

contextualized, are usually not seen as Muslim by the Muslim community. C4 believers identify themselves as followers of Isa the Messiah (or something similar).

C5: Christ-Centered Communities of "Messianic Muslims" Who Have Accepted Jesus as Lord and Savior. C5 believers remain legally and socially within the community of Islam. Somewhat similar to the Messianic Jewish movement. Aspects of Islamic theology that are incompatible with the Bible are rejected, or reinterpreted if possible. Participation in corporate Islamic worship varies from person to person and group to group. C5 believers meet regularly with other C5 believers and share their faith with unsaved Muslims. Unsaved Muslims may see C5 believers as theologically deviant and may eventually expel them from the community of Islam. Where entire villages accept Christ, C5 may result in

"Messianic mosques." C5 believers are viewed as Muslims by the Muslim community and refer to themselves as Muslims who follow Isa the Messiah.

C6: Small Christ-Centered Communities of Secret/Underground Believers. Similar to persecuted believers suffering under totalitarian regimes. Due to fear, isolation, or threat of extreme governmental/community legal action or retaliation (including capital punishment), C6 believers worship Christ secretly (individually or perhaps infrequently in small clusters). Many come to Christ through dreams, visions, miracles, radio broadcasts, tracts, Christian witness while abroad, or reading the Bible on their own initiative. C6 (as opposed to C5) believers are usually silent about their faith. C6 is not ideal; God desires his people to witness and have regular fellowship (Heb. 10:25).

Nonetheless, C6 believers are part of our family in Christ. Though God may call some to a life of suffering, imprisonment, or martyrdom, he may be pleased to have some worship him in secret, at least for a time. C6 believers are perceived as Muslims by the Muslim community and identify themselves as Muslims.

*"Insider" pertains to the local Muslim population; "outsider" pertains to the local non-Muslim population.

REFLECTION AND DISCUSSION

1. Where would you draw the line within this spectrum?
2. What approach would you take in teaching C6 people?
3. A friend of yours has decided to engage in Muslim evangelism using a C5 approach and asks for your advice. What would you say?

tions should be asked by every missionary early in his or her career (adapted partly from Muck 1993): First, What kind of role do you take? Second, What does it mean to take other religions seriously?

What Kind of Role Should You Take?

Let's imagine a new missionary named Jim. Shortly after arriving in a Middle East destination, Jim purchased local clothing and tried to find ways to blend in wherever possible. Basing his actions on Paul's desire to become all things to all people in order to win some (1 Cor. 9:22), Jim attended a local mosque, performed the associated

rituals, and prayed in Muslim fashion five times daily. At the same time, he looked for opportunities to talk carefully with others about his faith in Christ in such a way that they would not be offended. When asked what religion he followed, he simply stated that he is one who submits to God.

How do you feel about Jim's activities? What do you think the local Muslims would feel if they thought that Jim was misrepresenting himself to them? Is this what Paul meant when he said that he became all things to all people? Jim's case illustrates the fact that missionaries can take on different roles in their attempts to reach others for

Christ, but that questions about the legitimacy of their roles also must be discussed (see sidebar 18.1).

In what follows next we describe seven roles that the missionary can play in relating to those of other religions. Although each of these roles has advantages and disadvantages, missionaries at different times in their ministries may need to take on a number of them.

The first role is that of *adherent* or *insider*. This is the position that Jim took; he adopted the habits, practices, and rituals of the adherents of the religion. Over the course of Christian history this role has been judged inappropriate for the missionary because typically it involves deception, which is unbecoming to a follower of Christ. In thinking this through in Jim's case, it is helpful to consider what your feelings would be toward a Muslim who apparently came to Christ, joined your church, and then began quietly trying to convert selected members of your youth group to Islam (see Parshall 1998). You probably would not be pleased with this turn of events! Missionaries who are tempted to take an insider role should carefully consider all of the implications lest they find themselves in a position of denying Christ in order to maintain the role.

The second role is that of *seeker* or *inquirer*. A seeker is one who explores religious teachings with the intention of considering conversion. Nicodemus played this role in his discussion with Jesus (John 3). Again, ethical issues arise that make it difficult for the missionary who has no intention of conversion to adopt this role in a non-Christian setting.

A missionary who follows this model may take on the role of the seeker who pursues ultimate truth. Evangelicals generally have rejected this approach, asserting that in Christ truth has been revealed, and the Christian who denies Christ for another religion has turned away from the truth.

A third role, related to the second but one step removed, is that of *explorer*. Recent shifts in mainline and ecumenical mission circles have resulted in an emphasis on interreligious dialogue. Dialogue essentially refers to an interpersonal exchange in which neither side tries to convert the other, though both seek to learn about the other and to teach the other about themselves through the process of mutual exchange (see Stott 1975b, 60–61; Pierson 2000). In fact, dialogue is so important in ecumenical circles that the *Dictionary of the Ecumenical Movement* (Lossky et al. 1991) contains four articles on it. Dialogue is idealized as a means by which a Christian may learn how to become a better Christian through a mutual exchange of teachings with, for example, a Hindu. In fact, it allows for the risk that a Christian may convert to another religion because of what he or she discovers while in dialogue. A preordained conclusion to dialogue is not allowed; both parties come not to convince or persuade, though persuasion may occur.

Many missionaries do engage in fruitful dialogue with non-Christians. But ultimately the role of explorer, if no persuasive element is allowed, falls short of God's call to Christians to invite people to repent, turn to Christ, and worship God. Missionaries may at times take on the role of the explorer, but they need to move beyond that role if they want to obey Christ.

The fourth role is that of *reporter*. Reporters are outsiders whose job is to accurately describe or report the religion they encounter. They may be thought of as social scientists of religion who try to be as objective as possible. Their focus is on understanding and describing rather than on evaluating or judging.

The missionary who takes on this role must beware of "relative" objectivity—that is, subjectivity disguised to look objective. Often, missionaries take on this role during deputation as they explain to their home churches about the people among whom they minister. They must be careful not to paint an exaggerated or untrue picture or to play to stereotypes held by members of their home churches. Although missionaries are not to become advocates for another religion, they can serve as voices of moderation when appropriate to ensure that those who pray for them properly understand the adherents among whom they live.

The fifth role is an extension of the reporter, that of *specialist*. Specialists essentially are reporters who go beyond the normal reporting method and specialize in one religion or one aspect of religion. Missionaries may need to specialize their engagement of a religion to the particular forms it takes where they serve. They also may choose to become experts in a particular element of religions (such as symbolism [see Zahniser 1997]) for the purpose of developing better-contextualized methodologies to help draw people to Christ.

The sixth role is that of *advocate of a new religion*. At times the missionary may serve as a type of gadfly who irritates and stimulates adherents of other religions toward change in the hopes that people will turn to Christ. In taking on this role, the missionary respects people of other religions but is willing to continuously and gently prod and challenge them to consider the consequences of belief systems and practices. Paul's sermon before the Aeropagus (Acts 17) models this approach. He expressed appreciation for the beliefs he found, but he used them as a stepping-stone toward the teachings of Christ.

This role brings the discussion back to the issue of dialogue. Examples in the Bible frame dialogue as an element of proclamation rather than portray it as an end in itself (see Stott 1975b, 60–64). This provides a biblical approach to dialogue. As advocates of a new religion, missionaries approach non-Christians in a spirit of charity and humble acceptance of the fact that they do not know all truth—indeed, all missionaries have much to learn. At the same time, however, missionaries possess not only some truth; they possess the very truth granted by divine revelation. It is this truth that Jesus calls Christians to lovingly and respectfully communicate. As they do so, they must remember that it is not their job to see that those with whom they dialogue accept the truth. That is a role that God reserves for the Holy Spirit, who alone works in the hearts of people.

Though missionaries may temporarily take on the role of seeker, they eventually must move beyond that role to engaging non-Christians by calling them to Christ. To do any less is to deny the fundamental nature of Christ's command to disciple all nations.

The seventh role is that of *apologist* or *antagonist*. Many among previous generations of missionaries assumed that this was the only role that a missionary should play. Being an antagonist is sometimes necessary. For example, religious practices that are morally reprehensible and deeply dehumanizing, such as the burning of widows (see Walls 2002, 24–25), infanticide, and slavery, should be, and have been, vigorously opposed. In cases such as these, the role of antagonist is one that fits well with

301

the prophetic models found in the Old Testament.

A potential weakness in taking on this role is that the missionary's opposition to another religion may turn into inappropriate attacks and unnecessary demeaning of its adherents. At times, those who are more outspoken in their antagonistic role deny or overlook good things that may be said about non-Christian religions. Sometimes, they do this because of their zealous desire to change people or because they fear that to admit any good is to compromise. Other times, they fear that they will lose their entire argument if they give any ground. Christians need not be defensive about the truth claims of the gospel. After all, the Bible does not present truth in a defensive way. It simply presents the story of Jesus.

Additionally, the missionary who takes on the apologist role should be willing to acknowledge that all religions have mixtures of good and bad, and that he or she will do well to avoid unnecessary offense in the proclamation of truth to non-Christians. A missionary can be uncompromising without being vindictive or mean-spirited. By focusing energy on positively living and teaching the truth rather than constantly attacking lies, missionaries will be more effective in encouraging people to change allegiances and follow Christ (see Sjogren 1993; 1996).

What Does It Mean to Take Other Religions Seriously?

Several attitudes are important if missionaries are to look at the religions of others seriously. Though they do need to take other religions seriously, they should not lose sight of the fact that God has made them ambassadors of Christ who are sent to call people to leave their religions, follow Christ, and worship him. Even as missionaries do this, however, cultivating and keeping the following attitudes as their orientation will help them in their role as ambassadors.

RESPECT

Good missionaries handle with care the religious beliefs of the people they serve. These beliefs are deeply held, and out of respect to those people missionaries should respect their religious beliefs. This is not the

> *Isn't it time that we missionaries part company with those who roll this word heathen under their tongues as a sweet morsel of contempt? Shall we Christians at home or in mission fields be courteous in preaching the gladdest tidings on earth, or not? . . . It is time that the followers of Jesus revise their language and learn to speak respectfully of non-Christian peoples.*
>
> Lottie Moon (Allen 1980, 201)

same as agreeing with the beliefs; it simply means that missionaries are careful not to demean or disrespect the people who follow them.

HUMILITY

Additionally, missionaries should cultivate and work to maintain a humble attitude. This does not mean that they pretend not to know Christ or to believe that he is the only way a person can enter a relationship with God. Rather, it means that they encounter those of other religions fully aware that they themselves have deep limitations as human beings and do not have all the answers.

Humility provides a type of reality check. Some get caught up in the trap of thinking that they have nothing to learn from adherents of other religions. Often, non-Christians indeed do have things to teach missionaries, especially about ways of living appropriately in the culture of the adherents.

The sad reality is that Christian history displays some deep flaws, which missionaries must acknowledge. For example, those who minister among Muslims must come to grips with the brutality of the Crusades (see chapter 7) and not try to cover over or deny that Christians have been abusive toward Muslims in the past.

SENSITIVITY

Missionaries rarely are sensitive enough about the religious commitment of others, and all too often they are oversensitive about their own. Sensitivity means not only understanding the worldview of others, but also connecting with their feelings and frustrations. Sensitivity does not mean that the missionary never says anything that would hurt or offend another. Truth does hurt sometimes. But it is radically different to hear truth lovingly offered than to experience it as a cudgel used to hammer people down. Sensitivity here means that missionaries do their best to avoid *unnecessary* offense by their words, attitudes, or actions.

ADVOCACY

In the early stages of your ministry it is appropriate that you refrain from advocacy until you know more clearly what the people actually believe. Knowing the general beliefs of a religion typically is not enough for you

---

SIDEBAR 18.2
TERMS USED FOR FOLK RELIGIONS

Robert Schreiter
(Adapted from Schreiter 1985, 124–25)

The following chart lists various terms that have been used to describe folk religions. The number of terms reminds us that the concept, while basic, is somewhat fluid. Some of them were coined to avoid pejorative connotations, while others simply were trying to better describe the phenomena involved. Generally, missionaries have used the term *folk religion* more often than any other.

Popular Religion: Not popular in the sense of what is fashionable, but in the sense of what is of the people.

Religion on the Ground: A more recent term coined to avoid some of the pejorative connotations associated with other terms.

Little Tradition: Used in relation to the "great" traditions that are the more orthodox, doctrinally based and priestly executed religions. Little traditions are local; great traditions are universal.

Folk Religion: Refers to religion "of the people," though with additional connotation of the lower strata of society as the particular "people." The romantic idea involves folk wisdom embodied in proverbs, stories, and myth. The political idea involves a romantic notion of purity untainted by modernity. It is oriented on the earthly, material needs of daily life (see Küng and Ching 1989, 47).

Common Religion: The more formal and doctrinal aspects of a religion generally are the domain of specialists. Common religion, on the other hand, is composed of the baseline of the average person's religious response to the daily needs of life.

303

to know what the local "on the ground" expressions of that religion are. Missionaries should take the time, not to mention the courtesy, to get to know the actual beliefs of those among whom they minister. You may formally study the religion of the people prior to your arrival, but do not assume that what you learned is what they actually believe and practice.

The role of advocate is one that you certainly will need to play as you call others to come to Christ. However, *how* you advocate is as important as *what* you advocate. The cross is already a stumbling block to adherents of non-Christian religions; don't add to that stumbling block a type of advocacy that demeans or denigrates people made in God's image and for whom Christ died. After all, your goal is not to defeat them, but to woo and win them for Christ.

RELIGIOUS CHALLENGES

The challenges offered by the major religions of the world are the biggest that the church will face in the future. Even just understanding non-Christian religions in all their complexity poses a difficult challenge to the missionary. In this section we will explore five of the most important religious issues faced by missionaries today: (1) folk religions, (2) syncretism, (3) salvation in non-Christian religions, (4) toleration of and cooperation with non-Christian religions, and (5) religious persecution.

Entire books have been written on each of these areas. We cannot trace all of the arguments and discussion here. Instead, we will try to provide a basic outline for each issue in the hope that you will be better prepared to face the challenges that they present.

Folk Religions

All religions incorporate formal belief systems maintained by religious leaders. This does not mean, however, that the practices of a religion's adherents are all the same. In fact, the practices of followers can vary widely from the practices of those who occupy centers of religious power. A wide variety of terms has been coined to distinguish the local expressions of religion found among the populace from the more formal religion practiced by the religious elite (see sidebar 18.2).

Folk religions are a mixture of local religious traditions ("little traditions") often intermingled with animistic beliefs on the pragmatic level (see Van Rheenen 1991; Blaschke 2001). They tend to be pragmatically oriented. The most important question for the average follower is not "Is it true?" but "Does it work?" A general comparison of formal and folk religion is offered in table 18.1 (Burnett 1988).

TABLE 18.1
CONTRASTING FORMAL AND FOLK RELIGION

Formal (High) Religion	Folk (Low) Religion
Answers cosmic questions: origin of universe, meaning of life	Answers everyday issues: sickness, drought, war
Written text with fixed system of beliefs	No written text; myths and rituals
Specialist leadership roles	Informal, no specialists
Central institutions: church, mosque, temple	Few institutions
Formal training	Apprenticeship type of training
Formalized moral teaching	Amoral system, pragmatic

The beliefs and associated practices of folk religion often are found at the social periphery rather than at the core. This is seen in Christianity, for example, where the practices and beliefs in local churches contrast with the beliefs and practices in denominational and educational centers.

Additionally, individuals often are orthodox on the surface but have belief systems and religious practices built on an animistic and folk religious core. Many missionaries have noted how Christians in other parts of the world adopt a veneer of Christianity overlaying an unchanged core system of beliefs that may or may not correspond to true biblical faith. There is perhaps no area where this more consistently appears than that of ancestral beliefs and practices, and missionaries will do well to work hard to understand the local ancestral beliefs to better understand how Christian faith is worked out by people "on the ground."

The beliefs and practices of folk religion are inherently syncretistic—a blending of the formal with the local. They also have endurance because they are more fluid and amenable to change as circumstances fluctuate in the lives of the adherents. Though changing with time (as local traditions change), the general orientations to life that they offer tend to persist even through major religious change. For example, many African Muslims practice ancestral veneration, as do many African Christians. Missionaries who overlook the thought and practices of folk religion often will be unaware that they continue even in the lives of church members. This is an area that no missionary can afford to ignore!

Syncretism

Another challenge brought by the non-Christian religions of the world is that of syncretism. Most simply defined, *syncretism* refers to the replacement of core or impor-

tant truths of the gospel with non-Christian elements (Moreau 2001c).

A quick look at the practices of Israel in the Old Testament shows how God views syncretism. God called Israel and set them apart from the rest of the nations because of the idolatrous practices found among the nations. Israel's responsibilities included avoiding syncretism; God even commanded Israel to destroy those nations because he knew that the Israelites would adopt their practices if they were allowed to survive, and this in spite of his commands to avoid them (Exod. 23:23–33; Deut. 18:10–14). Unfortunately, Israel did not obey God. Among other things, they engaged in shrine prostitution (1 Kings 14:24), intermarriage (Ezra 9:1–2), idolatry (Ps. 106:35–39), and witchcraft (2 Kings 17:16–17). The grim reality is best captured in 2 Kings 17:41: "Even while these people were worshiping the LORD, they were serving their idols."

The New Testament church tended to be more faithful. There are examples of syncretism by non-Christians (Acts 8:9–24; 14:8–20; 28:1–7) as well as Christians (Col. 2:13–19; Rev. 2:14), and there also are warnings to the church to be on guard against syncretistic practices and teachers (e.g., 1 Cor. 10:20; 2 Cor. 11:13–15; 1 Tim. 6:3).

Missionaries working among a people who have come to Christ from another religion inevitably will have to face syncretistic practices. One key to resolving issues of syncretism is for the missionary to ensure that the local church members have the resources necessary to make their own decisions rather than making the decisions for them. If the missionary focuses on developing the church to the stage where the decisions are made by the community of indigenous believers as they carefully explore the Scriptures, then the community will be able to serve as a self-correcting one long after the missionary is gone. On the other hand, the missionary who retains personal control over the power of decision-making fosters dependence in the local church. The church will be less equipped to make wise decisions once the missionary is gone (see Priest 1994).

Salvation in Non-Christian Religions

What is the eternal fate of those who faithfully follow their own religion and have never heard of Christ? Are they destined to spend eternity separated from God, as Christianity traditionally has taught? In an increasingly pluralistic and global world, that position is no longer seen as right. In fact, Christianity's claims to absolute truth

> *The whole character of the missionary's message is determined by his attitude toward the non-Christian religion that he has to wrestle with.*
> Johan Herman Bavinck (1948, 109)

now are challenged even in what were previously considered "Christian" cultures. How should the missionary respond?

Throughout the history of the church the Christian position on the salvation of people apart from Christ has been simple, clear, and consistent: Jesus is the only way to God (John 14:6), and there is no other name by which people can be saved apart from Jesus (Acts 4:12).

In more recent times questions have arisen: Is Jesus the only way to God? Are non-Christian religions completely false? Would God send those who never heard of Jesus to hell because they did not believe

in him? Furthermore, academic debates on God's openness have stirred strong feelings among evangelicals, with some maintaining that people who genuinely follow their own faith should not be seen as automatically condemned by God (see Pinnock 1994; Clendenin 1995).

Ultimately, Christians go to the Bible as their source for answers to these and related questions. However, they should do so not in the interests of finding theoretical answers, for their decisions may have an eternal impact. Therefore, they should tread cautiously before declaring a shift in the traditional Christian approach to non-Christian religions.

A reasonably clear biblical picture of non-Christian religions is painted in the Old and New Testaments. In the Old Testament God set Israel free from Egypt and commanded them to enter Canaan, conquering the peoples there because those people engaged in abominable practices (Lev. 18:24–25; 20:23). Christians dare not overlook the fact that Israel's possession of Canaan is at least in part a judgment against the religious practices of the people in the land.

Furthermore, Israel was a people in a covenant relationship with God, and that covenant was explicitly monotheistic, scripturally based, and exclusive (see Greenway 1999, 70–71). In the New Testament the statements about Jesus' uniqueness and exclusivity as the only way to God (John 3:36; 14:6; Acts 4:12; 1 Tim. 2:5; 1 John 5:12) (see Fernando 2001, 14) weigh heavily against a broadly inclusivistic approach to the religions.

Paul, in Rom. 1–3, also addresses issues of those who adhere to other religions. There he notes that people who have not heard of Christ are judged differently from those who have (Rom. 2:6–15). However,

CASE STUDY:
THE BUDDHA PEDESTALS

Lee-Lim Guek Eng
(Hiebert and Hiebert 1987, 220–22 [used with permission])

"I don't know what to make of them," Stephen said to himself as he thought about the statues of Buddha he had seen in the homes of the church elders. "Are they idols, or are they symbols of national loyalty? In either case, do they not undermine the local Christians' allegiance to Christ? And what should I do? Should I raise the issue in the annual meeting of the churches next week, or should I leave it up to the elders to decide on the matter? But do they as new believers really understand what is at stake here?"

Stephen Ling, an American-born Chinese, had come as a missionary to Nong Pai in northeastern Thailand to minister to the new Thai Christian community there. With a theological degree and training in evangelism and discipleship by a Christian organization in his background, he was excited about his new assignment. He had worked hard on learning the local language and culture and now felt at home in the administrative center where he lived.

The work had been started five years earlier by Jerry and Sue Lannin, American missionaries. It had grown to 550 believers in 49 congregations that met in local homes. Each church was composed of from two to twelve families and led by an "elder." Staff at the administrative center, located in Udon Thani, the capital city, coordinated the work of the existing churches and planned new evangelistic outreach. When the Lannins retired, they invited Stephen to take charge of their work. One of his chief tasks was to train the elders. Each week he visited a number of them in their village homes and helped them prepare for the services they would conduct in their homes the following Sunday.

Stephen's first visit was to the home of Seum, the young elder of Nong Pai, to help him study the apostle Paul's doctrine of grace. Seum ran a general store and lived in the quarters attached to the rear of the store. Worship services were held in his large living room. In the entry Seum had hung two rows of pictures. In the top row were photographs of the military graduation class of one of his family members; the queen of Thailand, the king, and the crown prince; a collective picture of the head monks of the Thai monastic order and Thai military officers; and a military recruiting poster. Under them hung magazine and calendar pinups of pretty Thai girls in bathing suits. On the far right of these was a statue of the Buddha. In later visits Stephen found that this was typical of most village homes, including those of Christians, for in the minds of the people in that part of Thailand there was a close tie between Thai nationalism, the royal family, the military, and Buddhism.

At first Stephen had hoped that the weekly Bible teaching would persuade the Christians to get rid of their Buddha pedestals. But most of them, including the elders, kept the pedestals as an act of patriotism and an expression of political loyalty to the king. Stephen realized that local history played an important part in their decisions. The northeastern part of Thailand had a long record of invasions and political and military instability, and the people wanted to affirm their allegiance to the government that had brought them peace and stability.

Now, four months later, Stephen was making his regular visit to Nong Pai to meet with Seum and several other elders. When Stephen asked them why they kept their Buddha pedestals, Seum pointed out that neither he nor his family performed rituals at the Buddha shrine in order to gain merit. Though he affirmed the biblical teaching that Jesus Christ eliminated the need for merit-making, he said, "I am a Thai and a loyal subject of our king. So I keep the Buddha pedestal to show my solidarity

(continued)

307

with my neighbors, my town, and my country." Wassana, a senior elder, defended Seum's position by appealing to Paul's doctrine of Christian liberty found in Galatians and his discussion of eating meat offered to idols in his letter to the Corinthians.

Back at the center, Stephen questioned the decision of the elders, and wondered whether such a decision should be left in their hands. They looked to him for biblical instruction, yet in this matter they seemed sure of themselves. The annual meeting of the churches would be held in a week. Could he as the missionary let the matter lie? If not, what should he do? He did not want the Christians to be accused of disloyalty to their country, but he knew that non-Christians would consider them Buddhists if they kept their Buddha pedestals. Moreover, in the long run it would open the door to syncretism. Finally, after considerable prayer and study of the Scripture, Stephen decided to …

his blanket condemnation of all people because they fail to live up to the light that they have (Rom. 1:18–32; 3:19–20) does not leave much "wiggle room" for those who teach that non-Christians who are sincere believers in their own religions can be saved (see Kane 1978b, 133–37). Roger Greenway, former missionary to Sri Lanka, summarizes Paul's main thrust:

> We see people everywhere desiring to know God and at the same time running away from God. This is the essence of all other religions. They substitute other gods for the only true and living God. The apostle Paul says that they know that God exists, but they do not worship him or give him thanks for all his blessings. They exchange the glory of the eternal God for images and worship them instead. (Greenway 1999, 73)

Toleration and Cooperation

Many Christian observers have noted that non-Christian religions offer good alternatives to the dehumanizing practices and ideologies of secular culture. When there is common ground that Christians share with non-Christians, is it possible for them to stand together? More broadly, what should our attitude be toward the non-Christian in relation to establishing just and civil societies? Are there areas in which missionaries can cooperate with people of non-Christian religions?

Through the history of the church Christians have believed that the alternative ways to God offered by non-Christian religions are ultimately false. This belief has been biblically founded in both the Old and New Testaments. Missionaries have a reputation, at least among North Americans, for being intolerant of people who follow other religions. In light of the biblical condemnation of non-Christian religions, what attitude should missionaries take toward people who follow different gods? An important word used in modern discussion is *tolerance*.

Certainly, *tolerance* is a term defined in context. When used in a largely Christian culture with minority religions, it will take on a different meaning than when used in a largely non-Christian (or anti-Christian) setting. In general, however, tolerating others means putting up with them in spite of disagreements. The missionary should ask whether or not Jesus' call to love our neighbors is fulfilled simply by tolerating them.

Scripturally, Christians are called not simply to tolerate, but to go further: they are commanded to love the followers of non-Christian religions. Jesus reminded his hearers that even the sinners love those who love them. His call to his followers is higher and harder. They are to love those who hate them, and this certainly applies to those who follow another religion and deny Christianity (Matt. 5:43–48; Luke 6:32–36).

Love in this case includes dialogue with non-Christians over important issues without coercive or threatening language or actions, performing acts of charity whenever appropriate, joining them in working for their benefit when they are oppressed, and demonstrating God's unconditional love for them in all circumstances. All missionaries should conform to this basic attitude; all should act out a love that invites people to come follow the Savior.

If a godly approach to non-Christian religions is one of toleration, how far does that toleration go? Can missionaries partner with Muslims in a campaign against pornography? Can they join forces with Native American religionists who cry out for respect for the environment? Can they cooperate with Buddhists who proclaim peace as the alternative to war?

Answers to these questions are complex, and they need to be taken on a case-by-case basis. Generally, however, the missionary should recognize that cooperating with others is less likely to harm the gospel message than is an intolerant attitude that communicates a posture of superiority. Joining non-Christians in civil causes can be an appropriate salt-and-light path for the missionary to take, and the benefits as well as the disadvantages should be weighed carefully in light of the growth of the kingdom of God in the decision-making process.

Religious Persecution

Finally, as missionaries seek to win people to Christ, adherents of other religions who are threatened by conversion will lash back. Religious persecution is on the rise, with little evidence that the trend will change anytime soon. What are the challenges of religious persecution, and how should the missionary respond?

Over the course of the past century few stories have held a greater range of implications for the missionary than that of persecution. Untold millions lost their lives simply because they happened to believe in Jesus. As we mentioned in chapter 4, it is estimated that more Christians were martyred from 1900 to 2000 (45.4 million) than all other centuries combined (24 million) (Barrett, Kurian, and Johnson 2001, 2:229). Although China probably holds more prisoners for Christ than does any other place (Nettleton 2002), persecution there results more from political ideology than from religious difference. Religious persecution,

> *Our greatest cause for rejoicing tomorrow will not be that we have been spared from trial and suffering but that Christ has been present to sanctify the trials to us and comfort us in them.*
>
> T. J. Bach (Watson 1965, 97)

on the other hand, is seen most frequently in contexts of Islam (Sudan, Indonesia, Pakistan, Saudi Arabia, Iran, Nigeria [see Shea 1997; Marshall 1997]), Hinduism (India and Nepal), and, to a lesser extent, Buddhism (Myanmar) and traditional oral religions (Africa, Oceania). Since the strongest persecution takes place within the 10/40 Window, missionaries may need to be ready to face even more persecution in the coming years.

CONCLUSION

The non-Christian religions of the world will provide the greatest challenge to the church for the foreseeable future. Missionaries must be equipped to face that challenge with charity and respect. They will need courage and insight from the Holy Spirit to face persecution and possibly even martyrdom. They will need wisdom to know when to cooperate and when to remain separate. They will need to know how to equip local churches to recognize and respond to syncretism. May God give them grace and staying power as they seek to proclaim his greatness and mercy and invite others to respond to his lordship over their lives.

The chapter's case study incorporates religion and culture, showing how difficult it can be to sort them out and what type of impact they can have on local churches and the missionaries who are trying to minister effectively among them.

19

Mission
and the Future

What will the immediate future bring for mission? Above all, it will bring an ongoing series of challenges. God's interest in mission ensures that it will not die out, but Satan's interest in mission ensures that it will have obstacles to overcome. There are at least four areas of challenge that tomorrow's missionaries probably will face: (1) theology, (2) geopolitics, (3) emerging models of the church, and (4) emerging models of mission.

THEOLOGICAL CHALLENGES

It seems almost certain that theological tensions will increase in the coming years. The larger cultural shift toward postmodernism and the ongoing relativization of truth even in the evangelical church will pose a challenge for the foreseeable future. In such a context missionaries may be tempted to give up, faced as they are with increasing resistance from peoples who not only do not want to hear the good news, but also even forcefully repel those who hope to bring it to them. Why bother, some will ask, to preach an outdated message that has lost relevance in the world?

Increasingly, the impact of postmodernism on theological thought will be felt, and not just in more ecumenical or liberal circles. Missionaries will be challenged to keep in perspective God's view of the world, and in sidebar 19.1 Jim Reapsome poignantly reminds all who would follow Jesus what that is.

GEOPOLITICAL CHALLENGES

As with theological challenges, it is almost certain that new ethical, and even globally threatening, issues will loom larger and larger in the near future. Biological warfare capabilities in the next half-century are expected to grow to the stage where a single maniac, with limited resources but technical know-how, bent on destruction, will be able to unleash a biological or even mechanical attack that can wipe out significant portions of the human population. Rogue governments not concerned with the consequences may very well launch nuclear attacks wreaking havoc across the globe. Hackers, whether on a personal vendetta or a government payroll, may escalate computer attacks to a level

SIDEBAR 19.1
MAKING LIFE OUR PRIORITY

Jim Reapsome
(Reapsome 1999, 40–42 [used with permission])

Every Monday night the guys who lived in the University Christian Union at the University of Washington in Seattle were summoned by our house parent, Charles (Chief) Peterson, to discuss our efforts in personal evangelism. Like a farmer collecting eggs, he expected us to produce. Chief always asked, "Any stories?" The peer pressure worked.

The UCU house was not a Christian ghetto, but a base from which we were to evangelize the university. Chief Peterson himself set the pace. (This was long before books about mentoring were written.) After we told our stories, Chief told his own, fresh from the front lines downtown where he worked.

In one, he had initiated a daily conversation with his regular parking lot attendant. It was short, simple, but enigmatic: "Have you got life?" The man was puzzled and usually talked about religion. Chief never argued or persuaded. He just tried to show the man that the issue was not religion, but life in Jesus Christ.

One morning, after a month of this, as Chief pulled into the lot the man dashed up to him, yelling, "I've got life! I've got life!" To me, this is much more than a story about how to witness to our faith.

Sure, we were all thrilled and rejoiced when Chief told us the outcome. But we learned that the essence of mission and evangelism is life.

Jesus said, "I am the way and the truth and the life. . . . I am the resurrection and the life. . . . I have come that they might have life, and have it to the full."

Yes, life is the main thing. It is what we are about, bringing life to people dead in their trespasses and sins. The gift of God is eternal life. Life is found in Jesus Christ and in no one else. If this sounds like the Old Fashioned Revival Hour, so be it. We need to know and act like the only thing on our mission agenda is life. A truly biblical mission agenda is not littered with a laundry list of good things Christians do. It's not strangled by a host of things charitable organizations do, worthy as they may be. Once we have choked life with machinery to run programs, we have missed what we are supposed to do.

Having spent hundreds of hours on mission agendas, I can tell you where much of our time, energy, and thought go. Not into producing life among the dead, but into mission business: personnel and support, property and taxes, relations with our partners overseas, and fund raising and recruiting at home. When will we wake up? The question is not, Where are we going to get money, recruits, buildings, and property? but, How many people are finding life in Jesus Christ? Does everybody in this mission organization know, believe, and act like life is the only issue?

What would we say at our international councils, field councils, and U.S. councils if we were asked for stories? What stories do our church-planting teams have? Our secretaries, pilots, radio technicians, nurses, teachers, linguists, accountants, well drillers, and relief workers? If we do not tell stories about people finding life in Christ, we ought to reconsider our purposes.

I once sailed across a fog-bound bay off the coast of Maine. We could see nothing, but the consistent clanging of the bells on the channel markers split the fog and kept us on course. The New Testament's channel marker is eternal life in Christ. That bell must crash around our ears and pierce the fog of irrelevance, or we will drift off into a sea of good-intentioned but meaningless mission business.

REFLECTION AND DISCUSSION

1. What is your main priority? How is this seen in the way you live?
2. What can you do to align (or maintain the alignment of) your priorities with God's priorities?

that makes them the most important battles being fought. Shutting down an economy or an important infrastructure may become the preferred method of attack, especially when conventional military options offer no hope of success. Even if there is no war—and human history indicates that the chances of that are bleak—environmental challenges will tax us to the best of our ability.

Missionaries may very well find themselves at the epicenter of devastation on a global scale unheard of in human history. Will they be prepared to minister in love in the midst of such tragedy? By God's grace they will, though the price may be higher than today's church can ever imagine.

CHALLENGES FROM EMERGING MODELS OF THE CHURCH

From the nonchurch movement in Japan to African Initiated Churches, from base ecclesial communities to Pentecostal churches in Latin America, and from the "New Apostolic Reformation" churches (Wagner 2000b) to Chinese house churches, new models of what it means to be church are springing up everywhere. These newer models pose significant challenges to the traditional denominational churches and even to the independent churches found in Western nations. They also pose new challenges and offer new opportunities for mission agencies.

These newer church models often are unfettered by preset agendas and presuppositions about mission. Their vibrant energy can be dangerously confined to an inward focus, or it can push out explosively beyond current mission frontiers. For good and for ill, they challenge the traditional models and methods, offering new ones and new ways of thinking about mission. They may very well be the fuel for the mission movements of the twenty-first century and beyond.

CHALLENGES FROM EMERGING MODELS OF MISSION

We anticipate an increasing tension between old and new models of mission over the next several decades. Mission agencies face daunting challenges in the future, not the least of which will be finding models to support missionaries financially that do not rely on the spare change of a wealthy American church. Both fairly and unfairly, churches are likely to become more critical of the agencies that represent the "old guard" and are viewed as staid and unchanging long after the time for meaningful reformation. Only the future will tell which agencies will make the adjustments necessary to ensure their vitality and which will succumb to the rising tides of change in culture and society. There is little doubt, however, that for those that do succumb, God will raise up new vehicles for his missionary agenda.

CONCLUSION

Thankfully, mission is God's priority, and it will remain so until Christ returns. The challenges that missionaries face may become increasingly daunting, but God transcends them all. It is our belief that God will provide the skills and gifts necessary through whatever ages and challenges come to reach the peoples of the world. That is God's agenda; may it increasingly become ours as well.

Reference List

Abbott, Walter M., ed. 1966. *The Documents of Vatican II*. Piscataway, N.J.: New Century.

Adeney, Bernard T. 1995. *Strange Virtues: Ethics in a Multicultural World*. Downers Grove, Ill.: InterVarsity.

Adeney, Miriam. 1987. "Esther across Cultures: Indigenous Leadership Roles for Women." *Missiology: An International Review* 15 (July): 323–27.

Adrian, Victor. 1967. "The Missionary Message of the Old Testament." In *The Church in Mission: A Sixtieth Anniversary Tribute to J. B. Toews*, ed. Abram J. Klassen, 17–32. Fresno, Calif.: Board of Christian Literature, Mennonite Brethren Church.

Allen, Catherine B. 1980. *The New Lottie Moon Story*. Nashville: Broadman.

———. 1994. "Charlotte (Lottie) Moon, 1840–1912." In *Mission Legacies: Biographical Studies of Leaders of the Modern Missionary Movement*, ed. Gerald H. Anderson et al., 205–15. Maryknoll, N.Y.: Orbis.

Allen, David. 1994. *The Unfailing Stream: A Charismatic Church History in Outline*. Tonbridge, England: Sovereign World.

Allen, Roland. [1912] 1962. *Missionary Methods: St. Paul's or Ours?* Reprint, Grand Rapids: Eerdmans.

———. [1913] 1964. *Missionary Principles*. Reprint, Grand Rapids: Eerdmans.

———. 1927. *The Spontaneous Expansion of the Church*. London: World Dominion Press.

Allender, Dan B., and Tremper Longman III. 1992. *Bold Love*. Colorado Springs, Colo.: NavPress.

Althen, Gary. 1988. *American Ways: A Guide for Foreigners in the United States*. Yarmouth, Maine: Intercultural.

Anderson, Allan H. 2001. *African Reformation: African Initiated Christianity in the 20th Century*. Trenton, N.J.: Africa World Press.

Anderson, Courtney. 1956. *To the Golden Shore: The Life of Adoniram Judson*. Boston: Little, Brown.

Anderson, Gerald H., ed. 1960. *The Theology of the Christian Mission*. New York: McGraw-Hill.

———. 1969. "Providence and Politics behind Protestant Missionary Beginnings in the Philippines." In *Studies in Philippine Church History*, ed. Gerald H. Anderson, 279–300. Ithaca, N.Y.: Cornell University Press.

Anderson, Neil. 1990a. *The Bondage Breaker*. Eugene, Oreg.: Harvest House.

———. 1990b. *Victory over the Darkness: Realizing the Power of Your Identity in Christ*. Ventura, Calif.: Regal.

Anderson, Neil, and Charles Mylander. 1994. *Setting Your Church Free*. Ventura, Calif.: Regal.

Anderson, Rufus. 1869. *Foreign Missions*. New York: Charles Scribner.

Arnold, Clinton. 1992. *Ephesians, Power and Magic: The Concept of Power in Ephesians in Light of Its Historical Setting*. Grand Rapids: Baker.

———. 1997. *Three Crucial Questions about Spiritual Warfare*. Grand Rapids: Baker.

Askew, Thomas A. 2000. "The New York 1900 Ecumenical Missionary Conference: A Centennial Reflection." *International Bulletin of Missionary Research* 24 (October): 146–54.

Athyal, Sakhi. 2000. *Evangelical Dictionary of World Missions,* ed. A. Scott Moreau, s.v. "Third World Women." Grand Rapids: Baker.

Augsburger, David W. 1992. *Conflict Mediation across Cultures.* Louisville: Westminster John Knox.

Augustine. 1972. *The City of God.* Trans. Henry Bettenson. Baltimore: Penguin.

Azariah, V. S. 1910. "The Problem of Co-operation Between Foreign and Native Workers." In World Missionary Conference, *Report of Commission I–VIII.* Vol. 9, *The History and Records of the Conference, Together with Addresses Delivered at the Evening Meetings,* 306–15. New York: Fleming H. Revell.

Bach, Thomas John, comp. 1951. *Pearls from Many Seas: Colorful Quotations for Message and Meditation.* Wheaton, Ill.: Van Kampen.

Barber, Benjamin R. 1992. "Jihad vs. McWorld." *The Atlantic Monthly Digital Edition.* Online: http://www.theatlantic.com/politics/foreign/barberf.htm [cited 1 July 2002].

Barber, William T. A. [1903?]. *Raymond Lull, the Illuminated Doctor: A Study in Mediaeval Missions.* London: Charles H. Kelly.

Barna, George. 1991a. *What Americans Believe: An Annual Survey of Values and Religious Views in the United States.* Ventura, Calif.: Regal.

———. 1991b. *Without a Vision, the People Perish.* Glendale, Calif.: Barna Research Group.

Barna, George, and Mark Hatch. 2001. *Boiling Point: It Only Takes One Degree.* Ventura, Calif.: Regal.

Barna, LaRay M. 1982. "Stumbling Blocks in Intercultural Communication." In *Intercultural Communication: A Reader,* 3d ed., ed. Richard E. Porter and Larry A. Samovar, 322–30. Belmont, Calif.: Wadsworth.

Barna Research Online. 2000a. "Americans' Bible Knowledge Is in the Ballpark, but Often Off Base." Online: http://www.barna.org/cgi-bin/PagePressRelease.asp?PressReleaseID=66&Reference=D [cited 1 July 2002].

———. 2000b. "The Year's Most Intriguing Findings, from Barna Research Studies." Online: http://www.barna.org/cgi-bin/PagePressRelease.asp?PressReleaseID=77&Reference=D [cited 1 July 2002].

Barrett, C. K. 1987. *The New Testament Background: Selected Documents.* San Francisco: Harper & Row.

Barrett, David B. 2001. "The Worldwide Holy Spirit Renewal." In *The Century of the Holy Spirit: 100 Years of Pentecostal and Charismatic Renewal, 1901–2001,* ed. Vinson Synan, 381–414. Nashville: Thomas Nelson.

———, ed. 1982. *World Christian Encyclopedia: A Comparative Study of Churches and Religions in the Modern World, AD 1900–2000.* Nairobi: Oxford University Press.

Barrett, David B., and Todd M. Johnson. 2001. *World Christian Trends AD 30–AD 2200: Interpreting the Annual Christian Megacensus.* Pasadena, Calif.: William Carey Library.

Barrett, David B., George T. Kurian, and Todd M. Johnson. 2001. *World Christian Encyclopedia: A Comparative Survey of Churches and Religions in the Modern World.* 2d. ed. 2 vols. Oxford: Oxford University Press.

Barry, Colman J., ed. 1985. *Readings in Church History.* Rev. ed. Westminster, Md.: Christian Classics.

Bartleman, Frank. 1980. *Azusa Street.* South Plainfield, N.J.: Bridge.

Basil the Great. 1968. "The Treatise de Spiritu Sancto." In *A Select Library of Nicene and Post-Nicene Fathers of the Christian Church.* 2d series. Vol. 8, *St. Basil: Letters and Select Works,* ed. Philip Schaff and Henry Wace, 1–50. Grand Rapids: Eerdmans.

Bavinck, Johan Herman. 1948. *The Impact of Christianity on the Non-Christian World.* Grand Rapids: Eerdmans.

Beach, Harlan P. 1906. *A Geography and Atlas of Protestant Missions.* Vol. 2, *Statistics and Atlas.* New York: Student Volunteer Movement for Foreign Missions.

Beach, Harlan P., and Charles H. Fahs, eds. 1925. *World Missionary Atlas.* New York: Institute of Social and Religious Research.

Beaver, R. Pierce. 1962. *Ecumenical Beginnings in Protestant World Mission: A History of Comity.* New York: Thomas Nelson & Sons.

———. 1968. "Missionary Motivation through Three Centuries." In *Reinterpretation in American Church History,* ed. Jerald C. Brauer, 113–51. Chicago: University of Chicago Press.

———. 1980. *American Protestant Women in World Mission: History of the First Feminist Movement in North America.* Grand Rapids: Eerdmans.

Beets, Henry. 1937. *Johanna of Nigeria: Life and Labors of Johana Veenstra, S.U.M.* Grand Rapids: Grand Rapids Printing Company.

Befus, David. 2001. *Getting with God's Program: Expatriates in International Ministry: A Critical Appraisal from a Missionary Kid/Mission Director.* Miami: Latin America Mission.

———. 2002. "Kingdom Business: A New Frontier in Missions." *Evangelical Missions Quarterly* 38 (April): 204–9.

Bell, Sandra, and Simon Coleman. 1999. "The Anthropology of Friendship: Enduring Themes and Future Possibilities." In *The Anthropology of Friendship,* ed. Sandra Bell and Simon Coleman, 1–19. New York: Berg.

Belliveau, Jeannette. 1996. *An Amateur's Guide to the Planet: Twelve Adventure Journeys and Lessons for the Contemporary United States.* Baltimore: Beau Monde.

Bernard, H. Russell. 1988. *Research Methods in Cultural Anthropology.* Beverly Hills, Calif.: Sage.

Beyerhaus, Peter. 1971. *Missions: Which Way? Humanization or Redemption.* Trans. Margaret Clarkson. Grand Rapids: Zondervan.

———. 1972. *Shaken Foundations: Theological Foundations for Mission.* Grand Rapids: Zondervan.

Beyreuther, Erich. 1955. *Bartholomaeus Ziegenbalg.* Madras: Christian Literature Society.

Blaschke, Robert C. 2001. *Quest for Power: Guidelines for Communicating the Gospel to Animists.* Belleville, Ont.: Guardian.

Bochner, Stephen, and Adrian Furnham. 1986. *Culture Shock: Psychological Reactions to Unfamiliar Environments.* New York: Routledge.

Bolt, Peter, and Mark Thompson, eds. 2000. *The Gospel to the Nations: Perspectives on Paul's Mission.* Downers Grove, Ill.: InterVarsity.

Bonk, Jonathan J. 1991. *Missions and Money: Affluence as a Western Missionary Problem.* Maryknoll, N.Y.: Orbis.

Borthwick, Paul. 1987. *A Mind for Missions: 10 Ways to Build Your World Vision.* Colorado Springs, Colo.: NavPress.

———. 1991. *How to Be a World Class Christian.* Wheaton, Ill.: Victor.

———. 1996. *Six Dangerous Questions to Transform Your View of the World.* Downers Grove, Ill.: InterVarsity.

Bosch, David J. 1980. *Witness to the World: The Christian Mission in Theological Perspective.* Atlanta: John Knox.

———. 1983. "The Structure of Mission: An Exposition of Matthew 28:16–20." In *Exploring Church Growth,* ed. Wilbur Shenk, 218–48. Grand Rapids: Eerdmans.

———. 1991. *Transforming Mission: Paradigm Shifts in Theology of Mission.* Maryknoll, N.Y.: Orbis.

Bowers, W. Paul. 1993. *Dictionary of Paul and His Letters,* ed. Gerald F. Hawthorne and Ralph P. Martin, s.v. "Mission." Downers Grove, Ill.: InterVarsity.

Boxer, C. R. 1969. *The Golden Age of Brazil, 1695–1750: Growing Pains of a Colonial Society.* Berkeley: University of California Press.

———. 1978. *The Church Militant and Iberian Expansion, 1440–1770.* Baltimore: Johns Hopkins University Press.

Boyd, Robert T. 1995. *Paul, the Apostle: The Illustrated Handbook of His Life and Travels.* N.p.: World Publishing.

Brewster, Tom, and Betty Brewster. 1986. *Community Is My Language Classroom!* Pasadena, Calif.: Lingua House Ministries.

Brockelmann, Carl, Moshe Perlmann, and Joel Carmichael. 1973. *History of the Islamic Peoples.* Rev. ed. New York: Capricorn.

Brockman, James R. 1989. *Romero: A Life.* Maryknoll, N.Y.: Orbis.

Brown, Alistair. 1997. *I Believe in Mission.* London: Hodder & Stoughton.

Brown, Dale. 1978. *Understanding Pietism.* Grand Rapids: Eerdmans.

Bruce, Alexander Balmain. 1971. *The Training of the Twelve.* Grand Rapids: Kregel.

Bruce, F. F. 1977. *Paul: Apostle of the Heart Set Free.* Grand Rapids: Zondervan.

———. 1988. *The Book of Acts.* Rev. ed. Grand Rapids: Eerdmans.

Bruce, Jack W., Jr. 2000. "Four Years in 45 Minutes." *Evangelical Missions Quarterly* 36 (January): 86–91.

Bryant, David. 1997. *Stand in the Gap: How to Get Ready for the Coming World Revival.* Rev. ed. Ventura, Calif.: Regal.

Buckland, Barbara. 1998. *History of Mission.* Boroko, NCD, Papua New Guinea: Bethel.

Budge, E. A. Wallis. 1928. *The Book of the Saints of the Ethiopian Church: A Translation of the Ethiopic Synaxarium Made from the Manuscripts Oriental 660 and 661 in the British Museum.* Cambridge: Cambridge University Press.

Burgess, Stanley M. 1989. *The Holy Spirit: Eastern Christian Traditions.* Peabody, Mass.: Hendrickson.

———. 1993. "Proclaiming the Gospel with Miraculous Gifts in the Postbiblical Early Church." In *The Kingdom and the Power*, ed. Gary S. Greig and Kevin N. Springer, 277–88. Ventura, Calif.: Regal.

Burnett, David. 1988. *Unearthly Powers: A Christian Perspective on Primal and Folk Religions.* Eastbourne, England: MARC.

———. 2000. *World of the Spirits.* London: Monarch.

Bush, L. Russ, ed. 1983. *Classical Readings in Christian Apologetics, A.D. 100–1800.* Grand Rapids: Zondervan.

Caldwell, Larry W. 1994. *Missions and You!* Manila: OMF.

Cameron, Nigel. 1970. *Barbarians and Mandarins: Thirteen Centuries of Western Travelers in China.* Chicago: University of Chicago Press.

Cardoza-Orlandi, F. 2002. *Mission: An Essential Guide.* Nashville: Abingdon.

Carey, S. Pearce. 1923. *William Carey, D.D., Fellow of Linnaean Society.* New York: George H. Doran.

Carson, Donald A. 1984. "Matthew." In *The Expositor's Bible Commentary*, ed. Frank E. Gaebelein, 8:3–599. Grand Rapids: Zondervan.

———. 2000. "Paul's Mission and Prayer." In *The Gospel to the Nations: Perspectives on Paul's Mission*, ed. Peter Bolt and Mark Thompson, 175–84. Downers Grove, Ill.: InterVarsity.

Chang, Hui-Ching, and G. Richart Holt. 1991. "The Concept of *Yuan* and Chinese Interpersonal Relationships." In *Cross-Cultural Interpersonal Communication*, ed. Stella Ting-Toomey and Felipe Korzenny, 28–57. Newbury Park, Calif.: Sage.

Chen, Guo-Ming, and William J. Starosta. 1998. *Foundations of Intercultural Communication.* Boston: Allyn & Bacon.

Chikane, Frank. 1988. *No Life of My Own: An Autobiography.* Maryknoll, N.Y.: Orbis.

Chinese Culture Connection. 1987. "Chinese Values and the Search for Culture-Free Dimensions of Culture." *Journal of Cross-Cultural Psychology* 18:2: 143–64.

Cho, Yong Joong, and David Greenlee. 1995. "Avoiding Pitfalls on Multinational Frontier Teams." *International Journal of Frontier Missions* 12 (October–December): 179–83.

Christenson, Larry, ed. 1987. *Welcome, Holy Spirit: A Study of Charismatic Renewal in the Church.* Minneapolis: Augsburg.

Chua, Elizabeth G., and William B. Gudykunst. 1987. "Conflict Resolution Styles in Low and High Context Cultures." *Communication Research Reports* 4 (June): 32–37.

Clendenin, Daniel B. 1995. *Many Gods, Many Lords: Christianity Encounters World Religions.* Grand Rapids: Baker.

Coggins, Wade T. 1984. "Evangelical Foreign Missions Association: A Brief History." Special Collections, Flower Pentecostal Heritage Center, Springfield, Missouri.

Conn, Harvie M. 1984. *Eternal Word and Changing Worlds: Theology, Anthropology, and Mission in Trialogue.* Phillipsburg, N.J.: P&R.

Considine, John J. 1925. *The Vatican Mission Exhibition: A Window on the World.* New York: Macmillan.

Cook, Harold. 1954. *An Introduction to Christian Missions.* Chicago: Moody.

Coote, Robert T. 2000. "'AD 2000' and the '10/40 Window': A Preliminary Assessment." *International Bulletin of Missionary Research* 24 (October): 160–66.

Corwin, Gary R. 1994a. "Training for the Frontiers: Who Does What?" *International Journal of Frontier Missions* 11 (January): 45–50.

———. 1994b. "The Church's Primary Role in Training for the Frontiers." *International Journal of Frontier Missions* 11 (July–August): 170.

———. 1997. "Women in Missions." *Evangelical Missions Quarterly* 33 (October): 400–401.

———. 1998. "Leadership as Pain-bearing." *Evangelical Missions Quarterly* 34 (January): 16–17.

———. 2000a. *Evangelical Dictionary of World Missions*, ed. A. Scott Moreau, s.v. "Burnout." Grand Rapids: Baker.

———. 2000b. "The Message of Short-Term Missions." *Evangelical Missions Quarterly* 36 (October): 422–23.

———. 2001. "Focus on the Missionary Family." *Evangelical Missions Quarterly* 37 (October): 418–19.

———. 2002. "The Root of All Kinds of Confusion." *Evangelical Missions Quarterly* 38 (January): 8–9.

Costas, Orlando E. 1982. *Christ Outside the Gate: Mission Beyond Christendom*. Maryknoll, N.Y.: Orbis.

Covell, Ralph R. 1986. *Confucius, the Buddha, and Christ: A History of the Gospel in Chinese*. Maryknoll, N.Y.: Orbis.

Cranfield, C. E. B. 1985. *Romans: A Shorter Commentary*. Grand Rapids: Eerdmans.

Crosby, Alfred W., Jr. 1972. *The Columbian Exchange: Biological and Cultural Consequences of 1492*. Westport, Conn.: Greenwood.

Culbertson, Howard. 2001. "Ten Commandments for Mission Trip Participants" Online: http://www.shorttermmissions.com/articles/ar005_int.html [cited 22 March 2002].

Cull, Paul. n.d. "Ten Commandments for Short Term Missions." Online: http://ourworld.compuserve.com/homepages/pcull [cited 21 February 2002].

Culver, Robert Duncan. 1984. *A Greater Commission: Theology for World Missions*. Chicago: Moody.

Cunningham, Mary B. 1999. "The Orthodox Church in Byzantium." In *A World History of Christianity*, ed. Adrian Hastings, 66–109. Grand Rapids: Eerdmans.

Curtis, Brent, and John Elderidge. 1997. *The Sacred Romance: Drawing Closer to the Heart of God*. Nashville: Thomas Nelson.

Danker, William J. 1971. *Profit for the Lord: Economic Activities in Moravian Missions and the Basel Mission Trading Company*. Grand Rapids: Eerdmans.

Davis, Leo Donald. 1987. *The First Seven Ecumenical Councils (325–787): Their History and Theology*. Wilmington, Del.: Michael Glazier.

Dayton, Donald W. 1987. *Theological Roots of Pentecostalism*. Peabody, Mass.: Hendrickson.

Deane, David J. n.d. *Robert Moffat of Kuruman*. Edinburgh: Pickering & Inglis.

Deere, Jack. 1993. *Surprised by the Power of the Spirit: Discovering How God Speaks and Heals Today*. Grand Rapids: Zondervan.

de Vaulx, Bernard. 1961. *History of the Missions*. Trans. Reginald Trevett. New York: Hawthorn.

Dick, Lois Hoadley. 1987. *Isobel Kuhn*. Minneapolis: Bethany House.

Dickason, C. Fred. 1987. *Demon Possession and the Christian*. Chicago: Moody.

Dickerson, Lonna. n.d.(a). "Planning for Success in Language Learning." Online: http://www.wheaton.edu/bgc/icct/pubs/planning1.pdf [cited 22 March 2002].

———. n.d.(b). "Getting a Jump Start on Language Learning before Leaving Home." Online: http://www.wheaton.edu/bgc/icct/slares/jumpstart.htm [cited 22 March 2002].

Dinges, Norman. 1983. "Intercultural Competence." In *Handbook of Intercultural Training*. Vol. 1, *Issues in Theory and Design*, ed. Dan Landis and Richard W. Brislin, 176–202. New York: Pergamon.

Dobbie, Robert. 1962. "The Biblical Foundation of the Mission of the Church." *International Review of Missions* 51: 196–205.

Dodd, Carley H. 1991. *Dynamics of Intercultural Communication*. 3d ed. Dubuque, Iowa: Wm. C. Brown.

Dollar, George W. 1973. *A History of Fundamentalism in America*. Greenville, S.C.: Bob Jones University Press.

Dollar, Harold. 1996. *St. Luke's Missiology: A Cross-Cultural Challenge*. Pasadena, Calif.: William Carey Library.

Douglas, Trevor. 1988. "Wanted! More Single Men." *Evangelical Missions Quarterly* 24 (January): 62–66.

Dries, Angelyn. 1998. *The Missionary Movement in American Catholic History*. Maryknoll, N.Y.: Orbis.

Dsilva, Margaret U., and Lisa O. Whyte. 1998. "Cultural Differences in Conflict Styles: Vietnamese Refugees and Established Residents." *Howard Journal of Communications* 9 (Jan–Mar): 57–68.

DuBose, Francis M., ed. 1979. *Classics of Christian Missions*. Nashville: Broadman.

Duffy, Joseph, ed. 1985. *Patrick in His Own Words*. Dublin: Veritas Publications.

Duin, Julia. 1994. "India's 'Billy Graham' Is Catholic." *Charisma & Christian Life* (November): 86, 88–89.

Dulles, Avery. 1995. "John Paul II and the New Evangelization—What Does It Mean?" In *John Paul II and the New Evangelization*, ed. Ralph Martin and Peter Williamson, 25–39. San Francisco: Ignatius.

Dunn, Edmond. J. 1980. *Missionary Theology: Foundations in Development*. Lanham, Md.: University Press of America.

Dussell, Enrique. 1976. *History and the Theology of Liberation: A Latin American Perspective*. Maryknoll, N.Y.: Orbis.

———, ed. 1992. *The Church in Latin America, 1492–1992*. Maryknoll, N.Y.: Orbis.

Dyer, Helen S. 1923. *Pandita Ramabai: Her Vision, Her Mission and Triumph of Faith*. Glasgow: Pickering & Inglis.

Dyrness, William A. 1983. *Let the Earth Rejoice! A Biblical Theology of Holistic Mission*. Westchester, Ill.: Crossway.

Edwards, David L. 1980. *Christian England: Its Story to the Reformation*. Grand Rapids: Eerdmans.

Ehrenström, Nils. 1967. "Movements for International Friendship and Life and Work, 1925–1948." In *A History of the Ecumenical Movement, 1517–1948*, 2d ed., ed. Ruth Rouse and Stephen Charles Neill, 545–96. Philadelphia: Westminster.

Elgstrom, Ole. 1994. "National Culture and International Negotiations." *Cooperation and Conflict* 29 (September): 289–301.

Elliot, Elisabeth. 1957. *Through Gates of Splendor*. New York: Harper.

———. 1958. *Shadow of the Almighty: The Life and Testament of Jim Elliot*. New York: Harper & Row.

Elmer, Duane. 1993. *Cross-Cultural Conflict: Building Relationships for Effective Ministry*. Downers Grove, Ill.: InterVarsity.

Engel, James F., and William A. Dyrness. 2000. *Changing the Mind of Missions: Where Have We Gone Wrong?* Downers Grove, Ill.: InterVarsity.

England, John C. 1996. *The Hidden History of Christianity in Asia: The Churches of the East before the Year 1500*. Delhi: Indian Society for Promoting Christian Knowledge.

English, David. 2002. "Today's Global Job Market: Nature of the International Job Market." Online: http://www.globalopps.org/downloads/Todays Global Job Market.txt [cited 5 November 2002].

Erdmann, Martin. 1998. "Mission in John's Gospel and Letters." In *Mission in the New Testament: An Evangelical Approach*, ed. William J. Larkin and Joel F. Williams, 207–26. Maryknoll, N.Y.: Orbis.

Erickson, Millard J. 1985. *Christian Theology*. Grand Rapids: Baker.

———. 1991. "The State of the Question." In *Through No Fault of Their Own? The Fate of Those Who Have Never Heard*, ed. William V. Crockett and James G. Sigountos, 23–33. Grand Rapids: Baker.

———. 1998. *A Basic Guide to Eschatology: Making Sense of the Millennium*. Grand Rapids: Baker.

Estep, William R. 1975. *The Anabaptist Story*. 2d ed. Grand Rapids: Eerdmans.

Eusebius Pamphilus. 1955. *The Ecclesiastical History of Eusebius Pamphilus*. Trans. Christian Frederick Cruse. Grand Rapids: Baker.

Evennett, H. Outram. 1970. *The Spirit of the Counter-Reformation*. Notre Dame, Ind.: University of Notre Dame Press.

Fee, Gordon D. 1987. *The First Epistle to the Corinthians*. Grand Rapids: Eerdmans.

Fernando, Ajith. 1995. *The Supremacy of Christ*. Wheaton, Ill.: Crossway.

———. 2001. *Sharing the Truth in Love: How to Relate to People of Other Faiths*. Grand Rapids: Discovery House.

Ferris, Robert W., ed. 1995. *Establishing Ministry Training: A Manual for Programme Developers*. Pasadena, Calif.: William Carey Library.

Fiedler, Klaus. 1994. *The Story of Faith Missions: From Hudson Taylor to Present-Day Africa*. Irvine, Calif.: Regnum.

Filbeck, David. 1985. *Social Context and Proclamation: A Socio-Cognitive Study in Proclaiming the Gospel Cross-Culturally*. South Pasadena, Calif.: William Carey Library.

———. 1994. *Yes, God of the Gentiles Too: The Missionary Message of the Old Testament*. Wheaton, Ill.: Billy Graham Center.

Ford, J. Massyngberde. 1988. "The Social and Political Implications of the Miraculous in Acts." In *Faces of Renewal*, ed. Paul Elbert, 137–60. Peabody, Mass.: Hendrickson.

Fortescue, Adrian. 1913. *The Lesser Eastern Churches*. London: Catholic Truth Society.

Foyle, Marjory. 1985. "Overcoming Stress in Singleness." *Evangelical Missions Quarterly* 21 (April): 134–42.

———. 1987. *Overcoming Missionary Stress*. Wheaton, Ill.: EMIS.

———. 2001. *Honourably Wounded: Stress among Christian Workers*. 2d ed. London: Monarch.

Fraser, James O. 1958. *The Prayer of Faith*. Kent, England: Overseas Missionary Fellowship.

Frizen, Edwin L., Jr. 1992. *75 Years of IFMA, 1917–1992: The Nondenominational Missions Movement*. Pasadena, Calif.: William Carey Library.

Fuller, Harold. 1996. *People of the Mandate: The Story of the World Evangelical Fellowship*. Grand Rapids: Baker.

Gairdner, W. H. T. 1910. *Echoes from Edinburgh, 1910*. New York: Fleming H. Revell.

Ganaka, Gabriel Gonsum. 1995. "Evangelization in the Church of Jos, Nigeria." In *John Paul II and the New Evangelization*, ed. Ralph Martin and Peter Williamson, 101–10. San Francisco: Ignatius.

Gannett, Alden A. 1960. "The Missionary Call: What Saith the Scriptures?" *Bibliotheca Sacra* 117 (January–March): 32–39.

Garrett, Bob. 1998. "The Gospels and Acts: Jesus the Missionary and His Missionary Followers." In *Missiology: An Introduction to the Foundations, History, and Strategies of World Missions*, ed. John Mark Terry, Ebbie Smith, and Justice Anderson, 63–82. Nashville: Broadman & Holman.

Garrett, Paul D. 1979. *St. Innocent: Apostle to America*. Crestwood, N.Y.: St. Vladimir's Seminary Press.

Garrison, V. David. 1990. *The Non-Residential Missionary: A New Strategy and the People It Serves*. Monrovia, Calif.: MARC.

Geanakoplos, Deno John, ed. 1984. *Byzantium: Church, Society, and Civilization Seen through Contemporary Eyes*. Chicago: University of Chicago Press.

Gehman, Richard J. 1999. *Who Are the Living Dead? A Theology of Death, Life after Death, and the Living Dead*. Nairobi: Evangel.

George, Timothy. 1989. "The Challenge of Evangelism in the History of the Church." In *Evangelism in the Twenty-First Century*, ed. Thom S. Rainer, 9–20. Wheaton, Ill.: Harold Shaw.

Gibson, Tim, et al. 1992. *Stepping Out: A Guide to Short Term Missions*. Seattle: YWAM.

Gill, Sam D. 1982. *Beyond "The Primitive": The Religions of Non-Literate Peoples*. Englewood Cliffs, N.J.: Prentice-Hall.

Gilliland, Dean S. 1983. *Pauline Theology and Mission Practice*. Grand Rapids: Baker.

Gilmour, James. 1895. *James Gilmour of Mongolia: His Diaries, Letters and Reports*. Ed. Richard Lovett. London: Religious Tract Society.

Glasser, Arthur F., and Donald A. McGavran. 1983. *Contemporary Theologies of Mission*. Grand Rapids: Baker.

Glenny, W. Edward, and William H. Smallman, eds. 2000. *Missions in a New Millennium: Change and Challenges in World Missions*. Grand Rapids: Kregel.

Gnanakan, Ken. 1989. *Kingdom Concerns: A Biblical Exploration Towards a Theology of Mission*. Bangalore: Theological Book Trust.

Goff, James R., Jr. 1988. *Fields White unto Harvest: Charles F. Parham and the Missionary Origins of Pentecostalism*. Fayetteville: University of Arkansas Press.

Gollwitzer, Heinz. 1969. *Europe in the Age of Imperialism, 1880–1914*. New York: W. W. Norton.

Gooding, David W. 1987. *According to Luke: A New Exposition of the Third Gospel*. Grand Rapids: Eerdmans.

Goodpasture, H. McKennie, ed. 1989. *Cross and Sword: An Eyewitness History of Christianity in Latin America*. Maryknoll, N.Y.: Orbis.

Graham, Franklin, with Jeannette Lockerbie. 1983. *Bob Pierce: This One Thing I Do*. Waco, Tex.: Word.

Gray, John. 1992. *Men Are from Mars, Women Are from Venus: A Practical Guide for Improving Communication and Getting What You Want in Your Relationships*. New York: HarperCollins.

Green, Joel B. 1994. "Good News to Whom? Jesus and the Poor in the Gospel of Luke." In *Jesus of Nazareth: Lord and Christ: Essays on the Historical Jesus and New Testament Christology*, ed. Joel B. Green and Max Turner, 59–74. Grand Rapids: Eerdmans.

Green, Michael. 1970. *Evangelism in the Early Church*. Grand Rapids: Eerdmans.

Greenfield, John. 1928. *Power from On High: The Story of the Great Moravian Revival of 1727*. Bethlehem, Pa.: Moravian Church in America.

Greenway, Roger S. 1999. *Go and Make Disciples! An Introduction to Christian Missions*. Phillipsburg, N.J.: P&R.

Gregory, Bishop of Tours. 1969. *History of the Franks*. Trans. Ernest Brehaut. New York: W. W. Norton.

Gregory the Great. 1969. "The Book of Pastoral Rule and Selected Epistles of Gregory the Great, Bishop of Rome." In *Nicene and Post-Nicene Fathers*. Vol. 12, *Leo the Great, Gregory the Great*, ed. Philip Schaff and Henry Wace, 1–243. Grand Rapids: Eerdmans.

Griffiths, Michael. 1981. *Get Your Church Involved in Missions: Some Suggestions for Ministers and Congregations Disenchanted with the Traditional Muddle*. Robesonia, Pa.: OMF.

Grisanti, Michael A. 2000. "The Missing Mandate: Missions in the Old Testament." In *Missions in a New Millennium: Change and Challenges in World Missions*, ed. W. Edward Glenny and William H. Smallman, 43–68. Grand Rapids: Kregel.

Grubb, Norman P. 1933. *C. T. Studd: Cricketer and Pioneer.* London: Religious Tract Society.

———. 1945. *Christ in Congo Forests: The Story of the Heart of Africa Mission.* London: Lutterworth.

Grudem, Wayne A. 1988. *The Gift of Prophecy in the New Testament and Today.* Westchester, Ill.: Crossway.

Grundmann, Christoffer. 1990. "Proclaiming the Gospel by Healing the Sick? Historical and Theological Annotations on Medical Mission." *International Bulletin of Missionary Research* 14 (July): 120–26.

Gudykunst, William B., and Tsukasa Nishida. 1986. "Attributional Confidence in Low- and High-Context Cultures." *Human Communication Research* 12 (June): 525–49.

Gudykunst, William B., and Young Yun Kim. 1992. *Communicating with Strangers: An Approach to Intercultural Communication.* 2d ed. New York: McGraw-Hill.

Gudykunst, William B., et al. 1996. "The Influence of Cultural Individualism-Collectivism, Self Construals, and Individual Values on Communication Styles across Cultures." *Human Communication Research* 22 (June): 510–43.

Guthrie, Stan. 2000. *Missions in the Third Millennium: 21 Key Trends for the 21st Century.* Carlisle: Paternoster.

Gutiérrez, Gustavo. 1973. *A Theology of Liberation: History, Politics and Salvation.* Maryknoll, N.Y.: Orbis.

Hafemann, Scott. 2000. "'Because of Weakness' (Galatians 4:13): The Role of Suffering in the Mission of Paul." In *The Gospel to the Nations: Perspectives on Paul's Mission*, ed. Peter Bolt and Mark Thompson, 131–46. Downers Grove, Ill.: InterVarsity.

Hahn, Ferdinand. 1965. *Mission in the New Testament.* London: SCM.

Hale, Frederick. 1993. "Insights from Norwegian 'Revivalism,' 1875–1914." In *Modern Christian Revivals*, ed. Edith L. Blumhofer and Randall Balmer, 101–17. Urbana: University of Illinois Press.

Hale, Thomas. 1986. *Don't Let the Goats Eat the Loquat Trees: Adventures of an American Surgeon in Nepal.* Grand Rapids: Zondervan.

———. 1989. *On the Far Side of Liglig Mountain: Adventures of an American Family in Nepal.* Grand Rapids: Zondervan.

———. 1993. *Living Stones of the Himalayas: Adventures of an American Couple in Nepal.* Grand Rapids: Zondervan.

———. 1995. *On Being a Missionary.* Pasadena, Calif.: William Carey Library.

Hall, Edward T. 1960. *The Hidden Dimension.* Garden City, N.Y.: Anchor.

———. 1973. *The Silent Language.* Garden City, N.Y.: Anchor.

———. 1981. *Beyond Culture.* Garden City, N.Y.: Anchor.

———. 1990. *Understanding Cultural Differences: Germans, French, and Americans.* Yarmouth, Maine: Intercultural.

———. 1991a. *The Dance of Life.* New York: Doubleday.

———. 1991b. "Monochronic and Polychronic Time." In *Intercultural Communication: A Reader*, 6th ed., ed. Larry A. Samovar and Richard E. Porter, 334–39. Belmont, Calif.: Wadsworth.

Hampton, Vinita, and Carol Plueddemann, eds. 1991. *World Shapers: A Treasury of Quotes from Great Missionaries.* Wheaton, Ill.: Harold Shaw.

Hansel, Tim. 1985. *You Gotta Keep on Dancing.* Elgin, Ill.: David C. Cook.

Hardesty, Nancy A., and Adrienne Israel. 1993. "Amanda Berry Smith: A 'Downright, Outright Christian.'" In *Spirituality and Social Responsibility: Vocational Vision of Women in The United Methodist Tradition*, ed. Rosemary Skinner Keller, 61–79. Nashville: Abingdon.

Harrison, Eugene Myers. 1967. *Missionary Crusaders for Christ.* Glendale, Calif.: Church Press.

Harvey, John D. 1998a. "Mission in Jesus' Teaching." In *Mission in the New Testament: An Evangelical Approach*, ed. William J. Larkin and Joel F. Williams, 30–49. Maryknoll, N.Y.: Orbis.

———. 1998b. "Mission in Matthew." In *Mission in the New Testament: An Evangelical Approach*, ed. William J. Larkin and Joel F. Williams, 119–36. Maryknoll, N.Y.: Orbis.

Hastings, Adrian. 1999. "150–550." In *A World History of Christianity*, ed. Adrian Hastings, 25–65. Grand Rapids: Eerdmans.

Hawthorne, Gerald F., and Ralph P. Martin, eds. 1993. *Dictionary of Paul and His Letters.* Downers Grove, Ill.: InterVarsity.

Hedlund, Roger E. 1985. *Mission to Man in the Bible.* Madras: Evangelical Literature Service.

Hefley, James, and Marti Hefley. 1981. *Unstilled Voices.* Chappaqua, N.Y.: Christian Herald.

Henry, Rodney. 1986. *Filipino Spirit World.* Manila: OMF.

Her, Mee. 1990. "Friends in Beds." In *Passages: An Anthology of the Southeast Asian Refugee Experience,* comp. Katsuyo K. Howard, 185–190. Fresno: Southeast Asian Student Services, California State University.

Heroes of the Cross. Vol. 2, *Pandita Ramabai, Mary Slessor, Rasalama and Heroes in Madagascar.* 1933. London: Marshall, Morgan & Scott.

Hesselgrave, David. 1973. "Identification—Key to Effective Communication." *Evangelical Missions Quarterly* 9 (summer): 216–22.

———. 1978. *Communicating Christ Cross-Culturally.* Grand Rapids: Zondervan.

———. 1987. "Fitting Third-World Believers with Christian Worldview Glasses." *Journal of the Evangelical Theological Society* 30: 215–22.

Hesselgrave, David J., and Edward Rommen. 1989. *Contextualization: Meanings, Methods, and Models.* Grand Rapids: Baker.

Hicks, Bryant. 1998. "Old Testament Foundations for Missions." In *Missiology: An Introduction to the Foundations, History, and Strategies of World Missions,* ed. John Mark Terry, Ebbie Smith, and Justice Anderson, 51–62. Nashville: Broadman & Holman.

Hicks, Scott. 2001. "Let's Be Honest about Missionary Marriages." *Evangelical Missions Quarterly* 37 (October): 420–21.

Hiebert, Paul. 1985. *Anthropological Insights for Missionaries.* Grand Rapids: Baker.

———. 1994. *Anthropological Reflections on Missiological Issues.* Grand Rapids: Baker.

Hiebert, Paul, and Frances Hiebert, eds. 1987. *Case Studies in Missions.* Grand Rapids: Baker.

Hiebert, Paul, and Eloise Hiebert Meneses. 1995. *Incarnational Ministry: Planting Churches in Band, Tribal, Peasant, and Urban Societies.* Grand Rapids: Baker.

Hiebert, Paul, Daniel Shaw, and Tite Tienou. 1999. *Understanding Folk Religions.* Grand Rapids: Baker.

Hill, Harriet. 1993. "Lifting the Fog on Incarnational Ministry." *Evangelical Missions Quarterly* 29 (July): 262–69.

Hitt, Russell T. 1959. *Jungle Pilot: The Life and Witness of Nate Saint.* New York: Harper & Brothers.

Hochschild, Adam. 1998. *King Leopold's Ghost: A Story of Greed, Terror, and Heroism in Colonial Africa.* New York: Houghton Mifflin.

Hocken, Peter D. 2002. *New International Dictionary of Pentecostal and Charismatic Movements,* ed. Stanley M. Burgess, s.v. "Charismatic Movement." Grand Rapids: Zondervan.

Hocking, William Ernest. 1932. *Re-Thinking Missions: A Laymen's Inquiry after One Hundred Years.* New York: Harper & Brothers.

Hodges, Melvin L. 1953. *The Indigenous Church.* Springfield, Mo.: Gospel Publishing House.

Hofman, J. Samuel. 1993. *Mission Work in Today's World: Insights and Outlooks.* Pasadena, Calif.: William Carey Library.

Hofstede, Geert. 1980. *Culture's Consequences: International Differences in Work-Related Values.* Beverly Hills, Calif.: Sage.

———. 1991. *Cultures and Organizations: Software of the Mind.* New York: McGraw-Hill.

———. 1998. *Masculinity and Femininity: The Taboo Dimension of National Cultures.* Thousand Oaks, Calif.: Sage.

Hogg, William Richey. 1952. *Ecumenical Foundations: A History of the International Missionary Council and Its Nineteenth-Century Background.* New York: Harper & Brothers.

Hoke, Steve, and Bill Taylor. 1999. *Send Me! Your Journey to the Nations.* Wheaton, Ill.: World Evangelical Fellowship.

Hopkins, C. Howard. 1979. *John R. Mott, 1865–1955: A Biography.* Grand Rapids: Eerdmans.

Howard, David M. 1976. *The Great Commission for Today.* Downers Grove, Ill.: InterVarsity.

———. 1987. *What Makes a Missionary.* Chicago: Moody.

Huff, Livingston. 2002. "Avoiding the Crash-and-Burn Syndrome: Toward a Strategy of Missionary Re-Integration." *Missiology: An International Review* 30 (January): 81–89.

Hughes, Philip Edgcumbe. 1962. *Paul's Second Epistle to the Corinthians: The English Text with Introduction, Exposition and Notes.* Grand Rapids: Eerdmans.

Hunter, Jane. 1984. *The Gospel of Gentility: American Women Missionaries in Turn-of-the-Century China.* New Haven: Yale University Press.

Hutchison, William R. 1987. *Errand to the World: American Protestant Thought and Foreign Missions.* Chicago: University of Chicago Press.

Ice, Thomas, and Robert Dean. 1990. *A Holy Rebellion: Strategies for Spiritual Warfare.* Eugene, Oreg.: Harvest House.

Irvin, Dale T., and Scott W. Sunquist. 2001. *History of the World Christian Movement.* Vol. 1, *Earliest Christianity to 1453.* Maryknoll, N.Y.: Orbis.

Jennes, Joseph. 1973. *A History of the Catholic Church in Japan, from Its Beginnings to the early Meiji Era (1549–1873): A Short Handbook.* Rev. ed. Tokyo: Oriens Institute for Religious Research.

John Paul II. 1990. *Redemptoris Missio.* Vatican City: Libreria Editrice Vaticana.

Johnstone, Patrick. 1998. *The Church Is Bigger Than You Think: Structures and Strategies for the Church in the 21st Century.* Pasadena, Calif.: William Carey Library.

———. 2001. *Operation World.* Carlisle: Paternoster.

Jones, A. H. M. 1978. *Constantine and the Conversion of Europe.* Toronto: University of Toronto Press.

Jones, Marge. 1995. *Psychology of Missionary Adjustment.* Springfield, MO: Logion Press.

Jongeneel, J. A. B. 1995. "The Protestant Missionary Movement up to 1789." In *Missiology: An Ecumenical Introduction,* ed. F. J. Verstraelen et al., 222–28. Grand Rapids: Eerdmans.

Kaiser, Walter C. 1996. "The Great Commission in the Old Testament." *International Journal of Frontier Missions* 13 (January–March): 3–7.

———. 1999. "Israel's Missionary Call." In *Perspectives on the World Christian Movement: A Reader,* 3d ed., ed. Ralph D. Winter and Steven C. Hawthorne, 10–16. Pasadena, Calif.: William Carey Library.

———. 2000. *Mission in the Old Testament: Israel as a Light to the Nations.* Grand Rapids: Baker.

Kane, J. Herbert. 1947. *Twofold Growth.* Philadelphia: China Inland Mission.

———. 1975. *The Making of a Missionary.* Grand Rapids: Baker.

———. 1976. *Christian Missions in Biblical Perspective.* Grand Rapids: Baker.

———. 1978a. *A Concise History of the Christian World Mission: A Panoramic View of Missions from Pentecost to the Present.* Grand Rapids: Baker.

———. 1978b. *Understanding Christian Missions.* Rev. ed. Grand Rapids: Baker.

———. 1980. *Life and Work on the Mission Field.* Grand Rapids: Baker.

———. 1981. *The Christian World Mission: Today and Tomorrow.* Grand Rapids: Baker.

———. 1986. *Wanted: World Christians.* Grand Rapids: Baker.

Kasdorf, Hans. 1984. "The Anabaptist Approach to Mission." In *Anabaptism and Mission,* ed. Wilbert R. Shenk, 51–69. Scottdale, Pa.: Herald.

Kealey, Daniel J. 1990. *Cross-Cultural Effectiveness: A Study of Canadian Technical Advisors Overseas.* Hull, Que.: Canadian International Development Agency.

Kealey, Daniel J., and Brent D. Ruben. 1983. "Cross-Cultural Personal Selection Criteria, Issues, and Methods." In *Handbook of Intercultural Training.* Vol. 1, *Issues in Theory and Design,* ed. Dan Landis and Richard W. Brislin, 155–75. New York: Pergamon.

Keyes, Richard. 1992. "The Idol Factory." In *No God but God,* ed. Os Guinness and John Seel, 29–48. Chicago: Moody.

Kidner, Derek. 1967. *Genesis: An Introduction and Commentary.* Leicester: InterVarsity.

Knowles, David, and Dimitri Obolensky. 1969. *The Middle Ages.* New York: Paulist Press.

Kohls, L. Robert. 1976. *Survival Kit for Overseas Living.* Chicago: Intercultural Networks.

Komroff, Manuel, ed. 1930. *The Travels of Marco Polo, the Venetian.* Garden City, N.Y.: Garden City.

Köstenberger, Andreas J., and Peter T. O'Brien. 2001. *Salvation to the Ends of the Earth: A Biblical Theology of Mission.* Downers Grove, Ill.: InterVarsity.

Kraft, Charles H. 1983. *Communication Theory for Christian Witness.* Nashville: Abingdon.

———. 1989. *Christianity with Power: Your Worldview and Your Experience of the Supernatural.* Ann Arbor, Mich.: Vine.

———. 1992. *Defeating Dark Angels: Breaking Demonic Oppression in the Believer's Life.* Ann Arbor, Mich.: Vine.

———. 1994. *Deep Wounds, Deep Healing.* Ann Arbor, Mich.: Servant.

———. 2000. *Evangelical Dictionary of World Missions,* ed. A. Scott Moreau, s.v. "Power Encounter." Grand Rapids: Baker.

———. 2002a. "Contemporary Trends in the Treatment of Spiritual Conflict." In *Deliver Us from Evil: An Uneasy Frontier in Christian Mission,* ed. A. Scott Moreau et al., 177–202. Monrovia, Calif.: World Vision International.

———. 2002b. "Contextualisation and Spiritual Power." In *Deliver Us from Evil: An Uneasy Frontier in Christian Mission,* ed. A. Scott Moreau et al., 290–308. Monrovia, Calif.: World Vision International.

Kraft, Marguerite. 1995. *Understanding Spiritual Power: A Forgotten Dimension of Cross-Cultural Mission and Ministry.* Maryknoll, N.Y.: Orbis.

———. 2000. *Evangelical Dictionary of World Missions,* ed. A. Scott Moreau, s.v. "Women in Mission." Grand Rapids: Baker.

Kraft, Marguerite, and Meg Crossman. 1999. "Women in Mission." *Mission Frontiers* 21 (August): 13–17.

Kuhn, Isobel. 1947. *Nests above the Abyss.* Singapore: Overseas Missionary Fellowship.

———. 1956. *Ascent to the Tribes: Pioneering in North Thailand.* London: Lutterworth.

Küng, Hans, and Julia Ching. 1989. *Christianity and Chinese Religions.* New York: Doubleday.

Kuriakose, M. K., ed. 1982. *History of Christianity in India: Source Materials.* Madras: Christian Literature Society.

Kydd, Ronald A. N. 1998. *Healing through the Centuries: Models of Understanding.* Peabody, Mass.: Hendrickson.

Ladd, George E. 1974. *A Theology of the New Testament.* Grand Rapids: Eerdmans.

Ladipo, Yemi. 1989. "Developing an African Mission Structure." *East Africa Journal of Evangelical Theology* 8: 19–24.

LaGrand, James. 1995. *The Earliest Christian Mission to "All Nations" in the Light of Matthew's Gospel.* Grand Rapids: Eerdmans.

Lai, Patrick. 2001. "Tentmaking—In Search of a Workable Definition." Online: http://www.strategicnetwork.org/index.asp?loc=kb&id=9162 [cited 22 March 2002].

Lane, Denis. 1990. *Tuning God's New Instruments.* Singapore: World Evangelical Fellowship.

Lang, G. H., ed. 1939. *The History and Diaries of an Indian Christian (J. C. Aroolappen).* London: Thynne.

LaPoorta, Japie. 1999. "Unity or Division: A Case Study of the Apostolic Faith Mission of South Africa." In *The Globalization of Pentecostalism: A Religion Made to Travel,* ed. Murray W. Dempster et al., 151–69. Irvine, Calif.: Regnum.

Larkin, William J. 1998. "Mission in Luke." In *Mission in the New Testament: An Evangelical Approach,* ed. William J. Larkin and Joel F. Williams, 152–69. Maryknoll, N.Y.: Orbis.

Larkin, William J., and Joel F. Williams, eds. 1998. *Mission in the New Testament: An Evangelical Approach.* Maryknoll, N.Y.: Orbis.

Latourette, Kenneth Scott. 1941. *A History of the Expansion of Christianity.* Vol. 4, *The Great Century: In Europe and the United States of America, A.D. 1800–A.D. 1914.* Grand Rapids: Zondervan.

———. 1967. "Ecumenical Bearings of the Missionary Movement and the International Missionary Council." In *A History of the Ecumenical Movement, 1517–1948,* 2d ed., ed. Ruth Rouse and Stephen Charles Neill, 353–402. Philadelphia: Westminster.

Lausanne Committee for World Evangelization. 1982. *Evangelism and Social Responsibility: An Evangelical Commitment.* Wheaton, Ill.: Lausanne Committee for World Evangelization; London: World Evangelical Fellowship.

Lawson, Michael. 1987. *Unfolding Kingdom.* Eastbourne, England: Kingsway.

Lehmann, Martin E. 1996. *A Biographical Study of Ingwer Ludwig Nommensen (1834–1918), Pioneer Missionary to the Bataks of Sumatra.* Lewiston, N.Y.: Edwin Mellen.

Le Joly, Edward. 1986. *Evangelization: Theory and Practice.* Bombay: St. Paul Publications.

Levine, Robert, and Ellen Wolff. 1985. "Social Time: The Heartbeat of Culture." *Psychology Today* (March): 28–35.

Lewis, Jonathan, ed. 1996. *Working Your Way to the Nations: A Guide to Effective Tentmaking.* 2d ed. Downers Grove, Ill.: InterVarsity.

Liefeld, Walter L. 1984. "Luke." In *The Expositor's Bible Commentary,* ed. Frank E. Gaebelein, 8:795–1059. Grand Rapids: Zondervan.

Lindsell, Harold. 1970. *An Evangelical Theology of Missions.* Rev. ed. Grand Rapids: Zondervan.

Lingenfelter, Sherwood. 1996. *Agents of Transformation: A Guide for Effective Cross-Cultural Ministry.* Grand Rapids: Baker.

Lingenfelter, Sherwood G., and Marvin K. Mayers. 1986. *Ministering Cross-Culturally: An Incarnational Model for Personal Relationships.* Grand Rapids: Baker.

Lippy, Charles H., Robert Choquette, and Stafford Poole. 1992. *Christianity Comes to the Americas, 1492–1776.* New York: Paragon House.

Loane, Marcus L. 1970. *They Were Pilgrims.* Sydney: Angus and Robertson.

Longenecker, Richard N. 1971. *The Ministry and Message of Paul.* Grand Rapids: Zondervan.

Lossky, Nicholas, et al., eds. 1991. *Dictionary of the Ecumenical Movement.* Grand Rapids: Eerdmans.

Love, N. B. C. n.d. *John Stewart: Missionary to the Wyandots.* New York: Missionary Society of the Methodist Episcopal Church.

Lovett, Richard. 1899. *History of the London Missionary Society, 1795–1895.* 2 vols. London: Henry Frowde.

Lowe, Chuck. 1998. *Territorial Spirits and World Evangelisation? A Biblical, Historical and Missiological Critique of Strategic-level Spiritual Warfare.* Sevenoaks, England: Mentor/OMF.

Lum, Ada. 1984. *A Hitchhiker's Guide to Missions.* Downers Grove, Ill.: InterVarsity.

Lustig, Myron W., and Jolene Koester. 1996. *Intercultural Competence: Interpersonal Communication across Cultures.* 2d ed. New York: HarperCollins.

MacArthur, John. 1992. *How to Meet the Enemy: Arming Yourself for Spiritual Warfare.* Wheaton, Ill.: Victor.

MacDonnell, Joseph. 1989. *Jesuit Geometers: A Study of Fifty-six Prominent Jesuit Geometers During the First Two Centuries of Jesuit History.* St. Louis: Institute of Jesuit Sources.

Mangalwadi, Vishal. 1998. *Missionary Conspiracy: Letters to a Postmodern Hindu.* 2d ed. Carlisle: OM.

Manning, Brennan. 2000. *Ruthless Trust: The Ragamuffin's Path to God.* New York: HarperCollins.

Manschreck, Clyde L., ed. 1981. *A History of Christianity: Readings in the History of the Church.* Vol. 2, *The Church from the Reformation to the Present.* Grand Rapids: Baker.

Manzano, Jojo. 1994. *Mission Is for Every Church.* Manila: OMF.

Markus, Hazel Rose, and Shinobu Kitayama. 1991. "Culture and the Self: Implications for Cognition, Emotion, and Motivation." *Psychological Review* 98: 224–53.

Marlowe, W. Creighton. 1998. "Music of Missions: Themes of Cross-Cultural Outreach in the Psalms." *Missiology: An International Review* 6 (October): 445–56.

Marshall, I. Howard. 1978. *The Gospel of Luke: A Commentary on the Greek Text.* Grand Rapids: Eerdmans.

———. 2000. "Luke's Portrait of the Pauline Mission." In *The Gospel to the Nations: Perspectives on Paul's Mission,* ed. Peter Bolt and Mark Thompson, 99–113. Downers Grove, Ill.: InterVarsity.

Marshall, Paul. 1997. *Their Blood Cries Out: The Untold Story of Persecution against Christians in the Modern World.* Dallas: Word.

Martin, George. 1998. "Missions in the Pauline Epistles." In *Missiology: An Introduction to the Foundations, History, and Strategies of World Missions,* ed. John Mark Terry, Ebbie Smith, and Justice Anderson, 83–96. Nashville: Broadman & Holman.

Martin, Marie-Louise. 1975. *Kimbangu: An African Prophet and His Church.* Grand Rapids: Eerdmans.

Martindale, Wayne, and Jerry Root, eds. 1989. *The Quotable Lewis.* Wheaton, Ill.: Tyndale.

Martinson, Paul Varo, ed. 1999. *Mission at the Dawn of the 21st Century: A Vision for the Church.* Minneapolis: Kirk House.

Maslow, Abraham H. 1970. *Motivation and Personality.* 2d ed. New York: Harper & Row.

Massey, Joshua. 2002. "Hometown Ministry as Pre-Field Preparation." *Evangelical Missions Quarterly* 38 (April): 196–201.

May, Peter. 1959. "Towards a Biblical Theology of Mission." *Indian Journal of Theology* 8: 21–28.

Mayers, Marvin K. 1974. *Christianity Confronts Culture: A Strategy for Cross-Cultural Evangelism.* Grand Rapids: Zondervan.

McAlpine, Thomas H. 1991. *Facing the Powers: What Are the Options?* Monrovia, Calif.: MARC.

McDaniel, Ferris L. 1998. "Mission in the Old Testament." In *Mission in the New Testament: An Evangelical Approach,* ed. William J. Larkin and Joel F. Williams, 11–20. Maryknoll, N.Y.: Orbis.

McDonald, Hugh Dermot. 1981. *The Christian View of Man.* Westchester, Ill.: Crossway.

McGavran, Donald A. 1955. *The Bridges of God: A Study in the Strategy of Missions*. New York: Friendship.

———. 1965. "Wrong Strategy: The Real Crisis in Missions." *International Review of Mission* 54 (October): 451–61.

———. 1970. *Understanding Church Growth*. Grand Rapids: Eerdmans.

———. 1984. *Momentous Decisions in Missions Today*. Grand Rapids: Baker.

McGee, Gary B. 1997. "The Radical Strategy in Modern Mission: The Linkage of Paranormal Phenomena with Evangelism." In *The Holy Spirit and Mission Dynamics*, ed. C. Douglas McConnell, 69–95. Pasadena, Calif.: William Carey Library.

———. 2001a. "To the Regions Beyond: The Global Expansion of Pentecostalism." In *The Century of the Holy Spirit: 100 Years of Pentecostal and Charismatic Renewal, 1901–2001*, ed. Vinson Synan, 69–95. Nashville: Thomas Nelson.

———. 2001b. "Shortcut to Language Preparation? Radical Evangelicals, Missions, and the Gift of Tongues." *International Bulletin of Missionary Research* 25 (July): 118–23.

McIntosh, John A. 2000. *Evangelical Dictionary of World Missions*, ed. A. Scott Moreau, s.v. "Missio Dei." Grand Rapids: Baker.

McKinney, Lois. 1991. "New Directions in Missionary Education." In *Internationalizing Missionary Training: A Global Perspective*, ed. William Taylor, 241–50. Grand Rapids: Baker.

McNamara, Jo Ann, and John E. Halborg, with E. Gordon Whatley, eds. and trans. 1992. *Sainted Women of the Dark Ages*. Durham, N.C.: Duke University Press.

McQuilkin, Robertson, Jr. 1984. *The Great Omission: A Biblical Basis for World Evangelism*. Grand Rapids: Baker.

———. 2000. *Evangelical Dictionary of World Missions*, ed. A. Scott Moreau, s.v. "Reached and Unreached Mission Fields." Grand Rapids: Baker.

McSweeney, William. 1980. *Roman Catholicism: The Search for Relevance*. New York: St. Martin's Press.

Medary, Marjorie. 1954. *Each One Teach One: Frank Laubach, Friend to Millions*. New York: David McKay.

Meier, Johannes. 1992. "The Organization of the Church." In *The Church in Latin America, 1492–1992*, ed. Enrique Dussel, 53–68. Maryknoll, N.Y.: Orbis.

Meyendorff, John. 1960. "Orthodox Missions in the Middle Ages." In World's Student Christian Federation, *History's Lessons for Tomorrow's Mission: Milestones in the History of Missionary Thinking*, 99–104. Geneva: World's Student Christian Federation.

———. 1989. *Imperial Unity and Christian Divisions: The Church 450–680 A.D.* Crestwood, N.Y.: St. Vladimir's Seminary Press.

Miller, Darrow L., with Stan Guthrie. 1998. *Discipling Nations: The Power of Truth to Transform Cultures*. Seattle: YWAM.

Miura, Hiroshi. 1996. *The Life and Thought of Kanzo Uchimura, 1861–1930*. Grand Rapids: Eerdmans.

Moffett, Samuel H. 1992. *A History of Christianity in Asia*. San Francisco: HarperSanFrancisco.

Moister, William. 1885. *Missionary Martyrs; Being Brief Memorial Sketches of Faithful Servants of God Who Have Been Put to Death Whilst Endeavoring to Propagate the Gospel of Christ, Chiefly among the Heathen, in Different Ages and Countries*. London: Moister.

Montgomery, Helen Barrett. 1910. *Western Women in Eastern Lands: An Outline Study of Fifty Years of Woman's Work in Foreign Missions*. New York: Macmillan.

Moorman, John. 1968. *A History of the Franciscan Order: From Its Origins to the Year 1517*. Oxford: Clarendon.

Moreau, A. Scott. 1990. *The World of the Spirits: A Biblical Study in the African Context*. Nairobi: Evangel.

———. 1995a. "The Human Universals of Culture: Implications for Contextualization." *International Journal of Frontier Missions* 12:3 (July–September): 121–25.

———. 1995b. "Religious Borrowing as a Two-Way Street: An Introduction to Animistic Tendencies in the Euro-North American Context." In *Christianity and the Religions: A Biblical Theology of World Religions*, ed. Edward Rommen and Harold Netland, 166–82. Pasadena, Calif.: William Carey Library.

———. 1997a. *Essentials of Spiritual Warfare*. Wheaton, Ill.: Harold Shaw.

———. 1997b. "Broadening the Issues: Historiography, Advocacy, and Hermeneutics." In *The Holy Spirit in Missions*, ed. C. Douglas McConnell, 121–35. Pasadena, Calif.: William Carey Library.

———, gen. ed. 2000a. *Evangelical Dictionary of World Missions*. Grand Rapids: Baker.

———. 2000b. *Evangelical Dictionary of World Missions*, ed. A. Scott Moreau, s.v. "Mission and Missions." Grand Rapids: Baker.

———. 2000c. "Putting the Survey in Perspective." In *Mission Handbook: U.S. and Canadian Ministries Overseas*, ed. John A. Siewert and Dotsey Welliver, 33–80. Wheaton, Ill.: Evangelism and Missions Information Service.

———. 2001a. *Evangelical Dictionary of Theology*, 2d ed., ed. Walter A. Elwell, s.v. "Missiology." Grand Rapids: Baker.

———. 2001b. *Evangelical Dictionary of Theology*, 2d ed., ed. Walter A. Elwell, s.v. "Phenomenology of Religion." Grand Rapids: Baker.

———. 2001c. *Evangelical Dictionary of Theology*, 2d ed., ed. Walter A. Elwell, s.v. "Syncretism." Grand Rapids: Baker.

———. 2002a. "Gaining Perspective on Territorial Spirits." In *Deliver Us from Evil: An Uneasy Frontier in Christian Mission*, ed. A. Scott Moreau et al., 263–78. Monrovia, Calif.: World Vision International.

———. 2002b. "A Survey of North American Spiritual Warfare Thinking." In *Deliver Us from Evil: An Uneasy Frontier in Christian Mission*, ed. A. Scott Moreau et al., 118–27. Monrovia, Calif.: World Vision International.

Moreau, A. Scott, and Mike O'Rear. 2001. "Virtual Missionary Care?" *Evangelical Missions Quarterly* 37 (January): 84–87.

———. 2002. "Relief and Development Helps." *Evangelical Missions Quarterly* 38 (January): 90–94.

Moreau, A. Scott, et al., eds. 2002. *Deliver Us from Evil: An Uneasy Frontier in Christian Mission*. Monrovia, Calif.: World Vision International.

Mott, John R. 1910. *The Decisive Hour of Christian Missions*. New York: Student Volunteer Movement for Foreign Missions.

Moule, C. F. D. 1959. *Idiom Book of the New Testament*. 2d ed. Cambridge: Cambridge University Press.

Muck, Terry. 1993. *The Mysterious Beyond: A Basic Guide to Studying Religion*. Grand Rapids: Baker.

Mueller, J. Theodore. 1947. *Great Missionaries to China*. Grand Rapids: Zondervan.

Mugambe, Jesse. 1989. *The Biblical Basis for World Evangelization: Theological Reflections on an African Experience*. Nairobi: Oxford University Press.

Müller, Karl, with Hans-Werner Gensichen and Horst Rzepkowski. 1987. *Mission Theology: An Introduction*. Trans. Francis Mansfield. Nettetal: Steyler.

Müller, Karl, et al., eds. 1997. *Dictionary of Mission: Theology, History, Perspectives*. Maryknoll, N.Y.: Orbis.

Mundadan, A. Mathias. 1989. *History of Christianity in India*. Vol. 1, *From the Beginning Up to the Middle of the Sixteenth Century*. Bangalore: Church History Association of India.

Murdock, J. N. 1888. "Woman's Work in the Foreign Field." In *Report of the Centenary Conference on the Protestant Missions of the World, Held in Exeter Hall (June 9th–19th), London, 1888*, ed. James Johnston, 160–68. London: James Nisbet.

Murphy, Ed. 1992. *The Handbook for Spiritual Warfare*. Nashville: Thomas Nelson.

Murray, Andrew. 1953. *With Christ in the School of Prayer*. Westwood, N.J.: Fleming H. Revell.

Muzorewa, Gwinyai H. 1990. *An African Theology of Mission*. Lewiston, N.Y.: Edwin Mellen.

Myers, Bryant L. 1993. *The New Context of World Mission*. Monrovia, Calif.: MARC.

———.1995. "Modernity and Holistic Ministry." In *Serving with the Poor in Asia*, ed. Tetsunao Yamamori, Bryant L. Myers, and David Conner, 179–91. Monrovia, Calif.: MARC.

Neely, Alan. 1999. "Saints Who Sometimes Were: Utilizing Missionary Hagiography." *Missiology: An International Review* 27 (October): 441–57.

Neely, Lois. 1980. *Come Up to This Mountain: The Miracle of Clarence W. Jones and HCJB*. Wheaton, Ill.: Tyndale.

Neill, Stephen. 1986. *A History of Christian Missions*. 2d ed. New York: Penguin.

Netland, Harold. 1991. *Dissonant Voices: Religious Pluralism and the Question of Truth*. Grand Rapids: Eerdmans.

Nettleton, Todd. 2002. "The Walk of Faith by an 'Evil Cult.'" *The Voice of the Martyrs*. March, 3–7.

Neuner, J., and J. Dupuis, eds. 1991. *The Christian Faith: In the Doctrinal Documents of the Catholic Church*. Bangalore: Theological Publications in India.

Newbigin, Lesslie. 1986. *Foolishness to the Greeks: The Gospel and Western Culture*. Grand Rapids: Eerdmans.

———. 1995. *The Open Secret: An Introduction to the Theology of Mission*. Rev. ed. Grand Rapids: Eerdmans.

Nichols, Alan, ed. 1989. *The Whole Gospel for the Whole World: Story of Lausanne II Congress on World Evangelization, Manila, 1989*. Charlotte, N.C.: Lausanne Committee for World Evangelization.

Nilsen, Maria. 1956. *Malla Moe*. Chicago: Moody.

Nuckolls, Charles W. 1991. "Culture and Causal Thinking: Diagnosis and Prediction in a South Indian Fishing Village." *Ethos* 19: 1–51.

Nussbaum, Stan, ed., 1998. *The Wisdom of African Proverbs: Collections, Studies, Bibliographies*. [CD-ROM]. Colorado Springs, Colo.: Global Mapping International.

O'Brien, Peter. 1976. "The Great Commission of Matthew 28:18–20: A Missionary Mandate or Not?" *The Reformed Theological Review* 135 (September–December): 66–78.

O'Donnell, Kelly, ed. 1992. *Missionary Care: Counting the Cost of World Evangelization*. Pasadena, Calif.: William Carey Library.

———. 2001. "Touring the Terrain: An International Sampler of Member Care Literature." *Evangelical Missions Quarterly* 37 (January): 18–29.

———. 2002. *Doing Member Care Well: Perspectives and Practices from around the World*. Pasadena, Calif.: William Carey Library.

O'Hara, Bill, and Carol O'Hara. 2002. "What about Cross-Cultural Marriage?" Online: http://www.missionsandmarriages.org/xculture.html [cited 24 July 2002].

Olson, Bruce. 1978. *Bruchko*. Altamonte Springs, Fla.: Creation House.

Olson, C. Gordon. 1998. *What in the World Is God Doing? The Essentials of Global Missions: An Introductory Guide*. 4th ed. Cedar Knolls, N.J.: Global Gospel Publishers.

Olthius, James H. 1985. "On Worldviews." *Christian Scholar's Review* 14: 153–64.

Origen. 1972. *Against Celsus*. In *The Ante-Nicene Fathers*. Vol. 4, *Tertullian, Part Fourth; Minucius Felix; Commodian; Origen, Parts First and Second*, ed. Alexander Roberts and James Donaldson, 395–669. Grand Rapids: Eerdmans.

Orr, J. Edwin. 1975. *The Flaming Tongue: Evangelical Awakenings, 1900–*. 2d ed. Chicago: Moody.

Otis, George, Jr. 1993. "An Overview of Spiritual Mapping." In *Breaking Strongholds in Your City: How to Use Spiritual Mapping to Make Your Prayers More Strategic, Effective and Targeted*, ed. C. Peter Wagner, 29–47. Ventura, Calif.: Regal.

———. 1997. *The Twilight Labyrinth: Why Does Spiritual Darkness Linger Where It Does?* Grand Rapids: Chosen.

Padilla, Rene. 1987. "Evangelism and Social Responsibility: From Wheaton '66 to Wheaton '83." In *The Best in Theology*. Vol. 1, ed. J. I. Packer and Paul W. Fromer, 239–52. Carol Stream, Ill.: Christianity Today Institute.

Page, Sydney H. T. 1995. *Powers of Evil: A Biblical Study of Satan and Demons*. Grand Rapids: Baker.

Palmatier, Aaron. 2002. "Spring Break Mission Trips: A Blessing or a Curse?" *Evangelical Missions Quarterly* 38 (April): 228–32.

Palmer, Phoebe. 1859. *Promise of the Father, or, A Neglected Speciality of the Last Days*. Boston: Henry V. Degen.

Parshall, Phil. 1998. "Danger! New Directions in Muslim Contextualization." *Evangelical Missions Quarterly* 34 (October): 404–10.

Paton, David MacDonald. 1996. *Christian Missions and the Judgment of God*. 2d ed. Edited with a short biography by David M. M. Paton. Grand Rapids: Eerdmans.

Pelletier, Allen L. 1999. "The Forgotten Missionaries." *Evangelical Missions Quarterly* 35 (April): 174–77.

Pelto, Pertti J., and Gretel H. Pelto. 1978. *Anthropological Research: The Structure of Inquiry*. 2d ed. Cambridge: Cambridge University Press.

Penney, Russell L., ed. 2001. *Overcoming the World Missions Crisis: Thinking Strategically to Reach the World*. Grand Rapids: Kregel.

Pentecost, Edward C. 1982. *Issues in Missiology: An Introduction*. Grand Rapids: Baker.

"Pentecost Has Come." 1906. *The Apostolic Faith* (September): 1.

Peretti, Frank E. 1986. *This Present Darkness*. Westchester, Ill.: Crossway.

———. 1989. *Piercing the Darkness*. Westchester, Ill.: Crossway.

Peters, George W. 1972. *A Biblical Theology of Missions*. Chicago: Moody.

Peterson, David G. 2000. "Maturity: The Goal of Mission." In *The Gospel to the Nations: Perspectives on*

Paul's Mission, ed. Peter Bolt and Mark Thompson, 185–204. Downers Grove, Ill.: InterVarsity.

Peterson, Eugene H. 1980. *A Long Obedience in the Same Direction: Discipleship in an Instant Society.* Downers Grove, Ill.: InterVarsity.

Peterson, Willard J. 1988. "Why Did They Become Christians? Yang T'ing-yün, Li Chih-tsao, and Hsü Kuang-ch'i." In *East Meets West: The Jesuits in China, 1582–1773,* ed. Charles E. Ronan and Bonnie B. C. Oh, 129–52. Chicago: Loyola University Press.

Petry, Ray C., ed. 1962. *A History of Christianity: Readings in the History of the Church.* Vol. 1, *The Early and Medieval Church.* Grand Rapids: Baker.

Phan, Peter C. 1998. *Mission and Catechesis: Alexandre de Rhodes and Inculturation in Seventeenth-Century Vietnam.* Maryknoll, N.Y.: Orbis.

Phillips, James, and Robert T. Coote, eds. 1993. *Toward the 21st Century in Christian Mission: Essays in Honor of Gerald H. Anderson.* Grand Rapids: Eerdmans.

Pierson, Arthur T. 1910. "The Edinburgh Conference." *Missionary Review of the World* 23 (August): 561–63.

———. 1917. "The Testimony of Foreign Missions to the Superintending Providence of God." In *The Fundamentals: A Testimony to the Truth,* ed. R. A. Torrey et al., 3:320–36. Los Angeles: Bible Institute of Los Angeles.

Pierson, Paul. 1998. "Local Churches in Mission: What's Behind the Impatience with Traditional Mission Agencies?" *International Bulletin of Missionary Research* 22 (October): 146–50.

Pierson, Steven J. 2000. *Evangelical Dictionary of World Missions,* ed. A. Scott Moreau, s.v. "Dialogue." Grand Rapids: Baker.

Pinnock, Clark H. 1994. *The Openness of God: A Biblical Challenge to the Traditional Understanding of God.* Downers Grove, Ill.: InterVarsity.

Piper, John. 1986. *Desiring God: Meditations of a Christian Hedonist.* Portland, Ore.: Multnomah.

———. 1993. *Let the Nations Be Glad! The Supremacy of God in Missions.* Grand Rapids: Baker.

———. 2003. *Let the Nations Be Glad! The Supremacy of God in Missions.* 2d ed. Grand Rapids: Baker.

Pirolo, Neal. 2000. *The Re-Entry Team: Caring for Your Returning Missionaries.* San Diego: Emmaus Road International.

Pollock, John. 1955. *The Cambridge Seven.* London: InterVarsity.

———. 1970. *Victims of the Long March.* Waco, Tex.: Word.

———. 1972. *The Apostle.* Wheaton, Ill.: Victor.

Potter, Philip A. 1991. *Dictionary of the Ecumenical Movement,* ed. Nicholas Lossky et al., s.v. "Mission." Grand Rapids: Eerdmans.

Powers, Janet Everts. 1999. "Your Daughters Shall Prophesy: Pentecostal Hermeneutics and the Empowerment of Women." In *The Globalization of Pentecostalism: A Religion Made to Travel,* ed. Murray W. Dempster, Byron D. Klaus, and Douglas Petersen, 313–37. Irvine, Calif.: Regnum.

Powlison, David. 1995. *Power Encounters: Reclaiming Spiritual Warfare.* Grand Rapids: Baker.

Priest, Robert J. 1994. "Missionary Elenctics: Conscience and Culture." *Missiology: An International Review* 22 (July): 291–315.

Priest, Robert J., Thomas Campbell, and Bradford A. Mullen. 1995. "Missiological Syncretism: The New Animistic Paradigm." In *Spiritual Power and Missions: Raising the Issues,* ed. Edward Rommen, 9–87. Pasadena, Calif.: William Carey Library.

Prokurat, Michael, Alexander Golitzin, and Michael D. Peterson. 1996. *Historical Dictionary of the Orthodox Church.* Lanham, Md.: Scarecrow.

Quenot, Michel. 1991. *The Icon: Window on the Kingdom.* Crestwood, N.Y.: St. Vladimir's Seminary Press.

Ramachandra, Vinoth. 1996. *The Recovery of Mission: Beyond the Pluralist Paradigm.* Grand Rapids: Eerdmans.

Rayanna, P. 1989. *St. Francis Xavier and His Shrine.* 2d ed. Old Goa, India: Bom Jesus Basilica.

Reapsome, Jim. 1999. *Final Analysis: A Decade of Commentary on the Church and World Missions.* Wheaton, Ill.: Evangelism and Missions Information Service.

Richard, H. L. 1998. *Following Jesus in the Hindu Context: The Intriguing Implications of N. V. Tilak's Life and Thought.* Pasadena, Calif.: William Carey Library.

Richardson, Cyril C., ed. 1970. *Early Christian Fathers.* New York: Macmillan.

Richardson, Don. 1974. *Peace Child.* Glendale, Calif.: G/L Regal.

———. 1981. *Eternity in Their Hearts.* Ventura, Calif.: Regal.

Rickett, Daniel. 2001. "7 Mistakes Partners Make and How to Avoid Them." *Evangelical Missions Quarterly* 37 (July): 308–17.

———. 2002. *Making Your Partnership Work*. Enumclaw, Wash.: Winepress.

Ritchie, Mark. 1996. *Spirit of the Rainforest*. Chicago: Island Lake.

Ritschl, Dietrich. 1991. *Dictionary of the Ecumenical Movement*, ed. Nicholas Lossky et al., s.v. "Ecumenism." Grand Rapids: Eerdmans.

Robert, Dana L. 1990. "'The Crisis of Missions': Premillennial Mission Theory and the Origins of Independent Evangelical Missions." In *Earthen Vessels: American Evangelicals and Foreign Missions, 1880–1980*, ed. Joel A. Carpenter and Wilbert R. Shenk, 29–46. Grand Rapids: Eerdmans.

———. 1991. "Christianity in Asia, Africa, and Latin America." In *Christianity: A Social and Cultural History*, ed. Howard Clark Kee et al., 757–64. New York: Macmillan.

———. 1996. *American Women in Mission: A Social History of Their Thought and Practice*. Macon, Ga.: Mercer University Press.

———. 2002. "The First Globalization: The Internationalization of the Protestant Missionary Movement Between the World Wars." *International Bulletin of Missionary Research* 26 (April): 50–66.

Rodríguez León, Mario A. 1992. "Invasion and Evangelization in the Sixteenth Century." In *The Church in Latin America, 1492–1992*, ed. Enrique Dussel, 43–54. Maryknoll, N.Y.: Orbis.

Roembke, Lianne. 2000. *Building Credible Multicultural Teams*. Pasadena, Calif.: William Carey Library.

Romano, Dugan. 1997. *Intercultural Marriage: Promises and Pitfalls*. Yarmouth, Maine: Intercultural.

Rommen, Edward, ed. 1995. *Spiritual Power and Missions: Raising the Issues*. Pasadena, Calif.: William Carey Library.

Ross, Andrew C. 1994. *A Vision Betrayed: The Jesuits in Japan and China, 1542–1742*. Maryknoll, N.Y.: Orbis.

Rottenberg, Isaac C. 1980. *The Promise and the Presence: Toward a Theology of the Kingdom of God*. Grand Rapids: Eerdmans.

Rowley, Harold Henry. 1945. *The Missionary Message of the Old Testament*. London: Carey.

Ruben, Brent D. 1982. "Human Communication and Cross-Cultural Effectiveness." In *Intercultural Communication: A Reader*, 3d ed., ed. Richard E. Porter and Larry A. Samovar, 331–39. Belmont, Calif.: Wadsworth.

Rufinus of Aquileia. 1997. *The "Church History" of Rufinus of Aquileia: Books 10 and 11*. Trans. Philip R. Amidon. New York: Oxford University Press.

Runciman, Steven. 1955. *The Eastern Schism: A Study of the Papacy and the Eastern Churches During the XIth and XIIth Centuries*. Oxford: Clarendon.

St. Kilda, Martin. 1993. *Near the Far Bamboo: An Insightful Look at Cross-Cultural Clashes through the Eyes of a Tentmaking Missionary*. Camp Hill, Pa.: Christian Publications.

Saldanha, Julian. 1988. *Patterns of Evangelisation in Mission History*. Bombay: St. Paul Publications.

Sanderlin, George, ed. 1992. *Witness: Writings of Bartolomé de Las Casas*. Maryknoll, N.Y.: Orbis.

Sanneh, Lamin. 1983. *West African Christianity: The Religious Impact*. Maryknoll, N.Y.: Orbis.

Satyavrata, Ivan M. 1999. "Contextual Perspectives on Pentecostalism as a Global Culture: A South Asian View." In *The Globalization of Pentecostalism: A Religion Made to Travel*, ed. Murray W. Dempster et al., 203–21. Irvine, Calif.: Regnum.

Savage, Robert. 1943. *Lord, Send Me!* Grand Rapids: Zondervan.

Scherer, James A. 1969. *Justinian Welz: Essays by an Early Prophet of Mission*. Grand Rapids: Eerdmans.

———. 1987. *Gospel, Church, and Kingdom: Comparative Studies in World Mission Theology*. Minneapolis: Augsburg.

Schmidlin, Josef. 1933. *Catholic Mission History*. Trans. Matthias Braun. Techny, Ill.: Mission Press, S.V.D.

Schreiter, Robert. 1985. *Constructing Local Theologies*. Maryknoll, N.Y.: Orbis.

Schurhammer, Georg. 1973. *Francis Xavier: His Life, His Times*. Vol. 1, *Europe, 1506–1541*. Rome: Jesuit Historical Institute.

Schütte, Josef Franz. 1980. *Valignano's Mission Principles for Japan*. Vol. 2, *The Solution (1580–1582)*. Trans. John J. Coyne. St. Louis: Institute of Jesuit Sources.

Seccombe, David. 2000. "The Story of Jesus and the Missionary Strategy of Paul." In *The Gospel to the Nations: Perspectives on Paul's Mission*, ed. Peter Bolt and Mark Thompson, 115–29. Downers Grove, Ill.: InterVarsity.

Segal, Marshall H., et al. 1990. *Behavior in Global Perspective: An Introduction to Cross-Cultural Psychology*. New York: Pergamon.

Shank, David A. 1994. *Prophet Harris, The "Black Elijah" of West Africa*. Leiden: Brill.

Shea, Nina. 1997. *In the Lion's Den: A Shocking Account of Persecution and Martyrdom of Christians Today and How We Should Respond*. Nashville: Broadman & Holman.

Shenk, Wilbert R. 1983. "Kingdom, Mission, and Growth." In *Exploring Church Growth*, ed. Wilbert R. Shenk, 207–17. Grand Rapids: Eerdmans.

———. 1984. "The 'Great Century' Reconsidered." In *Anabaptism and Mission*, ed. Wilbert R. Shenk, 158–77. Scottdale, Pa.: Herald.

———. 1999. *Changing Frontiers of Mission*. Maryknoll, N.Y.: Orbis.

Shibley, David. 2001. *The Missions Addition: Capturing God's Passion for the World*. Lake Mary, Fla.: Charisma House.

Shim, Chang-sup. 1998. "Assessing the Impact of Pentecostalism on the Korean Presbyterian Church in Light of Calvin's Theology." *Chongshin Theological Journal* 3 (February): 115–31.

Shorter, Aylward. 1972. *Theology of Mission*. Notre Dame, Ind.: Fides.

Sider, Ronald. 1990. *Rich Christians in an Age of Hunger*. Dallas: Word.

Siemens, Ruth. 2002. "The Tentmaker's Preparation." Online: http://www.globalopps.org/GO%20Papers/prepare.htm [cited 22 March 2002].

Siewert, John, and Dotsey Welliver, eds. 1999. *Directory of Schools and Professors of Mission and Evangelism in the USA and Canada 1999–2001*. Wheaton, Ill.: Evangelism and Missions Information Service.

———. 2000. *Mission Handbook: U.S. and Canadian Ministries Overseas 2001–2003*. 18th ed. Wheaton, Ill.: Evangelism and Missions Information Service.

Simonnet, Christian. 1988. *Théophane Vénard: A Martyr of Vietnam*. San Francisco: Ignatius Press.

Simpson, A. B. 1892. "The New Testament Standpoint of Missions." *Christian Alliance and Missionary Weekly*, December 16, 387–91.

———. 1915. *The Gospel of Healing*. Harrisburg, Pa.: Christian Publications.

Sine, Tom. 1991. *Wild Hope*. Dallas: Word.

Sjogren, Steve. 1993. *Conspiracy of Kindness: A Refreshing New Approach to Sharing the Love of Jesus with Others*. Ann Arbor, Mich.: Vine.

———. 1996. *Servant Warfare: How Kindness Conquers Spiritual Darkness*. Ann Arbor, Mich.: Vine.

Smedes, Lewis B., ed. 1987. *Ministry and the Miraculous: A Case Study of Fuller Theological Seminary*. Waco, Tex.: Word.

Smith, Ed. 2000. *Beyond Tolerable Recovery*. Rev. ed. Campbellsville, Ky.: Theophostic Ministries.

Smith, Richard. 2002. "A Testimony for Missions: Respect or Rejection?" *Evangelical Missions Quarterly* 38 (October): 480–88.

Speer, Robert E. 1909. *Servants of the King*. New York: Young People's Missionary Movement of the United States and Canada.

———. 1916. "The Panama Congress on Christian Work in Latin America." *Missionary Review of the World* 29 (April): 249–59.

Stafford, Tim. 1984. *The Friendship Gap: Reaching Out across Cultures*. Downers Grove, Ill.: InterVarsity.

Stamoolis, James J. 1986. *Eastern Orthodox Mission Theology Today*. Maryknoll, N.Y.: Orbis.

Stanley, Brian. 1990. *The Bible and the Flag: Protestant Missions and British Imperialism in the Nineteenth and Twentieth Centuries*. Leicester: Apollos.

———. 2001. "Christian Missions and the Enlightenment: A Reevaluation." In *Christian Missions and the Enlightenment*, ed. Brian Stanley, 1–21. Grand Rapids: Eerdmans.

Starkes, M. Thomas. 1984. *Toward a Theology of Missions*. Chattanooga, Tenn.: AMG.

Stearns, Bill, and Amy Stearns. 1991. *Catch the Vision 2000*. Minneapolis: Bethany House.

Stebbins, Tom. 1996. *Missions by the Book: How to Find and Evangelize Lost People of Every Culture on Every Continent*. Camp Hill, Pa.: Christian Publications.

Steffen, Tom. 1993. *Passing the Baton: Church Planting that Empowers*. LaHabra, Calif.: Center for Organizational and Ministry Development.

———. 2000. *Evangelical Dictionary of World Missions*, ed. A. Scott Moreau, s.v. "Training of Missionaries." Grand Rapids, Baker.

Stephens, May Agnew, ed. 1910. *Missionary Messages in Song*. Toronto: H. L. Stephens.

Stewart, Edward, and Milton J. Bennett. 1991. *American Cultural Patterns: A Cross-Cultural Perspective*. Rev. ed. Yarmouth, Maine: Intercultural.

Stewart-Gambino, Hannah W., and Everett Wilson. 1997. "Latin American Pentecostals: Old Stereotypes and New Challenges." In *Power, Politics, and Pentecostals in Latin America*, ed. Edward L. Cleary and Hannah W. Stewart-Gambino, 227–43. Boulder, Colo.: Westview.

Stibbs, Alan. 1959. *The First Epistle General of Peter.* Grand Rapids: Eerdmans.

Stormon, E. J., ed. 1987. *Towards the Healing of Schism: The Sees of Rome and Constantinople: Public Statements and Correspondence between the Holy See and the Ecumenical Patriarchate, 1958–1984.* New York: Paulist.

Storti, Craig. 1990. *The Art of Crossing Cultures.* Yarmouth, Maine: Intercultural.

———. 1997. *The Art of Coming Home.* Yarmouth, Maine: Intercultural.

———. 1999. *Figuring Foreigners Out: A Practical Guide.* Yarmouth, Maine: Intercultural.

Stott, John R. W. 1975a. "The Biblical Basis of Evangelism." In *Let the Earth Hear His Voice,* ed. J. D. Douglas, 65–78. Minneapolis: World Wide Publications.

———. 1975b. *Christian Mission in the Modern World.* Downers Grove, Ill.: InterVarsity.

———. 1999. "The Living God Is a Missionary God." In *Perspectives on the World Christian Movement: A Reader,* 3d ed., ed. Ralph D. Winter and Steven C. Hawthorne, 3–9. Pasadena, Calif.: William Carey Library.

Stransky, Tom F. 1991. *Dictionary of the Ecumenical Movement,* ed. Nicholas Lossky et al., s.v. "Missio Dei." Grand Rapids: Eerdmans.

Struve, N. 1960. "The Orthodox Church and Mission." In World's Student Christian Federation, *History's Lessons for Tomorrow's Mission: Milestones in the History of Missionary Thinking,* 105–18. Geneva: World's Student Christian Federation.

Student Volunteer Movement for Foreign Missions. [1891] 1979. *Student Mission Power: Report of the First International Convention of the Student Volunteer Movement for Foreign Missions, Held at Cleveland, Ohio, U.S.A., February 26, 27, 28 and March 1, 1891.* Reprint, Pasadena, Calif.: William Carey Library.

Sturgeon, Derrill. 1986. "The Rest of the Story Must Be Told." *Mountain Movers* (May): 11.

Sullivan, Francis A. 1992. *Salvation Outside the Church? Tracing the History of the Catholic Response.* Mahwah, N.J.: Paulist.

Taber, Charles R. 1991. *The World Is Too Much with Us: "Culture" in Modern Protestant Missions.* Macon, Ga.: Mercer University Press.

Talbot, C. H., ed. 1954. *The Anglo-Saxon Missionaries in Germany.* London: Sheed & Ward.

Tallman, J. Raymond. 1989. *An Introduction to World Missions.* Chicago: Moody.

Tannen, Deborah. 1990. *You Just Don't Understand: Women and Men in Conversation.* New York: Morrow.

———. 1991. *That's Not What I Meant: How Conversational Style Makes or Breaks Relationships.* New York: Ballentine.

———. 1994. *Gender and Discourse.* New York: Oxford University Press.

Tatlow, Tissington. 1967. "The World Conference on Faith and Order." In *A History of the Ecumenical Movement, 1517–1948,* 2d ed., ed. Ruth Rouse and Stephen Charles Neill, 405–41. Philadelphia: Westminster.

Taylor, Howard, and Mrs. Howard Taylor [Mary Geraldine Guinness Taylor]. [1932?]. *Hudson Taylor's Spiritual Secret.* Chicago: Moody.

Taylor, J. Hudson. n.d. *A Retrospect.* Philadelphia: China Inland Mission.

Taylor, Mrs. Howard [Mary Geraldine Guinness Taylor]. 1949. *Pastor Hsi: Confucian Scholar and Christian.* 20th ed. London: China Inland Mission.

Taylor, Richard W. 1994. "E. Stanley Jones, 1884–1973: Following the Christ of the Indian Road." In *Mission Legacies: Biographical Studies of Leaders of the Modern Missionary Movement,* ed. Gerald H. Anderson et al., 339–47. Maryknoll, N.Y.: Orbis.

Taylor, William. 1880. *Christian Adventures in South Africa.* New York: Phillips & Hunt.

Taylor, William D., ed. 1991. *Internationalizing Missionary Training: A Global Perspective.* Grand Rapids: Baker.

———. 1997a. "Introduction: Examining the Iceberg Called Attrition." In *Too Valuable to Lose: Exploring the Causes and Cures of Missionary Attrition,* ed. William D. Taylor, 3–14. Pasadena, Calif.: William Carey Library.

———, ed. 1997b. *Too Valuable to Lose: Exploring the Causes and Cures of Missionary Attrition.* Pasadena, Calif.: William Carey Library.

———. 2002. "Revisiting a Provocative Theme: The Attrition of Longer-Term Missionaries." *Missiology: An International Review* 30 (January): 67–80.

Telford, Tom. 1998. *Missions in the 21st Century.* Wheaton, Ill.: Harold Shaw.

———. 2001. *Today's All-Star Missions Churches: Strategies to Help Your Church Get into the Game.* Grand Rapids: Baker.

Thangaraj, M. Thomas. 1999. *The Common Task: A Theology of Christian Mission.* Nashville: Abingdon.

Thekkedath, Joseph. 1988. *History of Christianity in India.* Vol. 2, *From the Middle of the Sixteenth Century to the End of the Seventeenth Century.* Bangalore: Church History Association of India.

Thoburn, James M. 1903. *The Life of Isabella Thoburn.* Cincinnati: Jennings & Pye.

Thomas, Norman, ed. 1995. *Classic Texts in Mission and World Christianity.* Maryknoll, N.Y.: Orbis.

Thompson, Phyllis. 1971. *The Transparent Woman.* Grand Rapids: Zondervan.

Ting-Toomey, Stella. 1985. "Toward a Theory of Conflict and Culture." In *Communication, Culture, and Organizational Processes,* ed. William B. Gudykunst, Lea P. Stewart, and Stella Ting-Toomey, 71–86. Beverly Hills, Calif.: Sage.

———. 1989. "Intergroup Communication and Simulation in Low- and High-Cultures." In *Communication and Simulation: From Two Fields to One Theme,* ed. David Crookall and Danny Saunders, 169–76. Philadelphia: Multilingual Matters.

———. 1991. "Cross-Cultural Interpersonal Communication: An Introduction." In *Cross-Cultural Interpersonal Communication,* ed. Stella Ting-Toomey and Felipe Korzenny, 1–10. Newbury Park, Calif.: Sage.

Ting-Toomey, Stella, and Felipe Korzenny, eds. 1991. *Cross-Cultural Interpersonal Communication.* Newbury Park, Calif.: Sage.

Toews, J. B. 1967. "The Theology of Mission in Acts." In *The Church in Mission: A Sixtieth Anniversary Tribute to J. B. Toews,* ed. Abram J. Klassen, 1–16. Fresno, Calif.: Board of Christian Literature, Mennonite Brethren Church.

Travis, John. 1998. "The C1 to C6 Spectrum." *Evangelical Missions Quarterly* 34 (October): 407–8.

Triandis, Harry C. 1992. "Collectivism v. Individualism: A Reconceptualisation of a Basic Concept in Cross-Cultural Psychology." In *Readings on Communicating with Strangers: An Approach to Intercultural Communication,* ed. William B. Gudykunst and Young Yun Kim, 71–82. New York: McGraw-Hill.

Triandis, Harry C., R. W. Brislin, and C. Harry Hui. 1991. "Cross-Cultural Training across the Individualism-Collectivism Divide." In *Intercultural Communication: A Reader,* 6th ed., ed. Larry A. Samovar and Richard E. Porter, 370–82. Belmont, Calif.: Wadsworth.

Troutman, Charles. 1976. *Everything You Want to Know about the Mission Field, but Are Afraid You Won't Learn until You Get There: Letters to a Prospective Missionary.* Downers Grove, Ill.: InterVarsity.

Tucker, John. 2001. "Short-Term Missions: Building Sustainable Relationships." *Evangelical Missions Quarterly* 37 (October): 436–39.

Tucker, Ruth A. 1983. *From Jerusalem to Irian Jaya: A Biographical History of Christian Missions.* Grand Rapids: Zondervan.

———. 1988. *Guardians of the Great Commission: The Story of Women in Modern Missions.* Grand Rapids: Zondervan.

Tucker, Ruth A., and Walter L. Liefeld. 1987. *Daughters of the Church: Women and Ministry from New Testament Times to the Present.* Grand Rapids: Zondervan.

Ugolnik, Anthony. 1989. *The Illuminating Icon.* Grand Rapids: Eerdmans.

Unger, Merrill F. 1963. *Biblical Demonology.* Wheaton, Ill.: Scripture Press.

Van Engen, Charles. 1996. *Mission on the Way: Issues in Mission Theology.* Grand Rapids: Baker.

Van Engen, Charles, Nancy Thomas, and Robert Gallagher, eds. 1999. *Footprints of God: A Narrative Theology of Mission.* Monrovia, Calif.: MARC.

Van Rheenen, Gailyn. 1991. *Communicating Christ in Animistic Contexts.* Grand Rapids: Baker.

———. 1996. *Missions: Biblical Foundations and Contemporary Strategies.* Grand Rapids: Zondervan.

VanVonderen, Jeff. 1989. *Tired of Trying to Measure Up.* Minneapolis: Bethany House.

Verkuyl, Johannes. 1978. *Contemporary Missiology.* Trans. and ed. Dale Cooper. Grand Rapids: Eerdmans.

Veronis, Luke Alexander. 1994. *Missionaries, Monks and Martyrs: Making Disciples of All Nations.* Minneapolis: Light and Life.

Verstraelen, F. J. 1995. "Ghana, West Africa: Between Traditional and Modern." In *Missiology: An Ecumenical Introduction,* ed. F. J. Verstraelen et al., 65–87. Grand Rapids: Eerdmans.

Vicedom, Georg F. 1965. *The Mission of God: An Introduction to a Theology of Mission.* Trans.

Gilbert A. Thiele and Dennis Hilgendorf. Saint Louis: Concordia.

Wacker, Grant. 2001. *Heaven Below: Early Pentecostals and American Culture.* Cambridge: Harvard University Press.

Wagner, C. Peter. 1988. *The Third Wave of the Holy Spirit.* Ann Arbor, Mich.: Vine.

———, ed. 1991. *Engaging the Enemy: How to Fight and Defeat Territorial Spirits.* Ventura, Calif.: Regal.

———. 1996. *Confronting the Powers: How the New Testament Church Experienced the Power of Strategic-level Spiritual Warfare.* Ventura, Calif.: Regal.

———. 1997. "Contemporary Dynamics of the Holy Spirit and Missions." In *The Holy Spirit in Missions,* ed. C. Douglas McConnell, 107–22. Pasadena, Calif.: William Carey Library.

———. 2000a. *Apostles and Prophets: The Foundation of the Church.* Ventura, Calif.: Regal.

———. 2000b. *Evangelical Dictionary of World Missions,* ed. A. Scott Moreau, s.v. "New Apostolic Reformation Missions." Grand Rapids: Baker.

Walker, Jean, comp. 1980. *Fool and Fanatic? Quotations from the Letters of C. T. Studd.* Gerards Cross, England: Worldwide Evangelization Crusade.

Walls, Andrew F. 1994a. "David Livingstone, 1813–1873: Awakening the Western World to Africa." In *Mission Legacies: Biographical Studies of Leaders of the Modern Missionary Movement,* ed. Gerald H. Anderson et al., 140–47. Maryknoll, N.Y.: Orbis.

———. 1994b. "Samuel Ajayi Crowther, 1807–1891: Foremost African Christian of the Nineteenth Century." In *Mission Legacies: Biographical Studies of Leaders of the Modern Missionary Movement,* ed. Gerald H. Anderson et al., 132–39. Maryknoll, N.Y.: Orbis.

———. 1996. *The Missionary Movement in Christian History: Studies in the Transmission of Faith.* Maryknoll, N.Y.: Orbis.

———. 2002. *The Cross-Cultural Process in Christian History.* Maryknoll, N.Y.: Orbis.

Walsh, Brian J. 1992. "Worldviews, Modernity and the Task of Christian College Education." *Faculty Dialogue: Journal of the Institute for Christian Leadership* 18 (fall): 13–35.

Ward, Ted. 1984. *Living Overseas: A Book of Preparations.* New York: Free Press.

Ware, Timothy. 1963. *The Orthodox Church.* New York: Penguin.

Warne, Frank W. 1907. *The Revival in the Indian Church.* New York: Board of Foreign Missions, Methodist Episcopal Church.

Warneck, Johannes. 1909. *The Living Christ and Dying Heathenism: The Experiences of a Missionary in Animistic Heathendom.* Trans. Neil Buchanan. New York: Fleming H. Revell.

Warner, Timothy M. 1991. *Spiritual Warfare: Victory over the Powers of This Dark World.* Wheaton, Ill.: Crossway.

Water, Mark, comp. 2001. *The New Encyclopedia of Christian Martyrs.* Grand Rapids: Baker.

Watson, Tom, Jr. 1965. *T. J. Bach: A Voice for Missions.* Chicago: Moody.

Weiss, George C. 1977. *The Heart of Missionary Theology.* Chicago: Moody.

Welliver, Dotsey, and Minnette Smith, eds. 2002. *Handbook of Schools and Professors of Missions and Evangelism.* Wheaton, Ill.: EMIS.

Wenham, David. 2000. "From Jesus to Paul—Via Luke." In *The Gospel to the Nations: Perspectives on Paul's Mission,* ed. Peter Bolt and Mark Thompson, 83–97. Downers Grove, Ill.: InterVarsity.

Wheeler, Reginald. 1956. *A Man Sent from God: A Biography of Robert E. Speer.* Westwood, N.J.: Fleming H. Revell.

White, John. 1992. *Changing on the Inside.* Ann Arbor, Mich.: Vine.

Whittle, Deseree. 1999. "Missionary Attrition: Its Relationship to the Spiritual Dynamics of the Late Twentieth Century." *Caribbean Journal of Evangelical Theology* 3: 68–83.

Wiebracht, Dean. 1992. *The World Beyond Your Walls: A Manual for Mobilizing Your Church in Missions.* Manila: OMF.

Wiest, Jean-Paul. 1993. "Learning from the Missionary Past." In *The Catholic Church in Modern China: Perspectives,* ed. Edmond Tang and Jean-Paul Wiest, 181–98. Maryknoll, N.Y.: Orbis.

Wiley, A. L. 1906. "India: Revival at Ratnagiri—Extraordinary Scenes." *Mission World,* May 1, 19–22.

Wilkins, Michael. 2000. *Evangelical Dictionary of World Missions,* ed. A. Scott Moreau, s.v. "Discipleship." Grand Rapids: Baker.

Williams, Don. 1989. *Signs, Wonders, and the Kingdom of God: A Biblical Guide for the Reluctant Skeptic.* Ann Arbor, Mich.: Vine.

Williams, Joel F. 1998. "Mission in Mark." In *Mission in the New Testament: An Evangelical Approach*, ed. William J. Larkin and Joel F. Williams, 137–51. Maryknoll, N.Y.: Orbis.

Willis, Avery T., and Henry T. Blackaby. 2002. *On Mission with God*. Nashville: Broadman & Holman.

Wilson, Dorothy Clark. 1959. *Dr. Ida: The Story of Dr. Ida Scudder of Vellore*. New York: McGraw-Hill.

Wilson, J. Christy, Jr. 1986. "The Legacy of Samuel M. Zwemer." *International Bulletin of Missionary Research* 10 (July): 117–21.

Wimber, John. 1986. *Power Evangelism*. San Francisco: Harper & Row.

———. 1987. *Power Healing*. San Francisco: Harper & Row.

Wind, Anne. 1995. "The Protestant Missionary Movement from 1789 to 1963." In *Missiology: An Ecumenical Introduction*, ed. F. J. Verstraelen et al., 237–52. Grand Rapids: Eerdmans.

Wink, Walter. 1992. *Engaging the Powers: Discernment and Resistance in a World of Domination*. Philadelphia: Fortress.

Winter, Bruce W. 2000. "Dangers and Difficulties for the Pauline Missions." In *The Gospel to the Nations: Perspectives on Paul's Mission*, ed. Peter Bolt and Mark Thompson, 285–95. Downers Grove, Ill.: InterVarsity.

Winter, Ralph D. 1975. "The Highest Priority: Cross-Cultural Evangelism." In *Let the Earth Hear His Voice*, ed. J. D. Douglas, 213–241. Minneapolis: World Wide Publications.

Winter, Ralph D., and Steven C. Hawthorne. 1999. *Perspectives on the World Christian Movement: A Reader*. 3d ed. Pasadena, Calif.: William Carey Library.

Worcester, Mrs. John H. 1987. *David Livingstone*. Chicago: Moody.

Wright, Christopher J. H. 2000. *Evangelical Dictionary of World Missions*, ed. A. Scott Moreau, s.v. "Old Testament Theology of Mission." Grand Rapids: Baker.

Wright, G. Ernest. 1960. "The Old Testament Basis for the Christian Mission." In *The Theology of the Christian Mission*, ed. Gerald H. Anderson, 17–20. New York: McGraw-Hill.

Wu, Silas H. L. 2002. "Dora Yu (1873–1931): Foremost Female Evangelist in Twentieth-Century Chinese Revivalism." In *Gospel Bearers, Gender Barriers: Missionary Women in the Twentieth Century*, ed. Dana L. Robert, 85–98. Maryknoll, N.Y.: Orbis.

Xi, Lian. 1997. *The Conversion of Missionaries: Liberalism in American Protestant Missions in China, 1907–1932*. University Park, Pa.: Pennsylvania State University Press.

Yamamori, Tetsunao. 2000. *Evangelical Dictionary of World Missions*, ed. A. Scott Moreau, s.v. "Tentmaking Mission." Grand Rapids: Baker.

Yamamori, Tetsunao, Bryant L. Myers, and David Conner, eds. 1995. *Serving with the Poor in Asia*. Monrovia, Calif.: MARC.

Yamamori, Tetsunao, et al., eds. 1996. *Serving with the Poor in Africa*. Monrovia, Calif.: MARC.

Yates, Timothy. 1994. *Christian Mission in the Twentieth Century*. Cambridge: Cambridge University Press.

Yri, Norvald. 1978. *Quest for Authority: An Investigation of the Quest for Authority within the Ecumenical Movement from 1910 to 1974 and the Evangelical Response*. Kisumu, Kenya: Evangel.

Zahniser, A. H. Matthias. 1997. *Symbol and Ceremony: Making Disciples across Cultures*. Monrovia, Calif.: MARC.

Zernov, Nicolas. 1968. *The Russians and Their Church*. London: SPCK.

Zwemer, Samuel M. 1902. *Raymund Lull: First Missionary to the Moslems*. New York: Funk & Wagnalls.

Subject Index

Abraham, 31–32
Adam, 28, 30–31
Advancing Churches in Missions Commitment (ACMC), 249
Aeizanes, 101
Africasia, 13
Afghanistan, 13
Africa, 11–12, 140–41, 144, 271–73. *See also under specific countries*
agencies. *See* missions agencies
AIDS, 11–12
Alexander VI, 114
"all nations," 42, 43
Alopen, 93
ambiguity, 177
Americans. *See* North Americans
Anabaptists, 121
ancestral veneration, 305
Anderson, Neil, 288
Antioch, 53–54, 110
Arminianism, 165
art, 109
Asia, 111–13, 117–19. *See also under specific countries*
assimilation, 205–8
attrition, 257–58
authority, 43–44
Azusa Street Revival, 147–48

baptism
    and the Anabaptists, 121
    and disciple making, 45
    as magic, 100
    in transcultural settings, 50, 51
Barnabas, 54, 56–58, 164, 167–68, 265–66
Bartolomé de Las Casas, 116
beggars, 210–11
Belgian Congo, 126
Berg, Daniel, 149
Bethlehem Baptist Church, 86–87
Bible. *See* Scriptures
Bible institutes, 132
Billy Graham Evangelistic Association, 145
blind, 47–48
boarding schools, 216–17
Brainerd, David, 122
Bray, Thomas, 121
Buddhism, 307–8
burnout, 256
Byzantine empire, 99, 110, 111, 113

call
    to Abraham, 31–32
    and the community of believers, 164, 170
    as a definite event, 160
    to discipleship, 165
    to full-time ministry, 165–66
    and giftedness, 163
    guidelines, 169–70
    to holiness, 165
    to missionaries, 20, 159–71
    misunderstandings about, 159–64
    as a mystical experience, 162
    to Paul, 160–61
    relevance of, 163
    to salvation, 165
    in the Scriptures, 164–68
    and short-term assignments, 170
    to a specific assignment, 167–68, 170
    and success, 162
    as test of fitness, 162
    types, 164–68
    varieties of, 164, 169
Calvinism, 165
care. *See* missionary care
Carey, William, 43, 122, 123–24, 132, 246
Catholic Church, 103. *See also* Franciscans; Jesuits
    and the Celtic church, 104
    and the Counter-Reformation, 117–18
    missionaries to Asia, 113
    missionaries to the western hemisphere, 116
    mission of, 119–20, 130, 150–53
    as mystical experiences, 162
    and the New Evangelization, 149–50

345

Scripture Index